Making a Difference

Making a Difference

A Fifty-Year History of Kansas-Nebraska Southern Baptists

Marjorie Stith

PROVIDENCE HOUSE PUBLISHERS
Franklin, Tennessee

Copyright 1995 by the Kansas-Nebraska Convention of Southern Baptists

Biblical quotations are from the *Today's English Version* of the New Testament, 1966, American Bible Society.

Printed in the United States of America

99   98   97   96   95   5   4   3   2   1

Library of Congress Cataloging-in-Publication Data

Stith, Marjorie M.
    Making a difference : a fifty-year history of Kansas-Nebraska
Southern Baptists / Marjorie Stith.
        p.   cm.
    Includes bibliographical references and index.
    ISBN 1-881576-50-7
    1. Southern Baptist Convention—Kansas—History—20th century.
    2. Southern Baptist Convention—Nebraska—History—20th century.
    3. Kansas—Church history.   4. Nebraska—Church history.   I. Title
BX6462.4.K2S75   1995
286'.1781'09045—dc20   95-33630
                                                                         CIP

Photos throughout text provided courtesy of the Kansas-Nebraska Convention of Southern Baptists.

Cover design by Ernie Hickman.

Published by
PROVIDENCE HOUSE PUBLISHERS
P.O. Box 158 • 238 Seaboard Lane
Franklin, Tennessee 37067
800-881-5692

Contents

Abbreviations

ABC   American Baptist Convention
AIMA   American Indian Mission Association
BD   *Baptist Digest*
BSU   Baptist Student Union
BYW   Baptist Young Women
CASA   Court Appointed Special Advocate
CLA   Church Loan Association
CSM   Christian Social Ministries
DOAM   Director of Associational Missions
ENBA   Eastern Nebraska Baptist Association
ESB   *Encyclopedia of Southern Baptists*
GAs   Girl's Auxiliary; Girls in Action
KCSB   Kansas Convention of Southern Baptists
KCSBC   Kansas Convention of Southern Baptist Churches
KNCSB   Kansas-Nebraska Convention of Southern Baptists
KSBB   *Kansas Southern Baptist Beams*
KSBF   Kansas Southern Baptist Fellowship
KSBFN   Kansas Southern Baptist Foundation
KSU   Kansas State University
KU   University of Kansas
NAC   National Acteens Conference
NBC   Northern Baptist Convention
OBU   Oklahoma Baptist University
OU   Oklahoma University
RAs   Royal Ambassadors
SBB   *Southern Baptist Beams*
SBC   Southern Baptist Convention
SEC   Securities and Exchange Commission
U.S.   United States
UNL   University of Nebraska, Lincoln
WCC   Webster Conference Center
WMU   Woman's Missionary Union
WNBA   Western Nebraska Baptist Association
WSU   Wichita State University
WU   Washburn University
YWA   Young Women's Auxiliary

Preface

IWANT TO EXPRESS MY APPRECIATION FIRST OF ALL TO THE people who have gone before us, on whose shoulders we stand as Baptists in Kansas and Nebraska—people who labored against incredible odds.

Thanks to the people who have shared pieces of their lives and many remembrances to make the story come alive, who have taken time to answer questions in writing, in interviews, and on the phone.

Without Yvonne Keefer this story could not have been written. Thanks to her sharp eyes, many spelling errors missed by the computer spell-check were spotted, commas were added and deleted appropriately, and run-on sentences were divided into two or three. Thanks to her keen mind, errors in dates and places and names were kept to a minimum. Thanks to her fund of stories, there is a chuckle here and there. Her stories also attest to her sensitive, caring relationships with scores of people all over the Kansas-Nebraska Convention of Southern Baptists (KNCSB). In addition, because of her work, we offer several informative appendices.

Thanks to Peck Lindsay who gave me the opportunity to tell the story of fifty years of Kansas history and shared his experiences with me. Thanks to Pat McDaniel, Mark Clifton, Harold Conley, John Hopkins, Terry McIlvain, Sue Lindsay, Roy Moody, Harry Taylor, and Andy St. Andre, who helped me understand the work of the KNCSB. They talked and explained, read and corrected the manuscript, and supplied answers to scores of questions.

Thanks to the members of the Anniversary Committee who planned this celebration: Roger Criser, Ron Pract, Carol Smith, Mary Jo Troughton, Gordon Dorian, and James Shope, in addition to the KNCSB staff. A special word of appreciation to the chair of the committee, Harold Inman, who, in addition to all his other contributions, did his best to eliminate southern colloquialisms from this record.

Thanks to all those who have "brought forth" *Southern Baptist Beams* (SBB), *Kansas Southern Baptist Beams* (KSBB), and the *Baptist Digest* (BD) through the years. These publications proved an invaluable source of information. A special thanks to James Shope, long-time historical secretary of the Convention, for his information and encouragement.

Thanks to Anita Wilson who typed thousands of words from sometimes hard-to-understand taped oral histories and interviews. Thanks to Vashti Jones who always seemed able to find answers to sometimes inconsequential questions, who copied and recopied the manuscript in all stages of doneness, and who helpfully assisted the editorial staff of the publisher.

Thanks, also, to family and friends for their patience and support as "the book" took shape.

To all of these, this book is dedicated.

One more word. The story is told from the perspective of the teller. It is a topical story, not a chronological one. I have written what has been shared with me, as I have understood it. As you read, no doubt you will wonder why some things are included and why others are left out. You will remember events, people, and circumstances which have not been mentioned. It did not seem possible to tell everything; I chose examples to spotlight and illustrate areas of concern and achievement.

I hope the story will go on and on. I encourage you to reminisce and to record what you remember of the past, along with important things that are happening now. These are the stories that will make great telling in Volume II— the next fifty years.

> Remember your former leaders, who spoke God's message to you. Think back on how they lived and died (Heb. 13:7, TEV).

1

From a Fellowship to a Convention

THE 1940S WERE YEARS TO BE REMEMBERED. A TWENTY-POUND watermelon cost eighty-eight cents. A ten-pound bag of potatoes was a quarter. Coffee was thirty-nine cents a pound; beef roast, twenty-eight cents. Dairies bragged about new machines that would produce homogenized milk; thus, everyone who drank milk would get a fair share of the cream.

No new cars had been made during the war and prices on used cars were sky-high. One headline suggested that if prices kept rising, horses might return to Kansas City. There was gasoline rationing; tires were retreaded. Everyone was encouraged to buy bonds. Kansas State College at Manhattan changed its admission policy to make it easier for returning GIs. Western Union and Postal Telegraph had just negotiated a merger. A year later Edwin H. Land first demonstrated the Polaroid Land camera, which could produce a black-and-white photograph in the unheard of time of sixty seconds. The exploits of Alley Oop, Freckles and His Friends, and Boots and Her Buddies appeared on the comic pages. "Out Our Way" and Major Hoople in "Our Boarding House" were popular. Alice Faye, Anne Southern, Bette Davis, and Lana Turner graced the silver screen and were top names in Hollywood. Don Ameche and Vivian Blaine were "romantically involved." Greer Garson and Walter Pidgen had just made their twenty-sixth film, *Mrs. Parkington.*

Ads invited men and women to come to work at the Kingsbury Ordnance Plant in La Porte, Indiana. Tuttle Creek Dam was not even on the drawing board. The Big Blue flowed along uninhibited. White coats and soft, frilly prom dresses were high style.

D-Day was June 6, 1944. Alf Landon was active in Kansas Republican politics. In November Franklin Delano Roosevelt was elected to a fourth term as President of the United States, easily defeating Thomas Dewey. Roosevelt died in 1945; Harry Truman became president. On August 6 an atomic bomb

11

was dropped on Hiroshima; two days later, another was dropped on Nagasaki. On August 14 Japan surrendered, and the shooting part of the war was over. GI Joe came home, and Rosie the Riveter went back to the kitchen. We picked up the pieces of a world that would never be the same again.

The formal story of Southern Baptists in Kansas and Nebraska was just beginning at this time. By faith, grit, determination, and with a longing to see churches in every town and hamlet in the state, Kansas Baptist pastors and laity alike did what some said could not be done.

Long before 1944 there were Baptist churches in Kansas which cooperated with the Southern Baptist Convention. These churches subscribed to Baptist doctrine and principle, and they supported Southern Baptist programs by gifts through the Cooperative Program. They had become disgruntled with stands taken by the Northern Baptist churches on alien baptism, affiliation with the Federal Council of Churches (later reorganized as the World Council of Churches), and lack of evangelistic fervor. At the same time, these churches saw themselves as victims of "state missions in reverse." They were members of Baptist associations in Oklahoma and Missouri which could not, or would not, open new work in Kansas because of the "Comity Agreement" between the SBC and the Northern Baptist Convention (NBC) in parceling out the territory above and below the Mason-Dixon Line.

The first comity agreement between Northern and Southern Baptists had taken place in 1894 and was called the Fortress Monroe Comity Agreement, because of the site of the meeting. The SBC had requested the meeting to give attention to educational and evangelistic work among Negroes and to territorial limits of operation of the NBC in the South.

Three points of agreement were reached: (1) it was not good for two different Baptist organizations to establish missions in the same territory; (2) when each group had work in the same area, there should be no strife between them; and (3) each body would avoid establishing work in a territory where the other was already working. The "territory" limits were not clearly established at this time, nor were they so established at any later comity conference. The general idea was an imaginary line south of Delaware, Pennsylvania, West Virginia, Ohio, Indiana, and Kansas and through the middle of Illinois and Missouri—the Mason-Dixon Line. No attention was given to the division of southern territory west of Texas.

With the growth of the country, large numbers of Southern Baptists went from the South to other areas and organized Southern Baptist churches. They wanted help from and affiliation with the SBC. New Mexico was the trouble spot. When the Home Mission Board began to respond to the requests of churches in New Mexico, Northern Baptists complained of violations of the Fortress Monroe Comity Agreement. Another comity conference was planned.

A committee from the Home Mission Board, SBC, and the Home Mission Society, NBC, met in Washington in 1909. It was agreed that the Home Mission Board would take over all the mission work in New Mexico, and reimburse the Home Mission Society for what it had spent in this area. This was contingent upon the consent of the New Mexico Baptist Convention. They agreed also that "the question of territorial adjustment be considered settled for at least five years."

When this agreement was presented by the Home Mission Board to the SBC for ratification, an additional clause was added: "That nothing in the statement would be so construed as to limit any church, association, or any other Baptist body in the free exercise of the inalienable right to make such alignment for co-operation as would, in its judgment, be for its own good and for the furtherance of its work." The Home Mission Society rejected the agreement because of the "clarifying clause on free self-determination of churches and other Baptist bodies."

The disagreement between the SBC and the NBC caused a split in the New Mexico Convention. This action underscored the need for another comity conference. So a joint committee met in Old Point Comfort, Virginia, in 1911 and again in Hot Springs, Arkansas, in 1912.

Three principles emerged from these meetings: "(1) The giving of financial aid by a denominational organization should not impair the free autonomy of any church. (2) Denominational organizations should sacredly regard the rights of sister organizations and churches to the end of promoting unity, harmony, and free self-determination. (3) Baptist bodies should never hinder or injure the work of any other Baptist group" (White, 1958).

W. R. White, who wrote the article on comity agreements, listed the following "facts and principles" which emerged from his study: "(1) The independence and autonomy of local churches and voluntary and advisory nature of denominational bodies among us make rigid disciplines incongruous and impossible. (2) The immigration of thousands of Southern Baptists into the North and West has produced a new situation. (3) The tremendous switch in the strength of the American Baptist and Southern Baptist Conventions calls for adjustments. (4) Most of our problems have arisen from our not being sufficiently realistic in a changing situation. (5) There is a great reservoir of good will at the heart of, and in the leadership of, each group sufficient for Christian fellowship and Christian orientation" (White, 1958).

White's 1958 summary statement contained no reference to "territory lines." Echoes of the earlier Fortress Monroe Agreement, however, must have still been ringing in the ears of many Southern Baptist leaders when Kansas made its petition for affiliation with the SBC. In fact, at the 1948 SBC meeting in St. Louis, Missouri, White brought a report for the Comity Committee which had been appointed the preceding year. He stated there had been an exchange of "points of irritation and problems in a most fraternal and Christian manner" (Hamm).

White's report to the Convention included this paragraph: "There are many people who misunderstand us, who live in the North, and there are many people who live in the South who misunderstand splendid people and churches in the North, and many of those misunderstandings were dissolved; and we discussed and came to know the facts first hand. And, may I say that there are points in which we differed, of course, but I trust that at those points where we differ, in the future we shall differ in a Christian spirit. We greatly becloud (confuse) the witness of Baptists, North and South, and the total witness of Baptists, often because of the undesirable relationships that exist between us, particularly in local situations here, there, and yonder. We think that is wholly unnecessary. We do not have to compromise our convictions to still be Christian in our spirit and relationship."

In many places in "Northern Baptist territory," there were Southern Baptist churches. As early as 1900, Memorial Baptist Church in Pittsburg, Kansas, had affiliated with Missouri Baptists (Shope, n.d.). In 1911 the Wirtonia Baptist Church, organized in 1892 (later known as First Baptist Church of Crestline), had aligned with the Spring River Association in Missouri. This church "set the pattern" for other churches in Kansas to become part of Southern Baptist associations, even though they had to cross the state line to do it. According to Lynn Clayton, editor of the *Baptist Digest* (May 30, 1977), "these stubborn churches were determined to show their autonomy. . . . They did not feel at home in 'Northern' churches."

Next to move was Lawton in 1914, Arma in 1922, and Macedonia, sometime later. The pastor of the Sixth Street Baptist Church in Galena had a part on the Spring River Baptist Association program in 1929, although there is no record that the church was a part of the association (Shope, n.d.).

Burden Baptist Church, organized before 1885, left the NBC in 1919 to affiliate with an Oklahoma association. Trinity Baptist Church of Chanute affiliated with the Northeast Baptist Association in Oklahoma in 1923. Pastors and members of that church were active in the association (Shope). In 1927 Baxter Springs, organized in 1872, affiliated with Oklahoma, followed in 1937, 1938 and 1939 by First Baptist of Chetopa, First Baptist Treece (constituted in 1925 or 1926), Coffeyville Emmanuel, and Chautauqua.

N. J. Westmoreland, the executive secretary-treasurer of the Kansas Convention of Southern Baptists (KCSB), wrote about the beginning of the Emmanuel Baptist Church in Coffeyville on the fifteenth anniversary of that church (*KSBB*, August, 1950). The church was organized in 1935 with twelve charter members who could not in good conscience remain in the only other Baptist church in town, which was affiliated with the NBC. They were modern-day pilgrims seeking to follow their own hearts, even though they were the objects of derision by the church from which they withdrew.

They were not aware, according to Westmoreland, of the precedent already set by Southern Baptists in Northern Baptist territory. They did not know "that in 1907, 226 churches in Illinois had withdrawn from the Northern Baptist Convention to affiliate with Southern Baptists in 1910. They did not know that New Mexico Baptists linked with Southern Baptists in 1912, with most of their churches coming from Northern Baptist ranks. They did not know that a similar action occurred in Oklahoma in 1914. They did not know that the Missouri Baptist Association severed its ties with the Northern Baptist Convention in 1919 to affiliate solely with the Southern Baptist Convention. Nor did they know that Baptists in Arizona had organized a Convention to affiliate with Southern Baptists in 1929. . . . They did not know that already the churches at Arma, Lawton, Wirtonia near Crestline, Baxter Springs, Trinity in Chanute, Treece, and Burden were cooperating with the Southern Baptist Convention." Even so, that day in 1935, the twelve charter members laid their hands on the Bible and pledged to be true to the New Testament and stand by this newly organized church in Coffeyville.

By 1943 ten churches in Kansas were cooperating with six associations in Oklahoma (Gibson, 1958, p. 718). The churches belonging to the Spring River Association in Missouri developed a group cohesiveness, but there was little fellowship among the Kansas churches affiliated with Oklahoma associations. A number of Kansas Baptist churches died "a'borning"; others (Liberal, Arkansas City, Cherryvale, Alden, Topeka) had sprung up among thorns of "aloneness" and "reproof" which had choked them. There had been no one around to hear their cries or minister to their needs. Records of several early Southern Baptist churches are filed away in the "dead-city file" of Kansas.

The fellowship and group consciousness among the churches affiliated with the Spring River Association in Missouri were likely due to the work of Frank Medearis, who served Kansas Baptists for thirty-one years—as pastor of the First Baptist Church of Burden (1915-22; 1933-41) and as missionary in Spring River Association (1923-33; 1941-46). When Medearis died in 1964 (*BD*, July 11, 1964), Westmoreland wrote a glowing tribute, noting that "of the twelve Southern Baptist churches in Kansas at the time of the organization of the Kansas Convention of Southern Baptists, he had performed a significant ministry in behalf of six of them."

While Medearis was pastor of Burden Church, he led them through a number of "destiny-determining decisions in a statesman-like manner" (*BD*, July 11, 1964). The church was a member of the NBC, and was "confronted with the appeal to participate in the Inter-Church World Movement, a fantastic inter-denominational fund-raising campaign in which Northern Baptists were to participate and from which they were to draw a proportionate share." The Burden Church decided they could not take part. Medearis went to the Northern Baptist annual meeting in Colorado in 1919 where this plan was adopted, and to the SBC in Atlanta where it was rejected. Burden withdrew from the NBC and affiliated with the SBC and the Perry Association in Oklahoma. As it turned out, the inter-church movement failed miserably; the NBC lost about $2.5 million.

Even under handicaps, new churches were formed among people who longed for fellowship with other like-minded believers. Westmoreland, in the first program (1947) for the WMU State Missions Day of Prayer, summed up the situation: "This establishment, affiliation, and growth of 12 Southern

Baptist churches in Kansas that had given more than $43,000 unsolicited to Southern Baptist causes through 35 years, all without any human planning and without many persons knowing that as many as six of them existed at any one time, is a marvel of marvels" (Westmoreland, Day of Prayer).

On the occasion of the Seventh Anniversary of the KCSB, Orbie Clem wrote an editorial dealing with beginnings (*KSBB*, March 19, 1953). He pointed out that he and Westmoreland had come to Kansas the same year, 1940—Westmoreland, to the eastern part of the state, Coffeyville, and Clem to the western part, Ness City, where he organized Trinity Baptist. Clem's church was a member of the Northwestern Association in Oklahoma, but the distance to the associational meetings was too great to continue this fellowship. Clem invited Clyde Fowler, pastor at Burden, to join him in writing letters to the other Baptist pastors in Kansas suggesting a breakfast meeting at the Oklahoma Convention meeting. Westmoreland and Clem met each other at that first breakfast meeting.

In 1944 the breakfast meeting came to pass. Pastors of five Kansas Southern Baptist churches (J. H. Ray, Chautauqua; N. J. Westmoreland, Coffeyville Emmanuel; Orbie R. Clem, Ness City Trinity; Clyde Fowler, Burden; and Bill Magar, Ellinwood Calvary) met to discuss this desire for fellowship, and the urgency of the mission needs in Kansas. Out of their conversation came the idea of a Kansas Southern Baptist Fellowship (KSBF). They talked and dreamed and schemed. Meetings, planned for early the following year, did not take place because of the rationing of tires. Two hundred fifty miles seemed too great a distance for a fellowship meeting on retreads! Pastors and youth from three other churches were on hand, however, at the fifth annual Youth Camp, sponsored by the Coffeyville Church in July 1945: Burden, Ellinwood, and Chautauqua. The fellowship was good, the need was deep, so the dream stayed alive.

THE KANSAS SOUTHERN BAPTIST FELLOWSHIP

The pastors met the following year, 1945, again at the Oklahoma Convention. Plans were finalized for a fellowship meeting, this time in concert with an evangelistic conference at Burden, November 26 and 27, 1945. During the Thanksgiving holidays, N. J. Westmoreland, pastor at Emmanuel in Coffeyville, attended the Training Union Conference in Missouri to contact Kansas Baptist churches affiliated with that Convention. This was the first announcement made outside the state of Kansas about a meeting of Kansas Southern Baptists.

On November 26, when time came to begin the meeting, in addition to the people from Coffeyville, there was only one other person present, a member of the Burden Church. Finally, the pastor from Burden, who had been conducting a funeral, appeared, the people from Ness City arrived, and the meeting began. Later, Ellinwood folk came, bringing along Ray Lansdowne, the missionary from Salt Fork Association in Oklahoma. He was enthusiastic about a revival held at Calvary Baptist Mission in Russell, where a number of people in the community and the oil-field camps had made professions of faith. His wonderful testimony lifted the people and made them forget the small number in attendance and remember the great task before them, and the power of the Holy Spirit. Westmoreland (State Mission Day of Prayer) spoke the sentiment of the group, "What God was doing at Russell, we were sure He wanted done in hundreds of places."

Out of this gathering of four churches, Burden First Baptist, Ellinwood Calvary, Ness City Trinity, and Coffeyville Emmanuel, came the formal organization of the Kansas Southern Baptist Fellowship (KSBF) (*SBB*, December 3, 1945). Chautauqua is included in the list in the *Encyclopedia of Southern Baptists (ESB)* account (Gibson, I, 1958, p. 719); Ness City is omitted. There is no doubt that Ness City was represented. Orbie Clem, pastor of that church, spoke often during the proceedings, led a discussion, and brought a message on "Opportunities in Western Kansas."

The first order of business was a motion by Clem that Ray Walker, pastor of First Baptist Church, Burden, be elected moderator. He was elected by acclamation. "Brother Clem" was nominated by Westmoreland for "temporary clerk." Clem responded, "I believe this would be a good job for a woman," whereupon Mrs. Orbie Clem was nominated and elected. Westmoreland was elected temporary vice moderator. Later in the meeting, William Magar, pastor of Ellinwood Calvary, was elected treasurer of the group.

Still later, Clem moved that those who had been elected as temporary officers remain in office until the close of the September 1946 general meeting. Also at this meeting, Mrs. J. D. Williamson was elected chairman of Women's Assembly (handwritten minutes from fellowship's organizational meeting).

At subsequent meetings, before the general organization meeting in March, the name was changed to Kansas Woman's Missionary Union (WMU), officers were elected, and Mrs. Clem was named executive secretary. The WMU was auxiliary to the Convention from its formation until 1957, when it became a department of the KCSB.

At the beginning of the Monday evening session at Burden, Walker announced that the superintendent of the Burden High School had "postponed the Junior play until another night so that it would not conflict with our meeting" (from typed minutes of the November meeting). A committee, made up of the pastors present, was appointed on "plans and policies . . . and suggestions for this body to follow in the months ahead." Mrs. Clem was "authorized to make a report of this meeting and mail it out to the churches."

An account in *Beams* (December 3, 1945) presented a slightly different roster of elected officers: Ray Walker, Burden, moderator; O. R. Clem, Ness City Trinity, vice-president; Bill Magar, Ellinwood Calvary, treasurer; and N. J. Westmoreland, Coffeyville Emmanuel, secretary. The purpose was "to promote fellowship, acquaint the people with the field which awaited missionary action, and to set the stage for a final organization authorized by the churches."

An engaging insight concerning the "Kansas organization" plan was furnished by Darold Morgan (Tape, 1994), who was a member of the Emmanuel Baptist Church in Coffeyville where Westmoreland was pastor. He remembered "N. J. and Wanda putting me in their old beat up Ford and driving across Oklahoma into West Texas one hot summer in 1942 in order to introduce me to Hardin-Simmons University, N. J.'s alma mater, which turned out to be a home for me as well."

Morgan thought that one of the things that pushed toward a state convention, even with a small number of churches in Kansas, and the lack of sympathy toward border states organizing conventions, was Westmoreland's "great disdain for the leadership of the Oklahoma Baptist Convention," with which several Kansas churches were affiliated. The Oklahoma Convention was building an elaborate Convention headquarters in Oklahoma City, and "N. J. had the conviction that they were wasting what little mission money came from Southern Baptist churches." At the time, Emmanuel Baptist Church was affiliated with the Delaware-Osage Association in northern Oklahoma.

The first decisions of the infant Fellowship were to choose an official name, KSBF; schedule general meetings in March, July, September, and at least two zone meetings before the first general meeting; and "arrange a weekly news sheet" which was to be mimeographed until other plans could be made. Emmanuel Church at Coffeyville lent its mimeograph machine, a college student was hired to do the typing, Westmoreland was assigned temporary editing responsibilities, and the first issue was December 3, 1945. This continued until March when Orbie Clem became editor.

Thus, *Southern Baptist Beams* was born. The mimeographed paper was published until July, when the first commercially printed four-page edition, published monthly, made its appearance. By May 1946 the name was changed to *Kansas Southern Baptist Beams*. Clem served as editor without pay for a time, and then was paid fifty dollars, for two issues per month. In 1953 a seven-man board of directors was authorized by the Convention. The following year, the board recommended that the name be changed to *Baptist Digest*; Hoyt Gibson was named editor. In 1958 the board was dissolved and the *Baptist Digest* editor became directly responsible to the Executive Board (*Annual*).

At that first meeting of the Fellowship, an offering of $41.60 was received, half to be used to publicize Southern Baptist work in Kansas and half to be sent to Orval Reid to pay off a debt on a print shop in Mexico in order to keep it in operation. Reid wrote a warm and encouraging letter which was published in the *Beams* (January 17, 1946). The debt on the print shop had already been paid; the money was used to publish one hundred thousand two-page gospel tracts.

Zone meetings were planned in 1946, at Baxter Springs in January and at Ness City or Ellinwood in February. General meetings were also scheduled during 1946: March in Chetopa and July in Coffeyville, again in connection with the Youth Camp. A third general meeting was planned for Burden in September, when a new association would be formed. At this time there were thirteen churches in Kansas with "at least" four preaching points (*SBB*, December 3, 1945).

The January Zone meeting was not without difficulty. According to an article in the *Beams* (January 30, 1946), a misty rain began on Sunday afternoon and a sharp north wind forced temperatures down, presenting hazards for the Emmanuel group who were planning to attend the meeting. "Not a few people prayed for a weather change," Westmoreland wrote. By late afternoon the mist stopped; the clouds had broken by night. Perfect weather was the order of the day for the Baxter Springs meeting.

A full slate of Zone officers was elected, representing six churches: Chetopa, Burden, Treece, Baxter Springs, Coffeyville, and Lawton. There was a glorious program of preaching, singing, and testimony about the work God was doing in the churches. The welcome address by the host pastor, H. Ellis Ogden, set the pace for anticipating history-making events. James Shope, pastor of the Calvary Baptist Church in Columbus, and long-time director of missions in Tri-County Association, remembers Ogden as a versatile person— a well beloved pastor, an ardent visitor who called on everybody, not just Baptists, and who wrote songs and played a musical saw.

The Fellowship was still a body composed of members-at-large, not of churches; there was discussion of the appropriate next step. Orbie Clem, from the Western Zone, appealed for the organization of a Convention, and according to N. J. Westmoreland (*SBB*, January 23, 1946), his appeal was "profoundly logical and with great conviction."

On Tuesday afternoon the Fellowship was thrilled by the historical account of Southern Baptist work in Kansas as given by Brother Medearis, pastor of the Burden Church which had left the NBC in 1919 and affiliated with an association in Oklahoma.

Two items on the program were especially noted (*SBB*, January 23, 1946; *Annual*, 1946): "Most soul stirring was the gloriously rendered song 'It Is Well With My Soul' by the dedicated voice of Mrs. R. W. Preboth of Airlane Church, Wichita." She was a radio singer. Second, "President Max Pendley brought the closing address on 'Baptists and the Bible.' No address was signified as the 'Convention' sermon, but all present will surely remember it as such."

Sunday School and Training Union work were discussed. Mrs. J. D. Williamson spoke on the objectives of WMU and challenged Southern Baptist churches in Kansas to put two missionaries on the field during the four months of 1946 preceding the general meeting in Burden. This challenge was accepted (*SBB*, February 4, 1946).

The Fellowship suggested that the churches raise twelve hundred dollars to put missionaries to work in the Western and Eastern Zones during three months of the following summer, and encouraged each church to elect two messengers to attend the meeting at Chetopa. These goals were carefully presented as a challenge, not a command, from the Fellowship.

At the Zone meeting held at Baxter Springs in February 1946, the decision was made to go forward with the formal organization of a Convention of Southern Baptist Churches in Kansas. There was no need to wait until September. The general meeting scheduled at Chetopa in March was to be C-Day.

A committee of pastors was appointed (*SBB*, January 30, 1946) to draw up articles of faith and a constitution which could be sent to the churches for ratification or rejection before the general meeting at Chetopa. Seeds had been planted and were beginning to sprout for a formal, permanent organization, and for the direction it would take.

Meeler Markham (Thesis) reported the Western Zone meeting at Ellinwood on February 8 and 9. Ewell Kirksey, pastor of First Baptist Treece, spoke on "Why the Southern Baptist Movement," presenting compelling reasons for action. At 10:00 A.M. the Constitution Committee met to set in place the organizational and administrative framework of the Convention. At the same time, the women met to set in motion the missions emphasis that would forever mark the Convention.

Addresses on "Present and Future of Southern Baptists" were presented for the Eastern Zone by N. J. Westmoreland and for the Western Zone by Bill Magar, Ellinwood. This meeting was strangely overlooked by the editor of the *Beams*, except to say that "the meeting was marked by anxiety to make the union of the separated churches a permanent thing. A group of wonderful people were falling in love with each other, and with a great missionary task, and like lovers who plan the setting up of a home, they couldn't wait for the wedding date."

The Constitution Committee set about its task. Westmoreland reported that, after some initial work, the constitution was written in one twelve-hour day, with time out only long enough for meals, which were served by the "good women of the Burden Church." The time frame, alone, seems something of a miracle.

Another great decision made early on, at one of the Zone meetings, was to attempt to organize twenty-five new churches by the time the SBC met in 1947. The strategy was to schedule three-week revivals in twenty-five cities where Baptist churches did not exist. With two tents and a week between each revival, this could be accomplished in thirteen months. The plan was presented to the churches through the mimeographed news letter (*SBB*, Febuary 4, 1946). The article closed with these words: "Your comments will be appreciated on this subject."

And so it began, a little leaven in the lump. The president of the Fellowship, Ray Walker, pastor at Burden, along with a deacon of the Coffeyville Church, made a tour of the thirteen churches which were in existence in January 1946. The constitution was sent to the churches for ratification or rejection. Plans for the general meeting at Chetopa were completed. There was talk of changing the meeting place to Wichita, where the facilities were perhaps a little better. The Chetopa Church was not completed; only the basement was usable. Westmoreland stood firm. To meet in a church in the making would symbolize for the messengers the purpose and goals of the new organization.

KANSAS CONVENTION OF SOUTHERN BAPTIST CHURCHES

Nobody thought it could be done so quickly. When the Fellowship was formed in November 1945, the strategy originally adopted was to be ready to take the next formal step about September 1946. "Ready" came in March 1946. There was rejoicing in Kansas and in Oklahoma (Delaware Osage Association) over the progress Kansas Southern Baptists had made.

Part of the push undoubtedly came from the perceived need for evangelism in Kansas. "Alarming" statistics were presented in various ways in the *Beams* with great regularity: "Under the Northern Baptist Convention there is only one Baptist out of every 72.9 persons in California; one Baptist out of every 18 in Arizona, one out of every 20.7 in Kansas, while in Oklahoma [Southern Baptist territory] there is one Baptist for every 5.7 persons" (March 20, 1946).

Another item gave these figures: in a selected group of five counties, there were "more than 370 towns in Kansas that did not have a Baptist church"; and that "Northern Baptists had lost 181 churches in 25 years, and that only 25 new ones have been organized in the same period."

In another five-county area, there "are 262,200 people and only 35 Baptist churches with a total membership of 12,728, or one Baptist out of every 20 people. Those 35 Baptist churches are in 27 of the towns of above 100 population, leaving 21 towns of more than 100 population that have no Baptist church. There are 54 villages of less than 100 population that have no Baptist church. In four larger cities there is a definite need for at least 12 other Baptist churches. This makes a total of 87 points including rural communities that have not the Baptist message in them" (*SBB*, March 20, 1946).

C. B. Coleman, "who has preached in Kansas for more than forty years," reported that there were more than three hundred towns in Kansas with no Baptist church. Along the southern border of the state, alone, there were five cities of at least fourteen thousand people where there was only one Baptist church and some of them with less than 175 in Sunday School and most with under 250. In one area, where there was an estimated seventy-five thousand people, less than two percent were active Baptists. Westmoreland concluded, "It is evident that Kansas and the North U.S.A. are not going to become pagan—to a deplorable extent they are *already* PAGAN. Other denominations in this same section have not made a commendable contribution to the moral uplift of the social order. Southern Baptists of Kansas need only to look to see the most white of harvest fields" (*SBB*, January 6, 1946).

Later, at the time of the constitution of a church at Osawatomie, Westmoreland highlighted the mission opportunity of Southern Baptists by pointing out that in the seven surrounding counties there were forty towns of more than one hundred people, in twenty-five of which there was no Baptist church. This was in the area surrounding Ottawa University, the only college in the state supported by Northern Baptists. In the area only three churches had been organized since 1890, and none since 1919. "All of this area," he lamented, "was within 100 miles of the Kansas City Seminary [Central Seminary, not Midwestern!]" *(KSBB, November 1946).*

ORGANIZATION

March 19, 1946, rolled around. This time the people were ready. One hundred twenty-five messengers and visitors gathered in the basement (the only part of the church completed at the time) of the church at Chetopa. To become a member of the new Convention, the church presented a letter of petition which stated adherence to the articles of faith and adoption of the constitution and by-laws of the Convention. These letters were acted upon by those present, and messengers from all such churches were seated. There is not total agreement on which churches were there, nor the number, nor identity of churches who were charter members.

Charles Max Pendley, chair of the Credentials Committee, read the roll call of the messengers and the churches they represented. He added a postscript after each church was identified as to whether or not it had ratified the constitution and/or adopted the articles of faith. Nine churches answered roll call; all but one, Ellenwood, Calvary, indicated a desire to be a part of the Convention: Chetopa, First; Coffeyville, Emmanuel; Wichita, Airlane; Ness City, Trinity; Treece, First; Chautauqua, First; Wirtonia, First; and Burden, First. Only five of these churches had ratified the constitution. According to the registration list from that meeting, persons were also present from Arma, Baxter Springs, Oswego, Pittsburg, Scammon (no church here), and two visitors from Oklahoma and Missouri. That made a total of twelve churches in attendance, with eight becoming charter members.

In an item headlined "21 Years Ago" in the *Digest* (March 25, 1967), nine churches were listed as charter members in this new Convention. The editor added this note after listing the nine churches: "The Ellinwood pastor claimed his church had voted only tentatively to be a part of the new Convention and led them to decline participation. The Wirtonia Church later declared they had not voted to be a part of the new Convention. Thus only seven churches participated from the start. Both [Ellinwood and Wirtonia] affiliated later."

The best evidence (Westmoreland, 1958) shows that seven churches became charter members of the KCSBC: Ness City, Trinity; Burden; Chautauqua; Coffeyville, Emmanuel; Treece; Chetopa; Airlane (later called First Southern, Wichita). Seven churches made an official commitment to the Convention at that extremely important March 1946 meeting.

First Baptist Church of Chetopa, Kansas, in which the Kansas Convention of Southern Baptist Churches was organized on March 19-20, 1946. N. J. Westmoreland, the first executive secretary-treasurer of the KCSBC, believed that organizing the Convention in a church under construction at that time (only the basement had been completed) would symbolize the thrust of a new Convention.

Arma expressed some desire to be a part of the Convention at a later date. Baxter Springs did not wish to join because four of their members held offices in the Spring River Association in Missouri. There was no report from Lawton or Macedonia. The Russell Mission was not yet a constituted church. One of the churches, which seemed originally in favor of being a part of the new venture, withdrew, with only a statement that the members did not wish to cooperate with the Convention. This church became aligned with KCSB at a later time.

The organization did not come to pass without opposition. One pastor, who had seemed keen on the idea from the very first, thought that the formation of an association affiliated with Oklahoma, rather than a Convention, would be wiser. Westmoreland (1947) presented four choices: (1) Do nothing, continue to operate as in the past, and forget about Kansas and its needs; (2) maintain affiliation with Missouri or Oklahoma and the Kansas Baptist Fellowship, which would put a double burden on people and churches; (3) organize an association affiliated with either Oklahoma or Missouri, in which case there would be no ability or authority to speak to Kansas mission needs; or (4) organize a separate Convention and ask the SBC to recognize us as such.

Fortunately, for the future of Kansas and Nebraska Baptists, the fourth choice prevailed. The Kansas Convention of Southern Baptist Churches became a reality. In 1947 the name was changed to Kansas Convention of Southern Baptists. The name was changed again, in 1973, to the Kansas-Nebraska Convention of Southern Baptists (KNCSB).

Officers were elected: Ray Walker, Burden, president; O. R. Clem, Ness City, vice-president; Mrs. O. R. Clem, recording secretary; R. Preboth, Airlane, Wichita, statistical secretary; and Brother Gillespie, a layman from Burden, historical secretary (*SBB*, March 27, 1946). By action of the Executive Board and vote of the Convention, N. J. Westmoreland, pastor of Coffeyville, Emmanuel, was elected executive secretary-treasurer. He served in this capacity part-time and continued as the pastor of Coffeyville Emmanuel.

At a special Executive Board meeting on June 8, 1946, in Linwood Park in Wichita, Westmoreland was prevailed upon to become the full-time executive secretary-treasurer of the new Convention, which position he accepted and held until 1969. That same month, the first Evangelistic Conference sponsored by the Convention was held in the First Southern Baptist Church of Wichita, with Home Mission Board representative, J. L. Aders, as the speaker.

The fledgling Convention was off and running. At the March organization meeting, a Unified Budget was adopted, with eighty-five percent allotted to state missions and fifteen percent to Southern Baptist causes through the Cooperative Program, a plan about like those of the Missouri and Oklahoma State Conventions. The fifteen percent would be increased on or after the time the KCSBC was accepted by the SBC (*SBB*, April 1946). The first check, in the amount of $60.63, to the Cooperative Program of the SBC from the KCSBC was mailed on October 4, 1946.

THE FIRST ANNUAL MEETING, OCTOBER 1946

The Executive Committee was instructed by the messengers at the Chetopa meeting to set forth an "official program" of missions and prepare a Calendar of Activities for the year. The program for 1946 included Eastern and Western Zone conferences (April/May, July, September, and December), an Evangelistic Conference in connection with six or more simultaneous revivals in Wichita, Youth Camp, annual State Convention, and Youth Convention. Southern Baptists in Kansas and Nebraska have been "on the go" ever since.

Much earlier, Westmoreland had posed several critical questions concerning the direction of the Convention or Association (*KSBB*, January 6, 1947): "(1) Shall we clarify the Articles of Faith on alien immersion and closed communion and other such doctrines? (2) Will our mission program include more than a missionary at work on the field in Kansas? Shall we establish a fund for aiding the purchase of mission station property? (3) Are there not orphan children in Kansas as well as Oklahoma City or Dallas that need Baptist care? (4) How long will we have to wait before a Bible Chair is

N. J. Westmoreland, elected in March 1946 as the first executive secretary-treasurer of the Kansas Convention of Southern Baptist Churches, served until 1969.

established in some properly located college where student preachers could get their training near to their churches?" These questions would guide the Convention in many decisions in the years ahead.

Orbie Clem assumed the duties of editor of the *Beams* on April 24, 1946. In an early issue, he explained his view of the KCSBC. He thought it critical to explain at every opportunity that the term "Southern" did not mean churches that belong only in the South. He defined it simply as a term that distinguished particular beliefs and practices held, both by Southern Baptist churches in Kansas and by many other churches all over the territory of the north. "More than likely, if time continues, the day shall come when in states throughout all the United States those churches will form Conventions as we have" (*KSBB*, May 1, 1946). These words make him sound like a prophet or the son of a prophet.

From time to time "open doors" were reported in the *Beams* (May 9, 1946). One letter reported a newly formed church in Syracuse, west and south of Ness City. The pastor expressed interest in the new movement in Kansas. He told about his son, a Southern Baptist preacher, who, with another Southern Baptist preacher, was living at Ulysses, fifty miles away. They were members of the Syracuse church because this was the church nearest to them. He thought that more than half the members in the new church were Southern Baptists.

In 1946 the first summer Youth Camp under the sponsorship of the Convention was held at Cedar Bluff, overlooking the River Verdigris, north of Coffeyville. Young people from Treece, Chetopa, Coffeyville, Chautauqua, Burden, Winfield, Wichita, and Ness City were in attendance along with a group from Oklahoma. Westmoreland wrote (*KSBB*, July 1946), "The majestic view of the river valley, the rich resources and the city of Coffeyville in the distance, are of never-ending inspiration. We are completely withdrawn from the world and here among the beauties of nature many mountain top experiences are had." The camping trail is still a high priority of the leadership of the Convention. The first land purchased by the Convention, in 1952, was a 130-acre tract southeast of Quenemo on the Marais des Cygne River for a state assembly.

The first annual meeting of the KCSBC was held at Burden on October 14-16, 1946. One of the amenities especially noted in the *Beams* was the up-to-date public address system only recently installed. The cost of a printed annual report of this meeting was borne by the Baptist Convention of New Mexico. Reports of the 1947 annual meeting at Airlane in Wichita and the 1948 annual meeting at Emmanuel were evidently summarized in the *Beams*. After 1948, there were specially printed proceedings and reports.

At the first annual meeting, four churches offered letters of petition: Calvary, Russell; First Southern, Winfield; Southside, Wichita; and First, Cambridge. All were newly organized and all had full-time pastors (*KSBB*, November 1946). Cambridge had been organized on Friday, October 11, just before the Convention began. Keith Hamm was the pastor. L. Clifford Wells came to this meeting from Topeka because he had read an announcement about it in the *Topeka Journal*. No one in southeast Kansas knew there was a Southern Baptist church in Topeka. According to Keith Hamm, everyone was thrilled.

The articles of faith defined the Convention as a purely cooperative body, furnishing means by which the "the churches of Christ in their sovereign capacity could work together in promoting all enterprises in Missions, Christian Education and Benevolence, as are a part of the Great Commission." However, the Convention reserved the right to refuse to seat the messengers of any church found corrupt in faith or practice, or because of the "personal attitude or character of the messengers."

The by-laws provided that all sessions of the general Convention "shall be opened with suitable devotional exercises and closed with prayer"; "preachers employed or aided by the Convention . . . shall be of good standing and tried piety and shall be members or become members of Baptist churches in Kansas." It was further ordered that "no appeal for funds shall be made at any session of the Convention nor shall collection be taken at such meetings except by a special order of the Convention." At almost every meeting, some change was made in the by-laws and suggested for the constitution, which could be amended the year following the presented change. The original constitution and by-laws were rewritten and new ones adopted in 1955.

At almost every Convention, from 1949 to 1970, the year in which Roy Hollomon retired, he made a report on temperance as executive secretary of Kansas United Dry Forces. At the 1946 meeting, the temperance report was read by J. H. Ray, who "discussed it fervently and at length." The report was adopted after it was strengthened by an amendment stating that Baptists shall "altogether," instead of "as far as possible," refrain from doing business with those who deal in alcoholic beverages.

This subject was of grave importance to Southern Baptists in Kansas, especially as distribution of liquor impinged on the armed forces. Several later resolutions spoke to this issue quite pointedly. A Thought for the Day in one issue of the *Beams* (November 1946) touched on this subject: "A certain graveyard was always kept locked, but a notice on the gate read: 'The Key to the graveyard will be found in the tavern.'"

Evidently the opening devotional at that first annual meeting, delivered by "Gene Leftwich, First Church, Burden, a fifteen-year-old preacher boy," made a great impression; it was mentioned in the minutes and a summary was printed in the *Beams*. He was one of several youth from the Burden Church who had been "called out" for the ministry. When he had finished his presentation, "Rev. C. B. Coleman, veteran preacher, made a short talk on the value of young Christian workers, using Gene as an example" (*Annual*, 1946).

Emmett L. Whitaker, manager of the Baptist Convention of New Mexico Press, was the speaker. His message was "timely and encouraging," excerpts of which were published (*KSBB*, November 1946): "A phrase from a poem of Clovis Brantley, in his book *God Can*, says: 'because they can, they must.' You can, and because you can, you must. Your evangelistic fervor is a mark of

Southern Baptists. . . . The first Convention of Southern Baptist churches is being held in the center of the world as pictured in a fold of a world atlas I glimpsed yesterday. Let us feel truly this is the center, even as Jerusalem was the center from which the thinking of the disciples radiated to the uttermost parts. You have the message Kansas needs. Let's go forth with that message. Not with silver and gold of which we have none, but with the abundant power of the Name, the Message, the Presence, and Power of our Leader who lives, arisen, victorious, and leading on to victory."

The evening session of that first annual meeting was one to be "long remembered and cherished by those present," for several responded to a call for salvation and rededication. Even though it closed late in the evening, the messengers from the East and West Zones of the Convention territory assembled separately and set the framework for the organization of two associations. Associations—another stone was set in place.

Associations proliferated as churches were organized for fellowship and shared tasks. In 1994 there were fourteen associations in the two-state area. To trace their "ancestry" is to understand the pattern of church development in Kansas and Nebraska. Western Association was disbanded in 1947 when two new associations were formed: Wheatland and South Central. In 1956 Smoky Hill Association was formed, uniting five churches from Wheatland and the Eastern Nebraska churches, including the First Southern Baptist Church (Southview) of Lincoln, which was the first Southern Baptist church in Nebraska. In 1958 churches in eastern Nebraska left Smoky Hill and formed Eastern Nebraska Baptist Association (ENBA). Wheatland was disbanded in 1954 when churches joined the new Central Association or Smoky Hill Association. George W. Truett, a new association, was formed in 1948 and disbanded in 1953. Out of this grouping of churches in 1953 came Kaw Valley Association and Kansas City Association. The original Southeastern (Eastern Zone) Association formed in Burden in 1945 was dissolved in 1949 to form Twin Valley and Tri County Associations. In 1954 a group of churches from Kaw Valley, along with churches from Twin Valley Association, formed Blue Stem Association. In 1966 the churches in western Nebraska left the Colorado Convention and aligned with the Kansas Convention, forming the Western Nebraska Baptist Association (WNBA). In 1952 High Plains Baptist Association came into being. It was disbanded in 1953, and in 1954 three associations were formed in this area: Southern Plains, High Plains, and Cheyenne. Cheyenne was dissolved in 1964 to form, along with churches from the Wheatland Association, the new Central Association. Southern Plains and High Plains were united in 1970 in the Western Kansas Association. In 1994 Western Nebraska became Sandhills and Platte Valley Associations, and in 1995 the Panhandle Fellowship was formed (Gibson, 1958; Shope and Smith, 1982; Westmoreland 1971).

At the annual meeting in 1946, several important pieces of business were transacted. The Convention adopted a book store. Already there was a privately owned Baptist book store in Wichita, at 719 Hydraulic, operated by

Lonnie Wells, a young layman in the Airlane Church. At the annual meeting he proposed turning the store over to the Convention, which would retain him as manager with his salary coming out of a share in the profits. The joint sponsorship with Wells continued for about two years. For thirty-seven months it was solely owned and operated by the Convention. In October 1951 (*Annual*), the Sunday School Board bought the assets of the book store and operated it until May 15, 1963, at which time it was closed. A committee was formed (*BD*, June 8, 1963), and at the annual meeting a resolution was framed which asked the Sunday School Board to reopen a Baptist Book Store in Kansas (*Annual*). This did not happen.

The Convention office was established, first as only an address: KCSBC, P. O. Box 729, Wichita Kansas. This was before the days of zip codes. The first "place" was the residence of the Westmorelands on Hydraulic Avenue, which also housed the Baptist Book Store in the "front" room, and the Convention office in a bedroom. In August 1949, a five-room building was rented at 244 1\2 North Main in Wichita. Later, in 1952, a building at 231 North Main was purchased and renovated for a headquarters building.

As the Convention grew, space needs increased. The beautiful headquarters at 3000 West Kellogg in Wichita was dedicated in 1963. For financial reasons and in order to more centrally locate headquarters among our churches and members, the Kellogg building was sold and the Convention office was moved in 1977 to 5410 West 7th Street, Topeka.

At the first annual meeting (November 1946), the officers elected included: president, Ray Walker; vice-president, Orbie R Clem; and executive secretary-treasurer, N. J. Westmoreland. These had all served as officers of the Fellowship and were reelected. Mrs. George Mitchell was elected recording secretary, since Mrs. Clem, who had been elected to this position in November, had been named executive secretary of WMU. G. W. Morrison, Coffeyville, was elected statistical secretary, and R. H. Maultsby, Wichita, historical secretary. In addition, R. H. Gruver, F. P. McDaniel, and Lonnie Wells were elected as Brotherhood president and Baptist Training Union and Sunday School secretaries, respectively. They served without pay.

THE FIVE-YEAR PLAN AND THE 100 CLUB

At the September 1946 meeting in Winfield, the Executive Board voted to adopt and promote a plan to organize one hundred new churches in the first five years of the Convention, which was appropriately called the "Five-Year Plan." Annual goals were set: first year, eight new churches; second year, thirteen; third year, nineteen; fourth year, twenty-seven; and fifth year, thirty-three. To fund this venture, the 100 Club was formed.

The goal of the Five-Year Plan was not fully realized, but notable strides were made. According to the report in the 1950 *Annual*, there were fifty-six churches and ten missions, representing marvelous growth from the original seven churches and one mission of five years earlier. A new Five-Year Plan was voted into place, and growth continued. At the end of 1994, there were 320 churches and missions, or an average net growth of 6.5 per year.

Through the years churches and missions have flourished for awhile and then vanished or changed. Some missions were started over and over again, under the auspices of various churches, and finally succeeded. Ogden Baptist is a prime example. This church grew out of a mission which had been begun and closed by a number of different churches in Smoky Hill Association. It is now a fully constituted church with a fine building, built by volunteers, partially financed through the Revolving Church Loan Fund of the Kansas-Nebraska Southern Baptist Foundation. In other instances, economic upheavals and population shifts have swallowed up churches and mission opportunities. Still the concern for preaching points to share the story of Jesus goes on. Evangelism continues to be a chief concern of Kansas and Nebraska Southern Baptists.

Membership in the 100 CLUB, patterned after the 100,000 Club of Southern Baptist debt-paying days, was made up of those who agreed to make a monthly contribution to the fund that was to help finance new churches growing out of the "Five Year Plan." Memberships included individuals, groups, classes, and churches both inside and outside the state. Contributions ranged from one dollar per month to as high as anyone pleased. A suggestion was made that there were churches and individuals in Oklahoma, Texas, Missouri, Arkansas, and other Southern Baptist states which could and would give from five dollars to twenty-five dollars or fifty dollars monthly and never miss it. The money was to be used to help support pastors in new churches until the churches could do this without help. From October 1946 through May 1947, $465.46 was given through the 100 Club. Two new churches, Osawatomie and Southside Wichita, were given help to the extent of $7.50 to ten dollars per week. Westmoreland longed for several hundred members who would give thousands of dollars which "will enable these new churches to have a fighting chance to live and thrive" (Day of Prayer Program, 1947).

Clem had earlier written an editorial suggesting that every Baptist give one day's wage each month to state missions. He figured the average daily wage to be at least five dollars. If just one hundred people agreed to this, it would mean five hundred dollars per month which would put two full-time men on the field in addition to Westmoreland. It did not seem unreasonable to him that two or three hundred would respond. Of course, any who could not give a full day's wage were invited to give what they could. He pointed out that California Southern Baptists were already following such a plan. WMU had already sponsored the first State Mission Day of Prayer.

In the report of the executive board in 1950, Westmoreland stated, "In forty-five months . . . $5,383.94 had been given through the 100 Club to help strengthen new Southern Baptist churches in Kansas. It . . . provided salary supplement, in some measure, to 25 pastors, who served (at different times) 20 new churches and missions. Where possible, the aid has been given over a period of time" until the church was strengthened. Gifts to the pastors ranged from a dollar a month to at least one gift of six hundred dollars in one month. The most consistent out-of-state member was a student at Oklahoma Baptist University (OBU) in Shawnee. An Oklahoma pastor was cited as giving the largest gift, with checks totaling six hundred dollars. First Baptist, Bethel was recognized as the church making the largest gift, $954.33 in the previous year.

The goal of one hundred churches was reached in 1954. W. F. (Bill) McKean, who came to Kansas in 1952 as pastor of First Baptist Church of Mulvane, reported that he attended the organization, "under a shade tree," of the Southern Baptist church in Douglass, the one hundred and first Southern Baptist church in Kansas. On the same day, the church in El Dorado, the one hundredth church, was organized.

From the very first, the Convention has been on the move. When the organization was only eight months old, there was a full-time executive secretary-treasurer, an official news publication, eighteen churches, a plan of action, a unified budget, associational framework, a book store, and a deep concern for mission outreach.

But this was not without opposition, from both within and outside the state. This opposition caused the editor of the *Beams* to explain the policy of that publication: "The material appearing in this publication shall not be restricted to that which carries the endorsement and expresses the views of the editor and/or other Kansas Baptist personnel. Nor shall any attempt be made to assume a straddle-of-the-fence attitude for the sake of safe-guarding relations with other religious bodies" (*KSBB*, October 1946).

An editor of a Baptist paper in a southern state had refused to publish anything about the organization of a Southern Baptist state convention in Kansas. The southern editor considered such an organization in Kansas as an encroachment on Northern Baptist rights.

In 1947, during the Topeka Evangelistic Crusade, nine simultaneous revivals were held in the Topeka area. Marjorie Moratto, then Marjorie Moore, shared revealing insights into this effort. She came to Kansas in that summer with her pastor, L. L. Peninger, to play the piano in one of the revivals, in the Seabrook area. Since there was no building, a man who owned a piece of land next to his filling station gave permission to use it. They built a stage, got a piano from somewhere, and hauled in benches. She and Mrs. Peninger sewed colorful little capes for the Booster Band, which was made up of young children. The beginning date was set, they visited, and people came. The only crisis was the mosquitoes—so big, and so many! The leaders passed out citronella so everyone would rub it on before the start of singing and preaching. The revival, typical of many others, was scheduled for two weeks, but kept going on and on indefinitely. Finally, it became a regular once-a-week meeting in a schoolhouse, from which the Seabrook Baptist Church emerged. This may have been the reason many churches were organized; revival meetings went on and on, so the people organized a church to rest a bit.

This experience may have caused Peninger to leave his Oklahoma pastorate and come to Kansas as bivocational pastor of a church in Topeka. Gene Strahan, the first state missionary, reported that Peninger was an automobile salesman in Topeka. "In fact," he said, "he sold me the best automobile I have ever owned."

Strahan also said that Peninger was a "strong supporter of missions and led the churches he pastored to be mission minded. He was a stabilizing force in the area among the young pastors . . . encouraged them and gave them wise counsel" (written communication).

This experience also put Kansas in Moratto's system, so when she finished her senior year at OBU, she contacted the Westmorelands about returning. This was 1948, and Westmoreland told her the Convention needed an office secretary. The Westmorelands were still living on South Hydraulic, just a couple of houses from the First Southern Baptist Church. They graciously invited the new employee to live in their home.

That fall at the annual meeting of the Convention, she was elected secretary and manager of the book store. She reported that she was really not equipped to do any of the jobs she filled: secretary, bookkeeper, and store manager. All she had "going for her" was her desire to be in Kansas and to be a part of the Lord's work here. After a few paychecks she was able to rent a room for herself, which freed the bedroom space for an office for the next employee of the Convention, W. E. Russell, who became the first secretary of religious education, February 1, 1949.

Later, Moratto went to Golden Gate Baptist Theological Seminary, as secretary to Fred McCaulley, Home Mission Board representative for a number of western states, and as a student at the seminary. She said, "My love for Kansas remained just as deep during the time when I was in California. Of course, I can look back now and see that the Lord was preparing me to get back here and do just a little bit more for Him. I got my education; I got my preacher man (Harry Moratto); I got my experience as pastor's wife; and then, again through the influence of Dr. Westmoreland, Harry and I were called to King's Highway Baptist Church in Wichita. Just ten years after leaving the state I was back again."

Once more, she began to type for Westmoreland, first during the evenings and then part-time when her children were in school. Next she became bookkeeper and finally assistant editor of the *Digest*, where she remained until after the financial crisis.

These were not easy times, and the worst was still ahead. The goal of the Convention was to be recognized by and accepted into the SBC. That was the next hurdle. Fortunately, that goal would be achieved soon.

SOUTHERN BAPTIST CONVENTION AFFILIATION

The KCSBC made formal application to the SBC in 1947. The formal letter of petition was read to the Convention by Secretary Porter Routh: "For the recognition of this Kansas body of Southern Baptists as a cooperating constituency of the Southern Baptist Convention" (*Annual*, SBC, 1947). At the time, there were eighteen affiliated churches with a membership of 1,600 in Kansas. Additionally, there were three other Baptist churches in the state, with 1,160 members, still affiliated with the Missouri Baptist Convention. Gifts to Southern Baptist causes, including the Cooperative Program and home and foreign missions, had totaled $949.49. The petition also stated: "Our establishment of 8 new churches during the first year of our organized existence and our unsolicited gifts to Southern Baptist work through Oklahoma and Missouri for 136 years, totalling more than $42,000, attest to our missionary zeal."

At this Convention, a committee was appointed "To Consider the Kansas Application." E. H. Westmoreland, from Houston, Texas, was named chairman. He was no relation to Kansas' Westmoreland, but when he gave his report to the Convention the following year, he admitted that he would not mind being a kinsman of such a fine person. On the committee was a man from each state affiliated with the SBC.

In a pamphlet published by the KCSBC, Westmoreland eloquently answered the question, "Why Southern Baptists in Kansas?" He cited the early practice of Kansas Baptist churches aligning with the SBC in Missouri "in protest of the spiritual laxity of their former associates." He called attention to the fast growth of churches since the Convention was formed and to the 368 towns in the state with no Baptist church: thirty-five of these had more than one thousand people; seventy-three had more than five hundred; and 260 had more than one hundred. In Southern Baptist "territory," one out of every five persons was a Baptist; in Northern Baptist territory, only one out of every fifty was a Baptist. In addition, he pointed to the loss of Northern Baptist churches and the lack of organization of new ones. From 1919 to 1944, Northern Baptists in Kansas had a net loss of 152 churches. From 1934 to 1946, only two new Northern Baptist churches had organized in Kansas.

He was concerned that even though Northern Baptists had been in Kansas for ninety-two years, they had no orphans' home, reported only $336 in hospital ministry in 1944, and made "no mention of ministerial training in their Convention *Annuals* of 1939, 1941, or 1944, in their report of the only Baptist College in the state."

On top of their "non-Missionary spirit," he pointed to their "certified heresies in Baptist doctrine," "foreign baptism" and "infant baptism" as reasons for the organization of another Baptist body in Kansas. "It is easily seen that Baptists who lose their conscience on New Testament baptism, also lose their conscience on the principles for which Baptists have long stood. Baptists who lose their reason for contending for the distinctive principles of the New Testament also lose their desire to establish new churches and the zeal to maintain their old ones."

Orbie Clem was equally verbal. He told of his encounter with a leader in one of the southern states who protested the organization of churches in Kansas and suggested that Southern Baptists would resent Northern Baptist action in our territory. Such an argument grew out of the Comity Agreement between the Northern and Southern Baptist Conventions. Clem assured him this would not be the case, because, he said, "Baptists are champions of religious liberty like no one else on earth" (*KSBB*, April, 1947). As an afterthought, he wished he had reminded this protester that Northern Baptists had operated a school (Bacone) in Oklahoma for many years. Oklahoma Baptists "have been very unselfish in their approval and support of this institution."

In that same issue (*KSBB*, April 1947), Clem quoted from a publication that came to his desk from the Council on Finance and Promotion of the NBC. The writer bemoaned the fact that Southern Baptist churches and even associations and state conventions were being established in Northern Baptist territory. This was particularly true, the author stated, in Arizona, California, and Illinois and was "becoming true in other state areas, such as Kansas." Because of these encroachments, the NBC had appointed a committee to meet with a similar committee from the SBC "in order that some action be taken to correct this situation." Clem must have been chuckling as he wrote his editorial comments:

> These aggressorous Baptists!—especially the preachers. Looks like they just will not stay at "home" and behave themselves. Looks like you can't teach them anything. Instead of staying in the place where others say they belong, and minding their own business, the boys just will slip out and climb over the fence and go fishing. No matter how much the would-be papas fuss about it, the scalawags still go fishing. They say the fence isn't hard to climb over because there really isn't a fence. Somebody tried to build one once upon a time, but the thing wouldn't stand up. And those fellows—why they'll fish just anywhere in that stream. They say there are plenty of fish for all who can catch 'em. Yeah, they've got the notion that "crick" don't belong to anybody except the One who made it, and they say that neither the fishermen nor those who just claim to be fishermen made it. Every once-in-a-while somebody'll speak before they think twice and tell 'em they can't fish in that bend of the "crick"! Then those Baptist brothers will ask them if they own that fishin' hole. Of course, they have to own up that they don't because they have no papers to show as proof.

Keith Hamm was one of the pastors present in 1948 when the question of affiliation of the KCSB with the SBC came to the floor. He had the presence of mind to pay a man five dollars to wire record the business session. There were no tape recorders in those long ago days. Hamm had come to Kansas in June 1946. He was one of the first Home Mission Board student summer workers to be appointed to work in Kansas. Two others served with him that summer: Stanley Gasswint and Charles Coleman. Hamm's first pastorate was at Cambridge.

Hamm set down the events of the 1948 Convention and gave a verbatim account of the session in a pamphlet titled "The Battle for Recognition." He began his account by stating, "Hilarious messengers stood by the thousands, expressing their hearts' desire to make the Kansas Convention of Southern Baptist Churches a fully recognized cooperating constituency. As I look back on that grand moment, I counted it then, as I do now, my life's most thrilling and meaningful experience."

Representatives had attended the SBC in 1946 in Miami with the hopes that the new Kansas Convention could be recognized. They were told that they would have to wait for the Convention in St. Louis the following year. They went back in 1947 to St. Louis with a letter of petition. At that Convention, a committee was appointed to bring a report to the 1948 Convention, which would meet in Memphis, Tennessee.

Early in the year four members of the committee, including the chairman, came to Wichita and spent about two hours with the Kansas Convention Executive Committee, listening and asking questions. Afterwards, unknown to the committee members, the visitors had lunch and a conference with the pastor of the First (Northern) Baptist Church in Wichita. It is unclear whether they were "asking permission" of this pastor to heed the Kansas request, or if they were trying to persuade Dr. F. B. Thorn to lend his prestige to the new organization by leading his church into the Southern Baptist fold. Thorn seemed sympathetic to the idea, but could not bring that church into the new Convention, since he had promised, when he was called as pastor, he would not do this.

Later, Westmoreland and seven Kansas pastors went to a meeting with the entire Convention committee. After much discussion the committee informed the Kansas representatives that they were not going to recommend that the Kansas Convention be accepted into the Convention at the Memphis meeting.

The promise of a negative report did not stop the Kansas brethren. The Kansas "battle cry" was "Add a State in '48." They went to Memphis with forty dollars which had been authorized for a Kansas exhibit. Behold! There were no exhibit spaces left. Undaunted they found a building supervisor who knew about a hat-check room which he allowed the group to use, free of charge.

Hamm got a piece of light-green beaver board, and the group worked till 1:30 the next morning setting up the exhibit. The big Kansas map, lighted with two floodlights, showed where the churches (thirty-five by now) were located, the towns and counties where there was no Baptist church, and some of the larger towns, such as Topeka and Wichita, where additional Baptist churches should be organized as soon as conveniently possible.

The booth was a hit. Groups almost constantly stood around the exhibit listening to the Kansas story. Even when the Kansas folk went home, the booth was left standing as a silent witness to the opportunities for evangelism and service in Kansas.

Evidently, real politicking took place among the pastors present at the SBC meetings in 1947 and 1948. Hamm recalls N. J. Westmoreland making his appeal to messengers for a favorable vote, holding up four fingers on his left hand as he presented reasons for acceptance: (1) There is a great need; (2) there are great opportunities; (3) good results can already be seen; and, (4) there is need for the work of Southern Baptist boards in Kansas: the Home Mission Board, Sunday School Board, and Annuity Board.

Anticipation and interest built during the Convention. The question came up often, "Do you think Kansas will make it this year?" The hall was packed when it was time for the business session. An overflow hall was provided.

Stemming from the 1946 petition from Kansas, By-Law 17 had been changed at the St. Louis Convention (Hamm, 1993). It provided a more definite process for receiving new constituents. Along with a letter of petition giving particular information, and appointment of a review committee (which had been followed in the Kansas matter), it also provided that only when a convention reached a membership of twenty-five thousand would it be represented by membership on boards and agencies.

Chief players on the floor that afternoon were Louie Newton, SBC president; L. E. Barton, parliamentarian; Bill Smith, president of the Baptist Bible Institute in Lakeland, Florida; Ollie Robinson, a faithful pastor in Southeastern Oklahoma; W. R. White, "a most influential man among Southern Baptists, who was President, and then Chancellor, of Baylor University"; and, of course, E. H. Westmoreland, chair of the examination committee and pastor of South Main Baptist Church in Houston, Texas. The stage was set. Lights! Camera! Action!

First came the report of the Comity Committee, chaired by White, and made up of members of both the NBC and SBC. White asked that the committee be continued, although some conclusions and agreements had been reached, because "developments have come into the forefront which can make obsolete some of the things we have discussed, and will require a restudy of the whole situation should this development materialize." The "development" turned out to be a consideration of a possible merger between the NBC and the Disciples. If this were to come to pass, it would "completely change the territorial problem and the whole question of comity."

Hamm suggested that this announcement, although the merger did not take place, may have stirred some thinking "in the right direction" for the Kansas position. He counted it a breakthrough for a favorable vote. The motion for the continuation of the Comity Committee was passed.

The report of the Committee to Consider the Kansas Application came immediately. The chair prefaced the recommendation with statements concerning the "Baptist brethren" of Kansas. They were vitally interested in a definite program of missionary activity. They were characterized by spiritual fervor. They had a conviction that the work could best be accomplished through the agency of the SBC.

So far, so good! Then came the BUT! Kansas represented only the tip of the iceberg, so to speak, of the whole "Comity Agreement" problem. While the committee realized that the "territory now occupied by our Convention includes Baptists who hold doctrinal positions in accord with the historic position held by Southern Baptists . . . [who] are desirous of a more aggressive missionary and evangelistic program than their present denominational relationship affords . . . [who] like us, oppose any affiliation with the Federal Council of Churches and any Comity Agreement which limits missionary endeavor . . . [who] like to use our literature . . . [who seek] pastors trained in Southern Baptist Seminaries . . . [who use similar] methods in organized work." Even so, perhaps to soften what they would recommend in regard to the Kansas application, the preliminary recommendation, in light of the larger problem which had repeatedly been encountered by the Convention in recent years through the application for recognition by Baptist constituencies outside the southern area, stated "that the Convention now set itself to the task of setting forth principles and procedures by which it will be guided in its decision on all such applications in the future."

With that apology, the committee was ready to make its final report. In short, it was not now, not full recognition. While the whole loaf was withheld, a few crumbs were offered. Any Southern Baptist church could affiliate with the Convention and be entitled to one messenger, if it contributed to the work of the Convention during the year preceding the annual meeting. Any cooperating church could even have one additional messenger for every 250 members or for each $250 paid to the work of the Convention. No church could have more than ten messengers.

While withholding recognition as a cooperating constituent "pending further development," all agencies and boards of the Convention were to have the privilege of administering whatever aid to the churches in Kansas they "deemed advisable."

And then came a formal recommendation that the Convention appoint a committee of seven members to study the larger problem of receiving new cooperating constituencies "in the United States and its territories." These words were lifted directly from the Convention constitution.

The motion got a second, and then the chairman complimented the Kansas committee and discussed each of the recommendations, pointing particularly to the "fluid state that now obtains in Kansas." It was this consideration that caused the committee to recommend that recognition be deferred, to "await further developments." One of the developments waiting in the wings in Kansas was the idea that the Northern Baptists in Kansas were considering withdrawing from the Federal Council of Churches.

Westmoreland (E. H. not N. J.) suggested that the wording of By-Law 17 be made more explicit than simply to instruct the committee to investigate "all matters pertaining to the request." He confessed the committee was "at a loss" to know what was meant by "all matters." He raised several questions about what the committee was to do. Should they go and examine the position of the churches and the leaders as to their theological beliefs? Should they investigate the spirit in which they cooperate with other Baptist bodies in the state? Should they discover whether there was a spirit of antagonism or one of good will?

The chair was informed by the Committee on the Order of Business that five minutes remained for discussion. Newton recognized Bill Smith of Florida.

Smith's comments deserve bronzing: "Brother President and members of the Convention: that was a most polite way to say 'No,' but that isn't what is in my heart. I want to tell these struggling brethren of Kansas that we are coming to help you, and I . . . [tremendous amount of applause], Brother President, I move that recommendation two of the report of the Committee to Consider the Kansas Application be changed to read as follows: 'Whereas, Kansas Southern Baptists have met all constitutional requirements for recognition as a cooperating constituency of the Southern Baptist Convention, we recommend that they be recognized as such at once with all constitutional privileges likewise becoming effective.'" And here there was another sudden burst of applause, loud and long.

Then the chair recognized Ollie Robinson of Oklahoma, who seconded the motion. He spoke of the difficulties faced in Kansas and the great way in which Westmoreland had led the Convention, and at no little sacrifice. There was more applause, so much that Newton tapped his gavel to quiet the messengers.

One man rose to speak in opposition. Fortunately, or unfortunately, Hamm wrote, the floor microphones did not work very well so that neither the messengers on the floor nor persons on the platform could hear him distinctly. He offered an amendment which was ruled out of order, with another amendment already on the floor. Time for the business session was extended for ten minutes.

J. B. Rounds, the first executive secretary of the Baptist General Convention of the State of Oklahoma, spoke in favor of the amendment. He commented that this was the third SBC meeting the Kansas Baptist brethren had attended with the hope of affiliating with the Convention. He finished by stating, "They have met the requirements of this Convention, and I feel that whatever we do regarding the reception of other people, that Kansas has waited long enough and ought to be received." His statement was met with great applause.

Ralph Harris from Missouri was recognized, again at a floor microphone and not easily understood. Years later, Hamm met a man who was sitting next to Harris on that day. His question concerned the leadership in Kansas.

He saw them as a group of young fellows who were not sure of what they were doing. He felt the SBC should respect the present boundary line and accept the committee's original recommendation.

The chair recognized Pat Murphy, pastor of First Baptist Church, Cushing, Oklahoma. He was an impressive fellow, always in the middle of politics in Oklahoma government, black hair combed straight back, dark heavy-rimmed glasses, wearing a seer-sucker suit, holding a flat-topped straw hat in his left hand, and waving his right index finger at Louie Newton to get his attention.

After a few satirical remarks concerning the "fluid situation in Kansas," he asked, "How do we get the previous question before the house?"

L. E. Barton, the parliamentarian, answered, "I call for the previous question." The "call for the previous question" is used to cut off debate and bring to a vote the amendment and then the main question. The Convention voted "the previous question," which passed.

The amendment from Bill Smith was read. Newton suggested a standing vote. "Those who are in favor," he said, "of the adoption of the amendment will please stand in this hall, and in the other hall, so that both Secretaries may know the vote." Thousands stood in favor of the amendment. When opposition was called for, there were only a scattered few who stood. Again there was loud applause, as Newton said, "The amendment prevails."

After the amendment, the main motion received almost unanimous support. Then a messenger from Oklahoma was recognized who moved that a committee be formed to bring a report at the Convention the following year in Oklahoma City to rename the SBC The Baptist Convention of the U. S. A. He stated his reason, "Because for four years we have been fighting about this thing, and Oregon and Canada and others want in, and the Great Commission says to go into the uttermost part of the earth." The motion was seconded.

Before the chair could call for a vote, Barton stepped to the microphone and said, "I guess it is alright, but our purpose is expressed in our Constitution, and says that this Convention is for the purpose of eliciting, combining, and directing the forces of the Baptist denomination and churches in any part of the United States. It is already nation-wide." The motion was lost. The name of the Convention would remain the same.

The Convention made important changes at the Memphis meeting, which went further than recognizing another state as a constituent of the Convention. There would be no more discussion of a comity agreement. No longer would Southern Baptists see themselves confined in any way, certainly not to the South. The Convention territory was broadened to include the United States and its territories. The following year, 1949, the Oregon-Washington Baptist Convention was recognized without any opposition or debate. In a few years Ohio, Indiana, Michigan, Colorado, Alaska, and Hawaii would be received. The fact that these Conventions were cooperating constituents of the SBC opened the way for establishing and encouraging new churches in these areas. By 1986 there were thirty-seven state Conventions. All fifty states are now affiliated with either a regional or state Convention through which churches cooperate in organized work.

Hamm finished his report with this paragraph: "But the amazing fact of it all is this: who would have thought that seven Southern Baptist churches in the month of March, 1946, could constitute a state Convention and in two years and three months this new state Convention would lead forth the entire Southern Baptist Convention to a nation-wide view and understanding of expanded home mission work into 31 other states, and make it truly nation wide? But it did happen!"

Apparently the first SBC president to visit Kansas was R. G. Lee in 1952. It was five years after Kansas became a part of the SBC before a Kansan appeared on its program. On February 15, 1953, announcement was received that George D. McClelland, pastor of Immanuel Baptist Church in Wichita, had been designated to bring the scripture and prayer for the opening session of the SBC at Houston, Texas, that year.

Just eleven years after Kansas was accepted as a constituent of the SBC, in 1959, another Ebenezer was raised: the KCSB passed the twenty-five thousand membership mark, which entitled the Convention to representation on the Boards and Committees of the SBC (*BD*, April 1959). A goal adopted in 1956, "A full-grown state in '58," was achieved. The slogan was conceived by W. A. Burkey, secretary of missions, and John Havlik, secretary of evangelism, and widely used throughout the Convention. The goal was actually reached in time to be announced at the November 1958 meeting of the Kansas Convention, held in Topeka.

Rang Morgan, pastor of Sharon Baptist Church in Wichita, and president of the KCSB, presented a walnut gavel to Brooks Hays, president of the SBC, for use during the 1959 SBC meeting. The walnut lumber from which the gavel was made came from the Pottawatomie Indian Baptist Mission building just outside Topeka, built in 1848. This building marked the first organized mission work of the Domestic Mission Board (now Home Mission Board) of the SBC in Kansas.

Actually, the number 25,093 was verified for Southern Baptists in Kansas and Nebraska by a telephone call from J. P. Edmunds in Nashville, Tennessee, in 1958 (*BD*, November 1, 1958). Paul Allison, assistant executive-secretary of the Kansas Convention, suggested that Kansas churches designate a mid-week service as a time of thanksgiving for this growth. "Pastors should explain to the people how much this means to the work, and how much more can be accomplished."

That same issue of the *Baptist Digest* (1958) contained a summary of the exciting and impressive twelve and a half years of growth of the KCSB: "The original seven churches have multiplied to become 135 plus 27 missions. Church property was valued at $54,278; now the assets are $4,746,850. Gifts to all causes from the churches have totaled $7,673,671, and the Convention's total receipts come to $1,223,277 through September."

Another view of progress was given the following year in the *Digest* (June 20, 1959): "The Convention has its own air-conditioned office building in the Wichita business district . . . a staff of 25 full-time employees . . . 138 churches . . . 25 missions . . . and 13 associations with an estimated membership of 28,000." The previous year churches had baptized 2,054 persons and received offerings totaling $451,190.

Westmoreland conceded that our size "in every wise does not compare favorably with the other states of the SBC" (*BD*, October 25, 1958). He believed, however, that "we have many things that occasion justifiable pride in the achievements of our churches and members." Several churches had baptized more than one hundred per year; a number of churches less than ten years old had reached a membership of one thousand. "Among our pastors are men who would be favorably accepted in any pulpit in the Convention. Within the churches we have leaders whose training and capabilities would be coveted by any church." Most important to Westmoreland was the fact that "the new membership mark should signify that we have a spiritual striking force for evangelism in Kansas and Nebraska that God can use for notable progress in subsequent years."

Rang Morgan, president of the KCSB, was the first Kansan to serve on the SBC's Committee on Committees (*BD*, June 6, 1959). By 1961 (*BD*, March 11, 1961), Kansas became eligible for "full representation." Previously, the Convention had been represented only on the four boards and the Executive Committee. By-law changes were completed which allowed constituencies reaching a membership of twenty-five thousand to be represented on more committees. The KCSB had come of age by the help of God.

And so the "Convention dream" was realized. Organized Southern Baptist work was in place in Kansas. This, of course, was not the real beginning of a Southern Baptist presence in this place. We were here long before the turn of the century, even before the Civil War.

2

In the Beginning

CORONADO, IN 1541, THE FIRST WHITE MAN IN WHAT IS NOW Kansas, came seeking the fabled cities of Cebola. According to one historian of early Kansas (Sharpe, 1939), while he did not find the cities of gold "he did find a fabulously rich plain, almost equal [to] the land visited by the spies sent out by Moses." Five Indian tribes inhabited Kansas at that time: Kansa, Osage, Pawnee, Apachee, and Wichita. Later, these were joined by the Kiowa, Comanche, Cheyenne, and Arapaho. The Osage and Pottawatomie, along with other tribes (later labeled Emigrant tribes by the U.S. Government), lived east of the Missouri River.

White people continued to come to the territory as farmers and explorers. In 1819 Zebulon Pike marched through Kansas and in the main Pawnee village on the Republic River; he officially raised the Stars and Stripes over the Territory of Kansas for the first time (Sharpe, 1939).

Baptists from the beginning have been an evangelistic people, a Great Commission people. Very early they were at work throughout the new Union establishing congregations, forming associations, and doing missionary work among the Indians and the struggling churches on the frontier (Armstrong and Armstrong, 1979).

But it was the decision of Ann and Adoniram Judson who were on their way to India to work with William Carey, a Baptist missionary sent by English Baptists, that rallied American Baptists to form a foreign missionary society. After study of the Scriptures, the Judsons concluded Carey was correct in his stand on baptism. Since they could not continue to serve with the Congregational Society which had commissioned them, they appealed to Baptists in America for support.

Thus it was that in 1814 delegates from eleven states and Washington, D.C., met in Philadelphia and organzied one grand general missionary society, in which all Baptist groups could cooperate. So was born the General Missionary Convention of the Baptist Denomination in the United States of America for Foreign Missions. According to the constitution, meetings were to be held evey three years, so it came to be known as the Triennial Convention.

The stated purpose of the oganization was to minister to both the "heathen" and the "natives." This was interpreted to include Indians and settlers on the frontier. In the early days of the Convention, however, the emphasis was on foreign missions almost to the exclusion of the needs of the Indians.

The conflict over slavery and whether or not slave-holders could be appointed as missionaries by the America Baptist Home Mission Society was a major cause for the organization of a separate convention of Baptists in the South. However, the deemphasis on home missions, uneven representation of southern churches on the boards, and what Baptists in the South saw as lack of attention to the mission needs of the South and West, particularly among Indians, were also reasons for the organization of the Southern Baptist Covention in 1845 (Armstrong and Armstrong, 1979).

Isaac McCoy was the undisputed pioneer and guiding force of whatever home mission activities the Triennial Convention supported among the Indians. McCoy was born in 1784 in Pennsylvania, but grew up in Kentucky. In 1803 he married Christiana Polk, certainly one of the most astute things he did. After they were married, they moved immediately to Indian country, where McCoy worked with the Miami tribe. He supported himself as a wheelwright before he became a Baptist minister in 1810. Christiana spent much time alone, as evidenced by some of her letters to McCoy while he was on the road, which he was much of the time. He made some twenty-two trips to Washington, D.C., on horseback. There were thirteen children, many of whom died at birth or very early in their lives, whom Mrs. McCoy cared for, parented, and buried, with little help from Isaac. A memorial statement said of this woman, "In the mission, Christiana was mother, teacher and missionary. She was also business manager, financial board, superintendent of agriculture, court of appeals, and family physician" (*Kansas-Scrapbook*, Vol. 14). Later, in 1817, McCoy was officially appointed for a one-year term by the Triennial Convention; and he was then appointed to another term in 1829 with his friend, Johnston Lykins.

A great concern of Isaac McCoy was the situation in which Indians lived, with encroachment from every side by white settlers. His dream was to relocate the Indians living east of Missouri to a reservation west of the Missouri River, giving them a land of their own from which white settlers would be forever barred. It would be an Indian state. Indians were troubled by the white man's whisky, sale of which resulted in "the most shameful orgies," and by his diseases, cholera and smallpox, which took deadly toll on the lives and welfare of the red man. McCoy believed the Indians could not be evangelized until they were protected from the white man.

His passion for the salvation and welfare of the Indians came at a time when "most people looked upon Indians as somewhat less than human, putting them in the same category as panthers, polecats and other varmints of which the land had to be cleared. They were hated, feared, despised" (McCoy, 1840).

Berkhoffer (1970), in his introduction to the reprinting of McCoy's *History of Indian Baptist Missions,* had this to say about McCoy and his dreams: "He sought nothing less than a portion of the trans-Mississippi West as a permanent Indian State, with himself as ruler. In his mind, the welfare of the Indians was intimately bound up with the Baptist religion, the establishment of a new country for them, and his own advancement. . . . To achieve his scheme, he used whatever means came to hand, whether it was the Baptist Mission patrons, the political furor over Indian removal, or the establishment of a new missionary society."

Even though his target goal was the well-being of the Indians, McCoy never learned any Indian languages and was often tricked by the interpreters he had to depend on, some of whom had no desire for the Indians to be moved or "civilized." Berkhoffer (1970) stated that even after twenty-three years of work among many tribes, McCoy had no insight into Indian attitudes and customs. At the end of his service, he was as oblivious to this as he had been when he had begun. "In this blindness he was like most other Americans. In the end, McCoy's book [*History,* 1840] shows him to be a nineteenth century American first, and a missionary only second."

In 1820 McCoy moved to Fort Wayne, Indiana, where he began a school with twenty-five students. By the end of year, thirty-two were enrolled. Here Johnston Lykins, who later married McCoy's daughter, began his service, which he continued for a quarter of a century, first as a blacksmith, then as a teacher, and finally as a physician.

Even though McCoy was quite frugal with the funds sent to him, there was never enough money. Without the board's consent, he wrote to many churches to ask for more support. He was convinced that the mission board, by failing to supply all his needs for establishing stations among all the tribes, had "deliberately sacrificed Indian missions for the more glamorous overseas effort" (McCoy, 1840).

At one of the Baptist Foreign Missionary Society meetings, when McCoy was pleading for the Indian cause, two hundred dollars was collected for foreign missions and only $51.25 for Indian missions. At this same meeting, arguments arose about what hymn book would be used, an eastern one, or one from the west, which McCoy considered another affront to Indian missions.

Berkhoffer (1970) suggested that McCoy "urged patrons to expand their Indian operation beyond their desires and their financial means." Since Baptists were not as liberal as he needed them to be, he turned to the Federal Government, because interest was high in Indian relocation.

The Chicago Treaty in 1820 between the U.S. Government and the Pottawatomies, and later with the Ottawa Tribe, made available a square mile of Pottawatomie territory for a mission site. The government agreed to spend one thousand dollars per year for fifteen years to support a teacher and a blacksmith at the Pottawatomie site. For the Ottawas there was a promise of one thousand dollars per year for ten years to support a farmer, as well as a teacher and a blacksmith, along with allocation of some cattle and farming implements. The board approved three teachers for schools for Pottawatomie, Ottawa, and Miami; McCoy became superintendent. The station operated by the group that moved from Ft. Wayne, Indiana, to the Pottawatomie site on the Osage River was called Carey, located at Grand Rapids, Michigan; the one for the Ottawas was called Thomas, located at Niles, Michigan. Later, in 1846, a new mission site was established for the Pottawatomie beyond the river in Kansas near Topeka.

In 1823 the manual training school at Carey Mission was opened with thirty students. McCoy, in his 1840 *History*, described it: "Our school house was without floor, shutters to the doors, or chimney. We burned a log fire within, around which we all sat, greatly annoyed by the smoke and cold."

McCoy's work many times included working out agreements between Indian tribes about land division. At one such agreement, a fascinating ceremony took place to "seal the bargain." The meeting ended in a "reciprocity of good feelings." One group of Indians offered, and the other group accepted, white porcelain beads, tied to a piece of tobacco. The meaning of the ceremony was described as "making a white road between the parties, which is to be kept clean" (Wyeth, 1995).

The Missouri Territory was opened in 1812, which made the relocation of Indian tribes of great importance. When Missouri applied for statehood in the 1820s, as a slave state, great argument exploded, which resulted in the Missouri Compromise. This allowed Missouri to join the Union as a slave state and Maine to join the Union as a free state, which kept the "balance" between slave and free states in the U.S. Senate. The Missouri Compromise also prohibited slavery in the land acquired through the Louisiana Purchase (1823) north of a line that roughly followed the southern border of the state of Missouri, but with the exception of the state of Missouri. This extended the "Mason-Dixon Line" which had been set in 1763, and was known as the demarcation between the slave and free states.

This great land beyond the Missouri was the place that McCoy wanted to locate the "emigrant" tribes, those tribes that lived to the east of the river. The relocation process was a sad and painful story. For example, when the Pottawatomie, a peaceful tribe, albeit they fought on the side of the English in the War of 1812, were to move to Kansas (1846), they had to face the warring Pawnee who did not want them in their territory. The Pottawatomie were victorious, but at a great price. When the removal or relocation was "accomplished," it did not take. By 1854 the Kansas-Nebraska Act set the boundaries of the Kansas Territory: "the 40th Parallel on the north, Missouri on the East, the 37th Parallel on the South, the crest of the Rocky Mountains on the west." This act also annulled the Missouri Compromise in that it gave these territories self-determination in the matter of slavery.

When Indians were moved again from the Kansas Territory to Oklahoma, "the Red Man's Land," many of the Pottawatomie chose to sell the holdings which had been allocated to them in 1854 and to move. A small group elected to stay in Kansas on a "diminished reservation" which is located even today about twenty miles northeast of Topeka.

This legislation also set Kansas as a battleground between "freedom" and "slavery" people. Settlers moved in to hold it as a "free" state, and others came to make it a "slave" state. Little attention was given to the rights of Indians in this matter. It was in 1861, when Kansas joined the Union as a free state, that the Indians were finally and fully dispossessed.

Westmoreland (1955) outlined the development of missions in Kansas in this fashion: 1831, a mission among the Shawnees where greater Shawnee Mission is today, with Johnston Lykins and John Pratt as leaders; 1833, a mission among the Delaware where Edwardsville is today, with Ira Blanchard as leader; 1837, a mission among the Ottawa, from which the city of Ottawa and Ottawa University came, with Jotham Meeker as leader; 1837, a mission among the Pottawatomie six miles below Ottawa in Linn County, near Marais des Cygne River, with Robert Simmerwell as leader; and 1846, the mission near Topeka for the Pottawatomies, including the Pottawatomie Baptist Manual Labor School.

THE AMERICAN INDIAN MISSION ASSOCIATION

By 1842 McCoy concluded that the American Home Mission Society of the Triennial Convention was not interested in the Indian work; it was too far away. Many Southerners were of the same opinion. So the American Indian Mission Association (AIMA) was organized at Ninth and O Baptist Church in Cincinnati, Ohio, with McCoy as executive secretary, headquarters in Louisville, Kentucky, and an official publication called *Indian Advocate*. Westmoreland (1955) called the new association "wellborn" and gave a "roll call" of Southern Baptist "greats" who were involved in and supportive of this undertaking: Dr. W. B. Johnson, who was to lead in organizing the SBC in 1845, Basil Manly of Alabama, James M. Pendleton of Kentucky, Humphrey Posey of Georgia, William Baldwin of Kentucky, and James H. Bagby of Kentucky. Isaac T. Tichenor, who served as agent for the association, presented its work to the Mississippi Baptist Convention in 1848, and was chairman of the committee to bring a report on new fields of work. Johnston Lykins and Robert Simmerwell were enthusiastic about this turn of events; John Pratt, Jotham Meeker, and Ira Blanchard were not at all pleased with the new organization. They did not approve McCoy's "high-handed" methods of getting things done.

McCoy's *History* (Alexander, 1981) sheds light on this position: "After the seat of the board of missions was located in Boston, the acting members manifested an unyielding aversion to boarding schools. First they were objected to on account of the expense of attending them. And secondly, because the proper work of the missionary was spiritual, and a boarding school would involve too much of what was secular."

The following year (1843), McCoy petitioned the Triennial Convention to recognize the American Indian Mission Association on an equal par with the Baptist Foreign Missionary Society and the American Baptist Home Mission Society. The Boston Board, however, would have nothing to do with this upstart, unauthorized group. They had no intention of turning over the Indian work west of Arkansas and Missouri to the new group. Their attitude was one of toleration at best. The AIMA was well received and supported by churches in the South, who thought they had been shortchanged by the distribution of home missionaries by the American Baptist Home Mission Society.

The "new kid on the block" began sending out missionaries: David Lykins was appointed to work at the Wea Mission, near the present site of Paola, Kansas; and Johnston Lykins, who had been discontinued by the Boston Board and was working as a government physician, was appointed to work with the Pottawatomies. In 1844 the association appointed Robert Simmerwell because he, too, had been dropped from the missionary roster of the Boston board when he offered to work without missionary pay and live on his blacksmith salary so that the board could send another missionary, which they did not do. McCoy had met Simmerwell in 1824 in the East. Simmerwell agreed to locate at the Carey Mission, and in Buffalo purchased needed supplies: seed, wheat, flour, and salt; in Detroit he purchased steel and iron for the blacksmith shop. Robert Simmerwell was a skilled blacksmith, a practical farmer, and a good mechanic. He supervised the erection of the stone building at the Pottawatomie site near Topeka. Simmerwell's youngest daughter was likely born in this building, the first white child born in the Kansas mission.

A "modern" sideline to this family concerns Simmerwell's daughter, Sara. When the Simmerwells left the mission, they became charter members of the Auburn Baptist Church, which was organized in 1855, or a little later. Sara married Isaac Baxter, who became a member of that church on February 31, 1867, and was baptized the following day. Their grandson, W. A. Baxter, led that church to affiliate with the Southern Baptist Convention (SBC) in 1948.

ELIZABETH MCCOY

In 1844 Elizabeth (Eliza) McCoy, daughter of John McCoy, great Baptist layman, and niece of Isaac McCoy, along with her friend Sara Ann Osgood, were appointed, Eliza to work among the Pottawatomie and Sarah Ann to work at Wea Mission. Eliza was probably the bridge between the "old" order and the "new," and, although she was not officially employed by the SBC, she was certainly the first woman to be appointed in her own right, and not as

Elizabeth "Eliza" McCoy, teacher at the Pottawatomie and Wea Indian Missions, niece of home missionary Isaac McCoy.

the wife of an appointed missionary. She was also the first appointed woman missionary to work at a mission which came to be an official part of the SBC when the work was transferred from the AIMA to the Board of Domestic Missions of the SBC in 1855.

Her salary for her first year was one hundred dollars and was subscribed by the women of the First Baptist Church of Talladega, Alabama. In addition to her salary and traveling expenses, her nephew (McCormick, 1892) reported that she received fifty dollars a year for "sundries," which assisted greatly. This was also the day of "missionary barrels." So gifts and surprises arrived from time to time, some useful, others not.

McCoy had been born in 1813, the seventh of ten children. When she was sixteen, she united with a Baptist church. Her father was a devout man and an able supporter of his missionary brother, Isaac McCoy. John McCoy and his wife were active in the church, but left the congregation when it fell under the influence of Alexander Campbell and repealed the "Articles of Faith" which were the foundation upon which the church had been constituted. Deacon McCoy and a few others formed the Silver Creek Baptist Church in Clark County, Indiana, which was taken into the Lost River Association in Washington County. Later, he and four others were excommunicated from the church because they failed to conform to advice of the association which opposed missionary and benevolent societies. The battle was over missions, Sunday School classes, tract societies, and temperance, which the association decreed were of the devil and his work.

John McCoy opposed this view. He said (McCormick, 1892), "Sir, you might as well expect to turn the water of the Ohio River upward by standing on its banks at the falls, and throwing straw by straw into its currents, as to expect to stop the good influence of Sunday Schools and missionary societies." The staunch little group was received into the Salem Baptist Church.

This was the home in which Elizabeth McCoy came to maturity. Evidently she adored her father and highly respected her uncle, Isaac McCoy. In addition, she was well educated, particularly for a woman of her era. When she was about twenty, she became a pupil at the County Seminary in Wellington, Indiana. Later, she graduated from Hanover College where she met her life-long friend, Sara Ann Osgood, who was later her associate in missionary service. Three years later, she attended the seminary at Charleston, Indiana.

In 1835 her mother died and, according to her nephew (McCormick, 1892), it became the responsibility of this daughter to take care of her father's household. During this time she was also employed as a school teacher until her father remarried.

In 1844, Elizabeth McCoy, at age forty-one, volunteered for mission service among the Indians who were being relocated to Kansas. She and Miss Osgood were accepted. They were "set apart" by the Lost River Church with an "appropriate service."

They left Louisville on a steamboat for Westport Landing, Missouri, near present Kansas City. The trip took three weeks; the fare was twenty-five dollars. Miss Osgood had been assigned to the Stockbridge tribe, but for some reason was sent to the Wea Mission (in Kansas near the Missouri border) and served there until she died in 1852.

McCoy went first to the Pottowatomie Mission School on the Osage River, which was located fifty miles southwest of Westport. A letter, which her nephew included in his *Memoir* (McCormick, 1892), was likely written while she was at the Osage Mission School:

> The only school among them, except mine, is a boarding school conducted by the Catholics. Owing to a number of the Indians being under the necessity of taking their families some distance from home to seek their daily food by hunting, my school is small. Yet it affords

me much pleasure to labor for the instruction of a few of the poor, unfortunate children of the forest. If I can be useful it will more than be compensated for: "For all the losses I sustain, of honor, riches, friends." We have also a small Sabbath-school, and on each Thursday afternoon a female prayer-meeting, and regular preaching on the Sabbath and on Wednesdays.

In a letter to her father, she talked about the land in which she served (McCormick, 1892):

My dear Father: Your more than welcome letter was received in due time. . . . My school, though small, requires the greater portion of my time. I think I am not mistaken in saying it is the most tiresome and trying to my health of any employment I could have, to be tied down from day to day with from five to twelve scholars. For while the labor is not sufficient to keep the mind and body in lively exercise, it prevents an engagement in anything else.

You request me to give you a description of the country, the population and number of white families. Owing to my recent arrival here you will not expect an accurate description. The Pottawatomie country is perhaps as beautiful as any uncultivated country could be. The soil is invariably good. As there is scarcely any boggy or marshy land, it wears a healthful appearance. The growth of timber on the low lands consists of black walnut, hackberry, buckeye, white and red elm, red-bud, ash, black and white hickory, pawpaw, and lynn. On the uplands are found abundantly all the various kinds of oak common to Indiana. Hazel bushes, plum, crabapple, wild cherry, and persimmon grow in the margin of the prairies in great abundance, also the winter grape.

In another letter to her father, she told of some of the experiences on the trip to the new mission station for the Pottawatomies:

Cousin Lykins' fever kept up all day, when his chill came on again about four o'clock. We then concluded to stop for the night, but had to leave the road more than half mile to get to the timber; and when we came to it, we found it a dreary, dreary place. The timber was all in a ravine, and we had to leave the wagons and go down a steep bank, where we found the ground wet, and without grass or leaves. But it was the only chance. While the men made a fire, Sara and I ran off a distance to gather what grass we could to spread under the bedding; stretched a tent and made a bed for cousin Lykins, who was growing worse rapidly. He soon fell into a stupor, so that we could scarcely rouse him enough to take a sip of water. We did not know that he would live until morning; and there we were alone in the wide prairie, far from any house, without knowing what to do for his relief. All we could do was to watch, with solicitude, first him, and then the approach of day. But a Merciful Providence was with us. The next morning found him better. As early as we could we resumed our traveling and reached here about three o'clock in the afternoon. We found the house very much out of repair, and altogether dirty. . . . But we went to work and soon made one room comfortably clean. But as we could not repair roofs nor stop cracks, we suffered from a snow-storm that blew in upon us a few days afterwards. Our floor, and often our heads and shoulders, would be white with snow that fell through the roof. We would sometimes retreat from one corner to another, but all efforts to escape the blast were in vain. We were compelled to take it as it came. But the storm is over. We have our other room cleaned, and for the present are comfortable. The Indians, we think, will soon be located, and everything appears favorable; if we can only meet with the necessary aid from home.

In these makeshift quarters they took seventeen Indian children, because "the Indians so pressed us. . . . How are we to take care of so many, under so many disadvantages, I cannot tell, and felt almost frightened when thinking of it. But when children are brought, and I am told they have no mother, and how they have been treated, and what they have suffered, I cannot refuse."

By 1849 there were twenty-six children in the school near Topeka, and still the new building was not ready. (It was completed sometime in 1850.) She stayed at this mission until 1852, when she began to work at the Wea Mission, upon the death of Miss Osgood. In 1853 she returned to her home. There were two reasons for her resignation: the lack of support from the churches and her father's declining health. After his death, she ministered to other family members, making a home in Franklin for her niece and nephew so they could attend Franklin College, and then moving to Texas in 1874 to live with her brother, where she lived until his death in 1887, and hers, four years later.

There is one more facet of her life that must be highlighted. When her brother died, he left to her his estate of fifty thousand dollars. In the four years she lived after that, she was able to make gifts, in cash and property, to various causes totaling $75,195. Her list of bequests showed where her heart was: one-third of the balance of her estate went to the SBC for foreign missions, one-third went to the American Baptist Home Mission Society, and one-third went to the Texas State Board of Missions. A gift of property valued at thirty thousand dollars was given to Southern Baptist Theological Seminary. Other gifts went to Buckner Orphans' Home in Texas, First Baptist Church of Dallas, Baylor University, and Franklin College.

At her death there were a number of memorial services, including one at Baylor University where Dr. George W. Truett read the following tribute: "Miss McCoy's life very strikingly illustrates the great truth that Christianity is to impress the world more by what it *is*, than by what it *says*, or even by what it *does*."

He went on to say, "Her gifts to missions will forever enable two men to preach the gospel in Texas; two more to preach it to the Indians; and still two more forever to preach it in foreign lands." It might have been a far better prediction for Truett to have suggested that Elizabeth McCoy's gifts, along with others like them, would send women, as well as men, to tell the good news here, there, and everywhere.

McCormick (1892) summed up her life in this fashion, "She was guest, friend, advisor, advocate, helper, aunt, guardian, and lover of a large number of relations in Clark County, Indiana." We can add to this list: committed to her duty, missionary to the Indian children, and financial manager of no small merit.

POTTAWATOMIE BAPTIST MANUAL TRAINING SCHOOL

Although she served for a time at Wea Mission and at the Manual Training School for the Pottawatomies on the Osage River, Elizabeth McCoy's main work was at the Pottawatomie Baptist Manual Training School near Topeka. In 1849 the AIMA reported that the Pottawatomie mission on the Osage had the following personnel: Johnston Lykins, physician and teacher; Robert Simmerwell, blacksmith; and Mrs. Simmerwell and Elizabeth McCoy, teachers. There were twelve students in attendance; McCoy conducted "classroom exercises in addition to a Sabbath school and female prayer meetings" (Barr, 1977).

By that time the mission was looking forward to the move to a permanent location where they hoped there would be more gratifying results. The Pottawatomies were given two years from the time the treaty was signed to move from Council Bluffs on the Missouri and on the Osage to their new country purchased from the Kanzas.

Lykins first arrived in Kansas in 1831 to establish a mission among the Shawnees, but there was no money for a building. Money was available in 1832, and work was begun in earnest. He became the editor of an Indian language paper, *Shawnee Sun*, which was printed by Jotham Meeker, who brought the first printing press to Kansas. Lykins was a linguist and had translated Matthew and Acts into the Pottawatomie language. A paragraph in the *Proceedings of the American Indian Missions Association* for 1844 gives information about his translation work: "These translations were designed not only for the use of such as could already read, but also to be used as a school-book for those who desired to learn to read. It is printed in the *New System* in which the idea of *spelling* is excluded. The types are merely characters, denoting sounds and the various positions of the organs of speech, while speaking. An unlettered Pottawatomi can thus learn to read in a few days."

When the time came for the Manual Training School to be built in the new location for the Pottawatomies, Baptists were the choice for the management "contract." Baptist advantages were evident in the correspondence dealing with this decision: Baptists were the first to establish a mission and school among this tribe (with particular reference to the Carey Mission); they had published the scriptures and other elementary works; there was "existence of a partiality for them by many of the Pottawatomies; . . . [they had] demonstrated unabated interest in their welfare and their strong desire to continue their labors among them" (quoted from Barr, 1977). All these were considered when the choice was made as to who would operate the school at the new Pottawatomie site. There was also to be a Catholic school in the area. When the AIMA received word of this decision, the corresponding secretary of the board responded, "I am instructed by the Board to inform you, that they not only *desire* but are *very anxious* to engage in the enterprise" (Barr, 1977).

The new school was to accommodate ninety pupils; the government would appropriate annually $4,500, and allocate fifty dollars per year for each child who was boarded, clothed, and educated. There was to be a "reasonable compensation for day scholars." There was also an allocation of five thousand dollars for permanent buildings and "agricultural improvements." The AIMA promised to "cheerfully add to the money appropriated by the Government for this purpose, whatever sum is usually required in such cases" (Barr, 1977).

The following personnel were assigned to the new school: Johnston Lykins, who became superintendent; John M. Ashburn (arrived in 1850) who had "extensive literary qualifications" and who would be teacher and preacher and in charge of the male department; Elizabeth McCoy, in charge of the female department; and Rev. Noediah Dille and his wife from Oswego, Iowa, who were replaced by John Sanders and his wife. He was to be in charge of "farming and mechanical departments" and was also to preach. Mrs. Dille was to be in charge of the "domestic department." Robert Simmerwell (first assigned to Wea Mission) and his wife were also part of the staff by the time the buildings were completed.

The school evidently opened in temporary buildings in the fall of 1848. A letter from Elizabeth McCoy indicated that she was ready to end the "vacation" as soon as possible and begin the school in the temporary building. "Due to limited means and accommodations there were sixteen pupils at the school, eleven being girls. In addition to the Pottawatomies, there was a full-blooded white girl, who was the step-daughter of a Pottawatomie man. Subjects being taught at the school consisted of reading, writing, geography, and arithmetic. The pupils were also instructed in domestic duties like sewing and other needle work. Religious instruction and sabbath school also formed an integral part of the curriculum" (Barr, 1977).

Lykins wrote in the fall of 1849 that the building was to be of stone, which he hoped would be both permanent and convenient. As it turned out, he probably achieved the first goal far better than the second. The building had three floors: the first, or basement, as he designated it, and second floors were 85' X 35' with walls on the first floor two feet thick and one-and-a-half feet thick on the second. On the first floor were four rooms: a cook's room with a central fireplace, two dining rooms (one for boys, the other for girls), separated by a north-south hallway, and a steward's room. The second floor had two classrooms, one for girls with a central fireplace, and one for boys with no fireplace. There were also four dwelling rooms for faculty, which were separated by an east-west hallway. The attic or third floor was 85' X 20' and featured a flush-gable monitor which set it apart from other institutional structures of the nineteenth century, giving the building a distinct profile. Lykins may have chosen this style because of economy or because it had the appearance of a basilica. There were sleeping rooms here for boys and for girls, which could be entered only by stairways from the classrooms below, and a small mission office. There were sixty doors and windows in the structure which was built of fine grained limestone, probably from nearby out-croppings and which weathered to a pale yellow or rusty brown. It was built at a cost of $4,800, which was paid by the United States Government. That building still stands today on the grounds of the Kansas Historical Museum.

By 1849 the school had gained nationwide attention. Joseph H. Ware in his *The Emigrants Guide to California,* published in 1849, reported that "about ten miles above [the Kansas crossing] there is a mission station of the M. E. [Baptist] Church where any blacksmith work can be done, which accidents may have made necessary."

When Lykins made his first report to the Indian commissioner about the school, he proposed that the name be changed from the Pottawatomie Baptist Manual Labor Training School to the McCoy Academy to honor Isaac McCoy. There was no response to this suggestion; evidently, a name change was not satisfactory to the Office of Indian Affairs.

In addition to the main stone building, several others were built about the same time, all of hewed logs, some with one or two "good stone chimneys" and others with none. There were houses for laborers, a kitchen, meat house, and a root room. Costs ranged from $351 (a large house with two chimneys) to thirty-five dollars for a lodging room for hired men.

The farm was also developed at this time. Lykins reported sixty acres of plowed land, with twenty-five acres in corn, one in potatoes, and two in beans and other vegetables. Thirteen thousand rails and stakes had been made and placed. There were to be twenty-five acres sowed in wheat and forty acres left for pasture.

The goings and comings to the mission were not easy. Ashburn wrote about his trip to the school: "By the mercy of God we arrived safely with all our things. We found the new building with two floors laid, doors and

Pottawatomie Indian Mission, probably the oldest standing building in which the Home Mission Board, SBC, did mission work, is undergoing restoration in 1995. The Kansas Historical Museum is located on its grounds.

windows in, plaster on the walls of the second story. The family rooms are impaired. I have been laboring very hard to facilitate the completion of the house. I have gotten me a room nearly ready to go into; we will put on the last coat of plaster tomorrow. The lime has eaten into my fingers so badly that they bleed" (Barr, 1977).

By 1850 there were thirty students enrolled. The buildings were completed in April of that year, and a full staff of eight was in place.

The plan was that the school would be self-supporting, so work was the order of the day for everyone, staff and students, each sex working with tools thought to be appropriate by the white man. "Older boys cut wood, made fires, fed cattle, cared for the cows, and worked in the fields at planting, hoeing, and harvesting. Little boys carried water and assisted in feeding the cattle. Girls cooked, baked, washed and ironed clothes, swept the buildings, made beds, spun, knitted and wove, made candles, and processed meats" (Barr, 1977).

The schedule for the day was incredible: up at 5:00 A.M. to wash, dress, and have devotionals. The big girls skipped the latter in order to prepare breakfast. Breakfast came next; then all the girls, except the dishwashers, went to the classrooms to knit or sew. The boys went to the fields. At nine o'clock, everybody assembled for lessons, which went on until noon. After lunch there was a period of recreation, followed by more lessons until 4:15, when the big girls cooked, the little girls sewed, and the boys went back to the fields until the evening meal at 5:30. When supper was over, there was a brief worship service and an exercise period. Afterwards, the children returned to the classrooms where they prayed and sang until bedtime at 8:00.

One way to assure support for the school was to enlist donors who would give generously. When children came to the school, they were given the English name of a person who had made a gift to the mission. So, for a certain specified gift each year, a donor could have a child named in his/her honor.

Whipping, which was the common practice in some white schools, was not used in the mission school. Instead, quite unusual forms of punishment were utilized, such as imprisonment, long periods of standing in uncomfortable positions, and sitting with a hood over one's head. Banishment from school was the result for sexual and other "gross offenses."

There were a number of half-French Pottawatomies; therefore, McCoy wrote her father to see if he could find people who would be willing to buy five French Bibles. Evidently, John McCoy could find no donors, so he paid for the Bibles himself and sent them. Also, an interpreter was added to the staff to help teachers communicate with new students.

The school faced several difficulties: cholera, smallpox, arguments with the fur-traders who wanted to keep Pottawatomies from attending school, accusations against Johnston Lykins about his work in general, particularly his procedures during the cholera epidemic, and his mishandling of funds. He was supported by many of the missionaries and filed a suit for libel against those who had bought charges against him. Nonetheless, these things led to his dismissal in 1852.

Even with all the difficulties, by 1850 the school had seventy students; in 1851 there were ninety enrolled. Inroads were being made with adult Pottawatomies. A friend of Mrs. Simmerwell (who was at this time at the Wea Mission), living near the Pottawatomie School, wrote her that she enjoyed attending prayer meetings with the women, which were held on Thursday afternoons. She told her that two Indian women also met with the group, which was an encouraging sign. However, attendance at preaching outposts was small.

The chief work of the AIMA was evidently with the Wea, located near Paola, and the Pottawatomie, in a mission located on 320 acres about six miles west of Kansas Avenue, Topeka's main street, which became Sixth Street. The first location of the Pottawatomie School was devastated by the flood of 1844, which Westmoreland described as worse than the floods of 1903 or 1951.

When that flood came, two hewn log houses were badly damaged, and were later moved to another location and repaired. Perhaps the worst clean-up job was that reported by Barr (1977). Hundreds of buffalo carcasses were washed down against the mission houses and had to be carted away. The stench was dreadful and the water supply was polluted.

THE BOARD OF DOMESTIC MISSIONS, SBC

The AIMA, organized in 1842, continued to function until 1855, when it made formal petition to the SBC, which had been organized in 1845, to take over this work. There were probably two reasons for this. Isaac McCoy died in 1846 and no one "rose up" to take his place of leadership. In addition, the SBC was made up of churches in the South which had been the chief support of the association. These churches could not afford to support two home mission societies and increasingly chose to give their support to the SBC, which was engaged in all sorts of mission activities.

So in 1854, negotiations began with the Board of Domestic Missions of the SBC. The leadership of the American Indian Association was desperate. If help did not arrive soon, they would be forced to give up the institution to the government and "surrender Baptist influence in that part of the nation."

Per Baptist custom, a committee of five was appointed to study the situation and bring a report to the 1855 Convention. When the committee brought its favorable report, there was a motion to accept. The committee had made careful plans. There was a time for "ernest discussion," a message on Indian missions by H. F. Buckner, who was secretary of the American Indian Mission Association, and an offering totaling $294.55, Even so, the motion was lost by a vote of sixty-five to sixty-three. However, a motion was made to reconsider this business the following day, May 15, 1855, at which time it passed: "Resolved, That the Convention accept the transfer tendered by the American Indian Mission Association. Resolved, That the Domestic Mission Board at Marion, Alabama, be charged with the conduct and management of all matters appertaining to the Indian Missions, and the continuance of the same, within the sphere of operations. Resolved, that prior to the consummation of said transfer, the Board of the American Indian Mission Association, shall make a full exhibit of its condition to the Marion Board" (Westmoreland, 1955).

A second motion was passed that day: "Resolved, That the Board of Domestic Missions be instructed to occupy Kansas as a field of missions as soon as practicable." This motion may have been born out of the concern for the white settlers pouring into Kansas Territory at that time, as well as for the Indians. With the Kansas-Nebraska Act, which opened the door to white men beyond the Missouri, the dream of Isaac McCoy for an Indian State was forever shattered.

At the meeting the following year, another resolution was adopted:

> Resolved, that the Board of Domestic Missions be instructed to occupy Kansas as a field of missions as soon as practicable. The civil and political condition of that territory has rendered it, until recently, entirely impracticable to obey the instructions conveyed in the foregoing resolution. In December last, Rev. J. H. Luther of South

Carolina, was appointed to this field. It was deemed advisable by the Board that he spend most of the winter in an agency on behalf of his contemplated mission, to which he yielded. About the 10th of March, he embarked for his new field. No tidings from him since his arrival on the field.

What will be the result of this effort, none of us can tell. The board regards it in the light of an experiment, made in compliance with the instructions of the Convention. The policy of the Territory is not yet settled; the trials are not yet ended; human foresight is not sufficient to disclose the end—when, or where, or what it shall be. The missionary sent out has all the requisites of success so far as human instrumentalities are concerned (Westmoreland, 1955).

Luther did not go into Kansas in 1857 after he was appointed, because he saw the turmoil over the slavery problem to be so great he felt it unwise to enter the area. He operated a school for young ladies in Kansas City for more than three years with over a hundred students enrolled. At the beginning of the Civil War, he moved to the interior of Missouri and served two churches as pastor. He was the first editor of a journal for Missouri Baptists, *Missouri Baptist Journal*, which he began in 1866. In 1878 he became pastor of a church in Texas and after that was elected president of Baylor Female Institute.

For a while the Pottawatomie Manual Training School was unoccupied, no missionaries or students were present. In 1856 John Jackson (probably one who had been appointed by the AIMA) was sent to work with David Lykins, who was described as superintendent of all Baptist missions in the Kansas Territory. The Indian agent and others noted some improvement in the school after the SBC took charge.

In 1856 Governor Jon W. Geary visited the Pottawatomie Baptist Mission and issued a Thanksgiving Proclamation for the whole Territory "as a day of general thanksgiving and praise to almighty God for the blessings vouchsafed to us as a people." He commented that he found "many bright-eyed, intelligent-looking Indian children exhibiting great aptness in learning" (Barr, 1977).

A report for 1857 shows John Jackson as superintendent, J. G. Thomason as boys' teacher, and Matilda Arnent and Malinda Holloday as girls' teachers. There was an enrollment of sixty-three students. Repairs were being made on the building and farm. In 1858 there were ninety-eight children enrolled. By this time the government was greatly in arrears with allotments for each student. The accounts remained unpaid; 1861 dawned and with it came war. In the latter part of 1860, Jackson wrote apparently both to the commissioner of Indian affairs and to the corresponding secretary of the board about the condition of school finances: "At the end of the present quarter all that will be due me from the government will not clear me of debt. I shall realize nothing from the farm—no corn, no potatoes—no vegetables of any kind. I have been at the expense of cultivation and received no return. I have cattle and hogs, but no feed for them. From the farm the school has, formerly, received a great part of its support. This support is altogether cut off for this season; and the government allowance will not sustain the school. Unless some additional assistance can be furnished I shall be compelled to dismiss the school at the end of the next quarter. . . . In view of the foregoing facts will not the Department either raise the present appropriation per scholar or make a special appropriation of some $500 to assist in the present emergency?" (Barr, 1977).

No help came. Neither the government, nor the Baptists wanted to spend more money on the school, since it seemed inevitable there would be a new treaty which would require a new location for the school. So on March 21, 1861, the school was disbanded by Jackson, who had been in charge for six years.

The next SBC appointment was Woodlief Thomas, who worked at Delaware City, located on the north edge of the Delaware Reservation, from October 1, 1857, to October 3, 1858. Westmoreland (1955) shared a bit of history about Delaware City, Kickapoo, and Leavenworth. There was great controversy over where the county government was to be located. In the first election, Delaware City polled the most votes and county offices were built. Two years later a second election was held, this time giving Kickapoo the victory. But for some reason the election returns were taken to court, and Leavenworth came out victorious. The only traces of Delaware City and Kickapoo today are in the dead-city file. These were wild and lawless frontier towns when Thomas was appointed.

Thomas organized a church in Delaware City with sixteen members, which grew to twenty-four by the time he left. During this year he organized the Baptist association in Kansas at Atchison, which was known as the East Kansas Association of Baptists. He helped frame the constitution of the "first ever Baptist association in Kansas." It read in part as follows: "A widespread destitution of Baptist preaching prevails in Kansas. In the boundaries of the association several of the important river towns and most of the inland villages are entirely destitute of preaching by ministers of our denomination. Many of the populous rural districts are also destitute. The Home Missionary Society and the Board of Domestic Missions of the Southern Baptist Convention have done and are doing something to supply this destitution, for which we are very grateful. Wickedness and dissipation, vice and immorality in their worst forms prevail to an alarming degree."

Thomas gave up his appointment in Kansas because of the "severity of the climate." He became a missionary in Austin, Texas. According to weather reports of that era, the winter he spent in Kansas was quite pleasant, but the preceding two winters had been bitter ones. He evidently thought two mild winters in a row were too much to hope for.

In 1859 the *Proceedings of the Southern Baptist Convention* indicated that there were no missionaries in Kansas. Westmoreland (1955) pointed out that this was incorrect. At that time the Pottawatomie Indian Mission at Topeka was under the direction of Board of Domestic Missions and so was the Wea Mission, near Paola. Both had been operated by the SBC since June 1855 when they were transferred from the AIMA. In 1859 it was reported that the Pottawatomie Reservation had seventy-three pupils enrolled. This mission had been in the Topeka area since 1847.

By 1861 there were seventy-eight pupils in the Pottawatomie Mission School, but the situation was difficult. The drought of 1860 had forced people to go back to their southern homes. The Pottawatomies were given the opportunity to become citizens, so the large reservation was soon to disappear. The SBC was seen as a part of the Confederacy and no longer eligible for U.S. Government aid for their school. Additionally, the government was behind in its allocation per pupil for two quarters. From necessity, the school was closed (Westmoreland, 1955).

Although Southern Baptists had been operating the school for ten years, they did not own this land. At the time of the treaty with the Indians and the dispersal of land, the government promised 320 acres of land to the denominations responsible for the schools. Since the SBC was identified with pro-slavery and with the Confederacy, when the treaty was fulfilled eight years later, the title to the Pottawatomie School and the 320 acres of government land were given to the American Baptist Home Mission Society rather than to the SBC Board of Domestic Missions (Westmoreland, 1955; Barr, 1977).

THE HOME MISSION SOCIETY

In 1865 the Baptist Home Mission Society made a formal claim for this 320-acre plot and, since there was no Southern Baptist claimant, the land was deeded to them. In 1866 the school was in operation again. The following year another treaty was signed with the Indians which provided a new home for the Pottawatomies. The Prairie Band did not emigrate, and they still live in Kansas in Jackson County. The school was kept in operation until 1867 when the Pottawatomies were situated in Indian country. In 1869 plans were submitted to the Baptist Home Missionary Society for renovation of the building for a hospital, which never materialized. That same year the land was offered for sale.

THE LAND

Now what happened to the land? It was officially deeded to the American Baptist Home Mission Society in 1869. In 1873 it was sold to R. I. Lee for $9,600. The price was thirty dollars per acre, payable at two thousand dollars each year, with interest on the unpaid portion at ten percent per annum (Barr, 1977). Lee's great love was the improvement of trotting horses; and the land he acquired, which he called Prairie Dell Farm, suited his purposes admirably. He built a fine two-story house of native stone at the north of the Manual Training School, and modified the original stone structure for his fifty horses. A number of Lee's stallions were nationally famous, and his brood mares were the best in Kansas (Barr, 1977). His most famous trotter, named Robert McGregor, for which he paid $33,250, was known as the "Monarch of the Home Stretch."

Lee died in 1911, but the home and farm stayed in the family until 1919, when they were sold to Charles Hawk who sold them in 1922 to Elmer Lee. At this time other modifications were made in the building because of its unsoundness. The property was sold again in 1928 and again in 1946. The Carmeans raised horses and cultivated the grounds until the State of Kansas bought the property in 1973.

According to Barr (1977), "Currently a planning study is underway relating to the new museum complex for the state, and the old Manual Labor Training School building is to be rehabilitated on the exterior to that period when it served in one of the frontier efforts by a religious body, the Baptists, to educate and convert a native American group, the Pottawatomies." That renovation is almost completed. It is being financed by a grant from the Koch Corporation in Wichita.

SOUTHERN BAPTIST CONVENTION

After the school was closed, or actually moved to the new home of the Pottawatamies, there was no more evidence of Southern Baptists in Kansas until 1900, when Memorial Baptist Church in Pittsburg affiliated with Spring River Association in Missouri (Shope, SBC Historical Commission records). There is no record of this church after 1903. In 1911, on September 6, Wirtonia (now Crestline) Baptist Church applied for membership in the same Missouri association. There were twenty-seven members with sixty-one in Sunday School. In 1922, on September 3, Trinity Baptist Church of Chanute, Kansas, was received into the Northeast Baptist Association of Oklahoma. By the time the Kansas Fellowship was formed, in 1945, at least twelve churches in Kansas affiliated with one association in Missouri and four associations in Oklahoma.

Lynn Clayton, editor of the *Baptist Digest* (*BD*, May 30, 1977), wrote of his visit to the Baptist Pottowatomie Mission, this first mission post in Kansas:

I felt humble, yet proud. Humble because they gave us so much. Proud to be named with them.

I tried to imagine what the building was like when its ministry was in full swing. Indian children lived there. They dreamed, slept, suffered the terrible pains of homesickness, played.

The fields around the school must have been under constant exploration by inquisitive children who felt so much a part of them. The creek was fished, waded, fallen into, jumped.

I wanted Robert Simmerwell and Johnson Lykins, the mission directors, home that day. I wanted to visit with them—ask them about their work, and why they came. Their presence seemed just that real.

But I did walk away with a part of that mission in my heart. The spirit of the work that went on in that place became, in a sense, mine. The determination to see the people of this Land know Christ, is mine. The faith that built a work where nothing stood before, is mine. The spirit to serve where God says, is mine.

No, I will never be another Simmerwell or Lykins. My faith and determination and sacrifice are dwarfed by theirs. But they are proof texts of the kind of person I want to be.

3

The Bond Fiasco

T HE YEAR WAS 1973; THE TIME WAS TUESDAY EVENING OF THE
twenty-eighth annual session of the Kansas-Nebraska Convention of
Southern Baptists at Bellevue, Nebraska. It was party time! Pat and
Gladys McDaniel, with their son, Ricky, and daughter, Tina, were presented
to the group. According to the minutes of that historic meeting (*Annual*),
"Charles Hawley, pastor of the First Baptist Church, Bellevue, Nebraska, presented Mrs. McDaniel a corsage of white carnations with blue tips and Mr.
McDaniel a boutonniere of a white carnation and blue tips," along with a love
gift of $2,500. A three-tiered cake was on display with the wording: "We Love
You Pat and Gladys." Although the cheering crowd in the auditorium of the
Bellevue Church called for a speech, Pat McDaniel, not given to long orations
nor fiery sermons, made only a brief comment and finished this way: "You
folks are being awfully kind to us by giving me a lot of the credit for something you've done" (*BD*, November 1973). After the evening session, the cake
was cut amid continued rejoicing.

What was the special occasion? McDaniel was neither joining the
Convention staff, nor was he leaving. It was the end of a rocky time in our
history, through near annihilation to jubilant victory. The final five years
(1968-1973) of this trail are his story. But back to the beginning, where all
good stories start. Once upon a time. . . .

THE BEGINNING

When the Kansas Convention of Southern Baptists was formed, the chief
concern of N. J. Westmoreland and the men who closely surrounded him was

63

evangelism, winning people to Jesus Christ. Whatever it took to accomplish that goal—personnel, programs, buildings, help from Southern Baptist agencies, camp experiences—Westmoreland set out to get. The first state-wide Simultaneous Revivals, led by C. E. Matthews of the Home Mission Board, took place in June 1948, in connection with an early meeting of the infant Convention. One of the early acts of the Convention was to purchase 130 acres on which to develop a state assembly. The Five-Year Plan and the 100 Club were initiated to begin new churches and support pastors.

With a gift of one hundred dollars from D. G. Cockrum of Knoxville, Tennessee, a Revolving Building Loan Fund was established on October 12, 1948 (*SBB*, March 8, 1951). In December of that year, the first area missionary to be supported jointly by the Home Mission Board and the KCSB, D. E. Strahan, began his work (*KSBB*, March 19, 1953).

In 1949 the Kansas Southern Baptist Foundation (KSBFN) was created when a committee brought proposed articles of incorporation and by-laws for approval by the messengers. It was not until 1952, however, that the charter was granted (*Annual*, 1953). In January 1953 the Baptist Church Loan Corporation of Texas voted to permit Kansas to participate in their loan program.

The first loan from the Texas Association was made to the King's Highway Baptist Church in Wichita. Four other churches quickly qualified for loans totaling $127,000 (*KSBB*, October 29, 1953).

The stage was set. There was a great urge to meet the needs of Kansans for churches where the word of God would be preached, the beginning of a fund to loan to churches, and the means to make increased amounts of money available through a plan that would make possible more churches in places where they were needed. All this would be available for groups who could not otherwise afford necessary expansion.

KANSAS SOUTHERN BAPTIST FOUNDATION

The KSBFN (Minutes, KCSB, 1949) was a non-profit corporation with the following purposes: "To encourage and motivate the making of gifts, donations and benefaction by deed, will, gift, annuity, contract or otherwise, and to receive and use the same in promoting, supporting, maintaining and fostering the various causes, objects and agencies now or hereafter fostered, created or officially sanctioned by the Kansas Convention of Southern Baptists, wherever located, including but not limited to the following: Baptist Children's Home; Baptist Student Centers; Baptist Bible Chairs; the Revolving Building and Loan Fund; the 100 Club (Pastors' Aid Fund); and proposed rescue missions for Wichita, Kansas City, and Topeka."

The charter, constitution and by-laws of the foundation were adopted in 1949, and trustees were elected. This action came too late for the foundation to get into action for that year, so the work proposed was done by the executive secretary and the Executive Board (*Annual*, 1950). Even in the 1951 report (*Annual*), because of "technical factors in its inauguration, the requirements for its operation were not met at that session [1949] and still have not been fully set in order." Indications were that the foundation would get into full swing the following year. Howard H. Whatley was elected executive secretary of the first board of directors, which was appointed by the trustees.

The foundation, though not fully functioning, was busy about a number of things. It was authorized to receive gifts, bequests, and wills made for the promotion of any agency or work of the Convention. The foundation had the additional responsibility of developing a bond plan for building loans, which was projected to reach fifty thousand dollars (*Annual*, 1951).

The foundation's 1952 report (*Annual*) highlighted the Revolving Building Loan Fund, which had been in operation for four years. Texas WMU (in 1951) had added $2,500 to the original gift which had set up the Revolving Building Loan Fund. During 1951, additional gifts and designations had swelled the operating capital in the Revolving Building Loan Fund to almost $10,500.

During the previous two years, ten churches had been assisted, and work had been completed on the residence for the secretary of evangelism. Even at that time, there was a desire to provide a "construction" service to Kansas churches, but there were "major problems," which were not detailed in the minutes of the annual meeting.

That same year (1952) a little more than three thousand dollars came from the sale of the Student Center at Pittsburg, which had to be sold because of the expansion of the college. These funds were placed in the foundation, and then loaned to the Convention, at six percent interest, to remodel the new Baptist state headquarters offices in Wichita. At the same time the foundation was charged with the responsibility of directing a campaign to raise "between $10,000 and $20,000" for a new Baptist Student Center at Pittsburg. The campaign was to be "so conducted as not to affect the budget sources of our convention" (*Annual*).

By 1953 the Revolving Building Loan Fund had climbed to more than fourteen thousand dollars. Even so, a sour note was sounded: "Kansas Southern Baptists are sorely in need of $100,000 in building loan funds." Kansans were encouraged to seek out rich friends who might make gifts to meet this need (if possible!).

In 1954 the report again included this concern for more money: "The total of our Building Loan Fund is appallingly small, but the amount of help that has come from it is inspiring indeed. These facts place the urgency upon our need to bring the total to $100,000 shortly." Previously, this goal had been fifty thousand dollars, but needs on every hand were pressing in, and a feeling of urgency to be about Kingdom business of church building was apparent.

In 1956 Gordon Dorian was elected president of the foundation board. Gifts from the churches had made the Children's Home fund richer by $1,100. Kansas WMU had designated twenty percent of the State Missions Offering for this cause. The foundation had been authorized to sponsor, for the first time, a Thanksgiving Offering for the Children's Home Fund.

Another statement from this report bears repeating: "We regret to report that the Court gave an adverse ruling in the case of the Ella Cunningham will. We did not think it advisable to appeal the case, so this amount is lost to our Children's Home fund" (*Annual* 1956, p. 57). There is no other mention of this transaction, but it attests to the fact that the foundation was at work.

In 1958 the office of the KSBFN moved from Hutchinson to Wichita and "took its place among the other departments of our Convention" (*Annual*). At this time, the foundation was handling the Children's Home Fund ($15,557.65), Student Loan Fund ($246.00), Church Sites Fund ($1,398.42) earmarked for two churches, and the Revolving Building and Loan Fund ($20,271.38).

The reason for the move was that the executive secretary of the foundation, Howard Whatley, had begun to serve as executive vice-president of the Church Loan Association (CLA) of Southern Baptists. At the same time, a change in the charter of the foundation abolished the board of trustees and provided that the board of directors be elected by the Convention.

THE BAPTIST CHURCH LOAN CORPORATION OF TEXAS

One must go back a bit to understand the CLA. In 1953 the voice of the Baptist Church Loan Corporation of Texas was heard. The serpent entered the garden and approached Eve, the good people who wanted to work faster toward the evangelization of Kansas and Nebraska, and who believed that space was the answer. A questionable concept was receiving wide acclaim— that congregations grow to fill the space available. If the space is increased, people will follow.

In 1953 the Baptist Church Loan Corporation of Texas made loans of almost $150,000 to seven "qualifying churches." In the February 1953 (*Annual*) meeting of the Executive Board, the work of this corporation was presented by its executive secretary, A. B. White, and "plans were made to put it into operation in Kansas." This action was finalized at a special meeting of the Convention on February 24, 1953.

At that special meeting, after the usual petitionary letters were presented, messengers seated, music, and a devotional message, George McClelland, Kansas Convention president, introduced Dr. Westmoreland, who presented H. H. Whatley, chair of the Finance and Promotion Committee of the Executive Board. There were messengers from thirty-five churches on hand to hear what Whatley had to say.

Whatley moved that "the Convention agree to underwrite twenty-five percent of the loan granted any church by the Church Building and Loan Corporation of Texas and that a State Survey Committee be elected to serve with the Executive Secretary-Treasurer for the Kansas Convention in giving Convention approval for loans" (*Annual*, 1953). The Baptist Church Loan Corporation began to operate in Kansas.

The Survey Committee was made up of one member from each associa- tion selected by a committee appointed by the president. At the annual meeting in 1958, the Survey Committee was discontinued, and the responsi- bility for approving churches for loans was given to the KSBFN (*Annual*).

By the time the Baptist Foundation report was written for the 1953 Convention sessions in November, "more than $100,000 in loans [had] been approved for Kansas Southern Baptist churches." The report for 1954 showed seven more loans bringing the total to $142,350. At the same time loan appli- cations were being processed which would increase indebtedness by another $109,500 (*Annual*).

From one year to the next, there was high praise for the progress made possible by the Texas Corporation. At times it seemed the Texans were doing all this out the kindness of their hearts rather than as a quite profitable business venture.

The 1955 report of the Executive Board to the Convention stated, "The Baptist Church Loan Corporation of Texas has made loans to our churches, in original totals, amounting to $222,350 through July 31, 1955. In most cases, these loans have been larger than would have been obtainable from the Home Mission Board, and satisfied a need by which some of our more advanced churches have come into new strength and usefulness" (*Annual*, 1955).

"Our constituency has been befriended in the past year through loans made by the Baptist Church Loan Corporation of Texas: four churches— $132,000" (*Annual*, 1956). Under the general heading of "Acknowledgments of Out-of-State Financial Assistance," which included the Home Mission Board and Sunday School Board, was this further note: "The Baptist Church Loan Corporation reports that $353,350 in original contracts is now loaned to our Kansas churches" (*Annual*, 1957).

CHURCH LOAN ASSOCIATION OF SOUTHERN BAPTISTS

By this time the church bond business was booming. In an interview (1994), Pat McDaniel pointed out that in the late 1950s and early 1960s there was a tremendous need for church financing. In Kansas-Nebraska there was a veritable industrial revolution during these years. Beech, Boeing, and Cessna aircraft industries were burgeoning and bulging with new orders. There were jobs galore. Oil fields were being opened in western Kansas. Uncle Sam was transferring Air Force personnel to Schilling in Salina, Forbes in Topeka, Offutt and the Strategic Air Command Base in Bellevue, a base in Grand Island, and missile sites in the western parts of Nebraska and eastern Kansas around Topeka. There was a tremendous influx into this area of

Okies, Arkies, and Texans, who had grown up in Southern Baptist churches and were looking for their counterparts, which some of the natives of Kansas and Nebraska called "y'all clubs." On a given Sunday morning, as many as three or four new families might show up in some little store-front Baptist mission looking for a place to worship. With all this inflow of Southern Baptists, there had to be more churches—which meant money, money that had to be borrowed in order to build NOW.

When these little, unknown Southern Baptist groups went to banks or savings and loans or insurance companies to borrow money, the lenders said "Southern *who*?" They did not know who we were and were not about to loan us money and then have to foreclose on a church. It was just not good public relations to do that sort of thing. It was in this financial void that the bond industry blossomed.

Church bonds, a vehicle already in place, were readily available to churches all across the nation. The A. B. Culbertson Company, of Fort Worth, Texas, was among a dozen or so of the largest bond issuers in the nation. Two churches in Wichita, Olivet and Sharon, were the first in Kansas to make extensive use of bond programs through the ABC program (*Annual*, 1958). Bonds were easy to sell; Olivet sold sixty thousand dollars worth in nine days. Other churches followed. Because of the tremendous success of these efforts, there was an immediate push for bonds all over Kansas and Nebraska. At this juncture, it was decided that we had best get into a church bond program on a Convention-wide basis.

In an editorial in the *Baptist Digest* (April 1, 1967), Westmoreland wrote in great detail about how the decision to accept the plan presented by A. B. Culbertson was made. After the successful bond sales in Wichita, Westmoreland offered to make a recommendation to the Executive Board that rent-free space be offered, if Culbertson would put a representative in Kansas. Culbertson, a noted Baptist layman of Texas and head of the bonding company, did not respond to this until November 12, 1957. The preliminary meetings of the annual meeting were already going on at Immanuel Baptist Church. He and an associate, "at their own expense," came to Wichita and asked Westmoreland to meet with them in their hotel room. Westmoreland continued:

> They presented to me a plan that Mr. Culbertson, being an attorney, had devised and offered to the Baptist General Convention of Texas, but which had been laid aside in favor of other financing plans. He presented the concept of the Church Loan Association and then offered, for a fee of 5% of each bond sale, to care for the legal work, train the first Executive Vice-President of the Church Loan Association, and pay his salary. Most of the day was given to consideration of the plan. There seemed to be no way to avoid the feeling that hasty action about a tremendous matter was being

demanded, and there seemed to be no way to buy time for a thorough investigation. I missed all of the pre-Convention meetings. Late in the day, I took the idea to leading pastors of the Convention, namely members of the Executive Board, for informal consideration. As the idea was debated in our minds, the brevity of time demanded that we remember the integrity and experience of Mr. Culbertson, and the great need for building funds in our Convention territory. In a preliminary way, the idea was presented to the Convention in its first session, November 12, 1957, and adopted following the report of the Executive Board on Tuesday morning, November 13.

So in 1957 the Church Loan Association of Southern Baptists was born. H. H. Whatley agreed to head the CLA on a commission basis. Westmoreland went on to say that Howard Whatley was "eminently qualified" to head up the bond program. Whatley had come to Kansas, in 1949, from the First Church in Stratford, Texas, to be pastor of the First Southern Baptist Church of Hutchinson. He was "a business administration graduate of the University of Texas, and a business man for many years, even teaching in a business college." He was executive secretary of the foundation, and had served on possibly every committee, board, and agency of the Convention, and in the Wheatland Association. He was the Convention's president in 1955 and 1956.

Nobody intended this. To meet the requirements of Kansas churches was the original plan. In the October 1957 issue of *Baptist Digest*, there was an emphasis on the need for buildings. "Today's greatest need in the Kansas Convention is for space, for buildings, for a place to worship, for more class-rooms. Kansas Baptists are pushing out the walls of their present quarters, and they need to spread out.

"Several missions are meeting in only rented or borrowed quarters. Several missions are meeting in homes, waiting only for a day of victory when they have their own buildings.

"Indian Southern Baptist Church in Wichita became discouraged and many quit before they had the ground-breaking. . . . University Church in Wichita . . . waited four years for the day of victory."

H. H. Whatley included the following in his report of the CLA of Southern Baptists at the 1958 annual meeting (*Annual*):

One of the greatest obstacles to the growth of our Southern Baptist churches in Kansas has been the sad lack of a source of funds with which to purchase adequate property and to erect suitable buildings. Through the years of our organized life as a state Convention, our churches have obtained limited loans from the Home Mission Board, The Baptist Church Loan Corporation [Texas], banking institutions, and individuals. We thank God for all these and what they have done for our churches, but what they could do was not enough.

We set up our own Revolving Building Loan Fund which helped some, but did not have sufficient funds to begin to meet the need. Some money was loaned from the funds held by Kansas Southern Baptist Foundation, but these loans were of necessity short-term loans. Dr. N. J. Westmoreland, our Executive Secretary-Treasurer, and many of our leaders came to realize that we must have some kind of church loan fund or association that would have unlimited resources, that would understand the problems and needs of our own churches, and could make loans on a long-term basis. Several ideas were explored, but nothing we studied seemed to be the answer to our need.

. . . [The financing of Olivet and Sharon Churches worked so well] that Dr. Westmoreland was impressed to contact [A. B. Culbertson] concerning our need throughout the state. [Culbertson] indicated his willingness to help set up a church loan association in Kansas and on October 15, 1957, the Executive Board of our Convention passed a resolution authorizing a committee to be appointed with power to act toward the framing of a charter for such a church loan association under the supervision of Mr. Culbertson. Those named to this committee were Dr. N. J. Westmoreland, Rang Morgan and Gordon Dorian.

Dorian, president of the CLA board of directors (Interview, 1994) described Culbertson as a quite wealthy, retired banker who took a liking to the people in Kansas when he came to Wichita to talk with Olivet about the bond program. He liked the idea of working with a state convention and took Kansas under his wing. Culbertson set it up, and the board depended completely on his leadership. Dorian saw Culbertson two or three times a year since he was also serving as a trustee for Southwestern Baptist Theological Seminary. Culbertson was always gracious and reassuring. On one occasion he told Dorian, in answer to a direct question, that he had "built into the program" the provision for selling bonds to pay off bonds because he knew that to get started that would be necessary. Dorian trusted him; Culbertson was a banker and he loved Kansas.

According to Dorian (Interview, 1994), "Whatley [Executive Vice-President of CLA] would come in with recommendations and I'd call the Board together and we would get a quorum and listen to the recommendations and we'd, I'm sorry to say, rubber stamp them. They had done their home work and they did it well enough that they convinced us that these churches needed to get a start. The only way they would get a start was selling bonds and so we okayed it. Rang (Morgan) and I didn't know anything about it."

The 1958 *Annual* presented the first report of the CLA. Westmoreland wrote, "In less than one year [the CLA] has proven to be one of the most phenomenal projects. Brother H. H. Whatley, executive vice-president of the loan association, informs us that loans during the first year will likely exceed $400,000 and will excel the Home Mission Board and the Baptist Church Loan Corporation of Texas in total loans to churches."

To provide the necessary security for this guarantee [underwriting twenty-five percent of all loans], action was taken June 24, 1958, to establish a Security Fund. One percent of all Cooperative Program receipts per year was to be designated to this fund until it reached a total satisfactory in the wisdom of the Executive Board (*Annual*, 1958). The "satisfactory total" was never clearly defined. Nor was the one percent commitment kept. Dorian's memory is that the Convention voted to underwrite only one million dollars worth of bonds. There seems to be no record of this in the Executive Board's reports to the Convention, nor in motions approved. "Well, the thing just took off and it was two million, three million, four million, 4.5 million. N. J. would come to me and say, 'This is not right. We can't do this; we only voted to underwrite one million dollars.' But there was no stopping, it was catching on fire so fast" (Dorian, Interview, 1994).

In the January 4, 1958, issue of the *Baptist Digest*, Howard Whatley was quoted, "We have hold of something big—we are set up, not just for Kansas, but for all the surrounding states. Our goal for 1958 is to finance one church per month. Money-wise we hope to issue and sell at least $300,000 in bonds. Mr. A. B. Culbertson says that this is a low goal, and that we can do much more."

That year's (1958) *Book of Reports* included a chart showing the lines of authority and relationships among departments and agencies and employees of the Convention. The *Baptist Digest*, KSBFN, and the CLA were responsible only to the Convention, not to the Executive Committee nor the Executive Board of Convention. Each of these operated with a board of directors elected by the Convention. (That year, this was changed for the *Baptist Digest;* it no longer would have a board of directors, and became responsible to the Executive Board. Because of this action, the editor, Joe Novak, resigned.)

The report from the executive secretary-treasurer of the Convention stated, "No new loans have been made in 1958 by the Baptist Church Loan Corporation of Texas. The First Southern Baptist Church of Topeka has been first in the state to pay off a Texas Loan in full. We continue to be mindful of the $353,350 in original contracts loaned by them to our Kansas churches."

The messengers to this annual meeting (1958) approved the action of the Executive Board to authorize the CLA to extend operations to Southern Baptist churches outside the constituency of the KCSB, "providing that a separate prospectus be printed containing no guarantee of their payment by the Kansas Convention" (*Annual*, 1958, p. 17).

The bonds seemed a "sure thing!" According to a brief article in the February 22, 1958, issue of the *Baptist Digest*, the first bond was purchased by a retired Texas soap manufacturer, Earnest O. Gillam, who had been born on a Kansas homestead in McPherson County in 1884. The caption above the accompanying picture was "More Realistic Than Soap Bubbles."

University, Wichita completed bond sales in just three days (*BD*, May 7, 1958). The slogan for First Baptist in Mulvane was "Seventeen Thousand in Seventeen Days." The campaign was finished in three days (*BD*, July 26, 1958).

The bonds were easy to sell. In the early days of the CLA interest was two and one-half to three percent; church bonds began at five and one-half and six percent. Frugal Kansas and Nebraska farmers very soon learned about these church bonds, and literally knocked at the doors of the CLA asking to purchase them. A CLA representative could meet with two or three families in Somewhere, Kansas—families who were interested in the advancement of Kingdom business, families who wanted to make a Christian witness in their community—and say to them, "Money is no problem. If you want to build a church, we can get you the money and you can build your church. You sell the bonds and then we stagger payments on the first bond for maybe five years and the person holding the bond receives interest on it during that time and then starts receiving the principal. During that five years, your church will grow to the point that you will be able to repay the loan, so the bonds will be paid off."

"We will have cause to rejoice," wrote Westmoreland (*Annual*, 1959), "over the prospect of benefits which we shall receive through the establishment of the Convention Reserve Fund and the Church Loan Guarantee Fund. In these particular funds, we will have a total of $6,770 at the end of 1960. They will greatly aid in stabilizing weaker churches and the budget resources of our Convention." This same year the CLA reported loans of $794,500 to thirty Kansas Southern Baptist churches (*Annual*, 1959, p. 21). The total of $6,700 was a long way from twenty-five percent of this total, which had been guaranteed by Convention action. In less than two years, under the new plan with the A. B. Culbertson Company, more money had been loaned to churches for new buildings than had been borrowed from the Home Mission Board and the Baptist Church Loan Corporation of Texas "in the several years of their unusual assistance to our work."

Even though a reserve fund was authorized, the Kansas Convention was living from "hand to mouth." Because there was no money for a reserve fund in the Convention and no sinking fund in the CLA, it is no wonder that the house of cards came tumbling down.

In 1966 the federal branch of the Securities and Exchange Commission (SEC) in Fort Worth, Texas, became disturbed in regard to the almost out-of-control church bond program across the nation. For example, a church in New Orleans became involved with Broadway Bonds of Houston, a reputable first-rate operation. The New Orleans church discovered how easy it was to sell bonds. They built a huge day care center, bought around one hundred buses for a bus ministry, and built other large facilities. They sold so many bonds and were so in debt that they finally discovered it would take one thousand dollars every day just to unlock the door. Stories like this made the SEC concerned about church bonds in general and the CLA of Kansas Baptists in particular. Although a small number may have been worried, the majority of those on the Executive Board remained oblivious to our financial difficulties. From 1959 on, there were glowing reports and statements of gratitude for the help of the A. B. Culbertson Company. "Our debt of gratitude to the A. B. Culbertson Company of Fort Worth, Texas, continues to increase as they provide legal counsel, sound financial advice, and a sales outlet for some of the bonds for the Church Loan Association of Southern Baptists" (*Annual*, 1959).

According to the 1961 *Annual*, "The A. B. Culbertson Company continues to serve, as part of a ten-year contract, [as] the trustee of the Church Loan Association of Southern Baptists. This is a private corporation. Their technical assistance is prized quite highly by those who are acquainted with the ministry of the Church Loan Association." Some reference along this line was noted in every annual report for almost ten years.

In 1963 (*Annual*) changes were reported in the contract with the A. B. Culbertson Company. The company reduced its "off the top" fee of five percent to one-half percent, which made it necessary for the CLA to assume the responsibility to pay its executive vice-president, H. H. Whatley, salary and travel compensations previously borne by the A. B. Culbertson Co.

In 1965 (*Annual*) the CLA gave a summary report of the loans made since its inception in January 1958 through September 1965: Ninety-five churches financed; $3,300,000 bonds issued; $3,260,000 bonds sold; and $3,500,000 made available to churches. These figures are difficult to understand, but appeared in the CLA report. In the 1964-65 year alone, new loans were made to twenty-nine churches and a thirtieth had been approved.

As an additional service, a Construction Department was begun on May 1, 1965; Byron D. Tracy, Jr., was elected as supervisor of construction. He was formerly pastor of the First Southern Baptist Church, Fort Scott, Kansas, and had many years of construction experience. The purpose of the division was to help churches get better buildings at a lower price. Tracy's job was to meet with building committees in churches in Kansas and Nebraska, at their request, to provide planning information, help work out details of construction, and supervise the actual construction work, if churches wished (*BD*, May 15, 1965). During his first year of employment by the CLA, Tracy started construction on four churches, and had four others ready to start.

A note of warning was included in the 1966 annual report concerning financing this work. The work of the Church Architecture Department was handled through the CLA office. Hours were spent in consultation, and many miles were driven to help churches get the best in church sites, church buildings, and church furnishings. The materials, professional and technical advice, and architectural consultation received from the Church Architecture Department of the Sunday School Board were helpful. It was the CLA, however, that had to foot the bill, with money that came from the sale of bonds or the repayment of loans.

After the usual "numbers" in the 1966 report, the attitude of the CLA was expressed concerning loans for church buildings (*Annual*, 1966). The executive vice-president wrote, "All of the remainder of the story may not be heard this side of Heaven. However, much of it can be learned from the growth in Sunday School and Training Union, improved and enlarged worship services, increase in Cooperative Program receipts, and souls won to Christ because the Church Loan Association made it possible for the one hundred eleven churches to have adequate buildings and equipment."

By and large, 1966 was a good year for the Convention. The number of churches, members, and the value of church property all increased. Baptisms totaled 2,342. Cooperative Program receipts were up (5.8 percent), but the increase was not as great as for the preceding year (11.7 percent).

For the first time, in the 1966 *Annual*, a hint of difficulty clouded the horizon. Loans were not being paid as promptly nor as fully as expected. During the year, the Executive Board authorized the executive secretary-treasurer and associate executive secretary-treasurer directing the program of missions, in cooperation with the associational missionaries, to arrange conferences with the churches that were "behind on church loan payments with the hope of offering constructive assistance to strengthen their total work, and in turn to build their budgets and enable them to . . . care for their responsibilities and meet their commitments."

Suddenly, more trouble loomed as Cooperative Program receipts fell. Churches were not giving as many dollars nor as great a percentage through the Cooperative Program. Authority was given to the Convention president and executive secretary-treasurer to borrow amounts of up to five thousand dollars when necessary between meetings of the Executive Committee or Board to insure that the 1967 payrolls would be met (*Annual*, 1966).

By this time the staff of the CLA had increased: a full-time secretary, accountant, and secretary/assistant bookkeeper had been added. These were in addition to the executive vice-president and construction supervisor.

Cooperative Program receipts reported for 1966 came to a little more than $252,000, a gain of only 2.1 percent over the preceding year, and a monetary increase of only $5,341. The plateau in Cooperative Program giving was confronted after the 1967 budget had been planned, involving a goal of $271,505, which required the reduction of the budget by at least $19,340 for the year. In addition, not as much was forthcoming from the Sunday School Board as had been expected, which involved more cuts. The Convention had to operate in 1967 on nearly twenty-six thousand less than was anticipated.

A hold-over deficit in the budget of the previous year and an indebtedness of seventeen thousand dollars brought the total deficit to $58,100. Making reductions involving ten percent of a budget was not easy.

In order to deal with this problem, the Convention launched the "1,000 Club" to pay the debt on the Baptist Student Activities building at Lawrence. The plan was to enlist a thousand people who would give one dollar per month over their tithe. This would release $480 per month of Convention funds for other needs. These financial considerations became more important when the bond issue was faced the following year.

Because of problems cropping up in loan repayment, new rules for the CLA were instituted (*Annual*, 1967): The repayment schedule would not exceed twenty-five percent of the average weekly income based on the previous year's income. Payback ability would be based on the average payments of the ten- or fifteen-year schedules rather than the beginning payment. The beginning payment was a bit deceptive of the total obligation, since the payment increased, assuming church growth. The ratio of loan payback to weekly income could be increased only when the following items were carefully considered: pastoral leadership, economy of the community, membership income, spiritual health of the congregation, budget promotion, educational space, population potential increase, payment record of the church, and the use of a fund-raising campaign.

The maximum ratio would not exceed thirty percent of the average weekly income based on the previous year's income. It became more difficult to be approved for a loan. Further, in cases of missions and churches that did not qualify under the above regulations, underwriting by an established older church would be required.

But for the most part, things went on as usual. In the April 1, 1967, edition of the *Baptist Digest*, Westmoreland wrote the following editorial (only a part is quoted): "One of the phenomenal events that has made major contributions to the Kansas-Nebraska Southern Baptist Convention has been the institution and growth of the Church Loan Association. I count myself to have been exceedingly fortunate to have been able to lend my support to its formation, of my encouragement along the way. Its successes have reflected the dedicated work and genius of its Executive Vice-President, H. H. Whatley. The first church to be financed was the Immanuel Baptist Church, Great Bend, Kansas. . . . With the background of nine years of successful operations, we are reflecting gratefully upon these events."

DISASTER IN 1968—TIE A KNOT, AND HANG ON!

The twenty-third annual KCSB, meeting in the First Southern Baptist Church of Topeka, began on Tuesday, November 12, 1968, with the seating of 119 messengers, welcoming new churches into fellowship, receiving and sending greetings to other Conventions in session, hearing reports and messages from Brotherhood and WMU Departments, and Protestants and Other Americans United for Separation of Church and State. The Executive Board report dealt with plans for the twenty-fifth anniversary, policies relating to housing allowances for board employees, and to resolving conflict of interest concerns in regard to extra employment. A visitor from Mars at that afternoon session would have been lulled into believing all was well, and that it was "business as usual" for the KCSB. Fitting enough was the closing message from Garth Pybas: "Christ the Only Hope."

When the messengers returned for the Tuesday evening session, the axe fell. It is hard to tell how many expected it. Certainly not everyone in attendance did. Discussion of the crisis had taken place only in the Executive Board meetings. Perhaps some were all abuzz, but many of the messengers were astonished and angry by what took place. There had been little communication, even among the staff, concerning the crisis. Staff members did not know what would happen as far as employment was concerned until, inadvertently, a copy of the budget was found just before the meeting, in a wastepaper basket.

After a report on student work and some miscellaneous business, Tommy Grozier, pastor of First Baptist Church in Bellevue, Nebraska, and president of the Convention, "presented and discussed the Church Loan Association crisis." Paul Buchannon, attorney for the Convention, discussed the situation from a legal point of view. The gist of what they said was, "We are in debt up to our ears, guilty of criminal actions, likely to face bankruptcy with the possibility of losing seventy-seven churches, and of some of our staff facing prison sentences—unless we take drastic action."

The following resolution was read and later adopted:

WHEREAS, the Church Loan Association of Southern Baptists is a corporation formed and governed by the Kansas Convention of Southern Baptists for the purpose of making loans to the churches of this Convention; and,

WHEREAS, the Church Loan Association has financed its operations by the sale of church bonds to the general public; and,

WHEREAS, this Convention has by previous action guaranteed the loans made by the Church Loan Association to various churches of this Convention to the extent of 25% of such obligations; and,

WHEREAS, it now appears that the Church Loan Association is unable to meet its obligations to the bondholders as they mature, that at the present time its liabilities exceed its assets, and that under these circumstances immediate, drastic, and continued action by the Convention is necessary to protect the integrity of this Convention and its member churches; and,

WHEREAS, the Board of Directors of the Church Loan Association and the Executive Committee of the Executive Board of this Convention have made a study of this matter and further have asked the Home Mission Board of the Southern Baptist Convention for its advice, direction, and assistance;

NOW, THEREFORE, the Executive Board of the Kansas Convention of Southern Baptists recommends the following resolutions for adoption by this Convention:

BE IT RESOLVED:

1. The Home Mission Board of the Southern Baptist Convention be requested to refinance the office building property owned by this Convention so as to increase the indebtedness now owing on said property by the sum of approximately $100,000 and repayable as nearly as practicable at the same monthly rate as now required to retire the present indebtedness, the proceeds of this refinancing to go to the sinking fund of the Church Loan Association.

2. The Home Mission Board of the Southern Baptist Convention be requested to create a stand-by fund in the amount of $300,000 to be used, as required, to meet the obligations of the bondholders as they mature in the event funds of this Convention or of the Church Loan Association are not available.

3. That the Home Mission Board of the Southern Baptist Convention be requested to purchase at par a sufficient number of the church loans now being held by the Church Loan Association so as to provide adequate funds for the sinking fund through the calendar year 1969 with said purchases not to exceed $400,000.

4. That this Convention budget for 1969 the sum of $50,000 to be paid to the Church Loan Association for the purpose of meeting the obligations due the bondholders and operating expenses, and that such pledge be paid to the Church Loan Association monthly. This Convention shall continue to budget funds of not less than $50,000 per annum for a period of approximately ten years, or until such time as all indebtedness due the bondholders has been paid in full.

5. That in the event the Home Mission Board of the Southern Baptist Convention is called upon to expend any of the $300,000 fund created in Item 2 of this resolution, this Convention shall continue to budget the sum of $50,000 per year for the purpose of repaying the Home Mission Board any such sums it may have expended together with such additional sums that may be necessary to reimburse the Home Mission Board for any interest income it may have lost on said funds.

6. That the Church Loan Association of Southern Baptists enter into a management contract with the Home Mission Board of the

Southern Baptist Convention for a period of not less than ten years, or until all bondholders have been paid in full, and that such management contract provide that the Home Mission Board have full control of the affairs of the Church Loan Association.

7. That this Convention pledge to the Home Mission Board that it will not increase its present indebtedness or sell any of its assets without the express written consent of the Home Mission Board.

8. That the Convention pledge to the Home Mission Board that it will give the Home Mission Board its full Cooperation during the period of time that may be necessary to repay all the bondholders and will offer to the Home Mission Board the services of any employees of this Convention necessary to effectuate the purposes of this resolution.

9. That this Convention, acting by and through its president and secretary, and the Church Loan Association, acting through its proper officers, execute such documents as may be necessary to effectuate and to carry into effect the spirit and purpose of the resolution.

10. The Executive Committee of the Executive Board of this Convention be, and it is hereby, empowered to take such action as may be necessary to carry out and put into effect the spirit and general purpose of this resolution, which power shall include the power to change or alter the terms of the request made to the Home Mission Board of the Southern Baptist Convention as herein above set forth as may be necessary to meet the requirements of the said Home Mission Board.

To deal with the indebtedness, the Home Mission Board, through refinancing the office building (one hundred thousand dollars), setting aside an emergency fund to be used if necessary (three hundred thousand dollars), and buying bonds (one hundred thousand dollars), would make available five hundred thousand dollars to Kansas Southern Baptists. The Convention would pay fifty thousand dollars per year for bond repayment, which over ten years would mean five hundred thousand dollars. The report was accepted by the Convention.

The difficulty with the plan was that, a six-month study, completed in the early months of 1969 by Pat McDaniel, representative of the Home Mission Board, revealed this was not enough.

Stunned, saddened, and confused as the messengers must have been after the action taken that evening, the minutes reported that "a standing vote of appreciation was given to the Executive Committee, Board of Directors of the Church Loan Association, Dr. N. J. Westmoreland, President Tommy Grozier, the Home Mission Board personnel and attorneys, Mr. Bill Major and

Mr. Paul Buchannon, for the work done in setting up the above program" (*Annual*, 1968).

The hard work began as the budget for 1969 was presented. Staff reductions had been made to meet the stringent budget requirements. At that time, in addition to Westmoreland, who served as both executive secretary-treasurer of the Convention and as interim editor of the *Baptist Digest*, there was a staff of five plus secretarial support and CLA staff. Galen F. Irby, who came in February 1968 after Paul Allison had resigned in September 1967, served as associate executive secretary-treasurer and director of Missions and Stewardship Departments. Garth Pybas, who joined the staff in 1965, was secretary of the Departments of Evangelism and Brotherhood; Harold Inman, with the Convention since 1964, was secretary of Sunday School and Church Music; Ray Gilliland, who came in 1951, served as secretary of Training Union and Student Work; and Viola Webb had served since 1957 as executive-secretary of WMU.

Harold H. Whatley served as executive secretary-treasurer of the foundation (beginning in 1951) and executive vice-president of the CLA (beginning in 1957). He had been relieved of the latter position before the beginning of the 1968 annual meeting. At the request of the Executive Committee of the Convention, the office of executive secretary-treasurer of the foundation was vacated on April 1, 1969 (*Annual*). It operated with a board of directors only until Pat McDaniel became executive director-treasurer of both the KNCSB and the foundation (*Annual*, 1974).

A careful explanation was made that cuts in the Convention staff were related to positions, rather than personalities. The budget provided for Administration, a Department of Missions, Stewardship, and Brotherhood, a Department of Religious Education, and a Department of WMU. Even though President Grozier stated that no personalities were involved in the budget proposal, only positions, by this time it was "Convention knowledge" that Westmoreland was to continue as executive secretary-treasurer, Garth Pybas's Brotherhood responsibility was to be transferred to Galen Irby, the emphasis on evangelism would be transferred to Westmoreland, and all educational work would be under one department head, Harold Inman. WMU would continue unchanged.

As might be expected there was certainly not full agreement on these personnel decisions. One amendment to "keep Ray Gilliland rather than Harold Inman" was ruled out of order since it did not pertain to the motion, which was for the adoption of the budget. A motion to table the budget motion until Wednesday afternoon lost eighty-four to forty-two. Another motion to postpone action on the adoption of the budget until the personnel committee brought its report lost fifty-four to forty-two. The question was called, and the budget motion carried 117 to twenty-three.

Prior to the annual meeting (1968), there had been very little, if any, communication with Convention personnel over what was to be done to reduce staff. If there had been open discussion and planning together, the changes might have caused less heartache. One suggestion made to Ray Gilliland was that personnel changes would be made on the basis of seniority.

Gilliland (Interview, 1994) did not want to be a part of that sort of solution. He called his wife and discussed it briefly. She agreed with his decision. He would leave his position and follow his calling somewhere else. This was possibly never communicated to the Executive Board or to the Convention. Gilliland was ready to leave the Kansas Convention at that time for a number of reasons. During his continued study and work with students, he had come to theological positions that were not in keeping with viewpoints of Westmoreland. Gilliland respected Westmoreland as a friend and as a Christian gentleman, but could not agree with him in a number of instances. This was a particularly difficult situation, since Westmoreland had helped him in so many ways, as he had helped a number of other promising young men.

Ray Gilliland had grown up in Coffeyville, while Westmoreland was pastor of Emmanuel Baptist Church, which met for a while in a converted machine shop. The oil-changing pit had been cleaned and was used as a baptistry. It was there that Gilliland was baptized. Westmoreland had helped him get into Hardin-Simmons Baptist College in Abilene, Texas. On the way he had stopped at the Baptist Book Store in Dallas and bought Gilliland a Scofield Reference Bible to take to college with him. The Bible was paid for with a gift from the Adult Training Union in Emmanuel Church.

After college, Gilliland went to Southwestern Baptist Theological Seminary, but came back to Kansas six hours short of completing a degree. Ten years later the Convention granted him a sabbatical in order to finish this work. When he first came to Kansas, he worked at the Baptist Book Store and directed Camp Fellowship. Westmoreland invited him at the end of the summer (1951) to head the Department of Religious Education of the very young KCSB. Ed Russell had filled this position briefly in 1949 and 1950. Gilliland was called in 1951, which brought the paid professional staff to five. (At that time, in addition to Westmoreland, there was a secretary of the Department of Missions, W. A. Burkey; editor, Orbie Clem; WMU executive secretary, Mrs. Orbie Clem; and Gilliland.) Gilliland had all the Sunday School Board educational work under his wing until the growth of the Convention warranted an associate. Hilary Brophy was hired as an associate in this department in 1956; the work was divided, with Brophy becoming secretary of Sunday School and Vacation Bible School, and Gilliland being named secretary of Training Union and Student Work. Howard Halsell and Ray Conner followed Brophy, both with responsibilities in church music. In 1964 Harold Inman came to be secretary of Sunday School and Church Music.

Another reason for Gilliland to leave Kansas was that total responsibility for all the religious education emphasis demanded too much time away from home and would make necessary the curtailment of many activities which he had developed. It would be a little like cutting off a finger—which one? By this time, also, there was a great emphasis on church music, a forte of Harold

Inman, which was not in Gilliland's satchel of talents. When Gilliland left, he went to New York City as student director, working under the auspices of the Baptist Convention of Maryland-Delaware.

It was just as difficult for Harold Inman. He had been in the Convention family since 1964 and loved his responsibilities. A native of Texas, he had grown up in western Oklahoma in Hobart. He went to Oklahoma Baptist University and Southwestern Seminary. He was educational director in Calvary Baptist in Beaumont, Texas, when Sam Russell, director of missions in Wichita, asked him to come to Kansas for a Training Union Enlargement Campaign in 1960. One thing led to another; in 1961 Inman became educational director at Sharon Baptist in Wichita, where Rang Morgan was pastor.

In September 1964 (Interview, Harold Inman), Gordon Dorian talked to Inman about his becoming state Sunday School and Church Music secretary. He accepted these responsibilities in November of that year. With a shake of his head and a little grin, he recalled his first Vacation Bible School Clinic in February of the following year—the day before an ice storm descended on Kansas. The following day dawned clear, however, and the people came.

During those first five years money was tight. "It was not unusual for me to drive to Omaha or to Garden City or to Pittsburg or Kansas City, do a conference, and return home that night because I did not have enough money to pay for extra meals and a motel." This was true for all those on the Convention staff. It is no wonder, then, that Gilliland talked to Inman about the extravagance observed in the CLA vice-president's household. Selling bonds seemed to pay far better than straight work for the Convention.

Gilliland called Inman on the night before the annual meeting, after the unexpected appearance of the budget to be presented to the Convention, to tell him there would be only one position in the general area of religious education in the Convention and no longer a Sunday School and Church Music Department and a Training Union and Student Department. Inman's reply was that he would have his resignation ready the following day to allow Gilliland to continue as the department director, since he had been longer on the job. Gilliland counseled him not to do this. Gilliland felt that it was time for him to move to other fields.

Although staff relations were generally good, Inman was aware of the stress within the Convention leadership; there were some who had tried to "get Dr. Westmoreland fired." On at least one occasion, the Executive Board went into executive session, and Westmoreland thought he had been fired. It was not until that night, or the next morning, that someone told him he still had a job.

Inman believes the reason he was asked to stay on, rather than Gilliland, was because of the good relationship he had been able to maintain with Westmoreland. "Ray and Westmoreland did not have that kind of relationship, and both must bear some blame for that."

The stress of this situation—the bond issue, the financial condition of the Convention, and the personnel problem—took a physical toll on Inman. In addition, the work during the next two years was difficult. He was given assignments in Sunday School, Training Union, Church Music, Church Administration, Student Work, Church Library, Church Recreation, Family Ministry, and Church Architecture. The only concern of the Management Committee that was finally in charge was the bond situation, not the general work of the Convention. It was no wonder that he began to experience some health problems.

When R. Rex "Peck" Lindsay came to the Convention (1971), along with other responsibilities he took over student work, which came as a welcome relief to Inman. Then Harry Taylor (1974) came as director of Music and Recreation. This left Inman with what he loved best, training local associational and church leadership—equipping the saints.

Inman remained with the Convention until his retirement in 1991. That year the Convention honored him with a reception, and gifted him and his wife, Bobbie, with a cruise to Alaska. Since that time he has continued to serve, in a volunteer capacity, as the Church Building consultant, Senior Adult consultant, and as Volunteers in Missions coordinator. He remarked, "I've been able to stay fairly busy and fulfilled at the slower pace."

It must be said that the men involved in these difficult personnel matters, about which they had not been consulted, perhaps not even properly informed, performed their duties during the entire 1968 meeting in an admirable fashion. They presented reports, manned exhibits, led the music, preached, and behaved as Christian gentlemen in the midst of crisis.

The report of the Personnel Committee was moved from a scheduled Wednesday morning time-slot in connection with the report from the Executive Board to Wednesday evening during the usual time for the annual sermon. The Personnel Committee brought the following recommendation (*Annual*, 1968): "That the Evangelism Department be transferred to the Executive Secretary and the Department of Brotherhood be transferred to the Associate Executive Secretary, and that all Sunday School Board related departments in our Convention be combined into a Religious Education Department, effective January 1, 1969, and our present Sunday School Secretary be retained as Religious Education Director."

Garth Pybas, Mrs. Collins Webb, and Galen Irby were the other staff members affected by this report. Mrs. Webb was retained, perhaps in part because there was some financial aid from the Home Mission Board for her salary, and because it was the only position that had missions education of women, girls, and preschoolers as its chief goal.

Galen Irby, associate executive secretary-treasurer with responsibilities for Missions, Stewardship and Brotherhood, remained with the Convention until the end of 1969. His resignation letter was published in the October 18 *Baptist Digest*: "I thank God for the opportunity I have had to serve our blessed Lord with you. These 20 months have been a fruitful and rewarding experience in my life. . . . Other opportunities were mine at the time I came to Kansas. Some have asked if I wished that I had gone to another place to serve. My answer is and always has been no. I would not take anything for the challenge and opportunity that has been mine to serve in the Kansas Convention of Southern Baptists."

Garth Pybas, the other casualty of the budget cut, had come to Kansas in 1955 as pastor of First Southern, Topeka. The ten years in Topeka were satisfying, successful years. Pybas served in many capacities at both state and Convention-wide levels. He was president of the Kansas Convention in 1962-63. The church grew from thirty-seventh to first in Cooperative Program gifts, and from 250 to more than a thousand members with 650 baptisms. The church had an extensive ministry to the deaf, was involved in two building programs, and sponsored two missions: Emmanuel Baptist Mission and the Spanish Mission.

In 1965 Pybas accepted the responsibility to be director of Evangelism and Brotherhood of the Kansas Convention. During his tenure, there was high interest in the annual Evangelistic Conferences and a record number of baptisms. His personal reaction to the bond situation and the elimination of his position was that he felt it was a tragedy.

Just two weeks after he left the Convention staff, Pybas was called as pastor of First Baptist Church, Effingham, Illinois, where he served until 1980. At that time he retired from active ministry and moved to Oklahoma City, where he and his wife, Doris, united with the Southern Hills Baptist Church. Four months later he became part-time associate pastor of the church, where he served for eight years. Still, he and his wife are active in many phases of the church: teaching Sunday school classes, singing in the senior choir, and serving in the intercessory prayer ministry.

There were a number of amendments and substitute motions after the Personnel Report was presented, including one that Westmoreland be asked to resign, another that all staff be retained and asked to take a ten percent cut in salary (as Westmoreland had already offered to do the day before), and a third that there be more conferring about our needs and who could best fill them. All such motions were ruled out of order or lost. The main motion carried 139 to twenty-two.

A second motion, which urged that the Convention respectfully ask Westmoreland to resign, resulted in a secret ballot; the motion failed. Before the close of the session, Clint Dunagan, who had made the motion to request the resignation, moved that the Convention "pledge its sincere and earnest support to our Executive Secretary, N. J. Westmoreland." The motion carried. The Executive Board, along with Westmoreland, was called to the platform and given a standing vote of confidence and a pledge of support for the difficult year ahead.

Westmoreland's editorial, "The Story We Could Not Tell (*BD*, November 23, 1968), began, "Circumstances dictated that the churches not be informed of the plight of the Church Loan Association prior to the sessions of the 1968 state Convention. This directive was despite the fact that the deficits of the CLA had been obvious in the audits since early in 1964." He mentioned that deficits had been called to the attention of the Executive Committee and leaders of the CLA, but the trouble was "discredited." He mentioned actions taken to revise church loan policies and to encourage churches to keep payments current. It was not until January 1968 that the deficits were taken seriously by the CLA Board. After investigations had started, "the Convention was directed by the SEC that no announcement of any phase of the problem should be made until the messengers were in session and could act. Only this could avoid the possibility of bringing the CLA into foreclosure. Consequently, except for a few instances, the messengers had to wait until the Convention sessions to learn of developments. This precipitated shock, disbelief, frustration, and indignation before they could bring themselves to deal with the practical solutions demanded by the problem. This was not easy as members of the Executive Committee and messengers would testify. The messengers acted with unusual poise, faith and courage concerning a problem that few Christians have ever faced."

Personnel reduction, which was finally to include Westmoreland's resignation before the end of the following year, painful as it was, was only the tip of the iceberg in the vast sea of what to do and how to pay our bills and protect the bondholders. We were in mind-boggling trouble with the Securities Commissioner of the State of Kansas and the U.S. SEC because bonds had been sold, not only in Kansas, but also outside the state. These two agencies were engaged in arguments about who had the right to foreclose on the CLA, as well as the Convention, since the Convention had pledged to underwrite twenty-five percent of the bond indebtedness. It was their (SEC) goal to protect the bondholders. In the end, this turned out to be the real reason they did not foreclose, but gave us the opportunity to be as good as our word. We have to go to the minutes of the 1969 annual meeting and to interviews with those closely involved to understand all that happened.

PAT MCDANIEL

Pat McDaniel, whose background is in banking and finance, went to work at the Home Mission Board in the Church Loan Division in 1967 as a finance officer on a nationwide basis. Prior to that time he had been associate executive director of the Baptist State Convention of Michigan. He had not been in Atlanta three weeks when the head of the division handed him a Kansas-Nebraska *Annual* and asked him to look at the financial statements to see if there was anything wrong. When he examined the CLA statement, the Bond Sinking Fund was already sinking; it was twenty-three thousand dollars in the red then. His statement to the division director was, "I can't believe what I'm reading!" The Bond Sinking Fund is made up of loan repayments to pay bondholders interest and principle as the coupons become due and bonds mature. There was practically no money in the Bond Sinking Fund.

In less than six months (late spring of 1968), a call came from the SEC in Fort Worth from their senior trial attorney, Richard Hewett, to McDaniel at the Home Mission Board. He wanted to know if McDaniel knew anything about a bond program in Kansas and Nebraska. Hewett was alarmed at the situation both here, and in other places as well. From his perspective it looked like the entire church arena was awash in bonds, and he felt that sixty to seventy percent of the people were at risk of losing money. It was his job to protect them. He must have thought McDaniel or someone from the Home Mission Board could go out to Kansas and tell the Convention and churches "what for!" McDaniel chuckled, "I spent a good deal of Mr. Hewett's long distance money giving him a basic course in Baptist Autonomy 101."

Hewett next (summer, 1968) dispatched a group of his people to Wichita. They appeared unannounced on the doorsteps of the CLA office and spent two weeks going through records.

Then Hewett called Michael Quinn, Securities Commissioner of the State of Kansas, to warn him of the potential bombshell under his nose in Wichita. Quinn sent his crew to Wichita, and they came to the same conclusion: the CLA was beyond redemption. They invited McDaniel, Robert S. Kilgore, director of Division of Loans for the Home Mission Board, and the Home Mission Board lawyer to Fort Worth to talk about what to do with these seventy-seven churches in Kansas and Nebraska that had sold bonds to John Q. Public and could not pay them off. McDaniel's advice was to meet with the Convention officers and work out a plan. The plan must come from the Convention. It could not be imposed on them. He suggested that it would be in the SEC's best interests and certainly in the best interests of the bondholders to work out a payment plan rather than to foreclose on seventy-seven churches. They agreed to this.

By this time (late summer of 1968), the Convention office was like an armed camp, with the CLA blaming the Convention and the Convention blaming the CLA. Everyone attempted to shift the blame in a scary situation. For weeks the tension festered and grew.

Finally, an action plan was adopted. By executive order of the board, Tommy Grozier, pastor of the First Baptist Church in Bellevue, Nebraska, and president of the Convention, invited the Home Mission Board to come see what could be done to save the situation. This was the plan presented to the Convention at the 1968 annual meeting. It is important to remember that the Home Mission Board was invited, not imposed on the Convention by the SEC. McDaniel was the Home Mission Board's representative in this predicament. He came to Wichita in January 1969, brought his family, rented a house, and worked for six months to determine the extent of the problem

After the in-depth calculations and bond payment projections, he concluded that if all the churches who owed money dedicated thirty-five to forty percent of the income to bond payment (and they could hardly be asked for more), that would provide only about twenty-eight to thirty thousand dollars a month, not nearly enough. It was a nightmare. The CLA was $1.6 million short.

This stark reality led to the plan that was finally imposed on the Convention in 1969 by the Kansas Securities Commissioner, Michael Quinn. For the SEC, the safety of the bondholders was the bottom line. Quinn insisted that the CLA be placed under a management team, which could be suggested by the Executive Board, but had to be approved by him.

From January to August 1969, the management of the CLA was under the direction of the Home Mission Board through its agent, Pat McDaniel. His first act was to send a letter to all bondholders which disclosed that the CLA was insolvent. The bondholders were not to sell or trade their bonds. His careful study revealed that the KCSB had a deficit of $1.6 million.

By summer (1969), when the SEC understood the vastness of the problem, the Kansas Securities Commission wanted more direct control. Quinn requested the resignation of the Home Mission Board as "agent" and asked for a five-man team of managers who would be nominated by the Executive Board and approved by and responsible to the commission. This was not a request, but an ultimatum, and the Executive Board named a group of men from whom Quinn chose five. This group took charge of the CLA and of the KCSB in August 1969.

Gordon Dorian remembers that meeting well. All the Executive Board members were subpoenaed; twenty-five or thirty attended. By this time, he realized the gravity of the situation. He thought he would lose his house, his property, even face a jail sentence. "I was scared to death," he recalled. Since the CLA was a corporation, he and other board members need not have been afraid of losing their homes, just going to jail.

During that meeting, Quinn called into his office Dorian and W. E. Thorn, who was president of the Convention. Quinn issued an ultimatum: "Now here's what you're going to do. You're going back to Wichita and I'm going to give you one week and you're going to find five men, a lawyer, accountant, and others and these men are going to take over the Church Loan Association. They're going to run it. We're going to see if we can save this situation" (Dorian, Interview, 1994).

Dorian "went to everybody." Thorn, Ted Wilcox, and Don Scott went with him. "We all tried to find people to serve on this committee, but nobody wanted to do it." Finally, a list of ten men was pulled together, and delivered to Quinn. Quinn made the final selection.

THE FIVE-MAN BOARD OF MANAGERS

Senator Lester Arvin, chair of the five-man Board of Managers suggested by the Executive Board and approved by the Kansas Securities Commission, reported to the Convention at its 1969 annual meeting.

The CLA and A.B. Culbertson and Company were derelict in their duty to use ordinary prudent business practices and had failed to set up within the bond selling program adequate reserves to take care of the costs of commissions, underwriting fees, or defaults on the part of churches who were loaned money. During the period from 1958 to 1968, there were many violations of the Securities Act, including the sale of more bonds than authorized. To allow Southern Baptists in Kansas to function as a Convention and to occupy their properties and to keep the CLA from being placed into a court appointed receivership, the Kansas Commissioner ordered that it be managed by some responsible party. The responsible party chosen in January 1969 was the Home Mission Board of the SBC.

At the 1969 summer meeting, Quinn had summed up the situation: liabilities of the CLA exceeded its assets by $1.6 million; in ten years of operation, $5 million of church bonds had been issued; and 254 loans had been made to 115 churches totaling $3.5 million. When he proposed the five-man Board of Managers, he stated that if the bondholders' condition got any worse, the Securities Commission would have to take more drastic action (*BD*, August 16, 1970).

Quinn met with the men selected by the Executive Board and with Pat McDaniel and Robert Kilgore from the Home Mission Board. A few days later, Quinn made the final selection of members of the committee: Leo Poland, chairman of the Accounting Department, Wichita State University, and member of Hillside Baptist Church; Dick Phillips, president of Guarantee Title Co., Wichita, and member of Bel Aire Baptist Mission; Robert Hobson, co-owner of Donlevy Lithograph, Inc., and member of University Baptist Church in Wichita; Emit Ray, pastor of Immanuel Baptist Church, Wichita; and Lester C. Arvin, attorney, Senator, Kansas Legislature, and member of Metropolitan Baptist Church.

Quinn designated four others to be alternates: Ed Alsup, pastor of First Baptist Church, Haysville; and John LeFever, Glen Thompson, and Richard Glenn, all Wichita businessmen. Ed Alsup was the only alternate to serve on the Board of Managers. Emit Ray, the only pastor named to the board, left Immanuel in Wichita and moved to Miami, Florida. Alsup was named to this spot, and later served as president of the Kansas Convention.

Senator Arvin was elected chair; Emit Ray, vice-chairman; and Dick Phillips, recording secretary. The facts were these. The bonded indebtedness of the CLA was $1.6 million. Since the KCSB had guaranteed twenty-five percent of the loan, up to a million dollars, a cap that was not honored, it was in the mess up to its neck. The Kansas Securities Commissioner demanded that two thousand dollars each week be placed in the sinking fund, to be increased in January 1970 to three thousand dollars per week. This debt had to be paid first, before any other work could be done. About seventy-four churches were in default in payments. Some church buildings had been abandoned, were uninsured, and were being sold for taxes within the next few days.

The Board of Managers began its work by visiting all the agency heads in Atlanta and Nashville and then called a "summit meeting" of SBC leaders, agency heads, and executive secretaries of nearby state conventions. Arvin (Telephone Conversation) gives much of the credit for this plan to Owen Cooper, a layman from Mississippi, who was SBC president. Arvin, a member of the Committee on Committees at that time, had gotten to know Cooper, who was head of the Mississippi Chemical Company in Tupelo. As soon as Arvin became chair of the Management Committee, he called Cooper, who came to Wichita the next morning, and together, they set up the summit meeting, and contacted the executive secretaries of several state conventions.

Arvin also gives a great deal of credit to Emit Ray, who was able to talk with pastors across the Convention and help them understand the situation and what had to be done. He was able to pour "oil on troubled waters."

To deal with this enormous problem, the Board of Managers presented a three-point plan to the Convention in 1969: 1) further scale down the state mission program of the Convention and restructure the state staff (five hundred thousand dollars); 2) ask the Baptists of Kansas and Nebraska to pledge five hundred thousand dollars in a Strengthen Our Witness Campaign; and 3) look to other state conventions for help (five hundred thousand dollars).

In order to trim down Convention personnel, Missions, Brotherhood, and Evangelism Departments were combined with the duties of executive secretary-treasurer; functions of the executive secretary-treasurer of the foundation and the vice-president of the CLA were combined with those of executive secretary-treasurer of the Convention; money for associational superintendents of missions was cut, resulting in a number of resignations and combining of several associations; and Westmoreland was asked to resign.

Gerald Locke, who at that time was director of missions in Twin Valley Association, and Gaylon Wiley, who held the same position in Blue Stem Association, faced a situation in which many of the associational missions directors found themselves. Locke described the time when Irby directed the two men to decide who was to stay and who was to go as "anxious and nerve racking." Locke went to Ridgecrest to talk with home mission personnel about a place in the northeast. Before this could take place, Wiley called to say he was leaving Kansas to go back to Texas. Gerald Locke came back to Kansas, where he served Twin Valley and Blue Stem Associations, then Blue Stem and Smoky Hill Associations. After retirement as director of associational missions, the Lockes stayed in Kansas, serving the Americus Baptist Church, until 1991 when they returned to Missouri, from whence they had come in 1960.

Changes like these made it possible, beginning in January 1970, to place fifteen hundred dollars per week from Convention funds into the reserve fund—seventy-eight thousand dollars annually. This was less than the original three thousand dollars, but the Commissioner agreed to it. Including the amount ($170,186) already placed in the sinking fund by the Convention, this would bring the total to five hundred thousand dollars in five years' time.

A stewardship campaign was launched with the help of personnel and funds from the Stewardship Commission of the SBC. January 1970 was set as the "victory date" for campaign pledges to equal five hundred thousand dollars. It was called the Strengthen Our Witness Campaign, the purpose of which was to save our church buildings in Kansas and Nebraska, our reputation, and perhaps even our hides!

The campaign was wonderfully successful. On November 20 two checks arrived, one from an individual, Elmer Mundy, Kimball, Nebraska, and one from a church in Kansas, Mission Creek Baptist Church in Edwardsville. These tied for first place and "came from the two sources on which the success of the campaign rests: the church and the individual. Significant also was the fact that one check came from Nebraska and the other from Kansas" (*BD*, December 6, 1969).

The first pledge card arrived from the Cottonwood Falls Baptist Church in Blue Stem Association. The pledge was seven dollars per week, a total of $1,092 during the three years of the Strengthening Our Witness Campaign (*BD*, November 29, 1969). At the close of the first "Commitment Day" in the churches, December 21, $346,000 had been pledged. By the end of January 1970, churches of Kansas and Nebraska had pledged $672,108.62, which was well over the goal of five hundred thousand dollars. In the next five years $602,712 was actually given through the Strengthen Our Witness Campaign (*BD*, November 22, 1973). Pat McDaniel called this one of the most marvelous, sacrificial efforts that Southern Baptists had been involved in anywhere. The small struggling Southern Baptist churches in Kansas and Nebraska rose to the occasion and pledged more than the goal, and actually gave more than the goal.

Churches "behind" in Cooperative Program gifts made real efforts to "catch up." Although it may have been illegal, people holding bonds were asked to return these bonds as gifts to the Convention, and many did. Strong churches were asked to take smaller churches "under their wing" and help them pay back the loan. There was a spirit of "do or die" among the people. And we did it.

Gordon Dorian (Interview, 1994) recalled one church-helping-church story. A member of Olivet had gone to Hays to pastor a little church, which gave Olivet a tie to that church. They had a debt of thirty-four thousand dollars; Olivet voted to give them two percent of every week's budget until the loan was repaid. "We did this for so many years that it became natural and normal. We lost count of the years we had made that payment, until the church in Hays called and said they could make it on their own. Olivet voted to continue that budget item and call that two percent the 'pastor's fund' which I could use to help any church I wanted to help."

Other state conventions promised to help, if we could be successful in the Strengthen Our Witness Campaign, by making available to us up to five hundred thousand dollars, pledged over a five-year period. A committee to contact sister state conventions was appointed by the Executive Secretaries' Association and chaired by Earl Harding, executive secretary of the Missouri

Baptist Convention. Others on the committee were the executive secretaries of Georgia and Oklahoma. The committee made the crisis known to other conventions who pledged financial support in varying amounts. By 1970, $489,674.84 had been pledged to be paid over a five-year period. At that time $91,181 had come from thirteen conventions ranging from five hundred to fifty thousand dollars. The following year, seventeen states had made contributions, totaling $140,666. In 1972 another state joined; the total reached $193,166; by 1973, nineteen conventions had given three hundred thousand dollars (BD, November 23, 1973). Kansas owes a debt of gratitude to these Baptist groups who shouldered the burden with us: Alaska, Arizona, Colorado, Florida, Georgia, Hawaii, Indiana, Kentucky, Louisiana, Michigan, Missouri, New Mexico, New York, North Carolina, Northern Plains, Northwest, Ohio, Oklahoma, and Utah-Idaho (Annual, 1973). Twelve of these are new-work or pioneer areas, while seven are "old south" conventions.

James Shope, for many years historical secretary of the Kansas Convention, related a poignant story of one contribution. The young Alaska Baptist Convention received at its annual meeting an offering of five hundred dollars for the troubled Kansas Convention. Such action is reminiscent of the offering from the church at Macedonia to the folk in Jerusalem during Paul's time. Over the three-year period, Alaska contributed fifteen hundred dollars.

Because of Michael Quinn's desire that all administrative officers who had been part of the bond fiasco be removed, Howard Whatley, who had already vacated his position with the CLA, was relieved of his post as executive secretary-treasurer of the foundation, and Westmoreland was asked to resign, effective September 30, 1969.

Whatley had accepted a position with Friends University in Wichita, effective February 1, 1968. His job was in the Development Office, where he served as living endowment officer (BD, February 1, 1968).

Westmoreland had no intention of resigning; he wanted to ride out the storm in the position he had occupied since the Convention's beginning. The chair of the Board of Managers called and asked for his resignation, which was refused. Senator Arvin immediately drove to the Convention offices, found Westmoreland in his office, and, taking hold of his lapels, stated emphatically that his immediate resignation and vacation of the office space was absolutely necessary for his own survival and for the survival of the Convention. Only then did Westmoreland comply.

Gordon Dorian (Interview, 1994) quoted Quinn as saying, "'The reason he [Westmoreland] had to go as Executive Secretary is that he did not have enough clout or ability to make you all listen to him.'" Dorian regretted this point of view. He said, "I have always said, I cannot lay the blame for this debacle on N. J. I take a great deal of blame for not knowing what to do and not knowing how to watch the whole thing more closely. But I cannot blame him . . . he tried to warn us."

On Westmoreland's request, George Hair moved that the minutes of the Convention set forth the conditions under which Westmoreland's resignation came. His motion also included appropriate recognition for Westmoreland's years of service. This excerpt from Westmoreland's letter to Senator Arvin appeared in the minutes: "With the developments that have brought about the appointment of the Five-Man Management Committee, it is obvious that tremendous responsibilities requiring great expenditures of energy and time have been accepted by you and the other four men. Mindful of these demands upon the committee, and to cooperate in giving the committee complete freedom in all deliberations and actions, I am submitting my resignation as Executive Secretary-Treasurer of Kansas Convention of Southern Baptists to be acted upon at the discretion of you and the Committee" (*Annual*, 1969).

According to the minutes of the following year (*Annual*, 1970, pp. 19-22), Westmoreland asked for permission to speak to the Convention more fully about his resignation and the reason for it. He asked that his remarks be made a part of the official record. He called it a "correcting statement":

Item No. 49 of the minutes of the 1969 annual meeting of the Kansas Convention of Southern Baptist reads in part as follows: "that there be set forth in the minutes of this Convention the condition under which our former executive secretary resigned." A statement which follows that in the 1969 *Annual* was only a part of the letter of resignation and did not reflect the condition under which it was written. Since it amounts to misinformation, I have felt that to keep the records straight, the following facts should be made available to the messengers and churches related to our Convention. Because of the publicity that went out, many of my fellow workers in the churches felt that I had just grown tired of my task and quit or that I was guilty of bad conduct and had to find a way out.

First I must pay tribute to the life and ministry of the KCSB Executive Director, Pat McDaniel. What I have to say must not be construed to hurt his leadership in any way. There is no doubt that he has done more than anyone else to help the Convention solve the Church Loan Association problems. He deserves the full support of the KCSB constituency. I am not seeking salaried employment with the Kansas Convention of Southern Baptists.

I was in a good position late in 1968 to have my responsibility with the Church Loan Association appraised, testifying under oath to the Securities and Exchange Commission and before the Kansas Securities Commission. The factor of Baptist autonomy was understood and Kansas Securities Commissioner Quinn recognized it and said he would not destroy it. Because I had no vote with the CLA from early 1963 and no controlling power of any kind, because I had warned 7 of the 9 members of the CLA in a meeting and indirectly and because of the actions recommended and passed by the Executive Committee to help churches to keep up their payments and restrict the KCSB guarantee, I was not indicted nor was I ever confronted with personal reprisals by the regulating agencies. I was confident that if anyone dealing with me would be honest with the facts, I had no fear of litigation that might develop if the CLA went down. Furthermore, the Convention sustained my position in the 1968 session, an action that was violated by a group of pastors who tried to destroy my leadership in successive months.

The Five Man Committee appointed by Commissioner Quinn began its work near the 15th of August, 1969. On August 21, I was told by a spokesman of the Five Man Committee that the position of Executive Secretary-Treasurer of the Convention would be combined with that of the position that had been known as the Executive Vice President of the Church Loan Association. The Five Man Committee had been given the power by the Securities Commissioner and by the Executive Board to fire and hire all personnel.

On August 27, 1969, I was told by the same Five Man Committee spokesman to call for the resignations of the "staff members," and then present my resignation. Having been told six days before that my position would be abolished by structural changes, I was shocked to confront a forced statement of resignation. Why would they want my resignation from a position that did not or soon would not exist? I do not yet have the answer to this question, but circumstances and actions provide strong suggestions. Could they fear the reaction of the people with whom the executive secretary had served so long? If they did not, I did, and this fear was strong motivation with me after my work was ended. Letters were to reach him August 29.

I told the spokesman that I was not presenting a letter of resignation, when I wrote to him, a letter that I delivered personally. It was obvious that in a few days I would not have a job. My letter elaborated on this. He tore up the letter and I was confronted with tough, strong threatening language the type of which was a new experience to me. He would turn the CLA and the Convention into bankruptcy if I did not present a letter of resignation. He needed only to call Mr. Quinn and report my lack of cooperation to have the 74 delinquent churches lose their buildings and many pastors and laymen face losses though civil suits in almost endless litigation. I agreed to write a forced letter to avert disaster, but it took at least 30 minutes for quiet to reign.

I was to report back early Tuesday, September 2, after the long, Labor Day weekend. My next letter was as follows: "In compliance with your request and to contribute to the objectives of cooperation, I hereby submit my resignation as Executive Secretary-Treasurer of the Kansas Convention of Southern Baptists."

He tore it up. The loud, strong, threatening language ensued. "I didn't request your resignation. I suggested it," he said. I was maligned for not being able to follow though on communications. The session was rough, but shorter, and I was to return in the afternoon. The third letter was accepted, has been in the files of the Five-Man Committee, with one paragraph appearing in the 1969 *Annual*. The Five-Man Committee had a potential vacancy and a letter of resignation to go with it. It has been used widely as a point of reference, leading to many false impressions, and cast a dark shadow over my work with Southern Baptists.

The acceptance of the resignation by the Five-Man Committee came with much similar atmosphere. I had witnesses for the last round. One member of the Committee apologized for the actions of the spokesman along the way.

This statement will help my missionary fellow workers to know more of the strange events that have happened during the last year and that I did not run off from my job and calling. It will help them also to know that more than money was required to avert the disaster that threatened through the massive failure of the Church Loan Association. I did not attempt to tell of this earlier in a public manner for fear that fellow workers in the missionary enterprise would reel and refuse to participate in redeeming the CLA. Members of the KCSB staff were forbidden to discuss anything they knew about the resignation.

It was moved and carried that the transcript of Westmoreland's remarks be "felicitously accepted and that they be made a part of the records of this twenty-fifth anniversary session." After adjournment that evening, there was a reception for the Westmorelands.

Gordon Dorian, who was pastor of Olivet Baptist Church in Wichita, and president of the CLA Board, corroborated Westmoreland's statement in an interview with James Shope: "I did not know at the time that we were in such bad trouble. I knew we were way too far over in our commitment because we didn't have a million dollars to underwrite four million dollars. . . . [After a visit with Mr. Culbertson during which Culbertson assured him that everything was okay] I'd come back and tell N. J. that, and N. J. would shake his head and say, 'I don't think so.' But nobody would listen to N. J. I heard him talk to Whatley. He even talked to our Board and he tried to tell us, but nobody would listen to him. We were just full steam ahead."

So Westmoreland ended a quarter century as executive secretary-treasurer of the KCSB from its beginning in 1946. Much had happened in those years (*BD*, October 11, 1969): the seven beginning churches had increased to 197 with thirty-eight church-type missions. Property value had increased from sixty-one thousand dollars to nineteen million dollars. When the first annual meeting was held in November 1946, there were twelve churches that reported 133 baptisms for the year. In 1968 the 197 churches boasted 51,902 members and reported 2,731 baptisms for the year. Cooperative Program gifts had multiplied a hundredfold, growing from over two thousand dollars to two hundred thousand dollars. The acceptance of Kansas as a constituent of the SBC in 1948 was largely the result of Westmoreland's dream and work. During his tenure, first eastern and then western Nebraska churches joined forces with Kansas in Baptist work. There were other milestones to mark his ministry: an official state paper, an enlarged staff, attention to students on campuses across the state, language and ethnic missions with Indians and Spanish-speaking, emphasis on social ministry in urban centers, superintendents of missions (associational missionaries), and pastoral aid. In addition, he was a prolific writer, leaving articles, memos, reports, and editorials.

Harold Morgan, twin brother of Darold, recounted how Westmoreland had come to Kansas. The Morgan family had moved back to their old homeplace in Coffeyville in the early 1930s, after their father lost his job in Fort Worth, Texas. Harold reported their first Sunday morning in Emmanuel Baptist Church in this fashion: "Having come from the South, Dad sent me up to peek in the windows to see if it were a colored church. 'They're all white,' I said, as I returned to the car. Our family got out and trooped in to join the small group there. Every head turned as we walked down the wooden aisle."

After the pastor resigned, Morgan, Sr. was asked to contact "someone in Texas" about becoming the pastor. So, Morgan contacted Fred Swank, his former pastor, who recommended Westmoreland, who came "in view of a call." The church called him, and later he returned to Texas long enough to claim his bride. So it was in the early 1940s that Westmoreland cast his lot with Kansas and Nebraska Baptists. Nobody could have guessed at that time what a mark he would make on them.

After he left his post with the Kansas Convention, he turned to business and real estate, but he never was far away from Kansas and Nebraska Baptists. The Towne East Baptist Church of Wichita petitioned for affiliation with the KNCSB in 1975. Westmoreland was listed as pastor. He attended the annual meetings and served as historical secretary, and in that capacity was part of the Executive Board and Executive Committee.

In 1982 (*BD*, November) John Hopkins wrote an editorial titled "Leader Deserves Our Recognition," in which he suggested that the Convention honor Dr. Westmoreland by naming him executive director emeritus of the KNCSB. This was done at the annual meeting that year.

Hopkins characterized Westmoreland's years of leadership: "Standing tall among the people of God who have served His purpose in Kansas and Nebraska is N. J. Westmoreland. It was Westmoreland's leadership, insight, and commitment to the cause of Christ that permitted him a key role in founding our Convention. . . . This was not an easy task. It was a task where he had to assume the blame for many mistakes, but because he is the man he is, he was always quick to give God credit for victories won. . . . Westmoreland surely must have carried into retirement mixed feelings about the years he served God as our leader in Kansas-Nebraska . . . both important and difficult . . . years which gave us the firm foundation on which our work in the Midwest was built."

Westmoreland was born in 1914, converted at the age of thirteen, and baptized into Bird City Baptist Church in Texas when he was twenty-four. He graduated from Hardin-Simmons Baptist College and later received an honorary doctorate from East Texas Baptist College in Marshall.

He died in 1986 at the age of 72. The 1986 *Annual* of the Convention was dedicated to N. J. and Wanda Westmoreland. A memorial statement was included: "He was known and loved by hundreds of Baptists throughout the Kansas-Nebraska Convention of Southern Baptists. He loved the Lord supremely, his brethren warmly, and lost people with compassion. He was a dedicated disciple of his Lord. Marvelous is the fruit of his life. Blessed is his memory. His good works live on in the lives of those who knew him."

Gordon Dorian's tribute to Westmoreland is fitting: "He always loved the Convention. He loved the little churches and the little church pastors. His reasoning was the big churches didn't need him, so he never went around Metropolitan or Immanuel."

Kansas and Nebraska Baptists learned a lesson: everyone is responsible for the working of the Convention. During the miscellaneous business period at the 1969 Convention, an enlightening motion was made by George Roberts, director of missions in Kaw Valley Association: "That we ask the Management Board to prepare and present to the Executive Board for consideration by the Convention at its next annual session a business and financial plan designed to provide for our future fiscal soundness and for the constitutional representation on our boards and committees from the fields of business, finance, accounting, and law." Perhaps we were learning that men called of God to preach the gospel were not always equipped to handle all the other aspects of a corporate body. Christian men and women are equipped in many ways to do Kingdom work, gifts which need to be recognized and utilized in the orderly conduct of the business of the Convention and the business of churches.

The Board of Managers was also charged with the responsibility of finding an executive director for the Convention. Senator Arvin closed his report to the 1969 annual meeting with these words: "But what about leadership for the Convention and the Church Loan Association? Without strong, dynamic, business-like leadership we cannot exist. We know that a great spiritual leader is needed for our Convention. I, for one, have been praying that God will grant to His people such a leader. God will provide and we have been encouraged to believe from the President of the Convention and others that we will be supplied very shortly with such a man."

A NEW EXECUTIVE DIRECTOR

Pat McDaniel was elected executive director of the Convention and director of the CLA on March 1, 1970, by the Executive Board. He also served as editor of the *Baptist Digest*. Between March and the November meeting of the Convention, the Five-Man Management Board finished its work and was dissolved. They liked their job, and again it took firm, direct action by the new executive director to bring about their resignation. Strangely, there was no recorded welcome or introduction of the new director at the 1970 annual meeting. One sentence, in the Executive Board Report written by McDaniel, is given to this momentous change: "Pat McDaniel came March 1, 1970, as the Executive Director of the Convention and the Director of the Church Loan Association."

The term "Executive Director" was used in reference to McDaniel from the time of his appointment, even though the wording in the Executive Committee by-laws was not officially changed until 1974 from executive secretary-treasurer to executive director-treasurer (*Annual*).

At the annual meeting in November (*Annual*, 1970), the Convention voted to instruct the executive director to "compose and send an appropriate and official letter of appreciation to each man who served on our five-man Management Board, this letter to express our deepest gratitude for the outstanding service they rendered our Convention; also that such a letter of appreciation be sent to Mike Quinn, Securities Commissioner, for understanding and interested cooperation." The management of the Convention was back in the hands of Kansas and Nebraska Baptists.

In an interview, McDaniel shared some of his experiences during the seven years he served as executive director of the KNCSB. The Management Committee spent several months interviewing potential successors to Dr. Westmoreland. There were many applicants, but once they got out here, or talked to their friends, and discovered the immensity of the Kansas problem, they all declined. "There's many a slip twixt cup and lip," said the sage, and although there were a number of applicants, there were no takers for this job. Finally, the committee talked to Pat McDaniel about accepting this position, and discussed the problems he would have to help solve. He said, "I didn't have any better sense than to come, knowing full well what I was stepping into, but also knowing that the good Lord was in it and that He had a plan."

Pat McDaniel, Home Mission Board, SBC, employee who, beginning in 1968, helped resolve the bond crisis in the Kansas Convention of Southern Baptists. Elected executive director-treasurer of the Convention in 1970, he served until 1976.

By this time, McDaniel was enjoying his job with the Home Mission Board, and had just had a "dandy" increase in salary. He felt, however, unequivocally that the Lord wanted him to come to Kansas-Nebraska and go to work in this mess. "And it was a mess," he said. "There's no other way to describe it. But I felt very strongly led by Him. I thought He had a plan and so I decided that I would attempt with His help to go out and work where He was working."

This was not the first time McDaniel had felt "strongly led of the Lord" and accepted a hard job (*BD*, January 13, 1975). At twenty-two, he and his wife, Gladys, were living in Weatherford, and were members of the Northside Baptist Church. In a revival service with Hyman Appleman, McDaniel committed his life to the Lord—"this time for real," he said. Life took on new purpose; the thing that really mattered to him was Jesus Christ and His work.

Three years later, a bank in Weatherford, Texas, offered him a job, although he told them he did not know a "debit from a credit." He attended classes at night at the American Institute of Banking in Fort Worth, forty-four miles away. In his bank job, he started at the bottom, as a file clerk, and within three years was a bank officer, the youngest in Texas. Five years after he got into finance, he was elected vice-president of a savings and loan company.

All the while, he kept growing as a Christian, readily sharing his faith with others. He was elected a deacon and became Brotherhood director in his association, which led to exposure to "pioneer missions." He was caught up in it; he could not get away. He decided he would go to the great Northeast and as a layman become part of the solution. His pastor discouraged him, suggesting that the only way to really make a contribution to "pioneer missions" was as a preacher. So he enrolled at Southwestern Baptist Theological Seminary under what he considered "false pretenses," for the seminary did not know quite what to do with the avowed "called" layman.

A number of events led him and a "big preacher friend," Don Burton, to go to Michigan where there was great need. Seven people in Owosso, where Baptist work had failed twice, agreed to call Burton as pastor. They could not pay him. They had no place to meet. But they invited him to come. Burton went back to Weatherford, shared this with McDaniel, and the two families sold their belongings and went to Michigan.

McDaniel found a job in a bank twenty miles away; the big preacher worked in a steel mill in Owassa. They visited. They witnessed. Together they built a church. By the end of the year, 121 were enrolled in Sunday School. The church led the state convention in baptisms. For three years these two worked together.

Then it was moving time again. McDaniel was asked to join the staff of the Baptist State Convention of Michigan as assistant to the executive secretary. In four years another change came. Bob Kilgore, director of the Division of Church Loans at the Home Mission Board of the SBC, contacted McDaniel about a position as the board's first finance and loan officer on a nationwide basis. Thus, God's man was waiting in the wings to be used by God, front and center, in the crisis situation in Kansas. "God focused all of Pat's experience as a banker, churchman, denomination worker, and a man of faith on the Convention's problems. He carefully led the Convention back to financial soundness" (*BD*, January 31, 1975).

It was not easy. McDaniel confessed that to do a number of the things that were necessary he had to be tough when it would have been easier for him another way. He had to notify bondholders that they could not sell their bonds, discount them, or give them away. They would have to hold them. Some purchasers had "re-purchase agreements," which were illegal to begin with, and could not be honored. If a purchaser wanted a short-term bond and none was available, the CLA representative simply said, at the end of five years, "We will give you your money and re-sell the bond to someone else." Many people were depending on this impossible arrangement. Letters were sent to all the bondholders telling them of the legal rules by which they were to abide.

McDaniel told of meeting with a man in the hospital who had just had his leg amputated above the knee due to cancer. He had a bond with a repurchase agreement that was due, and no insurance. This was to be his means of getting out of the hospital. He had to be refused. The man died before his bond could be redeemed.

Pat visited an elderly man who invited him to his home to talk about his ten thousand dollars in repurchase agreements. After a bit of conversation, he invited his daughter to join them. The young woman wanted to go to college in the fall. Those bonds were meant as her ticket to an education. His request to honor the repurchase agreement was denied . . . another "unhappy Baptist."

Another task was to talk with churches about overdue payments and underpayments. Some churches took his admonitions "with a grain of salt," but after the fourth foreclosure (and that was all there were, just four), word got out and the churches began to decide they "might best improve their payment schedule." They did.

William F. McKean became pastor at Fort Scott in 1968, just as "the roof fell in." He was a member of the Executive Board. He recalled, "Every time we'd go to a Board meeting or Executive Committee meeting, Pat would look at us and say: 'Well, we've just uncovered another barrel of snakes.'" Finally, as in Ireland, the snakes were banished.

The 1970 Stewardship Report was an exciting one. Although Cooperative Program giving showed a dollar decrease during the preceding year, "it should be noted that during the same period, our churches have paid $141,916.86 to . . . the Strengthening Our Witness Campaign." The State Missions Offering and the Annie Armstrong Offering for Home Missions were more than the previous year, and the Lottie Moon Christmas Offering totaled almost forty-three thousand dollars, not much lower than the year before.

The 1971 *Annual* showed the Convention in improved financial position. On August 1, 1971, R. Rex Lindsay was hired to become director of Missions-Evangelism-Student Work of the KNCSB. He had been serving as superintendent of missions for the Eastern and Western Nebraska Associations.

In 1972 Cooperative Program receipts were above the year before, and $167,658 was given through the Strengthening our Witness pledges. The $2,526 State Mission Offering was also designated for the Strengthening Our Witness Campaign. The Lottie Moon Christmas Offering that year was the largest given to that point by Kansas-Nebraska Baptists: $64,138.03.

That year also, the Convention received $173,515.31 of a $197,500 court settlement with A. B. Culbertson and Company (former CLA trustee). More than $4,400,000 bonds were sold through the CLA, and the A. B. Culbertson Company and their representative were paid over $320,000 in commissions for selling the bonds and acting as trustees for the bondholders of the CLA.

VICTORY, 1973

The editors of thirty Baptist papers voted the Kansas crisis among the top ten news stories in 1969 (*BD*, January 3, 1970). "Financial Crisis Solutions Sought by Kansas Baptists; Five-Man Management Board Named; Fund Campaign to raise $1.5 million Begun" ranked number eight. Hurricane Camille damage to Baptist property, Caudill and Fite released from Cuban prisons, controversies over W. A. Criswell's book, proposed name change for Training Union to "Quest," problems with financing Baptist schools, and results of the Crusade of the Americas were stories that ranked above ours. It would have been heartening if the 1973 story of victory had also made the top ten.

The 1973 annual meeting of the Convention was at First Baptist Church, Bellevue, Nebraska. There was electricity in the air. A big party was scheduled after the evening session. Everything went along "as usual" Tuesday afternoon. One hundred six messengers were seated. There were changes in the order of business, an announcement of the Midwestern Baptist Theological Seminary luncheon, reports from the Historical Commission and Brotherhood Department, and a Bible study. All messengers, alternates, and visitors who had not registered were urged to do so.

The evening session began with the usual formalities. New pastors were recognized, Mrs. Anita Wilson was presented a service award, and then it was time for the combined Executive Board and CLA report. Edgar William Dwire, attorney for the Kansas-Nebraska Convention, spoke to this report.

He reviewed "where we have been" and how far we have come and then presented the following CLA resolution, which had been adopted by that board on September 17: "WHEREAS, it is in the judgment of the directors of this corporation advisable and most for the benefit of the bondholders of the corporation: 1. That the bonds of the corporation be called for payment on December 31, 1973; 2. That the Church Loan Association of Southern Baptists grant, assign, convey and set over unto the Executive Board of the Kansas

Convention of Southern Baptists, a Kansas nonprofit religious corporation, all monies, bills, notes, mortgages, contracts, agreements, books of account, office furnishing, leaseholds, and all other properties of every other nature and description owned or used by Church Loan Association of Southern Baptists on or before midnight, December 31 [1973]."

Other resolutions confirmed that the Convention would indeed take over all these obligations, and that the CLA of Southern Baptists be dissolved. In order for the Convention to meet the bond obligation of the CLA, there would have to be one more loan of five hundred thousand dollars which would be secured with the notes and mortgage proceeds received from the CLA.

With all the prosaic "Whereases" and "Be it resolveds," the bottom line was the bonds could be paid off—one hundred cents on the dollar. This was happening five years early—1973 instead of the target date of 1978. The Kansas-Nebraska Convention of Southern Baptists was solvent. We had met our obligations. We had kept faith with those from whom we had borrowed.

Because the debt was paid off early, the Kansas-Nebraska Convention was freed from its $1,250 weekly obligation, which made seventy-eight thousand dollars per year available for missions work. In addition, Dwire pointed out the following: "There will be a minimum interest saving of $35,000. All bondholders liability will be terminated and the bondholders will have the use of their money. There will also be an annual saving in attorney fees, audit fees, and administrative expense."

The necessary loan was obtained from Farmers and Merchants State Bank, Derby, Kansas and the Southwest National Bank in Wichita. As it turned out, only $157,000 was needed, and this loan was paid on June 7, 1974.

After a number of questions and clarifying explanations, Dwire offered the following resolution:

WHEREAS, it is in the judgment of the Messengers of the Kansas Convention of Southern Baptists that the Executive Board of the Kansas Convention of Southern Baptists should accept the assets and assume the liabilities of the Church Loan Association to be used for the redemption of the outstanding bonds of Church Loan Association of Southern Baptists,

NOW, THEREFORE, BE IT RESOLVED that the proper officers of the Executive Board of the Kansas Convention of Southern Baptists are authorized to accept and receive all assets of the Church Loan Association of Southern Baptists and authorized and directed to take such further necessary steps as may be necessary or proper to assume the outstanding obligations of Church Loan Association in the redemption of the outstanding bonds of Church Loan Association of Southern Baptists and obtain a loan of $500,000 to be used in the redemption of outstanding bonds of Church Loan Association.

BAPTIST Digest

SERVING KANSAS-NEBRASKA SOUTHERN BAPTISTS

Vol. 20—No. 22   3000 W. Kellogg Dr., Wichita, Kansas 67213   November 22, 1973

CLA BONDS CALLED!

"A miracle. Absolutely a miracle. There is no other way to explain it."

60,000 Southern Baptists in Kansas and Nebraska — and most other people who know the story — will agree.

The cause of the exclamation was the calling of $1.6 million of bonds issued by the Church Loan Association of the Kansas Convention of Southern Baptists. The bond calling signaled the victory of five years of prayer, agony, and sacrifice.

Five years ago in November, 1968, the Kansas convention (which serves the two-state area of Kansas-Nebraska) assumed the liabilities of its Church Loan Association (CLA) to keep from losing some 77 church buildings because of the CLA's insolvency. In 1969 the CLA had liabilities of $3,387,905.00 and assets of only $1,749,691.00, leaving a $1,638,214.00 deficit.

On January 28, 1969, the acting officers of the convention and CLA mailed letters to anyone holding any of the $4 million worth of bonds issued during the eleven year existence of the CLA. The letter disclosed that the Kansas Securities Commission and the Board of Directors of the CLA declared to the bondholders that the CLA was insolvent. The letter informed the bondholders that their bonds were not to be sold or traded.

Salvage begins

In order to salvage the situation, the Kansas Convention that year entered a management agreement with the Home Mission Board. The Board sent Pat McDaniel, later elected the state convention's executive director, to manage the CLA.

A program of recovery was outlined in the initial letter to the bondholders. In addition to sending Mr. McDaniel to manage the CLA the Home Mission Board agreed to place not less than $50,000.00 per year for ten years to apply to the operations and sinking fund of the CLA. The re-financing of the Kansas Convention's building by the HMB permitted placing $100,000.00 in the sinking fund of the CLA for the benefit of the bondholders. The establishment of a $300,000.00 stand-by reserve was funded for the CLA by the HMB.

In August of 1969 another letter was sent to bondholders to further appraise them of the CLA's — and their — situation. The Securities Commissioner of Kansas then placed the CLA under a 5-man board of managers. The management committee was appointed by the Commissioner to "(1) Manage the affairs of the Church Loan Association; and (2) Manage all

affairs within the Kansas Convention, of Southern Baptists which would relate to the Church Loan Association, including but not limited to budget controls, income, organization of the convention, etc."

SOW Born

The Stewardship Commission of the Southern Baptist Convention assisted the convention in a campaign, named the Strengthening Our Witness (SOW) Campaign, to raise money and pledged to offset the CLA deficit that had been assumed by the state convention. Within four months the people and churches of the Kansas Convention of Southern Baptists pledged $672,-108.00 through SOW Campaign. In addition other state conventions pledged $489,675.00 to be paid in a five year period. When these pledges were committed the five man committee recommended that Mr. Pat McDaniel be elected to serve as Executive Director of the convention and the CLA. The Executive Board unanimously elected Mr. Daniel and the five-man board dissolved.

In the following five years $602,712.00 from the Kansas-Nebraska churches and $300,-000.00 (either in cash or commitments to be funded by 1974) from other state conventions was placed into the CLA fund. The total was aided by

a settlement in favor of the CLA from A. B. Culbertson Co., Ft. Worth, Texas, original trustee and selling agent of the CLA, that netted $130,807.33 after legal fees and other expenses.

Further financial improvement came when some churches who had loans with the CLA refinanced through other agencies and paid off their indebtedness with the CLA. Also, four buildings were sold and their indebtedness paid.

One of the convention's financial advisors said, "Several factors, other than sacrificial contributions, made this victory possible. In the past five years prudent management, and wise investments of assets helped greatly."

'73 Convention Acts

At this year's convention messengers took the action necessary to call the bonds. T h e action included: Receiving a joint letter of commitment for a loan of up to $500,000.00 from The Southwest National Bank and Trust Company, Wichita, and the Farmers and Merchants State Bank of Derby, Ks. The loan was necessary to make possible the bond call. The Messengers authorized the convention officers to enter the agreement with the banks whereby up to $500,000.00 could be borrowed to pay off out-

standing bonds.

The convention also voted to assume all liabilities and assets of the Association and to dissolve the Association at midnight, December 31, 1973.

What It Means

Pat McDaniel, executive director, said, "Southern B a p-tist's history shows that they are people of faith who take crisis and turn them into victories in the Lord. We feel so much gratitude to so many. I know that difficult times have kept some state conventions from meeting their pledges. But I cannot help thinking that a great part of this victory belongs to the Southern Baptists of Kansas and Nebraska. These people individually could have done very little to save this convention. But they were good stewards of what God gave them. They gave one, two, three and five dollars a week to the SOW Campaign over and above what they gave to their churches. Their individual dollars flowed together and totaled over $602,912.00. And that is in addition to what has been record-breaking cooperative program giving across our convention during t h e s e five years."

In trying to summarize the impact of the bond calling on the state convention McDaniel said, "It means every bond-

holder will receive one hundred cents on every dollar they invested with the CLA. It means a recovery of our good name. It means $78,000.00 per year that was going into the CLA sinking fund will be freed for mission causes. Our morale should soar.

"We are now five years ahead of our regular program schedule. To think that five years ago we could have lost 77 church buildings. In these five years, churches using some of the 77 church buildings led our state in baptisms."

In the next 20 years approximately $1.2 million will come in from churches indebted formerly to the CLA and now indebted to the Kansas-Nebraska Convention. This money will be placed into the Kansas Southern Baptist Foundation for a revolving loan fund to assist churches in t h e convention's two-state area. The money will be carefully handled and available only for well-secured loans.

All legal and financial advisors were emphatic in stating that no loans would be forgiven. The same sound financial practices that saw the convention to the point of victory will be kept in force.

Good News Coverage

The convention action recived good secular press coverage. A news conference was held the day folowing the convention action to publicize the good news. The conference was conducted through the facilities of the Omaha Press Club. Two television stations, a radio station, and the city's daily newspaper covered the event. Present to present a news release and answer questions from the media were Pat McDaniel and Jim Martin.

Dr. Charles Bryan, representative from the Foreign Mission Board, was also interviewed on one of the television stations concerning the effect of Watergate on foreign missions—and the effect of the mid-east crisis.

Another news conference was conducted in Wichita the next week. The story was released on the major radio stations, a television station, and in the daily newspaper.

McDaniel said in the Wichita conference, "Five years ago when we got into trouble, the media, to borrow a phrase, left us to twist slowly in the wind. We are here today to do some unwinding."

Pictured are the officers of the organizations and institutions involved in the culmination of the CLA bond call. Left to Right: Lernard Smith, president of the Church Loan Association; Bob Powell, bookkeeper of the Church Loan Association; Pat McDaniel, executive director of the Kansas-Nebraska Convention of Southern Baptists and the Church Loan Association; Dale Easman, vice-president of the Farmers and Merchant State Bank, Derby, Ks., and members of the Church Loan Board; Gordon Johnson, executive vice-president and trust officer of The Southwest National Bank and Trust Company, Wichita, Ks.; Ed Dwire, legal counsel of the Convention and the CLA. The men are looking over the resolution passed by the convention that dissolved the Church Loan Association, effective December 31, 1973.

Front-page article in the November 22, 1973, issue of the Baptist Digest, *newspaper of the Kansas-Nebraska Convention of Southern Baptists, announcing the calling of Church Loan Association bonds, thus ending a major bond crisis in the Convention.*

H. E. Alsup moved the adoption of the joint Executive Board and CLA report, which was unanimously accepted. It was over! The crisis was past. Disaster had been averted. The bondholders would be paid every penny. Baptists were as good as their word. We had gone into the pit and come out— through the valley of the shadow of death! By the grace of God who had led us and our friends to do what needed to be done, we scaled the heights of joy.

The headline of the November 22, 1973, issue of *Baptist Digest* said it well, in large black letters, "CLA BONDS CALLED!" The full-page article began: "It was a miracle. Absolutely a miracle. There is no other way to explain it. 60,000 Southern Baptists in Kansas and Nebraska—and most other people who know the story—will agree."

A motion was made that a copy of the letter to the bondholders be included in the minutes of the twenty-eighth annual session. It was so ordered.

Then President Jim Martin presented Pat McDaniel and his family to the Convention. Flowers. Cheers. A gift. A standing ovation. These were the Convention's ways of saying thanks. Thanks to the man whose knowledge, work, and tough love, under God's leadership, brought Southern Baptists of Kansas and Nebraska through the fire and out on the other side, stronger and wiser than before.

KANSAS-NEBRASKA SOUTHERN BAPTIST FOUNDATION

As with the mythical phoenix, a beautiful bird that lived for a long time in the Arabian desert, consumed itself in fire, and arose from the ashes to start another long life, so it is with the Kansas-Nebraska Southern Baptist Foundation. This foundation was originally incorporated in 1952, although it had been in operation before that time. As early as 1948 a Revolving Building and Loan had been established. In 1952 the foundation held $6,167, was the beneficiary of one will, and had begun to raise money for the Baptist Student Center in Pittsburg, Kansas. As of 1960, the total assets of the foundation had grown to $50,727, held in six funds.

The first year the foundation showed assets of over a hundred thousand dollars was 1968 (*Annual*, 1968). The audit presented to the Convention showed ten funds totaling $102,458. One was the "Child Care Fund," which had originally been called the "Children's Home Fund," and was one of the earliest funds entrusted to it. It was money designated to build an orphanage, which was later deemed not feasible, nor was it necessary. The Convention designated the "Child Care Fund" to be used for foster homes, an adoption agency, and cottages to care for children. This too, proved not feasible. Thus in 1974, the Convention voted to add the fund to the "Missions Promotion Fund" so it could be used for mission causes in Kansas and Nebraska more suited to our needs.

This decision was another milestone. A children's home had been part of the Convention's thinking since its inception. Particularly was this true for

Westmoreland. The action of the Convention demonstrated we can certainly move in new directions when we are faced with different needs.

After Howard Whatley vacated the position of executive secretary of the foundation, it was operated by a board of directors until 1970, when Pat McDaniel was elected executive director of the KNCSB and also executive director of the foundation, followed by R. Rex Lindsay in 1977.

In 1972 (*ESB*, Vol. IV), just before the bonds were called, a study committee recommended that the foundation be continued but that changes be made in its organization and administration. The adoption of the report by the Convention was a landmark action. The Convention went on record as endorsing the idea of continuing the foundation; its work would be to promote giving, receive gifts, hold and invest them, and use them according to the wishes of the donor and the Convention for mission support. It was designated as the only agency of the KCSB to hold any property of any kind for endowment purposes.

In 1972, also, the KNCSB adopted a resolution instructing the Executive Board to transfer the Church Loan Fund remaining with the CLA of Southern Baptists to the foundation. This fund formed the corpus of the Revolving Building Loan Fund for new buildings and remodeling existing buildings for Baptist churches cooperating with the KNCSB. The interest earned is the money directed to mission work in Kansas-Nebraska.

These "changes" and others which grew out of the dreaming and thinking of McDaniel and Lindsay are the genius of the present foundation structure. The Convention will never find itself bogged down in another 1968 crisis.

The foundation is a subsidiary corporation of the Convention. It employs no personnel, and it does not own a building. Administrative expenses are paid by the Convention. Its board directs the use of money that becomes available through interest-bearing investments, from interest on loans made to churches, and by direction of the donor. Each year, from the proceeds of investments, the foundation makes grants to the Convention to be used for missions in Kansas and Nebraska. Grants vary from year to year depending on investment returns and Convention needs and requests.

The executive director of KNCSB is the executive director of the foundation. Each year the Convention approves the foundation's portfolio of funds.

Each year an independent certified audit is prepared, which is published in the annual *Book of Reports* and distributed to the messengers and churches. The foundation is not an institution, but a channel through which churches can be enabled to do a better job and all Southern Baptist causes can be strengthened.

At the same time (1972), the Executive Board of the Convention began to discuss the advisability of hiring an executive director for the foundation in order to lessen the workload of the executive director of the Convention. This person could also provide support to Convention staff in promoting the Cooperative Program and stewardship in general. The board also wanted to assign the specific responsibility for helping Kansas-Nebraska Baptists understand the opportunity of being good stewards even after their death.

This suggestion, as it was made, was never acted upon. McDaniel and Lindsay led the Convention to another plan.

In 1977 McDaniel resigned and accepted a position with the SBC Annuity Board. He was executive vice-president for ten years, took early retirement, and moved back to Kansas. At this time, Pat and Gladys McDaniel, of Topeka, and Charles and Janie Wood, of Wichita, operate as consultants to the foundation. They have assisted more than six hundred family units in Christian Estate Planning.

Also in 1977, when Peck Lindsay became executive director of KNCSB, Harold Conley was employed as business-administrator comptroller. This allowed the executive director of the Convention to continue to function as executive director of the foundation, but provided the skill necessary to handle the fiscal matters of the foundation and the Convention.

On December 31, 1994, the foundation had assets totalling $3,388,911 in twenty-eight funds supporting Southern Baptist causes in Kansas-Nebraska and around the world. The Revolving Building Loan Fund had twenty-nine outstanding loans totaling $1,609,099. Other funds had five outstanding loans totalling $99,608.

In 1994 the foundation gave $174,236 to the KNCSB for the direct support of field missionaries. The foundation made grants totalling another $28,875 for mission causes in Kansas-Nebraska and around the world. In the five years between 1989 and 1993, the foundation gave to KNCSB $708,708 for missionaries and $181,220 in grants.

In 1993 (*BD*, June 30, 1993), the foundation set up a cooperative project with the Church Extension Department. The foundation bought three modular buildings which are leased to churches which need help in providing the first unit of a building, or room for expansion. The lease will be for two or three years.

"Stewardship of possessions begins with the tithe, and offerings above the tithe, but the last evidence of Christian stewardship is the disposition of assets after death. A well conceived and properly implemented 'Christian Estate Plan' for the stewardship of an estate will result in the individual being able to do more for loved ones and more for God's kingdom. The Kansas-Nebraska Southern Baptist Foundation is ready and willing to provide assistance in 'Christian Estate Planning'" (Conley, Personal Communication). The foundation is alive and doing well.

4

The Nebraska Story

A STONE CHIMNEY NEAR A FARMHOUSE WEST OF BELLEVUE, Nebraska, is all that remains of the mission house of Moses Merrill, early Baptist mission pioneer. He was known to the Indians as "The-One-Who-Always-Speaks-the-Truth" (*BD*, June 20, 1967). Merrill and two helpers came from Michigan to the Nebraska area in 1833 in response to the efforts of the Home Mission Society of the Triennial Convention to provide a witness to the Indians (*BD*, May 30, 1977). Tradition has it that when Manuel Lisa, a Spaniard, came in 1805, ascended a bluff, and saw the beautiful plateau upon which he stood, he cried out "Belle vue!" which means "beautiful view" (Huddlestun, 1966). The English and even earlier the Indians, who used this place as a burial ground, must have thought the same. And so it has remained to this day. Bellevue was incorporated in 1823, and is the oldest city in Nebraska.

The Merrills "set the tone" for Baptist work in Nebraska when they arrived in Bellevue, where there was an Indian agency and a fur-trading post. Moses Merrill signed an agreement with the Indian agent to "perform the duties of Schoolmaster for the boys and girls of the Otoe and Missouri tribes of Indians diligently and faithfully" (Huddlestun, 1966). In addition to teaching, he worked hard at learning the language of the Otoes, to provide written materials for them, including Scripture translations, a spelling book, a reader, and a collection of hymns. His was a short ministry; he died four years after his son, Samuel, was born, which ended seven years of work.

According to Lynn Clayton (*BD*, May 30, 1977), seven days after their arrival, Mrs. Merrill opened a school for Indian children. Their life was hard; only a few children came to the school during the first few years. To win the confidence of the Indians, the Merrills provided food, seed, tools, clothing; they cared for Indians who were ill; and they moved with them to their new

106

village on the other side of Bellevue. They did not fully win the battle; some of the Otoes continued to believe the Merrills had evil spirits that made Indian people sick and brought bad luck.

On a hunting trip with the Indians in 1839, Merrill contracted a disease from which he never recovered. The following year he died and was buried on the east bank of the Missouri River. When the Missouri changed its course, his grave was washed away.

Clayton (*BD*, May 30, 1977) continued, "Merrill's Christian dedication and willingness to follow God's call to work in Nebraska still flavors the work of many who serve in the Kansas-Nebraska Convention of Southern Baptists. Modern-day missionaries have shouldered the work in much the same manner as Merrill. The difficulties modern-day missionaries face are more subtle than Merrill, but the hardships are just as real."

There is not a clear connection between the work of Merrill and the later history of Baptists in this region. Northern Baptists continued to work in Nebraska after the Southern Baptist Convention was organized in 1845. "In 1867, through a city land grant, property was given to the First Baptist Church of Bellevue. This church was the first Baptist church to be established in the state of Nebraska. . . . Through the years, the church flourished and then died completely" (*BD*, June 20, 1967). According to Huddlestun, the first Convention of Baptists in the state of Nebraska took place in 1867 in Bellevue. There is no record of the churches or number of messengers in attendance.

"Almost a hundred years later, Southern Baptists moved into beautiful Bellevue. Through circumstances known only to God, the group purchased the Salvation Army property for its building site . . . the site of the original First Baptist Church. . . . [Today] in the oldest and fastest-growing city in Nebraska, on the site of the oldest Baptist church in Nebraska, is located the largest-attended Baptist church of the state" (*BD*, June 20, 1967).

In 1868 there were nineteen Northern Baptist churches reporting 607 members; in 1894, 264 churches. By 1941 Nebraska churches affiliated with the Northern Baptist Convention had reached their peak membership, 24,413.

In May 1967, an article in the *Baptist Digest* commemorated Nebraska's Centennial celebration. Nebraska, an Otoe Indian word meaning "flat water," which was their name for the Platte River, became a territory of the United States by way of the Kansas-Nebraska Bill in 1854. The Nebraska Territory reached from north of Kansas all the way to the Canadian border and stretched between the Missouri River and the Continental Divide. When Nebraska became a state in 1867, the size was cut down a bit, to about 77,237 square miles. It is 462 miles at its longest point, and 207 miles at its widest point.

Nebraska is a land of variations: "fertile plains, watered valleys, plus 18,000 square miles of the Sandhills . . . sand and gravel reach to a depth of 800 feet, and 1,000 square miles of 'bad lands.' On the west are the foot hills of the Rocky Mountains" (*BD*, May 27, 1967). With its eastern urban area and its western area more akin to Colorado and Wyoming, it comes well by its title "Where the West Begins." There are hundreds of lakes in the Sandhills, attracting migratory birds and creating a fisherman's paradise. Although not native to the state, Nebraska is famed for pheasant hunting. Nebraska was home to great Indian tribes: Pawnee, Omaha, Ponca, Otoe, Iowa, and Missouri. Part of the great Sioux family, the Ogallala and Brule tribes, also called Nebraska home.

When the territory was opened, people flocked to Nebraska from Iowa, Illinois, Indiana, Ohio, and Pennsylvania. But it was the Kincaid Homestead Act of 1904 which assured the settlement of the Sandhills and the Panhandle regions. Anyone who would stay for five years and make improvements could claim 160 acres. Many came both from the states and from Northern Europe: Germany, Russia, Austria, and Switzerland. Later, immigrants came from Mexico, Italy, and Greece. The rich and poor alike staked their claims.

The Platte River valley marked the Oregon Trail, the ruts of which are still visible. The first continental railroad and, much later, Interstate 80 also followed this route. The railroad made an impact experienced by few other new states. At one time, cattlemen from Texas drove their herds to the railroad terminal at Ogallala. Cities grew along the route.

Air bases played a part in the growth of Nebraska. Eventually, the Strategic Air Command (SAC) was established at Offutt Air Base, adjacent to Bellevue, suburban Omaha. SAC headquarters that directed strategic bombing missions was located here, several stories underground. The growth of Omaha, plus the military demands of SAC, made the city of Bellevue one of the fastest growing cities in Nebraska.

An agricultural state, Nebraska was a corn grower, but after the introduction of winter wheat, it rivaled Kansas in wheat production. Sugar beets were grown with irrigation. The Sandhills region, covered with sage-grass, was suited to cattle production; Omaha became the nation's largest meat-packing center.

Another "claim to fame" for Nebraska is credit for naming a national holiday: April 22, Arbor Day. The idea to replace trees in Nebraska which had been destroyed by prairie fires was conceived by J. Sterling Morton, a newspaper publisher and politician. His home in Nebraska City is now a state historical park.

Nebraska is the only state with a unicameral legislature (one house); it is forbidden by its constitution to incur more than one hundred thousand dollars in debt; it had no sales tax before 1967. Two-thirds of the population live in cities and towns of more than 2,500; half live within fifty miles of Iowa, mostly near Omaha and Lincoln. More than half the counties have fewer than five thousand inhabitants with fewer than two people per square mile.

SOUTHERN BAPTIST BEGINNINGS IN NEBRASKA

Southern Baptists came late into Nebraska. J. R. Huddlestun shared a quote from Calvin Miller which put it quite well, "'When the early missionary traveled by canoe and on foot, the Jesuit missionary came. When trails had been made and men traveled by horseback, the Methodist preacher came. When the railroads were pushed west, the Lutheran pastor came. When they built the Jet Airports at Omaha and Lincoln, Southern Baptists came'" (Miller, quoted by Lockwood, 1965).

In December 1953, W. A. Burkey and an area missionary from Kansas traveled 1,340 miles at a cost of $126.50 on a tour of Iowa, Nebraska, and South Dakota. In Iowa they visited Ottumwa, Oskaloosa, Des Moines, Council Bluffs, and Sioux City; in Nebraska, the towns of Omaha, Blair, Lincoln, and Norfork; and in South Dakota, Springfield, Yankton, Sioux Falls, and "other major towns where Baptists have their strongest work."

At that time (1953) there were 175 American Baptist churches (before 1950 called "Northern") in Iowa and ninety-two in Nebraska. Burkey could not find information about North Dakota, but suggested that since Arizona already had work in that state, we should not attempt mission work there.

Burkey believed that "serious consideration should be given . . . to the opening of Nebraska as a definite missionary project. This should be done in conference with the Home Mission Board and upon approval of our Board to authorize our men to work in the state or to have a man placed in the state to carry on the program" (*Annual*, 1954).

The Executive Board of the Kansas Convention officially sanctioned beginning work in Nebraska in May 1955, following a recommendation from the Missions Committee (*Annual*). Kansas personnel were authorized to "answer calls for help and to assist" in any case in which the church was or could be affiliated with the Kansas Convention or one of the churches in this Convention (*Annual*).

At that May 1955 meeting, Burkey reported on his recent trip to Lincoln, Nebraska, where there were one hundred thousand people and only five Baptist churches. He saw a need for at least thirty additional points to be opened quickly.

In July 1955 Jack Stanton led the first Southern Baptist-sponsored revival in Nebraska at the First Southern Baptist Mission of Lincoln. It was not without problems; there was no building available until a couple of days before the meetings began, so publicity was cut short. They started out in the YMCA, but had to move during the week to the Welfare Society Building, and then on the closing Sunday back to the YMCA (*BD*, August 22, 1955). Even so, it was a great success, involving three summer student workers, and climaxed with the first baptismal service.

The First Southern Baptist Church of Lincoln (later called Southview) was constituted in September 1955 with thirty-four charter members, and petitioned Wheatland Baptist Association (Kansas) for affiliation (*ESB*, Vol. I).

The church really had "begun" four years earlier when the Wilmont Baptist Church of Oklahoma City had constituted the Carter Park Baptist Mission of Oklahoma City into a church. During the four years, the Carter Park Church had increased in membership, in stewardship, and in concern.

In early 1955 a member of that church, C. V. Jones, arrived in Lincoln, sent not by the church but by virtue of the fact that he was a staff sergeant stationed at Lincoln Air Force Base. He found no Baptist church and, like Paul at Ephesus, while he "made tents," he felt called to preach the word. He began to look for interested Baptists. He wrote his home church and with their permission opened a bank account in Lincoln under the name South Hills Southern Baptist Mission, in which he placed his tithe and offerings. Two bank employees saw this account, called Jones, and thus two more names were added to the list of Baptists.

On Easter Sunday the Joneses (Jones had been ordained by the Carter Park Baptist Church) opened their home on South 20th Street in Lincoln to eighteen people, constituting the South Hills Southern Baptist Mission. The work grew; space at the YMCA was rented and by January 1, 1956, the group, by that time First Southern Baptist Church, Lincoln, had a full-time pastor, Tom Hodgin, who accepted the challenge of "no salary and no house." Less than two years later, this group was able to buy a house and five acres on South 14th Street.

The young church was given forty copies of the *Broadman Hymnal* by the Home Mission board (Huddlestun, 1966), which marked a long and close association between the board and Nebraska churches, which were classified as "pioneer missions." Huddlestun wrote an illuminating note, "The business meetings show an intensive interest in details during this [early] period." The church had no baptistry, and was evidently using the one at Temple Baptist Church. In one business meeting action was taken to pay that church for use of the baptistry and use of the church for Lord's Supper services.

EASTERN NEBRASKA BAPTIST ASSOCIATION

In 1955 the First Southern Baptist Church (Southview) of Lincoln had affiliated with the Wheatland Association in Kansas. The next year, fourteen churches from this association formed a new association, Smoky Hill. This was due entirely to the large geographical area included in the association. The other churches which made up Wheatland Association joined Central Association. First Southern Baptist, Lincoln, Nebraska, was one of the churches dismissed from Wheatland Association in order to be a part of Smoky Hill. In the next two years, two other Nebraska churches affiliated with Smoky Hill Association: First Southern Baptist Church of Omaha and First Baptist Church of Bellevue.

Again, because of distance, in 1958 it was agreed that a Nebraska Zone could be formed within the Smoky Hill Association, with a view to organizing a new association as soon as possible (Huddlestun, 1966). Smoky Hill Association was "happy about its new baby and voted to give the Nebraska Zone $250 plus their gifts since April 1" (*BD*, July 19, 1958).

A formal petition went to the Smoky Hill Association in September 1958 for the formation of the Eastern Nebraska Baptist Association (ENBA). The request was granted. On December, 1, 1958, after the observance of their second annual Training Union "M" Night, six congregations met to officially organize the new association: First Southern (Southview), Lincoln; First Southern (Hillcrest), Omaha; First Bellevue; Immanuel Chapel, Lincoln; Plattsmouth Chapel; and Immanuel Chapel, Grand Island. Tom Hodgin, pastor of First Southern (Southview) Lincoln, was elected moderator; Tommy Grozier, pastor of First, Bellevue, was elected vice-moderator (Huddlestun, 1966).

In 1959 John Havlik, secretary of evangelism for the Kansas Convention of Southern Baptists, wrote a glowing piece about the first meeting of the ENBA. He labeled Tom Hodgin "Mr. Baptist of Nebraska," and praised the doctrinal sermon by Tommy Grozier, and the annual sermon "Shall These Bones Live?" by Jack Adkisson. He concluded, "I believe with Jack Adkisson, that 'these bones will live.' September 21, 1959, will go down as a historic date in the history of Southern Baptists in Nebraska" (*BD*, October 10, 1959).

At the second annual meeting of the association, the following churches presented petitions for affiliation: Bethel, Lincoln; Calvary, Beatrice; Immanuel, Grand Island; Plattsmouth; and Northside, Omaha. Tommy Grozier was elected moderator. At the third annual meeting a tenth church was recognized—La Vista Mission had become Southwest Baptist Church and called Jim Martin as pastor.

EASTERN NEBRASKA CHURCHES

Two issues of the *Baptist Digest* (July 18, August 15, 1959) featured "The Nebraska Story" with pictures and text by the editor, Joe Novak. In 1967 three issues of the *Baptist Digest* were devoted particularly to Nebraska (May 27, June 3, June 10): one to the Nebraska Centennial, one to the churches in Eastern Nebraska, and the last to churches in Western Nebraska. In addition, material in this section is taken from histories written by J. R. Huddlestun and Kit Morgan.

In the July 18 issue of the *Baptist Digest* (1959), the editor labeled First Southern (later called Southview), Lincoln, the "great-grandmother church" of the Nebraska work. The beginnings and development of the work in Eastern Nebraska, the editor wrote, read much like the book of Acts, where the people went everywhere preaching the Word.

The Lincoln church began a series of home fellowships in Omaha, the largest city in Nebraska, after the pastor found Wayne Amstutz. Amstutz worked for the Armour Company and had been transferred to Omaha from Oklahoma. The Amstutz family knew another family, the E.V. Smiths, who agreed to have a meeting in their home. At that first meeting there were nine people from Omaha, including one baby girl, Deborah, plus twenty-one from the Lincoln church. On the next Tuesday night they met at the YMCA and continued to do so each week until Sunday services began. Hodgin preached in Omaha at 8:30 on Sunday morning, and drove the sixty miles back to Lincoln for the service there; and laymen took care of other services in Omaha. After the church in Omaha organized in 1957 (it is now called Hillcrest Baptist Church), and called Jack Adkisson as pastor (who accepted it as a Macedonian Call), that church sponsored the work at Bellevue and Council Bluffs, Iowa (Huddlestun, 1966).

Adkisson, after a few years as pastor of Hillcrest, moved to Texas, earned a doctorate in education at North Texas State University, and was head of the Department of Education there, at the same time pastoring churches in Texas. After retirement he and his wife Robbie became part of the Mission Service Corps.

After brief service by another pastor, John Tucker, J. R. Huddlestun was called as pastor of Hillcrest, where he served for six years. He was from Georgia, and was at East Heights Baptist in Lawrence before he went to Omaha. After a short pastorate in Conley, Georgia, he went to Waleska, Georgia, where he pastored a church and taught history and philosophy at Reinhardt College.

To begin the Bellevue Church, First Omaha (Hillcrest) "lettered out half of its members." Then there were two churches reaching twice as many people. The church began with sixty-two charter members; six were civilian families, the rest were stationed at Offutt Air Force Base. Tommy Grozier was the first pastor. By 1967 there were 674 resident members with a Sunday School enrollment of 1,014. The church first met in the American Legion building; a small rented house nearby was used for the nursery. The next purchase was five construction sheds which were placed on rented property. Then a site was purchased with a Salvation Army building on it (*BD*, June 10, 1967).

Wendell Belew (Taped Report) held about five revivals in this church. "It was probably the most successful of the early pioneer churches. I remember at times it would receive over 200 members a year, and also lose that many! But it did grow and it has had as many as 800 enrolled in Sunday School." Certainly, a part of this was because of the in-and-out nature of the Air Force personnel. Belew also pointed out a unique quality of this pioneer church in that it had a "worldwide outreach. As members of the church were transferred to other SAC bases around the world, the church tried to keep in touch with them. It conditioned them to be missionaries wherever they ended up. In later years in my work with the Home Mission Board, I encountered members of the Bellevue Church who were stationed at Peace Air Force Base or other bases in the east and some of them were so dedicated to the Lord's work they went out as missionaries."

Bellevue church was in a strategic location, very near the enormous Offutt Air Force Base, home of Strategic Air Command, and also near the Capehart Housing area built by the government. There was so much growth at

Bellevue that the "daughter" was surpassing the "mother," First Southern Church of Omaha, in attendance and membership.

In 1959 Bellevue, with Tommy Grozier as pastor, had a mission in Plattsmouth. This church met in the Lion's Club Community Building and was organized with sixty-nine members. By 1967 the church buildings were valued at eighty-four thousand dollars and membership was 331. Calvin Miller was the first pastor (*BD*, June 10, 1967).

In 1957 First Southern began another work in Lincoln, which became Immanuel Baptist Church in 1959. An unusual plan was adopted for the beginning of this mission: only tithers were to leave First Southern to form the new mission. It took a little time, but "finally" the church agreed to this proposal (Huddlestun, 1966). After calling a pastor, Gerald Swaggerty, First Southern Lincoln reached out to Grand Island, ninety-one miles to the west. That mission, by 1959, had called a pastor, Gerald Rowe, and was sponsoring a mission in Kearney.

By 1967 (*BD*, March 18, 1967), when Bellevue celebrated its eighth anniversary, membership had grown from fifty-eight members to eleven hundred It was second in Cooperative Program gifts in the Kansas Convention and first in number of baptisms. This church suffered many of the same problems others churches experienced in unstable population areas. In 1966 they granted letters to 302 members who moved away due to reassignment of Air Force personnel. They kept at work and the following year reported eighty-seven baptisms and 230 additions by letter. Mrs. Ann Grozier, the pastor's wife, with a degree in religious education from Southwestern Seminary, was given high tribute for guiding the church in its religious education emphasis, which was credited for the phenomenal growth of the church. The church had begun three missions: Plattsmouth Baptist, with 331 members by 1967; Chandler Road Baptist, with 244 members by 1967; and West Side Baptist.

Immanuel, Lincoln was one of the "30,000 Movement" churches, a program to establish thirty thousand new Southern Baptist churches and missions between 1956 and 1964. This program was adopted in June 1956 during the annual SBC meeting as part of the Baptist Jubilee Advance (*BD*, May, 1962).

Grand Island has a fascinating beginning story. A layman, Mac McCarty, and his wife contacted Tom Hodgin (pastor of First Southern, Lincoln) through the Grand Island city hostess. Hodgin went the next day to visit with them, but it took eight months of praying and visiting before there were any visible results. The McCarty family wanted a Baptist church and just would not give up. He was the district superintendent for F. W. Woolworth stores in Nebraska and the surrounding area. The family put their tithe into a special account awaiting the formation of a Southern Baptist church. After the mission was formed in Grand Island, McCarty became Sunday School superintendent, his wife was Training Union director, and the three children were involved in the music program; it became a family affair.

Irvin Burlison, who had known Jack Adkisson in seminary, went to Grand Island as a pastoral missionary in 1960. Adkisson was pastor of the church in Omaha, and, along with others, "laid a hand on Burlison's shoulder." Burlison was a pastor in West Texarkana Baptist Church, in Texas, and had no desire to move, particularly to Kansas or Nebraska. After letters from Adkisson and McCarty, his wife encouraged him to go and have a look. At the same time, Westmoreland was asking him to consider being the associational missionary in Tri-County Association in Kansas. At that time, the mission at Grand Island was meeting in an old Christian Science church building, owned by a Catholic man who had moved it to the Forest Street site. The Christian Science people were building a new building on the old site. Burlison decided he did not want to move to Kansas, but was deeply impressed by the Grand Island situation, where there were many places nearby with no Baptist church at all.

At the end of three weeks, he had made no decision about the call to Nebraska. He confessed he did not know what to do. His wife, Dovie, said, "I'll tell you what I think about it. You won't be gone from here any time until they'll have a pastor to serve in your place. But in Nebraska, things are different. They are having a hard time getting someone to help them." And so the decision was made; the Burlisons went to Grand Island and stayed for twenty-one years.

In a 1965 issue of the *Baptist Digest* (July 24, 1965), N. J. Westmoreland wrote an account of what he called the "miracle of the month" regarding this church. Even though the church had a tract of land and an offer of building help from a team that had built churches in Washington and Colorado, the church was too small to qualify for loans for materials and too poorly housed to grow. Finally, help came from the Grand Avenue Baptist Church in Dallas, South Main Baptist Church in Pasadena, both in Texas, and from Immanuel Baptist Church in Wichita. These churches underwrote a loan of twenty-six thousand dollars from the Home Mission Board.

A hardware and lumber dealer of Clute, Texas, volunteered his experience as a contractor and buyer of building materials along with about two months of his time. A group of nine men and six women from First Baptist Church in Lake Jackson came on July 5, 1965. In six days they had erected the structure and almost completed the roof. As they left, a group arrived from Greenwood Church in Shreveport, Louisiana, along with friends of theirs from Marshall and Fort Worth, and Little Rock, Arkansas, who did the major portion of inside finishing. While part of the group worked on the building, others took a census and conducted a Vacation Bible School.

This group of Baptists, hard at work, far from home, caught the attention of the people. The Grand Island newspaper gave the story coverage; a stranger from Grand Island donated a day's work. A Lutheran pastor sent the story to his denominational paper.

The "Greenwood Church Plan" was of great benefit to the building crews, who returned to their churches with a testimony that made the missionary enterprise real. This experience would give them a handle on other mission opportunities. Westmoreland continued, "The benefit to the church in the mission area is likewise immeasurable. With a new building, they find themselves in a new world, on a new plane and facing a new horizon. The community is made dramatically aware of something dynamic in the new church."

A postscript to this account appeared in a 1966 issue of the *Baptist Digest* (July 23). The dedication service of their new building on July 10 was marked by the return of the original building crew from Greenwood Baptist Church in Shreveport, Louisiana, on its way to help start another building in Webster, South Dakota.

On another occasion the Grand Island Church received a gift of six hundred dollars from Bartlett Baptist Church in Texas. This money came from an endowment left with the stipulation that half the interest each year be used in Texas work and the other half on mission fields. We are indeed all bound together in marvelous ways by the love of and direction from God.

York Baptist Church was constituted in September 1964 with forty-two charter members after four years of nurturing by Immanuel at Grand Island. For a year a search went on for a Baptist family; not one was found. Finally, the Glen Kirklands moved to York from Oklahoma and began fellowship meetings in their home. By 1962 there was a full program of worship, Sunday School, Training Union, mid-week services, and visitation. The Grand Island pastor served the mission as well as Immanuel until 1963. Park Lyle was the first pastor called after the organization of the church in 1964.

Another story concerns the work at Kearney, a growing city with a college, agriculture, and industry. When Mrs. J. O. Kelly, former member of Emmanuel Baptist Church in Waco, Texas, found no Southern Baptist work in Kearney, she wrote her pastor and asked for the prayers of the church that something might open up. Her pastor put a note in the church bulletin concerning the Kelly family's request. Rang Morgan, pastor in Wichita, saw the bulletin and mailed it to Tom Hodgin, pastor in Lincoln, who passed it along to Gerald Rowe, mission pastor at Grand Island. Rowe immediately telephoned the Kelly family and called on them the following day. A couple of other families were located and a home fellowship, Calvary Baptist Mission, was developed. Rowe drove the thirty miles every Sunday morning and Tuesday evening to preach there, in addition to the work at Grand Island. There were also "institutional missions" in Grand Island: two in nursing homes and one in a home for sailors and soldiers. Rowe was also doing "preliminary work" in Hastings.

The second mission, which was called Ridgecrest, of the Omaha Church (Hillcrest) was at Council Bluffs, Iowa, and resulted from a request from the Missouri Baptist Convention to take on this task. Adkisson had an early service at the mission, then raced back across the river in time for the service in Omaha.

A number of other churches were reported in the June 10, 1967, issue of *Baptist Digest*. Bethel, Lincoln, was organized in 1960, and the next year was among the top ten of the KCSB in stewardship, ranking seventh in per-capita giving. The pastor, Robert Sieg, had to move out of his home in order to have enough room for Sunday School. In 1966 there were 163 members, and the church was sponsoring the Baker Avenue Baptist Mission, located adjacent to the Lincoln Air Force Base.

By this time, the Air Force base was closed and many of the houses were vacant, but the church remained hopeful. The church planned to be ready for the people who would at some time move into those vacant houses. The mission was meeting in a World War II chapel which was either given to, or sold to, the city of Lincoln for a token price. Bethel hoped that it could be bought for the surplus property price, but the city fathers changed their minds, and would only rent the building.

Chandler Road, Omaha (later called Chandler Acres), organized in 1965, recorded one baptism for every 2.2 members the next year. At the beginning the church used two "shell houses," residences built without any partitions, for later conversion into homes to suit the buyers. Gayle Wallace was the first pastor.

Harrison Street, Omaha held, a "name change" record among Nebraska churches. Since its organization in 1965, it had ministered under three different names. To begin with, it was called the LaVista Baptist Mission, sponsored by First Southern of Omaha. The mission was organized as Southwest Baptist Church, and called Jim Martin as the first pastor. By 1967 it had moved a long way from the tent meeting place in which the first Vacation Bible School was held, and as Harrison Street Baptist Church, had a membership of 125 and property valued at eighty-seven thousand dollars.

Northside Baptist began in 1959 as a mission of First Southern of Omaha, and was constituted as Northside Baptist Church in February 1960. R. Rex "Peck" Lindsay was called as pastor. In 1965, under his leadership, the membership divided. One group remained in the north central area of Omaha as Northside Baptist, and the other group went to the northwest section of the city and formed a mission. By staggering the times of services, Lindsay was pastor of both Northside Church and the mission. In March 1966, one year later, the mission became Terrace Drive Baptist Church. Lindsay continued as pastor of both churches until each had a first building unit. On top of all that, Northside sponsored another mission in Fremont, Nebraska, with its first meeting in a Jewish Synagogue. "Getting on with missions expansion" was a good way of succinctly stating the purpose of these churches.

Westside Baptist Mission, Omaha, began as a home fellowship in January 1966, sponsored by First Baptist of Bellevue. Calvin Miller, who had served the church at Plattsmouth from its organization in 1960, became the pastor in late summer of 1966. A year later they had two morning services and attendance of almost 150. They met at that time in two buildings which were auxiliary classrooms for one of the public schools.

Wendell Belew recalled that there was reticence on the part of some of the references Miller had listed about the wisdom of appointing Miller as a pastoral missionary in the Plattsmouth Church. They thought he was too closely identified in his theology with Midwestern Baptist Theological Seminary, Missouri Baptists, and Ralph Elliott, who had published *The Message of Genesis* (1961). Many pastors in Kansas and Nebraska knew Ralph Elliott as a very warm, spiritual person who contributed a great deal to the life of our churches. There were others who thought his commentary on the first eleven chapters of Genesis was nothing short of heresy. There was no little concern in Kansas and Nebraska over this matter.

Belew continued, "Westside Church in Omaha became one of the largest of pioneer churches that we have had within Southern Baptist life. It grew phenomenally—from ten members to more than 3,000— because of the abilities, I think, of Calvin [Miller]. He was a disciplined person who spent a lot of time in visitation and cultivative witnessing, and of course he is a unique preacher, as well as an administrator who was able to get the church going."

He also remembered Miller's first steps into the world of art and painting. He was visiting with him at one time and found Calvin painting with three stubby old brushes "that must have been pretty intolerable." Belew made him a gift of better painting materials and watched with joy the wonderful creativity blossom and grow. Miller's paintings have been recognized widely; he has been presented in one-man shows. In addition, "he has written more than two dozen books, some with more than a million copies sold; has had dozens of articles published in religious press and scholarly journals; and is one of Southern Baptists' most widely used speakers and lecturers" (*BD*, January 26, 1993). Miller continued as pastor of Westside Church for more than twenty-five years, and then went to Southwestern Seminary as professor of communications and ministries studies and writer in residence.

WESTERN NEBRASKA BAPTIST ASSOCIATION

In 1966 eight churches in the Western Nebraska Association, affiliated with the Baptist General Convention of Colorado, elected to move into the KCSB. These churches were affiliated with the Platte Valley Association and the Baptist General Convention of Colorado; the missionary was Robert Jolly. He was an employee of the General Baptist Convention of Colorado, and was responsible not only for the WNBA, but also for Eastern Colorado and Western Wyoming, a huge territory.

This long-standing division of Nebraska churches between two state affiliations had been at the suggestion of the Home Mission Board. Simply getting to them was no small feat. It is farther from Wichita, Kansas, state convention headquarters location at the time, to Scottsbluff, Nebraska, than from Wichita to Glorieta, New Mexico. The churches in western Nebraska were much nearer to the Colorado General Baptist Convention headquarters in Denver than to Wichita, Kansas. So, in the beginning, this division of Nebraska between Kansas and Colorado seemed a good idea.

In 1960 five churches in western Nebraska, members of the Platte Valley Association, organized the Western Nebraska Association of Southern Baptist Churches, which was renamed Western Nebraska Baptist Association (WNBA). The churches involved: Oak Street Baptist, Kimball (called First Southern Baptist until 1958, and by 1985 chose to relate to Wyoming rather than to WNBA); Calvary Baptist, Sidney; Egan Park Baptist, McCook; Bethel Baptist, Scottsbluff; and First Baptist Mission, Valentine.

CHURCHES OF WESTERN NEBRASKA

The June 3, 1967, issue of *Baptist Digest* was devoted to introducing the churches in Western Nebraska, which by that time had affiliated with the KCSB. The editor began the article by asserting, "It is predicted that this will be one of our most popular issues. Limitations of space make the story assume a brevity that is not good, but the spirit of the wonderful people of those churches seem to burst forth anyway." There were eight churches at the time. Almost all of them had experienced yo-yo growth because of the oil-field workers who poured into Nebraska and then left when their work played out.

"Distance Is a Way of Life" seems to be the hallmark of the people who work to strengthen the churches in western Nebraska. The editor gave two examples. The Elmer Copelands, members of Trinity Baptist Church, Benkelman, lived in St. Francis, Kansas, thirty-five miles away. He was Sunday School superintendent; they attended the midweek services and Sunday night services also. To chalk up 210 miles a week "church travel" was not unusual. Mr. Copeland had retired after forty years of work with Railway Express, then moved to St. Francis to be near a daughter. "Retirement" was put on hold when they found the church at Benkelman needed their support.

The Alton Jeffuses lived in Stratton, Nebraska; their church was Egan Park Baptist in McCook, which was thirty-five miles away. Mrs. Jeffus was the organist; he led music and took on other responsibilities as he was needed.

Calvary Baptist Church in Fort Morgan, Colorado, sponsored a mission at Kimball, Nebraska, which began with twelve people in October 1955, under the leadership of David B. Morris. First meetings were held in a schoolhouse three miles south of town. By February 1956, it became First Southern Baptist Church, which was changed to Oak Street Baptist in 1958. They built a sixty-thousand-dollar building with donated labor. High attendance records were set in 1956 with 118 and in 1959 with 218. Then the oil-field work took a tumble, and missile sites were closed. This took a toll on membership and attendance. This church has been aligned with the Cheyenne Wyoming Association since the late 1960s or early 1970s (Morgan, 1985).

Calvary Church in Sidney, a mission of Oak Street Baptist of Kimball, was organized in 1957 with forty charter members; Martin Kennedy was the first pastor. In this church also, oil-field workers and Air Force personnel provided leadership, money, and enthusiasm. When the workers were transferred, the church found itself loaded down with a $250 per month debt payment (a debt paid off in 1984). There was a dwindling membership and lessening community interest. After eight months without a pastor, Elmer Mundy accepted their call. He was paid twenty-five dollars per week plus housing, and found a part-time sales job. Later, he got a part-time job in a funeral home. He and others of the church pledged a double tithe in order to make the payments owed by the church. The church grew and started a mission in Chappell, a county-seat town twenty-five miles away which had no Baptist church of any kind. Andy Hornbaker was an early pastor of the Sidney church. Rushville (1959-1960) was a mission of this church, as were Egan Park (1958) and Valentine (1959). According to the Twenty Fifth Anniversary Report (Morgan, 1985), the mission was constituted as a church in 1975, but there was no further word. It was not included in the 1977 annual minutes of WNBA.

Bethel Baptist Church in Scottsbluff appeared almost spontaneously in 1957 out of home fellowships sponsored by Trinity Baptist Church of Scottsbluff. The group bought an abandoned hatchery, and in 1958 a church was constituted with thirteen charter members. In 1959 a pastor was called, and the hatchery was remodeled. This church, too, was dealt a blow by removal of oil-field workers and servicemen. Trinity, Scottsbluff, was a mission of First Southern Baptist Church, Greeley, Colorado, begun in June 1955 and organized into a church in November of that year. In April 1960 the Trinity building was destroyed by fire. The church was disbanded and the members "moved in" with their child, Bethel Baptist (WNBA Twenty-Fifth Anniversary Report, 1985). Alliance Baptist Chapel was a mission of this church, begun in 1978 and constituted as a church in 1983. Two other missions of Trinity were disbanded: Crawford (1962-1965) and Chadron Southern Baptist (1974-1984).

Calvary Baptist Church of Sidney sponsored a mission in McCook. One Sunday in November 1958, a small group met in the National Guard Armory; in August 1959, nineteen charter members constituted Egan Park Baptist Church. The Edmondsons, Colorado laypeople, helped the church acquire land at West Fourth and Q Streets. There was even an old building on the land which was remodeled for a temporary meeting place. By 1961 there was a parsonage and a church building with a seating capacity of two hundred, valued at eighty thousand dollars. In 1985 there were twenty-five active resident members (WNBA Twenty-Fifth Anniversary Report, 1985).

Trinity Baptist Church at Benkelman was begun as a mission of Egan Park in 1961 in the home of A. F. Kostanowski, and was officially constituted that same year with nineteen charter members (WNBA Twenty-Fifth Anniversary Report, 1985). Two families in the early church lived outside Nebraska: the Copelands from St. Francis and the Kent Ewing family from Bird City. In 1985 membership of this important church was thirty-one.

A second mission of Egan Park was Calvary Baptist in North Platte, begun in January 1960, and organized as a church in July 1961. Again, growth was reported as slow, "gains being regularly offset by the transfer of members." This transfer caused two "mission starts" by the Egan Park church, one in January 1960, the second in February 1961, before the organization of a church. The church has had a number of outreach programs through the years: a weekly thirty-minute radio program on a local Christian station; monthly Sunday afternoon vespers service at a retirement hotel; use of building for a day-care center for the handicapped; and use of building by the local school board until building was completed (Morgan, 1985).

The First Baptist Church, Valentine, was organized in 1960 under the leadership of a school teacher, Homer Rich, an ordained minister who was teaching science at the Valentine Rural High School. He contacted Robert Jolly, associational missionary, who encouraged Calvary at Sidney to sponsor a mission. Early, they attempted to buy an old Methodist church; an offer of eighteen thousand dollars, which was the price approved by the Home Mission Board, was rejected by the Methodists.

The organizational meeting was held in the Assembly of God church. "In October 1961, lots were purchased on Green Street for a future building site [in Valentine]. By January of 1962, the large home which had served as parsonage and worship center became too crowded, and they rented the old Methodist church for services. Later, they met in the basement meeting room of the First National Bank. By May, 1969 they were able to purchase a double-wide modular and locate it on their lot at 2nd and Green Streets. When they outgrew this space, the church purchased the old Catholic church at Norden, Nebraska, and after building a basement, they moved the church 28 miles, to Norden, and placed it over the basement. The trip took two days! A foyer was built between the church and the modular unit which was then converted to classrooms and nursery, pastor's office and rest rooms; the men of the church doing most of the work" (Morgan, 1985).

The Valentine Church fell upon hard times, pastors came and went, and for some years, there was no pastor. Valentine had a problem. It was hard to know the time of day in Valentine, and when meetings began. The dividing line between Central and Mountain Time Zones went down the main street of the town, so it was an hour earlier or later, depending on where a building was located. When Daylight Savings Time came around, it was even more difficult.

That could have been one of the reasons the group who had been part of the Valentine Baptist Church scattered, and the work was almost lost. Then in 1967 Dewey Hickey came from Arkansas.

Hickey has an interesting story. He grew up in Little Rock, felt called to preach, and for a good many years was a bivocational pastor. He worked on a dairy farm for about twelve years, then went into the insurance business. About 1967 he began to feel a tug toward full-time preaching, but he resisted since he had a good job, nice home, and a satisfying part-time ministry. Three churches in Arkansas approached him about coming in view of a call. He told them he was perfectly happy where he was.

Harriett helped him give it more thought when she said, "I married a minister, not an insurance salesman." The next day he approached the director of missions in his area to say that he would go anywhere and consider any church. He would go to the very next church which invited him. A man from Nebraska overheard this remark, and very soon he was invited to come to First Baptist Church in Valentine. There were fourteen people to hear him preach; a call was extended. When he went to the church on May 1, 1967, he discovered that there was only one family in the church. The other people who were there were visitors the family had rounded up to hear him preach.

At first any help from the Home Mission Board was denied him because he had not finished college. But Quentin Lockwood got together with Wendell Belew, and $150 a month finally came through. The first days were hard. Savings were used up. Hickey dug worms from the front yard of the house where he lived and sold them to the bait shop for two cents apiece. He fished and hunted to keep meat on the table. The very first day of the deer season he got his deer. He gave his Arkansas house away to a neighbor because he could not afford the payments and the taxes. With his last seventy dollars he paid the transfer of ownership costs. He stayed in Valentine five years.

Tom Wenig, who served as director of associational missions (DOAM) in the WNBA for twenty years, worked with Dewey on a plan to reach the ranchers in the Sandhills. One night Hickey's car broke down on the way home, he hitched a ride, and found a call waiting for him. The Home Mission Board was ready to allocate some Annie Armstrong money to the ranch ministry. What did he need, he was asked. He suggested that money be allocated to fix his car. Instead, the Home Mission Board bought a K-5 Blazer. Hickey began to go regularly to find and minister to ranchers. One of the new approaches he introduced, and which was continued, was Bible studies at ranches in surrounding areas. The only model he knew was that of the association and local church, so some of the ranchers to whom he ministered drove as much as sixty-five miles a couple of times a month into the church at Valentine.

Then the Home Mission Board appointed him a Church Extension Missionary in 1971, and raised his salary a bit. The ranch ministry grew and so did the church at Valentine. Hickey decided he really needed to get his education, so he went to a church in Fairfax, Oklahoma. He had to drive forty-five miles, but he was in school. However, the work grew so much in the church, with the addition of a coffee house ministry (which was fairly new then), there was little time for school. In fifteen months attendance at worship went from 155 to 275. There were fifty-five baptisms during that period, but not much progress on college hours. There was no time.

In 1973 Peck Lindsay invited Hickey to be Church Extension Missionary in Nebraska; the Home Mission Board was more helpful and told him "this time you can go to school with our blessing." So he went to South Sioux City and started a church there, now First Southern Baptist Church. During his tenure, two Mexican men appeared who wanted to begin a Spanish-speaking church and wanted to use space in the church.

Both of the Hickeys enrolled in school and completed their undergraduate degrees during the time they were in Sioux City. Then Hickey began to commute to Midwestern Seminary, 286 miles down the interstate. He was in Sioux City for five years, and again the church showed growth; there were a number of church starts.

In 1978 Lindsay, by then executive director of the KNCSB, invited Hickey to consider coming to Topeka to be director of Church Extension and Brotherhood. He was given the privilege of finishing his seminary work. He came and was in this position for eight and a half years, until 1986, when he was invited to be executive director of the Dakota Baptist Fellowship. Peck gave Hickey responsibility for the "200 by 2,000," which has been so successful. Hickey has also been successful in growth starts in the Dakota Fellowship. The ninety-four churches and missions of 1987 increased by twenty-five percent by 1994.

The Parkview Baptist Church in Lexington was organized in 1960 by a group who left the First Baptist Church (Independent) and originally affiliated with the General Association of Regular Baptists. They invited speakers from both the Regular and Conservative Baptist churches. One Sunday, somebody got the wires crossed up, and both of them were there. A charter member bought two lots at 11th and Park Streets; later, the Trinity Lutheran Church building was bought for eleven hundred dollars and moved to the lots. In 1966 there was a ten-month period without a pastor; membership declined. The church, with few members and little money, went to the KCSB for help. When new leadership came along, advances were made. By 1984 they were able to fully support a pastor. In 1985 there were eighty-four active members.

First Baptist Church, Ainsworth, was organized in 1964 as a mission of the First Baptist Church of Valentine. They bought a building site "in a nice residential neighborhood," ground was broken, but a building was not begun. In 1965 when the church was constituted, there was a membership of twenty-eight.

At that time, W. E. Fuller was pastor. He was a meat cutter in Valentine "to support his wife and their seven children." This meant driving forty-five miles to Ainsworth for services and ministry. "When the Valentine church was unable to secure a pastor, he stretched physical, spiritual, and financial resources to aid them, too, from August 1965 to August 1966. His car wore out, and he found it necessary to terminate his ministry at Ainsworth" (Morgan, 1985).

In 1977 Ainsworth was chosen as one of the key cities for the SBC Bold Mission Thrust. A youth choir from South Carolina came to the area, and in a survey found thirty-four prospective families, five of whom were Baptist.

First Baptist of Valentine was willing to begin again and start a Bible Fellowship (Morgan, 1985). "No later mention in WNBA Annual Reports on this work at Ainsworth, Nebraska . . . a small community located forty-five miles southeast of Valentine on Highway 20."

In the beginning one associational missionary served both associations—the whole state of Nebraska: Quentin Lockwood (1960-1967), R. Rex Lindsay (1968-1972), and B. Burt Potter (1972-1973). In 1973 two associational missionaries were placed in this territory. Tom Wenig came to serve the WNBA, and Harold Manahan worked in the ENBA. Manahan holds this position now; Wenig retired in October 1994.

Kit Morgan, associational historian of the WNBA, who wrote "Baptist History in the Making," closed the Twenty-Fifth Anniversary Report with these words: "The 'birthing' of a new work is never an easy task, and we who are a part of Western Nebraska Baptist Association owe a debt of gratitude to the many hardy Christ-led souls who often faced insurmountable trials, received cold receptions, and suffered extreme financial hardship to share their faith and God's love in the community about them.

"There have been many humble beginnings . . . in a chicken house converted to a church . . . a country school, even a 4-H building at a County Fair Grounds, but it mattered not the setting. 'For where two or three are gathered together in my name, there will I be in the midst of them.'"

NEBRASKA BAPTIST FELLOWSHIP

During 1965 and 1966, a stronger relationship developed between Eastern and Western Nebraska Associations. A fellowship meeting was held in October 1965 and another in May 1966. At a meeting of representatives of both associations in June 1966, careful plans had been made for a meeting in October for exchange of calendar events, ideas and programs, and fellowship between the two associations. At least seven Kansas Convention staff were to attend. Missionaries Quentin Lockwood (ENBA) and Robert Jolly (WNBA) worked closely with the pastors of the churches involved. Sam D. Russell, associate executive secretary of the Convention, wrote, "The future for Southern Baptists in Nebraska is greatly related to the degree of enthusiasm and dedication the people offer through their Associations and the Kansas Convention of Southern Baptists. Without question the final victory for Nebraska is a state Convention, but at no time do we want to cast a shadow on the cooperation of the people through our Kansas-Nebraska programs at this time, nor do we want to seem to imply any lessening of responsibility of the paid staff members of our Convention towards the farthest outpost of those whom we serve" (*BD*, July 9, 1966).

At the May meeting the pastors of Western Nebraska agreed to "challenge their churches to take steps to affiliate with the Kansas Convention to provide for better fellowship with the eastern Nebraska churches" (*BD*, July 2, 1966). N. J. Westmoreland described that meeting as one which marked a turning point for all future work in Kansas and Nebraska (*BD*, October 29, 1966). Sam Russell, Viola Webb, F. Paul Allison, and Westmoreland left on Friday afternoon for the meeting at Calvary in North Platte. Harold Inman was already in the area visiting churches. They encountered the predicted snow storm near Russell, Kansas. While it hindered their travel, it did not stop it. The storm was worse near Sidney and "some 3,000 utility poles were blown down between McCook and Benkelman, Nebraska."

Westmoreland must have smiled a bit as he reported that the raw weather had canceled most of the football games, but did not seem to affect attendance at the fellowship meeting of Nebraska churches. George Massengill of Oak Street Church, Kimball, presided; Calvin Miller, pastor of Omaha's Westside Mission, did a feature report on the churches. There were inspirational messages from Wendell Belew of the Home Mission Board, Robert Jolly, associational missionary employed by the General Baptist Convention of Colorado, and Sam Russell, who was associate executive secretary and director of the Department of Missions of the Kansas Convention. The traveling party from Kansas stayed over Sunday and spoke in four churches: Allison at Kimball, Webb at Benkelman, Russell at Sidney, and Westmoreland at North Platte.

The work in western Nebraska was said to be much like the work in western Kansas with widely separated towns and cities, long travel distances, a relatively small number of Southern Baptists, and an acute problem of shifting population.

The Nebraska churches presented letters of petition to the 1966 annual meeting of the Convention, in Coffeyville, Kansas, on November 15-17. The formal transfer took place at the close of the fiscal year, December 31, 1966. Eight churches made this transfer: First Baptist, Ainsworth; Trinity, Benkelman; Oak Street, Kimball; Egan Park, McCook; Calvary, North Platte; Bethel, Scottsbluff; Calvary, Sidney; and First Baptist, Valentine. At that time, there were thirteen churches from Eastern Nebraska already affiliated with the Kansas Convention.

This group of new churches also placed new constraints on the efforts of the Kansas Convention staff. Westmoreland pointed to the good work Colorado had done in a pioneer area, in addition to their responsibility for Colorado, a state as big as Kansas, plus serving in four other states, all equally large. He pointed out that Colorado staff had to travel farther on less allowance than Kansas staff. Thus, he concluded that we certainly could afford to do no less than Colorado had done for these churches, without it being a serious reflection on us. He finished by saying, "It is a great honor and privilege to be enabled to work for the churches of Nebraska. They ask no special favors of our Convention, but they are destined for a different role than the churches of Kansas. When they triple their present size, they will be ready to be constituted into a full-fledged state Convention. This could happen by 1970, and certainly will happen by 1976, the 20th anniversary of the beginnings in Nebraska" (*BD*, July 2, 1966).

SUPERINTENDENTS OF MISSIONS

In 1957 the Home Mission Board sponsored a mission program known as Pastoral Missionary Program. For churches chosen to be a part of this thrust, the board furnished a two-hundred-dollar a month salary supplement, and the state convention added another one hundred dollars, which was continued as long as the church began a mission every six months. First Southern in Lincoln and First Southern in Omaha were part of this program (*Annual*, 1957).

An early plan of the ENBA was the establishment of an associational mission program. It was increasingly evident that there was wisdom in having a person dedicated to the work of the association without pastoral duties, rather than relying solely on the pastoral missionary plan. After conferring with Meeler Markham, secretary of Missions, and John Havlik, secretary of Brotherhood and Evangelism, of the KCSB, a plan was formulated to have a missionary for the association. A target date of January 1962 was set, but there was too much excitement to wait that long. On June 26, 1961, the associational executive board extended a call to Quentin Lockwood, who was given the title "Superintendent of Missions" (Huddlestun, 1966).

Lockwood had a great deal of experience both with mission work and as a pastor. He came from the Hardwick Baptist Church in Georgia. He had served as a navigator in World War II and was injured in a crash in Italy. When he came home, he graduated with honors from Georgetown Baptist College and later graduated from Southern Baptist Theological Seminary in Louisville. He worked in the Kentucky mountains during this time, as a pastor, conducting Vacation Bible Schools and tent revivals. Later, he worked as a missionary for the Kentucky Baptist Convention. After graduation from the seminary, he pastored a mission in Ashland, Kentucky, which became a church during his four-year ministry. His wife, Alene, was a graduate of Georgia State College. There were three children, Chip, Susan, and John.

After several pastorates they went to Georgia, to the Hardwick Baptist Church. The Home Mission Board at that time was urging churches to send their pastors to pioneer areas to hold revivals and to encourage and motivate small churches in these areas (Taped Interview, Alene Lockwood). The Lockwoods went to Topeka to a "small struggling church" for two weeks. They found themselves so moved by the needs they saw that later, when Wendell Belew talked to them about going to Eastern Nebraska, where Lockwood would serve as DOAM, they were ready.

Within two weeks they had bought a house, traded cars, picked up their two teenaged children, whom they had left with Alene's parents, and reclaimed their dog, George. A bit later, the van arrived with the furniture they had left in storage. The associational office was in the basement of their Omaha home.

Lockwood remained in Nebraska as associational superintendent of missions until 1968, the first in Eastern Nebraska, and then in the entire state. At that time he was appointed to the Department of Pioneer Missions of the Home Mission Board as administrator in the Western United States (BD, February 3, 1968). In addition to starting new churches and doing all the other jobs required of a director of missions, an important contribution was the beginning of Omaha Baptist Center, of which Alene was the first director.

On March 3, 1968, Peck Lindsay was named area missionary for all Nebraska, where he served until August 1, 1971, when he became director of Missions-Evangelism-Student Work of the KCSB.

Lindsay is a Kansas-Nebraskan by profession, an Oklahoman by birth and family. His father worked in Oklahoma oil fields, so they moved to a number of places in the state; Lindsay went to OBU for two years. In the summer of 1957, he arrived in Omaha, Nebraska, as a summer missionary appointed by the Home Mission Board to work with Jack Adkisson. Adkisson had sustained severe head injuries in a terrible automobile accident and could not drive. So for five weeks, Lindsay was his hands and feet, visited, and worked in a mission of the church. The last five weeks of his assignment, he worked in Russell, Kansas, where the church was in great stress and near death because of a recent split. Lindsay said, "They figured a summer missionary couldn't hurt them any!"

By the end of the summer, there were about forty people coming to Sunday School. The people were so delighted that they asked Lindsay to come as their pastor and go to school at Fort Hays, which he did. He majored in English, and recalls only one bad choice with his schedule: he signed up for German in a town where the vast majority spoke it as their native tongue.

In 1959 a new church building was dedicated at Russell. Much of the work inside the concrete block building was done by the congregation. Everyone worked, including the young pastor, who was not a skilled construction person. He tells of an experience in which he knocked a hole in the wall as he moved a ladder into position and then spilled a bucket of pale blue paint over the white tile floor already in place in the sanctuary. A deacon working nearby commented, "It's a good thing you can preach good, or we wouldn't have any use for you at all."

Westmoreland, Hilary Brophy, and the area missionary all spoke during the Russell dedication service. This was a new site, as well as a new church building; the old building and old parsonage were sold. The church was begun in 1945 when it met in the City Service Recreation Hall. The first building was at West 5th and Ash Street. Finis O'Neal was the first pastor; another pastor was Earl Fine, a foreign mission volunteer who left for a "position in Nigeria, West Africa." That summer Lindsay and Sue Allen of Hinton, Oklahoma, were married, beginning a life of ministry together.

R. Rex "Peck" Lindsay, executive director-treasurer of the Kansas-Nebraska Convention of Southern Baptists since 1977, served earlier as missionary to both the Eastern and Western Nebraska Baptist Associations (1968-1971) and as missions director for the Kansas Convention of Southern Baptists (1971-1976).

A letter from Westmoreland was an answer to Lindsay's invitation to the dedication service, and his application for home mission service. Westmoreland accepted the invitation and, in response to the application for home mission service, wrote: "I shall dictate a statement concerning your work at Russell which should be a part of that application. I found no mention of the details of that achievement." It is probable that this is high praise indeed from Westmoreland. He was impressed that the church at Russell had grown from fifteen members to one hundred in Sunday School, had relocated, and had built a building using two new Convention programs: the Forward Program of Church Finance and the bond program.

By this time (1959), the mission Lindsay had worked with in Omaha during his summer missionary experience was ready to become a church and asked him to come as their pastor. The Lindsays went to Omaha and in 1960 the church, begun as a mission of First Southern Baptist, Omaha, became Northside Baptist Church with twenty-two charter members. After some years, Northside became Raven Oaks, and then, because of a change in the community, became Prince of Peace Church. While the Lindsays lived in Omaha, Peck completed his degree at Midwestern Seminary. During this time, Sue taught in an inner-city school and completed requirements for teacher certification. She also led the children's departments in the missions and later served the Nebraska Baptist Fellowship as director of religious education.

In 1968 Lindsay became superintendent of missions for the Eastern and Western Nebraska Associations; in 1971 he became director of Missions-Evangelism-Student Work of the KNCSB; and was chosen to be executive director of the KNCSB in 1977. After Lindsay left Nebraska, following a short term of service by Bert Potter, each of the associations in Nebraska employed a director of missions. Harold Manahan came to Nebraska from Southwestern Seminary to be the pastor of Chandler Acres Baptist Church in Omaha. From there he went to Alaska as a mission pastor. When asked how long he was in Alaska, Manahan's answer was "Long enough!" He was there about fifteen months, actually. After Bert Potter left Nebraska, and each of the Nebraska associations was ready to have a director of missions, Harold Manahan was called back to Eastern Nebraska, where he still serves.

In a celebration at Iglesia Bautista Hispana in Scottsbluff, on October 31, 1994, Tom Wenig was honored for twenty years of service as DOAM of the WNBA (*BD*, October 31, 1994). At this same meeting, WNBA was dissolved with the formation of two associations: Platte Valley and Sandhills, plus the Panhandle Fellowship. During his tenure as director of missions, Wenig travelled thirty-eight to forty thousand miles annually; WNBA was a big association, covering about sixty thousand square miles. While he served as director of missions, seven churches swelled to sixteen churches and three missions, pastoral tenure increased, language work began at Scottsbluff, and a new approach to Sandhills ministry was developed.

NEBRASKAN ELECTED KCSB PRESIDENT

In 1966 Tommy Grozier, pastor of First Baptist Church, Bellevue, Nebraska, was elected president of the KCSB at the twenty-first annual meeting at Emmanuel Baptist Church in Coffeyville, Kansas. Grozier was from Texas, educated at Baylor and Southwestern Seminary. He had held pastorates in Texas before coming to Nebraska and had served as vice-president of the Kansas Convention and was trustee of New Orleans Seminary. He went to Bellevue Church in 1958, when there were fifty-seven members. According to the *Baptist Digest* (December 3, 1966), "Today Bellevue Baptist Church is one of the largest churches in our pioneer areas with a membership of 1050." The church had property valued at $379,000. Nebraskans had served on the Executive Board, before this, and had even been elected officers. But Tommy Grozier was the first Nebraskan to be president of the Convention. That year one of the constitutional changes proposed was a name change for the Convention: "That Article I be amended to read, 'this body shall be known as the Kansas-Nebraska Baptist Convention.'"

KANSAS-NEBRASKA? OR KANSAS AND NEBRASKA?

This was not the first time "name change" had come to the floor of the Convention. At the 1958 annual meeting of the KCSB, a motion had been made by Jack Adkisson, pastor of the First Baptist Church of Omaha, to amend the constitution of the Convention as follows: "That Article I, which reads 'this body shall be known as the Kansas Convention of Southern Baptists' be amended to read: 'this body shall be known as the Kansas-Nebraska Convention of Southern Baptists." The sessions were "ahead of schedule" that day, thus President Rang Morgan recognized Adkisson to speak again about his motion.

Tom Hodgin, pastor of First Baptist Church (Southside), Lincoln, Nebraska, moved that the matter of changing the name of the Convention be referred to the Executive Committee for study and that a report be presented to the Convention the following year, a motion which carried. This was not the usual way of handling motions to amend the constitution. Other such proposals were simply automatically tabled, or recorded for consideration the following year, which was the manner set forth by which to amend the constitution. The following year, 1959, the minutes stated simply, "Motion concerning the change of the Convention's name to Kansas-Nebraska Convention of Southern Baptists: it is recommended [presumably by the Executive Committee] that no change in the Convention's name be made." The motion was approved. There was no explanation as to the reasons for the original motion nor for its rejection by the Convention.

Actually "more ink" was given to the discussion of a state song than to the name change. In 1958 Joe Novak, editor of *Baptist Digest*, made a motion that the Executive Committee of the Convention investigate the matter and make a recommendation to the Convention the following year of adopting "Kansas Land We Love" with its "several stanzas" as our Convention theme song. The motion carried. In 1959 it was recommended by the Executive Committee that the song not be adopted, this "despite its musical excellence," because of promotional problems created for our churches which are located in Oklahoma. There was surely some opposition from Nebraska as well. The song was printed, including the music, in the 1959 *Annual*.

Nothing more was said or done "officially" about the name change until, in 1966, Kenneth Combs, pastor of Emmanuel Baptist Church in Overland Park, Kansas, submitted an amendment to the Convention constitution: "That Article I be amended to read, 'this body shall be known as the Kansas-Nebraska Baptist Convention.'" He then spoke to the proposal. A parenthetical statement followed: "In accordance with requirements for amending the constitution as found in Article IX, the proposed amendment was made a matter of record." This was the year (1966) that Tommy Grozier was elected president of the Convention.

Before that meeting, Paul Davis, president of the Convention, wrote Lindsay asking him to consider such a change in the Convention constitution. It was his personal opinion that the best interests of both Kansas and Nebraska would be served if the two states became one Convention like Oregon-Washington. He felt this would forge a strong bond of unity between the two states in the "great task of reaching the people of Kansas and Nebraska for the Lord."

He pointed out that Article I would have to be changed to "This body shall be known as the Kansas-Nebraska Convention of Southern Baptists." The motion was defeated the following year.

Not everyone in Nebraska was in favor of such a move. The ENBA formulated a resolution which was presented to the messengers at the associational meeting. The "Whereases" included: the present arrangement had provided a long and fruitful relationship; Nebraskans had enjoyed a fair representation on the boards of the Kansas Convention; the staff had been unselfish in their services to Nebraska churches; the Pioneer Mission status would be changed; the Home Mission Board would no longer participate in the Annual Nebraska Fellowship meetings; and a name change would lessen the financial support from the Home Mission Board and other sources. "Be it therefore resolved: On this day, October 10, 1967, [messengers to the Association meeting] prayerfully suggest to the messengers attending the annual State Convention of the Kansas Convention of Southern Baptists, meeting in Kansas City, Kansas, that the proposed constitution amendment changing the name of the Kansas Convention of Southern Baptists be rejected."

It did not happen in 1967, 1968, or 1969. In 1970 a committee was appointed to review the entire constitution. This revised constitution was presented to the Convention in 1971 to be voted on in the 1972 session. One change proposed was in Article I: "This body shall be known as the Kansas-Nebraska Baptist Convention."

When the Convention met in 1972, one of the first motions made after the revised constitution was presented was that it be voted on in its entirety, rather than by sections. This was not unanimous, but the motion carried. Jim Martin, a Nebraskan, moved adoption of the revised constitution. Messengers spoke for and against it, for various reasons. A ballot was called for; adoption required a two-thirds affirmative vote. When the votes were counted, there were 120 yeas and 283 nays. The proposed constitution was not approved.

The name change, of course, was not the only issue with which messengers might have taken issue. Omitted from this revised proposal was any mention of "alien immersion," "open communion," and reference to affiliation with the National Council of Churches. Later in the meeting, Cecil Taylor moved an amendment to present at the 1973 annual meeting "that the present constitution be amended by striking the article including the terms 'alien immersion' and 'open communion.'" Still later, Bill Payne moved that the following amendment be presented to the 1973 Convention: "amend Article II, Section 5a to read 'any church which directly or indirectly affiliates with the National Council of Churches, World Council of Churches, or any other federating or other interdenominational agency *that is in conflict with the Baptist Faith and Message* must repudiate such affiliation before it can be recognized by this Convention.'" It was the underlined phrase that was to be the addition to the current section.

After two attempts to get a new constitution committee appointed to study and bring recommendations concerning these issues, both of which failed, R. C. Rayner recommended the following to be presented to the 1973 Convention: "that the constitution be amended to show the name of the Convention to be 'The Kansas-Nebraska Convention of Southern Baptists.'" Someone questioned the cost of a name change. The answer was that it could be done at an "approximate cost of $50.00." The messengers went home; they had defeated the proposed revision of the constitution about which many had questions. They also went home with three amendments to be considered the following year.

One of the resolutions presented to the 1972 Convention by the Resolutions Committee, and approved by the messengers, attests to the heat and vigor of the discussions during the meeting:

"WHEREAS there has been in this Convention a considerable difference of opinion regarding certain items discussed and,

"WHEREAS the Convention has been marked by a frank exchange of views during discussion of these items of business,

"BE IT RESOLVED that the messengers to this Convention join together in expressing their mutual respect and love to one another as brothers and sisters in Christ; and,

"BE IT FURTHER RESOLVED that we recognize the openness of this Convention to varying views as contributing to the strengthening of fellowship between the brethren and churches of our Convention."

At the 1973 meeting of the KCSB, messengers approved the Raynor motion, and the name of the Convention became The Kansas-Nebraska Convention of Southern Baptists. Regarding the other two motions, the first one, made by Cecil Taylor, concerning the deletion of Article II, was tabled because of difficulty in understanding exactly what was meant by the maker of the motion. The second, made by Bill Payne, which would have softened the prohibition of affiliation with other bodies, was soundly defeated.

This formal name change came the same year that Pat McDaniel and Edgar Dwire brought the wondrous news that the bonds could be paid off by the end of the year. It was truly a time for new beginnings for both Kansas and Nebraska.

To become or not become part of the KCSB was a hard question for Nebraskans, and perhaps for Kansans as well. Nebraskans were less traditional than Kansas Baptists. There was not as much concern over "alien baptism," "close communion," and "affiliation with the National Council of Churches" as there was through the years in Kansas among many pastors. Motions to take these phrases from the constitution were defeated many times. According to Lindsay, these were not issues among Nebraskans. "It was never in our constitution in Nebraska. The churches never saw it as a major issue. It was hardly ever discussed in Nebraska except to say, 'that's a Kansas problem; we don't want it here.'"

Nebraskans did not consider themselves "southern" and did not want to be so labeled. In most churches, "Southern" was not included in their names. They were Baptists, quite loyal to the Baptist Faith and Message, but southern they were not. Eastern Nebraska was far more urban and cosmopolitan than most of Kansas; western Nebraska was tied to the "cowboy" west.

During the time that the name change was being considered, the Kansas Convention was in trouble with a capital T. Nebraska was not interested in being too visibly identified with the Convention. Lindsay, who was by this time superintendent of missions in Eastern and Western Nebraska Associations, said, "We tried to act like we didn't know about Kansas and tried not to ever mention it up there. We did not have many churches that were in the bond program and the ones that we had were all current in their payments. We just acted like we never knew about it and hoped it never got in our papers . . . and it didn't much."

This is not to intimate that Nebraskans were not under the load with Kansans in this heartbreaking time. They were. Many Nebraska pastors were members of the Executive Board and had to deal with this problem head-on.

Two other reasons for this cautious approach concerned Nebraska's relationship to the Home Mission Board, and the aspirations of many of the people in the state for a full-fledged Nebraska Convention.

Nebraska was classified as a pioneer mission state, and worked directly with the Home Mission Board through its Pioneer Missions Department. This was in keeping with the board's policy of undergirding church extension. Nebraska was a prime target for this. Lindsay leaned back in his chair and smiled as he remembered those "free-flowing days."

"We didn't have to wait for the Kansas Executive Board to do anything. We could go right to the Home Mission Board. Wendell Belew directed that department; he was very close to Quentin Lockwood and others of us. So we'd go right to Wendell, tell him what we needed, and get action on it within 30 days—sometimes within a week. To become part of the Kansas Convention would have meant giving up that pioneer relationship with the Home Mission Board."

The thing that changed Lindsay's mind and others as well was the reorganization of the Home Mission Board. There was no more direct pioneer mission work; all resources from the board came through state conventions. Lindsay commented, "That's when I felt God was leading me to move to the Convention Office. If decisions regarding work in Nebraska were going to be made outside the state, I wanted to be in the chair where the decisions were made. Mr. McDaniel was kind enough to offer me that opportunity." Thus, R. Rex Lindsay was the first person added to the Kansas-Nebraska Convention staff after the CLA debacle, and the first staff member from Nebraska. He became director of Missions-Evangelism-Student Work in 1971.

From the very first, when Nebraska churches affiliated with the Kansas Convention, both Kansas and Nebraska thought that in ten years or so Nebraska would be strong enough and big enough to be a separate convention. Leaders in those early days saw this as the "ultimate goal," the "real victory." But the number of churches and the population made this direction not feasible. Nebraska leadership could not see their way clear to invest the kind of money it would take to set up the administrative structure necessary for a state convention.

So, in light of the way in which population in Nebraska grew and the changing policies of the Home Mission Board and other national agencies of the SBC, a dual Convention seemed the way to go. Even when this decision was made, there were pastors and other leaders who thought it would be better to align with Iowa, forming an Iowa-Nebraska Convention. They saw Nebraskans more closely related to Iowa culturally, geographically, and theologically, than to Kansas.

By the time the change in name came through, in 1973, the Home Mission Board policy had been revised; there was no more direct pioneer mission work. Particular guidelines for an independent state convention suggested by the board seemed unattainable in the near future: seventy churches with ten thousand members or fifty churches with 12,500 members; churches giving (average) at least ten percent of total budgets through Cooperative Program; and a fund established by the churches with which to begin convention operations. Nebraska had already fulfilled other regulations regarding cooperative relations. In addition, the CLA crisis was over and we could get on with mission work; and there was already talk of moving Convention headquarters to Topeka, which was a much better site considering the size of a two-state convention and location of the churches in both Kansas and Nebraska. And so it was accomplished—and we have all been strengthened and encouraged by this action.

Pat McDaniel engaged an agency in Wichita to design a new logo for the KNSCB. The twin flames rising up from the monogram laced within a half circle remind us that we are two parts of a whole. It also reminds us that we are enabled to do the work of the Lord in Kansas and Nebraska as we are empowered by the Holy Spirit. May we, too, be aware of what seems to be "tongues of fire" that come to rest on each of us.

In 1971 Lindsay wrote a series of four editorials in the *Baptist Digest* (March 6, 13, 20, 27) in which he set forth the needs of Nebraska churches and Nebraska people. These same things might very well be true for Kansas as well as Nebraska.

His first concern was with winning Nebraskans, not just displaced Southern Baptists. During the fifteen years Southern Baptists had been in Nebraska at that time, all the "easy places" had been reached. When we went into Nebraska, we found "little pockets of people who once were Southern Baptists, or who had married Southern Baptists, and with these we started a work. Like attracts like, and these seemed to attract more on a cultural than on a Christian basis. Often they were more proud of being Southern Baptist than of being Christian. They were more tied to a form of worship and a kind of program than they were to a personal Savior."

Lindsay's question was, "Could we bring a relevant Word from God to men whose culture is vastly different from that which spawned us? Can we win the people of the north whose religious and family heritage is different from ours, but who (like many on Southern Baptist church rolls) have never had a personal experience with Christ? Can we bring these to faith in Christ and membership in a Baptist church?"

He made suggestions for bringing this to pass. First, the pastor of the church must be there at the call of God. Pastors are the keys to indigenous growth, not because of what they are as pastors, but because of who they are as people. Pastors need to stay put longer in order to develop relationships and build trust. We must realize that we need to tailor programs to the needs of people, rather than squeeze people into program molds.

In the last two editorials, he presented and discussed the objectives of the Nebraska Fellowship: (1) To lead churches to so minister to the needs of the people of Nebraska that they may see by our deeds and know by our words that God cares for them and wants to redeem them unto Himself through His

Son, Jesus; and, to provide opportunities for fellowship among the pastors and churches of Nebraska; (2) To bring our churches to an awareness of the mission needs of Nebraska, and to lead them to share their methods, money, and members in an effort to meet these needs; and to function with a minimum of staff, so that the money shared in the churches may be kept in direct mission ministries; (3) To lead our churches into a concept of ministry which reveals itself through a concern for the totality of man (for his economic, emotional, physical, and spiritual needs); (4) To provide learning opportunities whereby the pastors and churches may become better equipped to do the work of ministry; and (5) To lead our churches in understanding the role and needs of their pastors, and to assist them in finding means whereby they can provide adequate salary, allowance, and housing. These are worthy goals for all of us who name the name of Jesus Christ and are part of His churches.

Kansas and Nebraska, a great team, each shares with the other, and both profit from the association. In many ways we are alike, in other ways quite different; and that is the genius of our Convention. We balance and strengthen each other. Perhaps that song suggested in 1958, "Kansas Land We Love," is not such a bad idea if we could change the title.

5

KN&SB

Campus Ministry

JON AND PRISCILLA SAPP, ALONG WITH THEIR DAUGHTER, Jennifer who was not a year old, agreed to spend a year in Zambia to follow up "Missions 80," a student ministry project. Preparation for this commitment made 1979 a busy year for them. Simply gathering and packing things they would need during that time was an awesome task. Brenda Hall (*BD*, March 24, 1980) wrote, "The cash register spewed forth its tape, a white paper coil that snaked its way down the counter-top. The electronic chatter of the machine echoed the prices read off by the cashier. Shoppers stared, amazed at the two carts piled high with groceries. Down the counter moved boxes of muffin mix, pounds of macaroni, tins of cocoa, boxes of powdered laundry bleach, and cases of whipped topping mix. Behind them came packets of powdered soft drink mix, aluminum foil, toothpicks, dishwashing detergent, spices, condiments and seasonings." Along with all this there were a year's supplies of disposable diapers, baby powder (which was five dollars a can in Zambia), baby oil, soap, and other infant-care items to be purchased, packed, and sent ahead to Zambia.

The Sapps, natives of Kansas, graduated from Kansas State University (KSU) in 1975, and worked as volunteers in the Baptist Student Union (BSU) program there until they moved to Topeka in 1977, where they became BSU directors on the Washburn University (WU) campus. There had been no BSU work on this campus since 1968, when Yvonne Keefer, who began the work on that campus in 1966, had resigned and moved to Lawrence. In addition to the work at WU, Jon earned a degree at Midwestern Seminary, and Priscilla worked as a secretary with the Kansas-Nebraska Convention until Jennifer was born.

The Africa project was not the first student missions outreach. A BSU summer missionary had been sent out in 1959, Dorothy Dehn from the

136

University of Kansas (KU), to serve in Hawaii. For her support, four BSU organizations—KU, KSU, Wichita State University (WSU), and Pittsburg—had raised $507.

Ray Gilliland reported (*BD*, April 18, 1959) that the "giving of the offering will be a featured part of the state Baptist Student Retreat, Camp Fellowship, Wichita, April 24-25, as will be the selection and commissioning of the student chosen."

The next report of student missionaries was in 1963 when three students from KSU, Kansas State Teachers College at Emporia, and Kansas State College at Pittsburg (*BD*, March 16, 1963) were sent to Hawaii and North and South Dakota. Students from six campuses had pledged $1,200 to help support these students. No BSU student missionaries were reported in the annual reports for 1964 or 1965. In 1966 (*Annual*, 1966) students from four campuses, Emporia, WSU, KU, and Pittsburg, went to Maryland, Hawaii, Arizona, and Pennsylvania. In 1967 eight students were supported, one in Guyana, the others in California, Texas, Montana, Washington, and Kentucky, where three students were assigned to a "Kentucky Work Camp." The students were from WSU, Fort Hays, KU, KSU, Pittsburg, WU, and the University of Nebraska, Lincoln (UNL). This was the first year a Nebraska student was appointed. In 1968 a team of four went to Shiprock, New Mexico, and six others went to Michigan, West Virginia, Wisconsin, Hawaii, Trinidad, and Guyana. The following year at least one student went to Switzerland. No indication of the campuses where the students came from was given in the report. After that time, students went on mission regularly, but, up to Missions 80, for the most part they went only to various parts of the United States.

MISSIONS 80

In the late 1970s, the campus ministers, from KU (Yvonne Keefer), KSU (Bob Anderson), and UNL (Brett Yohn) felt the need to help students catch a vision of world missions. These three, and Peck Lindsay, who was willing to try new directions, explored alternatives. Students of that time, part of the ME generation, seemed to be interested only in what affected *their* friends, *their* campuses, *themselves*. As the talk and planning continued, "Missions 80" took form: a short-term overseas missions program in which fifteen students and three BSU directors would take part.

In 1980 the Olympics were to be held in Moscow, and the first thought was to go to the Games to minister to the folk who came. This seemed too short a time for the expenditure of so much money, so the scheme was abandoned. The group contacted the Foreign Mission Board, and asked if they, three teams of five students, each headed by a BSU director, could be of service somewhere in the world for ten weeks in the summer of 1980.

Letters were sent from the Foreign Mission Board to mission fields over the world. Exciting invitations came from Zambia and Malawi, next-door neighbor African countries. By the end of October 1979, the teams had been selected and training begun. It was at this time that Zambia, which wanted two teams, asked that someone plan to stay for a year to do follow-up work.

With that prospect, Jon and Priscilla Sapp joined the group. They had hoped to become Journeymen missionaries with the Foreign Mission Board, but Jennifer's birth in July 1979 made them ineligible for that program (*BD*, March 24, 1980). "Missions 80" and a year in Zambia as Mission Service Corps volunteers gave them opportunity to pursue their missions dream. They volunteered to stay for the follow-up year in Zambia.

The Mission Service Corps had been initiated in 1977 at the suggestion of President Jimmy Carter, who believed the missionary force could be doubled in five years through wise use of volunteers. He spoke to the Southern Baptist Convention that year via video, and later sent a telegram encouraging the Convention agencies when a Mission Service Corps steering committee was authorized.

No money was allocated for this sort of mission venture, so the Sapps had to raise about fifteen thousand dollars for air fare, housing, food, and other expenses which would be incurred between June 1, 1980, and May 31, 1981. This was not an easy task, but they did it.

In 1980 Bob Anderson and Brett Yohn, ten students, and the Sapps went to Zambia; Yvonne Keefer and five students went to Malawi. The students were from KU, UNL, KSU, and WU. The teams traveled together to Kenya, spent a few days in Nairobi, and then went on to their places of service. In addition, students from KU, WSU, and UNL were sent that year to Alaska, Colorado, and Kansas; Jim Herron, WSU, was director of this group.

Brett Yohn wrote the following paragraph, which was included in the 1979 annual student work report: "Bold mission applied! For the past two years, the KNCSB staff and student ministers have been strategizing and planning with the Foreign Mission Board. This summer, the fulfillment of those plans will take place. . . . The funding ($50,000) of these projects is coming from the State Missions Offering, students' contributions, and special gifts from churches and individuals. God has burdened those in campus ministry to expose student leaders to world need and mission opportunity, believing God to call many to the harvest fields as a lifetime vocation."

The Zambia team spent time in Malawi in mid-summer; the Malawi team had a week in Zambia at the end of the summer; then they all headed home with a stop-over for a few days of rest and relaxation and debriefing in Amsterdam. They arrived home just in time to begin the fall term.

This project marked a renewed emphasis in summer student missions. Almost every year since, there have been Kansas and Nebraska students not only in the "hard" places in the U.S., but also overseas. All of them have come back to share with others a new vision of God at work in the world. In addition to Zambia and Malawi, students have served in Uganda, Canada, Korea, Philippines, Brazil, Hong Kong, Ecuador, Argentina, Ghana, Malaysia,

Dan Boeth, student missionary, gives his testimony in a Malawian school during Missions 80.

Russia, and Kazakhstan. Students have also served in the Journeymen Program of the Foreign Mission Board.

In 1989 (*BD*, August 28) eight Kansas and Nebraska students spent several weeks in a student-to-student cultural exchange with students in Hong Kong and South Korea. The midwesterners experimented with chopsticks and fried chicken feet. The Asians had an opportunity to practice English and find out about America. They talked about class rings, peanut butter and jelly, and shared family pictures. They also spoke of American, Chinese, and Korean values, and shared Christian values, as well.

These assignments have been good for students, good for the people with whom they served, and good for the ones with whom they have shared on their return. Two other significant things have grown out of this endeavor.

PARTNERSHIPS

Out of the contacts in 1980 grew a partnership between Kansas-Nebraska and Zambia and between Kansas-Nebraska and Malawi. Kansas-Nebraska was the first "new work" area to have a partnership with an overseas mission field. Through the ten years of those partnerships, which came to a close in the early 1990s, teams of Kansas and Nebraska men and women served in these countries for short-term periods. Kansans and Nebraskans have become more aware of and more involved with the missionaries and people of these countries than would otherwise have been possible. They have shared their vision in many ways back home.

Jon Sapp was the Zambia-Malawi coordinator from 1982 to 1983, when he and Priscilla were appointed by the Foreign Mission Board to Zambia. Yvonne Keefer was approved as KNCSB coordinator of the project in 1983.

The first year of active partnership (*Annual*, 1985) with the missions in Malawi and Zambia was 1985. Twenty-one persons representing thirteen churches were members of teams. That year, fifteen pastors and laymen went to Zambia for an evangelism project. They lived in seven villages teaching evangelism classes and holding revivals. Out of their efforts nine churches were started, and 359 persons professing Christ were recorded by name. Special work that year by other teams included a youth retreat for Missionary Kids, special projects with students, and help for the missionaries with computer programming. When the project closed, in 1990, seventy people had worked in Zambia and thirty-seven people had worked in Malawi. As significant as these contributions were, Keefer pointed out that "no less important are those members of churches who contributed the funds necessary to send these volunteer missionaries."

At the close of this partnership, the Foreign Mission Board asked Kansas-Nebraska to look into a partnership agreement with the Hashemite Kingdom of Jordan. Three members of the Convention staff went to Jordan to "discuss strategy with the Jordan Baptist Convention and the Baptist Society (Mission)." As a result, the Kansas-Nebraska Executive Board approved a partnership, which began October 1, 1993, and will continue through December 31, 1996 (*Annual*, 1993).

Already teams have gone to Jordan to take part in projects between the Jordanian Baptist Convention and the Southern Baptist representatives. The first team to Jordan (*BD*, December 20, 1993) was led by Andy St. Andre, KNCSB director of teaching and training. The team included two ministers of music, two pastors (one pair from Kansas, the other from Nebraska), and John Hopkins, KNCSB Christian social ministries consultant. The invitation came from Fawaz Ameish, president of the Jordanian Baptist Convention and pastor of the First Baptist Church in Amman, the capital city of Jordan.

The twelve-day program included a retreat for pastors, as well as key leadership in the churches, eight revivals, conferences with the pastors and missionaries, and daily visits to the school in Ajloun, which is the only institution still under the direction of the Foreign Mission Board. Trumpet-playing, six-foot-three-inch Jeff Brocaille of Westside Church in Omaha was a hit with the children. They loved his music, puppetry, and tales about his family, which includes a son named Jordan.

In addition, Kansas-Nebraska is the first "new-work" state to have a partnership with another "new-work" state. On January 1, 1994, we entered into such an arrangement with Nevada. Associations in Kansas and Nebraska were matched with like associations in Nevada with the goal of each contributing to the other. Directors of associational missions and state staff, plus other volunteers, have already visited in Nevada and worked with the leadership there. Jim Keefer was named coordinator of the Nevada Partnership.

MISSION VOLUNTEERS

Jon and Priscilla Sapp are examples of the other "fall-out" from the hands-on Missions 80 project of Baptist Student Unions. At the end of the year, the Sapps came back to the states and found that they had fallen in love with the people of Zambia and the work they were doing. So they volunteered as career missionaries of the SBC Foreign Mission Board. They were appointed to Zambia in 1983. After serving in the mission, Jon was appointed mission administrator in Zambia, and now he fills the position of assistant area director for Eastern Southern Africa with offices in Nairobi.

Jimmie Cobb, pastor of First Southern Baptist Church in Lawrence, was a member of an early team to Zambia. Later, he and his wife were members of the last team to serve in Malawi. Today, he and Carlene serve in Canada under the Foreign Mission Board. The long journey to the mission field began during this volunteer service in Africa. Yvonne Keefer recalled his saying, "I wake up in the night and hear the voices of the people in the village."

Even for those who did not "go back," there has been a difference. They have carried a mission vision which has changed their lives and actions in churches across Kansas and Nebraska and in other places where they live. The plan of helping students catch a world vision, conceived in the late 1970s, has paid off handsomely.

BAPTIST STUDENT UNION BEGINNINGS

Student work today is a big jump from the early days of beginning. Today there are BSU organizations on twelve campuses in Kansas and Nebraska. There are seven full-time student directors, four volunteer directors, and seven associates on these campuses. BSU began with two young men who had been involved in campus BSUs in Oklahoma. Keith Hamm and Charles Coleman came home from the war and decided to go to college with their GI allotment. They chose Pittsburg State Teacher's College in southeastern Kansas, which was a thriving institution. Hamm had served as a summer missionary with the Home Mission Board and wanted to remain in Kansas. To make ends meet, the two friends bought a house, full of old furniture, at the edge of the campus at 1111 East Cleveland. The house was authorized by the Kansas Convention in 1947 as the Pittsburg Student House and so designated in the State Missions Day of Prayer Program (1947), which N. J. Westmoreland wrote. There was enough room upstairs to house sixteen students, and a large room downstairs could be used for meetings and classes for thirty to forty students.

Keith Hamm (Interview, 1994) poured his life into that first BSU house, which was not in the best condition. He made repairs, cleaned it up, and made it livable. He said, "I worked on that place. I cleaned toilets, lavatories, and I don't know what all. We tore out the old coal furnace and replaced it with a gas furnace." According to Hamm, the Westmorelands for a time lived in the basement of this house. When the Convention met in Pittsburg in 1950, "a whole bunch of preachers stayed there. We rented out rooms; we made our payments, never missed a one; kept a little money ahead."

In the first three semesters of operation, Stanley Gasswint, also an early summer missionary of the Home Mission Board (*Annual,* 1949), and the first BSU director at Pittsburg, reported the dormitory was filled to capacity and the building was used as a meeting place for the new Trinity Baptist Church until a permanent building was secured. In each of the first three years of operation, "five young Baptist preachers" were able to work in churches in the area while they attended college, because they had a place to live in the Center. "These young men have had a part in the growth of all but one church in the Tri-County Association," the report concluded. By 1950, twenty-three students called the center "home."

D. E. "Gene" Strahan, the first state missionary, was particularly interested in student work. He made some input into the work at Pittsburg, at Haskell (Allan Morris came to Haskell at Strahan's invitation), and attempted to make a beginning at KU. He worked out of Pittsburg where he and his wife were among those who lived in the large two-story white house near the Pittsburg campus.

STUDENT CENTERS

In 1950 Westmoreland reported "the largest gift yet made" to the KCSB, which was the property that Hamm and Coleman bought and then gave to the Convention. The equity was about two thousand dollars. The total property was valued at $8,500, including furnishings. A committee was appointed to supervise the operation of the property as the Baptist Student Center. Coleman was on the committee, but resigned later in the year to attend Golden Gate Baptist Theological Seminary; Hamm was appointed in his place.

The Student Center was to be a place for young preachers to live while they went to school, which would provide pastors for needy churches around Pittsburg and make establishment of missions possible in the area. It was also a meeting place for a new church in Pittsburg. This was in addition to providing a "haven for Baptist student activities, a program that has been so profitable in states of the Southern Baptist Convention" (State Missions Day of Prayer, 1947).

Later, the house at 1111 East Cleveland was sold and the money set aside for the purchase of another house. Pittsburg State University was expanding and had completely surrounded the property. Westmoreland reported, "Since the college could eventually initiate condemnation proceedings and take the property at their price, the Board has considered it wise to get the highest possible price for our equity and retain the good will of the college." Hamm commented (Interview) concerning the sale, "The appraiser came, representing the state, and insisted we sell. The right of public domain took over our student center."

From the sale, $3,201 was turned over to the foundation to be invested until a time when a new Baptist Student Center could be secured. Also, a campaign was authorized to raise as much as twenty thousand dollars to build a Baptist Student Center there, with specific instructions that present Convention budget sources were not to be involved. At the same time, a campaign to raise money necessary for the beginning of the Baptist Bible Chair was authorized.

Another building was bought in Pittsburg in 1953 (*Annual*), located just off the northwest corner of the campus, at 1602 South Broadway. The purchase price, $7,500, was financed by the Citizens Bank of Weir.

The down payment for the Student Activities Building at Lawrence came from funds given by individuals whom Ray Gilliland had enlisted: a "Friends of Lawrence" group. The group did all sorts of fun things in order to raise money for the down payment for the house at 1221 Oread, which had been vacated by the Westminster Foundation (Presbyterian) when they moved into a new three-hundred-thousand-dollar property. In July 1960, the Executive Board of the KCSB approved the purchase of the building for $45,500 (*BD*, September 17, 1960). According to the 1960 *Annual*, "this property has figured in doubling the ministry of the BSU at our state university."

A dedication service was held on February 12, 1961; Charles Beck was Student Director (*BD*, February 4, 1961). The financing of the building was through ABC bonds. Space on the upper two floors of the building was rented to "men students" in order to pay the bonds plus utilities. Even so, when Anderine Farmer came as campus minister in 1962, she had an apartment in the building, as well. In 1961 the Convention borrowed two thousand dollars to complete necessary renovations to the building, which was to be paid back from proceeds from the State Mission Offering.

The center in Lawrence was sold in the wake of the CLA crisis. It was a big house with two floors of bedrooms. Three different student directors received living space in the house as part of their salary. The other rooms were rented primarily to international students.

Yvonne Keefer recalled finally being glad the KU Center had been sold. It was located in the "war zone" in 1970 when riots broke out on the campus.

There were snipers in windows of the buildings along the street with intermittent gunfire every night. She said (Interview), "I remember thanking God every night that I did not have 20 International students, for whom I was responsible, living in a building in the middle of that."

The Center at Emporia was purchased in 1964, the homeplace of a Mrs. Cornelius. When she married Oscar Stauffer of Stauffer Publications in Topeka, she was ready to sell the house at evidently quite a fair price. The Barbers from Texas, whose daughter, Maxine, was attending Emporia, made a substantial contribution. Maxine Barber served as president of Kansas Nebraska WMU, 1976-79. It is uncertain whether the money was used for the acquisition of the house or for its refurbishing. Galene Bozarth (now Turner) was the volunteer part-time campus minister. She was recruited by Ray Gilliland, and encouraged and supported by a group of eight faculty at Emporia, members of the Twelfth Avenue Baptist Church, who wanted to see a formal work with Baptist students on the campus. She came to Emporia with the promise of employment as a secretary in the library, a civil service job, which could not be given her because she was not a Kansan. One of the faculty took her credentials to the president of the university who "found" salary money from a fund which he administered. For a year she worked in the counseling department and then moved to another place in student personnel. The college contributed to the cost of making the Cornelius house handicapped accessible. After Bozarth married, she and her husband, Virdin Turner, had an apartment in the house until they left in 1969 (Verbal Communication with Galene Bozarth Turner). Dallas Roark became part-time volunteer. Through much of the time he served as faculty advisor.

The Emporia house was sold in the early 1970s. The house was old, with a wrap-around porch. Necessary repairs cost more than the Convention could afford (Verbal Communication with Mrs. Dallas Roark).

During the 1960s, there were five Baptist Student Centers: Wichita, 1818 North Yale; Pittsburg, 1602 South Broadway; Lawrence, Haskell, 140 Indian Street; the Baptist Activities Building at KU, 1221 Oread Avenue; and Emporia, 1109 State. The Convention had little money in any of these centers. According to the 1978 *Annual*, the state convention disposed of the BSU property on the campus at Pittsburg that year (1979), with the proceeds designated for BSU work in the Tri-County Association; KU's Activities Center and the one at Emporia were sold during the CLA crisis.

No other centers were acquired, although later on the foundation approved loans for homes of campus ministers. Campus ministers were encouraged to locate or remodel their homes so they could be used as meeting places for students. Student centers, as such, needed maintenance, which is expensive. More recent Kansas-Nebraska policy has been to use money for personnel, not for buildings.

What happens now is that Southern Baptist student groups rent space from American Baptist groups or some other student group. This is true to varying degrees at Lawrence and Manhattan. Of course, the lack of a building limits the kinds of programs and services available to students. It usually means not having a consistent and convenient meeting place which can be easily advertised and located. On the other hand, it pushes more activity into small dorm groups where students live and work and have their being.

HASKELL

Southern Baptist presence at Haskell was "student" work from the beginning of the involvement of the Home Mission Board there. The church grew out of the work with students, rather than the other way round.

From 1945, the year the Kansas Baptist Fellowship was begun, to 1955, Eileen and Victor Kaneubbe were the appointed home missionaries at Haskell Institute. Mrs. Kaneubbe is a Kansan, a graduate of Cherokee County High School in Columbus, Kansas. Her father, Roy Walker, was the first superintendent of missions in Tri-County Association. Mr. Kaneubbe's father is a full-blood Choctaw, his mother one-quarter Choctaw; he grew up in Oklahoma. The Kaneubbes have worked with Native Americans in Oklahoma, Mississippi, Arizona, and New Mexico since they left Kansas. Since 1986 they have been specially assigned missionaries located in Phoenix, Arizona. The Kaneubbes were followed at Haskell by Allan Morris, George Hook, Bill Crews, Tom Muskrat, James Goodner, Sam Morris, Fred Hollomon, Glenn Lawson, and Cloyd Harjo.

The building at Haskell was built as a student center, but now serves as the Baptist church. Haskell Institute, a government school for Native Americans, has operated since the turn of the century.

In the *Kansas Southern Baptist Beams* (December 1950), Mrs. Allan Morris (who with her husband were home missionaries) wrote that there were students on the campus from almost every state and from many denominations. There was a joint service on Sunday morning and denominational services on Sunday nights, with Northern and Southern Baptists taking turns. The freshmen, sophomores, and juniors were the responsibility of the Southern Baptists; Northern Baptists ministered to seniors and commercial students. Mrs. Morris lamented that the Northern Baptists were trying to make them quit: "they have a speaker from KU to speak to them for one Sunday evening, the next Sunday a party (or what they call a mixer). The third Sunday, their minister speaks. The last Sunday they go together for a movie."

When the students asked Allan Morris to have services like the Northern Baptists, he "told them he came to Haskell to preach the Word of God, and didn't come to entertain the students." Even so, they had one social each semester.

Mrs. Morris reported a number of rededications during the semester and one conversion, a first at Haskell. One of the girls planned to be a medical missionary to Africa. She concluded the article, "We have about 20 different tribes in our group. Some of the students sing in Indian for us, which we enjoy very much. It's a wonderful privilege to minister to our own nationalities. We're having wonderful services, although it gets discouraging sometimes."

For many years the Home Mission Board did what was called "direct mission work" (BD, January 30, 1960), which meant mission work within local state areas was carried on by personnel employed and supervised by the board, with no relationship to the local mission program. The philosophy changed: the board now operates through the missions department of local state conventions. The only direct work the board had in Kansas was Haskell Institute, a high school for Native American youth. In 1960 Bill Crews was a missionary appointee, and under the new policy of the board became an employee of the KCSB. While Crews was there, a beautiful parsonage and chapel were built with Annie Armstrong Offering dollars.

In 1962 change was begun at the institute to move it from a high school and vocational school to a two-year junior college (BD, October 27, 1962). Greater emphasis was placed on the vocational program, with less on the high school. In 1962 there was no new freshman class; each year another class was dropped. Haskell became an accredited two-year junior college. Emphasis continued on higher education, and by 1993, Haskell was a fully accredited four-year institution with a name change: Haskell Indian Nations University. In 1962 Tom Muskrat was the missionary and reported that Indian students from eighty-five different tribes and thirty-five states, including Aleuts and Eskimos from Alaska, were enrolled (BD, October 27, 1962).

Louise and Kenneth Holden (she a Creek, he a Chickasaw) went from First Southern Baptist in Lawrence to help begin Haskell Baptist Mission in 1965. A number of members from this church taught Sunday School classes and performed other services to get the mission started. The mission then and now is made up of Indian families in and around Lawrence. Many of them work at Haskell in various capacities. James Goodner was the Home Mission Board appointee when the mission was organized.

In 1988 (BD, October 24, 1988) a team of twenty-eight persons, accompanied by Cloyd Harjo, pastor of Haskell Indian Mission and Ken Townsend, director of missions in Kaw Valley Baptist Association, held Vacation Bible Schools and revival services on a Navajo Indian Reservation in New Mexico and Arizona. They worked in churches where there was no electricity or running water. A shower was rigged using a plastic milk jug with five holes punched in the bottom. It was filled with water, and held over one's head. It seemed to get the job done. This is putting faith into action. It was ever thus; those ministered to become ministers to others.

CHAIR OF BIBLE

Very early in the life of the Convention came the idea of a Chair of Bible at Pittsburg State Teacher's College, where Bible courses, carrying college credit, would be taught both for students enrolled in the college and for pastors not enrolled in school. This was the forerunner of Seminary Extension classes.

In the first year of the life of the Convention (*SBB,* January 6, 1946), one of the critical questions Westmoreland had raised concerning the direction to be taken was: How long would we have to wait before a Bible chair was established in some properly located college where student preachers could get their training near their churches?

For N. J. Westmoreland, "student work" was almost synonymous with preparing students for Christian service through formal Bible study. He was determined to set up a program that he called "the beginnings in Christian education" in the big white house across from the campus which would lead to a "Chair of Bible" at Pittsburg, offering credit courses to students and nearby preachers.

Westmoreland's dream stayed alive. In 1951 Foy O. King, pastor of the Southern Baptist church at Tulare, California, was elected professor of the Baptist Chair of Bible, but evidently never served in this capacity, probably because of lack of proper funding. That same year, there was a serious drop in enrollment at the college, which resulted in less renters and a drop in income for the Student Center. Churches were encouraged to sponsor young preachers who would attend college, enroll in the Bible classes, and live in the Student Center.

During 1951, $3,320 of the needed four thousand dollars, at that time the amount judged necessary for beginning a Chair of Bible at Kansas State Teachers College in Pittsburg, had been pledged. Hopes were high for its inauguration in September. Howard Whatley was elected by the Executive Board as professor of Bible, a position he declined. This might have been due to the fact that the program was not begun as hoped in September. It might have been due to the fact that already there was a Southern Baptist Foundation, of which Whatley became executive secretary in 1952.

That year, also, there were pledges of support for the Baptist Chair of Bible from the Baptist Sunday School Board, the Home Mission Board, Spring River Association in Missouri, Tri-County Association, and Neal Huff, a layman. Westmoreland reported that the president of OBU, John W. Raley, had given assurance that the school would work with the Convention toward the installation of a Chair of Bible at Pittsburg, if their aid was needed. They requested that the project be postponed until the spring semester of 1952, if we indeed wanted aid from them.

In 1952 a Board of Managers was appointed, and the Baptist Chair of Bible became a reality when, in August, Z. Liston Brister was elected professor. He was a graduate of OBU and Southwestern Seminary, and had served a number of churches in various capacities during college and seminary days. He was on the faculty of OBU for three years, teaching Bible and English, and was to return after a leave of absence to complete his Th.D. Because of the Korean War, there was a drop in college enrollment at OBU, so the invitation to return to a teaching position there was canceled. He chose to come to Pittsburg rather than accept a position he was offered at Hardin-Simmons. In addition to the Bible teaching, he also served as pastor of the First Baptist Church of Pittsburg and director of the BSU on the campus. The church was responsible for one-fourth of his salary, the Convention for three-fourths.

In an interview (1994), Brister shared the reason he accepted the position with the Kansas Convention, "Over two years earlier while I was teaching Bible in Oklahoma Baptist University, my alma mater, I had hosted Rev. Westmoreland in a Bible class in which he challenged my students to consider the mission opportunities of the new Kansas Convention for their future service careers. My students may have forgotten, but I had not."

Brister remained four years in this position, and then returned to a pastorate in Oklahoma. Later, he was in campus ministry at the University of Tulsa for fourteen years. He stated, "I never got student ministry out of my mind, not even entirely in my work as chaplain in an incarceration institution. And Kansas still has a big place in my heart."

Brister's (KSBB, July 24, 1952) election marked the "realization of an objective that has been deep in the hearts of Kansas Southern Baptists for more than five years." In 1955 two credit courses were scheduled: Old Testament History and Literature as a day class, with three enrolled for credit and two auditors, and Worship and Evangelism as a night class. Two men wanted to take an evening course, but they preferred Old Testament, so the course was changed to meet their needs. During the first three years, 1952 to 1955 forty-six were enrolled for credit and eleven enrolled for no credit. Out of the fifty-seven enrolled, forty completed the courses. In 1956 a course in church history was offered with fourteen enrolled for college credit plus six auditors.

Brister stated that during the first year, most of these Bible course students were not enrolled in college course work at Pittsburg. The students were pastors of smaller churches and persons feeling a call to serve who needed preparation. "The courses, accredited by Oklahoma Baptist University, included basic Bible teaching, preaching classes, and New Testament Greek. I think we tried Hebrew one semester." After a couple of years, OBU decided against the out-of-state extension center. Brister said, "We were not seriously harmed, however, for the Southern Baptist Convention's Seminary Extension Department took over the accreditation."

Keith Hamm (Interview, 1994) was in the office of Dr. Humphries, head of the Bible Department at Baylor University, and overheard a telephone conversation between Humphries and a person at Washington State College. The caller wanted to know if students could have credit at Baylor for Bible courses taught by a qualified teacher at Washington College. Humphries replied, "Yes, we're going to sponsor a Chair of Bible out there at no cost to the students." Hamm asked if the same thing could be done for Kansas and got an affirmative answer. There would be a registration fee of only four or five dollars per course. Westmoreland was a graduate of Hardin-Simmons, and, according to Hamm, would not accept this offer from Baylor. "A golden opportunity was missed," Hamm concluded.

In the *Baptist Digest* (April 7, 1954), Brister noted that a sure sign of an institution's "coming of age," no matter how small it still may be, was that a "product" of the institution returned to be a "principal speaker" at an event. Baptist student work at Pittsburg reached that point when Andy Hornbaker, a student at Southwestern Seminary, returned to lead the Trinity Church in revival services and speak in noonday meetings sponsored by the BSU. Hornbaker served as pastor of Trinity from 1962 to 1966, and in 1965 preached the Convention Sermon at the KCSB annual meeting.

When Hornbaker came to Pittsburg to go to school, he was a Methodist. During college years he felt called of God to enter the ministry and planned to attend a Methodist seminary. His sweetheart, Jo Ann Rhodes, a Baptist, had agreed to become a Methodist. In the summer after graduation, Andy was at home in a farming community in western Kansas, working in the local church, and getting ready for his fall study. In Brister's words (Taped Report, 1994), "He called me and said the Lord had led him during prayer to become a Baptist preacher and asked me to baptize him. He came for a weekend, the church accepted him for baptism, and we baptized him. Before the summer was over, he came back to Pittsburg, where we married him and Jo Ann on Friday, ordained Andy to the ministry on Sunday, and they went off to the Seminary." The Hornbakers have worked in a number of places, and for many years have been at the Holiday Baptist Church in Salt Lake City.

Every campus minister can multiply this story out of their ministry on college campuses. The goal of campus ministry is not to build a church, but to undergird students in such a way that they make contributions through the years to many churches, in Kansas and Nebraska and throughout the world.

EDUCATION COMMISSION

By 1955 (*BD*, June 16, 1955), many questioned the advisability of a Baptist Chair of Bible. The editor wrote, "In our moments of boasting, it is a delight to point to the Baptist Chair of Bible in the southeastern corner of our state. But when the financial status of the Chair of Bible meets our glance, some approve . . . some flinch . . . and some yell in the negative." There were those who said we would lose our testimony on the campus if we withdrew. Others said this was an unwise use of funds. There were less than five students enrolled in courses in 1954-55, and 7.8 percent of Convention funds were allotted to this. It was suggested in this editorial that when the Executive Board of the Convention began to give consideration to the 1956 budget, the Chair of Bible either be funded in a "respectable manner," or be discontinued.

A letter from George McClelland, who was pastor of Immanuel Baptist in Wichita, to the editor (*BD*, June 30, 1955) was a follow-up to this editorial:

". . . It might be well to emphasize the Baptist Student Union and Center at the college and at this time withdraw the Baptist Chair of Bible. This should not be done to in any way discredit the well-qualified and consecrated professor now employed. But if it is done, it should be done with the idea that the little money we have might be better spent to reach more people in another way."

Funding was continued for the 1956 year, with the provision that it would be reviewed at the end of the school year. It was funded in the 1957 budget to allow time for a survey of educational needs in Kansas.

So dear to the hearts of Convention leadership was the idea of formal accredited Bible course work at colleges and universities in Kansas that an Education Commission was established in 1954, with Howard Whatley as chair. The first action was to invite a blue-ribbon committee, with representatives from the Education Commission, SBC, officials of nearby universities, and student directors to make a survey of Kansas needs and possibilities in this arena. Little was done until 1957 when funds were made available for the study.

The results of the survey highlighted two thrusts: to encourage churches in college towns to call strong pastors and give the work of local BSUs high priority; and to urge Kansas Baptists to commit themselves to long-term planning and the establishment of a trust fund for the creation of a Baptist college, always keeping in mind their growth and resources.

In 1962 the conditions for starting a two-year Baptist college were outlined in the report to the Convention from the commission, including a minimum enrollment of three hundred students; sixty thousand Southern Baptist constituents in the immediate area to be served by the college; a minimum capital fund available of $1,200,000; and $125,000 available from Convention receipts annually for operating expenses. The commission's response to these conditions was classic: "The attainment of these conditions by our Convention is not yet in sight. The Commission, therefore, concludes that it would be premature to set a tentative target date for the establishment of a Baptist College" (*Annual*, 1962).

The commission was also working on the accreditation problem, both for courses taught on college campuses and for Seminary Extension courses. The plan was that OBU would grant credit which could be transferred to Wichita University. To do this, OBU required the teachers of the courses to meet the same qualifications as regular faculty members at the university and to have regular supervision, neither of which was possible at that point. The Student Work Department was encouraged to begin Seminary Extension classes where possible.

In 1964 a plan was worked out with OBU to place Stanley Nelson, pastor of University Baptist Church, in charge of Seminary Extension; he would teach one seminary class each semester. Credit would be transferred from OBU to WSU. That year, the Department of Philosophy at WSU changed its mind about the authenticity of this plan, but reversed the decision the following year. Also, by 1965, there was clear possibility of offering classes for credit at both Emporia and Pittsburg.

In 1967 the Education Commission submitted a proposed training plan to Midwestern Seminary for the preparation of student workers, with an internship at KU dealing with both national and international students, church, and community. A committee was appointed to study the plan, but there was no affirmation of the project in 1968, which was the last year the commission functioned.

In the meantime, the first Southern Baptist Seminary Extension Center to be established in Kansas prepared for classes in the fall of 1955 (*BD*, June 23, 1955) sponsored by the Sedgwick County Association. Anne (Mrs. Ray) Gilliland was named secretary. Three classes were planned: The Life of Christ and two courses in religious education. Classes were to be held at First Southern Baptist Church. In the spring term of 1956 (*BD*, January 19, 1956), three courses were offered in Bible, Religious Education, and Evangelism. Classes were held at the Immanuel Baptist Church. Teachers were George McClelland, Gordon Harms, and Rang W. Morgan. Diploma credit was offered from the five Southern Baptist seminaries for courses completed. Again in the fall three courses were offered taught by Gordon Dorian, Hillary Brophy, and Johnny Burnett.

The Education Commission had been at work since 1955, and had explored a number of avenues for Baptist education in Kansas. Seminary Extension classes, begun during this period, have continued through the years.

EARLY BSU WORK AT PITTSBURGH

When Z. Liston Brister came to Kansas, he was given the assignment of BSU work at Pittsburg, as well as teaching the Bible courses, and being pastor of First Southern Baptist Church in Pittsburg. A report of the first BSU Council in Kansas appeared in *KSBB* (October-November 1948). Keith Hamm was elected president. Brister continued, "The Baptist Student Union is made up of all of the Baptist students on a college campus where the BSU Council is elected for organized operation. The Council is the elected agency for the promotion of a spiritual program designed to tie the College student to the local church during his student days.

"The BSU Council is made up of some of the finest College students that our Lord has. They have been sponsoring noon-day prayer meetings in the Student Center for several months. Some are members of the Trinity Baptist Church, Pittsburg, and four of them are young preachers who serve in the nearby churches."

The following year (*KSBB*, November 1949), Westmoreland reported that the new college year at Pittsburg was begun with a reception for students and faculty at the Baptist Student Center. "The program was under the direction of Student Secretary Stanley Gasswint, and in cooperation with Rev. W. T. Coston, pastor of the Trinity Baptist Church." A special feature was fried chicken provided by Rev. and Mrs. Keith Hamm of the First Baptist Church in Arcadia. At that time, the Trinity Baptist Church allocated five dollars per month from their budget to the Student Center. Westmoreland hailed this as "truly a step forward in the realm of Christian Education and will make possible significant missionary contributions by the Pittsburg College ministerial students."

In this same issue, there was a request for names and addresses of students from Kansas Southern Baptist churches who were attending Kansas colleges. Devotional materials were available that would "contribute to their spiritual enrichment during college days."

STUDENT WORK DEPARTMENT

In 1949, just three years after its formal organization, the Convention hired the first secretary of religious education, W. Ed Russell. His major responsibilities were likely Sunday School and Training Union. There is no mention of his involvement in student work. He was in Kansas for about a year and then moved to a pastorate in Oklahoma.

On August 2, 1951, Ray Gilliland was elected secretary of the Department of Religious Education, taking responsibility for Sunday School, Training Union, and Student work, but not for the work at Pittsburg, which was considered a program unto itself. It was not until 1954, at the request of Brister, that this work came under the jurisdiction of the secretary of the Department of Religious Education. In 1957 the chair of Bible and extension classes also came into this department.

In recalling his first days in Kansas, Gilliland described himself as "green . . . completely . . . no knowledge of anything!" At Southwestern Seminary he had been a theological student and had had a few courses in education. He was young, a hard worker, and a quick learner. He came to Kansas to manage the brand new book store in Wichita and to direct Camp Fellowship near Wichita.

Gilliland, a native Kansan, characterized himself as a product of state missions. He had attended a Sunday afternoon service sponsored by the Emmanuel Baptist Church of Coffeyville, held at Witmer School. It was through relationships and friendships in that church that he became a Christian and later, at a youth camp sponsored by this church, experienced God's nudge to vocational Christian service.

Out of the efforts of Emmanuel Baptist Church came the Pleasant Valley Church located in the community where Gilliland grew up. In this church many of the members of his family accepted Christ and served.

Harold Inman assumed student work along with all other Baptist Sunday School Board assignments when the CLA crisis occurred and Gilliland's position was eliminated in 1969. R. Rex Lindsay joined the staff in 1971 as director of Missions-Evangelism-Student Work. He was the first person added to the staff after the bond disaster. He continued to have responsibility for student work, even after he became executive director of the Convention, until Roy Moody joined the staff in 1986 and a pilot project was begun with the Evangelism Section of the Home Mission Board.

Under the leadership of these Convention employees, and the men and women who have served as campus ministers, with and without pay, part-time and full-time, a number of things have come to pass in student work: organizational growth, enlarged campus programs, emphasis on personnel rather than buildings, freedom to develop varied programs according to campus needs, and emphasis on mission involvement.

PHILOSOPHY

In student work, the emphasis from the beginning has been on campus ministers and associates. Kansas-Nebraska has not put much money into student centers; there are none today in the two-state area. Our money has gone into personnel who can reach out to students, who really make up a special mission field, an "unreached people group" for the most part.

In the 1966 report to the annual meeting of the Convention, student work was recognized as a specialized ministry. As early as 1924, Frank Leavell, first Convention-wide student secretary, stated, "A very significant phase of this question which is difficult for the rank and file to grasp is the fact that our work is a missionary task; and not an educational task. It is a missionary task in which the Sunday School Board and the distinctly mission boards are directly, fundamentally, and vitally interested. It is a missionary task with an educational constituency."

Leavell pointed out the task of Baptist students on the campus: to make the gospel known. At the same time, the indispensable role of the churches is to nurture maturing spiritual, moral, and intellectual lives of both faculty and students.

Yvonne Keefer called student work a "strange phenomenon." Eighteen-year-olds who leave home and are "free" for the first time have a tendency to rebel and kick off the chains, to do their own thing. Part of the purpose of campus ministry is to be an anchor for those students so that everything is not "blown" in that first full taste of freedom. Campus ministry must give the student a way of continuing in religious growth. Students need a place to "re-group," and find support as they look at their values. Student work is an evangelism tool, as well, because of the tremendous need of so many students who are not Christians. Students who may have been in a local church, but have lost their zeal, need to be reclaimed.

BSU continues to be a link between the student and the local church. It is important for students to understand that "after college" they will need to find places of service and growth in churches in communities where they live and work. There is, however, some difficulty with this link concept at times: students may not feel welcome in a church; and/or the student campus minister may not feel comfortable or theologically compatible with the church, its pastor, or its program. Good student work places emphasis on this relationship and attempts to help students and churches recognize this responsibility.

Bob Anderson, student director at KSU since 1972, would like to see the day when every student has a definite, weekly, responsible commitment in a local church. Some churches are reluctant to give students this opportunity because of their youth, vacation times, other commitments. However, there are many "success" stories when this happens. Keefer reported that a student was elected by one church to serve on the search committee seeking a new pastor. She was elected not as a "token" student, but because of the strength of her commitment to that church. That is often the case.

One thing that may make "linking" more difficult to understand, particularly by local Baptist churches, is the diversity of the student population reached through campus ministry. In Kansas-Nebraska it is not an organization "of Baptist students, by Baptist students, and for Baptist students," as it may be in the "old South." It is a ministry to students who need to minister and those who need be ministered to. Outreach is not limited to Baptist students, but includes a heavy emphasis on internationals, and "whosoever will." For this reason, campus meetings or BSU rallies take on added significance. Student retreats, conventions, state and national meetings, Bible study, discipling, and the emphasis on summer mission opportunities form the centerpiece of today's student work.

Campus ministers work in their own way with students, utilizing their special gifts and training. Each campus has its own "personality" which must be understood and related to.

The first formal activity Gilliland did with student work was to organize a BSU on the Wichita campus in 1953. Already there was student work at Pittsburg, and the work at Haskell with Native American students. The first student convention was held in connection with the annual meeting of the Convention in 1953, on Tuesday evening at the Droll's English Grill on East Central in Wichita. William Hall Preston, associate secretary of the Department of Student Work of the Sunday School Board, who was also a guest at the Convention, was the speaker. Pastors from churches in college campus towns were encouraged to attend. In an item written by Brister, it was billed as "an attenuated version of what we expect to have in the future, but perhaps none in the future shall be of more importance in the history of BSU work in Kansas" (KSSB, October 25, 1953). Brister's words were prophetic.

The third Annual Student Convention was held in Lawrence, at the Student Union Building, again with William Hall Preston, and Earl Fine as missionary speaker. There were sixty-five in attendance. That year there was also a Spring Retreat at Lakeview Park with forty-five on hand.

Jane Ray Bean, from the Sunday School Board, was the "outside" speaker in 1957 when the group met, fifty strong, at Kansas State Teachers College in

Emporia. By 1960 attendance at the State Convention had grown to one hundred, with representation from the five campuses where there were directors. The following year, there were two hundred students at the Convention, which was at Haskell Institute. At the beginning of 1968, there were student directors on fourteen campuses, full-time, part-time, and volunteer. Ten students had gone that year to seven different areas in and outside of the U.S. to minister.

A Spring Planning Conference was instituted so that state officers could work together on the program for the following year. Students attended Student Week at Glorieta, an SBC-wide student conference. The Sunday School Board in 1962 (*BD*, April 14, 1962) announced that certain pioneer states, including Kansas, would be eligible to receive help for "workers" to be employed on selected university campuses. "An appreciable portion of each worker's time will be devoted to working with international students." The first State International Student Conference in Kansas was held in 1964 with thirty-eight registered, seventeen of them international students. The group met at the "Y" Ranch in Arlington. This conference continued through 1967.

Campus ministry paid a fearful price for the 1968 CLA debacle. Lost were all the salaried campus ministers; even volunteer work was reported on only eleven campuses. Ray Gilliland, the driving force for growth in this area in the early days, was gone. Harold Inman, a fine educator, was pulled in too many directions to give much time to student work when that responsibility was thrust upon him. Student centers, which had been acquired by various means, were swept away, the money used to pay debts to help keep the Convention afloat. No International Student Conference was reported for 1969. No Kansas-Nebraska students were chosen and commissioned for mission work for the summer of 1969. We can be grateful to a handful of strong volunteers and to committed student leaders who took seriously their positions of leadership on state BSU Councils and on campuses across the two-state area year after year.

STUDENT WORK COMMITTEE

In January 1972 (*Annual*), an ad hoc committee to study Baptist student work in Kansas and Nebraska was formed to recommend to the Executive Board a strategy for ministering to the college communities in the two-state area. Members included: Fred Hollomon, chair, Bob Dale, Fred Garvin, Lynn Clayton, Warren Willimeth, and Ernie Castro. Ex-officio members were Yvonne Keefer, John and Erma Bolan, Burt Potter, Bill Long, and Henry Smart.

The committee worked out a cooperative relationship with the BSU of OU, where Max Barnett was director. His dream was to place full-time personnel, trained in the OU program, on the campuses of all the Big-8 schools, with the exception of Oklahoma State University and Missouri. This was to be a two-year pilot project designed to develop ways to witness and minister to students on university campuses. It turned out to be of far longer duration.

During the time Bob Anderson was at OU, he was involved in what he called "campus ministry"—he led Bible study groups and was involved in BSU activities—and saw his own spiritual life mature. God gave him a "vision for students." This was during the time of the Vietnam war; after he finished his ROTC training, he spent two years in the military, part of that time at Fort Riley. The Andersons united with the College Heights Baptist Church and met John and Erma Bolan, who were part-time BSU directors, opening their home and sharing their lives with students at KSU. While Anderson was in Vietnam, a group from Oklahoma made a trip up through Kansas, Nebraska, and Iowa looking at universities that did not have full-time campus ministers. Fred Hollomon, pastor at Manhattan, was chair of the Student Work Committee of the Convention; Peck Lindsay was responsible for student work in the Convention.

Yvonne Keefer was already at work at KU, and she chose to stay in her position; therefore, no new person was sent there. John Bolan was part-time at KSU, so Bob Anderson, since he had some experience at Manhattan, went to Kansas State.

John and Erma Bolan came to KSU in 1966 as students in the graduate program, and stayed until 1973, employed as instructors at KSU and as part-time Baptist Student ministers. When Ray Gilliland discovered they were coming to Manhattan, he enlisted them in the BSU program. The Bolans and the students were "family." For the first part of their ministry, regular Thursday night meetings were held in their home; later the American Baptist Student Center was rented. Sunday night supper at College Heights Church in Manhattan was a regular activity, in part because this meal was not served in the dorms. There were picnics and other kinds of outings with the students, who, for the most part, attended College Heights. Little work, other than a once-a-week midday meeting and regular visiting, was done on the campus. Students participated in state-wide meetings, and looked forward to Student Week at Glorieta. One activity the students enjoyed, and so did the church, was the BSU Choir, which sang at the first service every week. It was not easy for the Bolans to give up this ministry with the students when the Oklahoma plan was inaugurated. They understood, however, the wisdom of having a full-time director, given the number of students involved, and the size of the campus. The Bolans stayed on for a year and then resigned, since Anderson was supported as a full-time director.

Brett Yohn, who had worked as a U.S.-2 missionary for the Home Mission Board, went to the UNL. In 1995 Bob Anderson and Brett Yohn were still in their positions at KSU and the UNL. Several other directors were placed on Kansas and Nebraska campuses from the OU program, such as Dave Barteaux at Pittsburg and Ray Crawford at Omaha.

Even before the 1971 Oklahoma plan, for the most part with volunteer and part-time directors, there were good programs and cohesiveness among the campuses. According to Keefer (Interview, 1994), "The students had a lot of joint projects. They held retreats twice a year, and had a tremendous emphasis on summer missions. We sent out eight to ten students each summer. Raising funds for these summer missionaries was a great game. One campus would have a party and invite all the other campuses to come. The parties were designed as both mission awareness events and fund raisers." Keefer shared the experience of one student who sold his car and gave the money to summer missions. His friends would find someone in a church who would buy it back and they would return it to him, only to have him sell it again. That spring the car was sold four times for summer missions money.

OKLAHOMA HELPS

The committee recommended the Oklahoma University plan to the Convention. Since Kansas-Nebraska was just coming out of the CLA problem, there was very little Convention money for the venture. The directors raised a large portion of their own support.

Bob Anderson (Interview, 1994) told of moving to Manhattan. His family and Brett Yohn's family transported their worldly goods from Oklahoma in a U-Haul. They "dumped" the Anderson household in Manhattan and then went on to Lincoln. "So," Bob concluded, "I have been on the field one day longer than Brett." That was in 1972.

Yvonne Keefer began her involvement with Baptists in Kansas in 1956 at College Heights Baptist Church in Manhattan right after she and Jim were married. Jim was with Southwestern Bell, so after a few moves, they landed in Wichita. During that time, they worked with the fairly young BSU at Wichita University. Mrs. Loren Belt, the wife of the DOAM, was the director. At that time, in addition to WSU, there was student work at Pittsburg, KU, Emporia, and it was just beginning at KSU.

After another series of moves, the Keefers returned to Topeka in 1966, and Yvonne began the BSU at WU, where she worked for two years. At this time, a transfer took them to Lawrence, where Yvonne was asked by Harold Inman in the fall of 1969 to become BSU director. Bill Marshall, who had been BSU director at KU for three years, was a CLA casualty. She was paid a "salary" of ten dollars per month, and fifty dollars per month for expenses connected with the program. The salary was increased little by little over the years. Yvonne remained at KU until 1983 when she became executive director of Kansas-Nebraska WMU.

Brett Yohn was a student at Southwestern Baptist Theological Seminary in Fort Worth when Max Barnett's Pilot Project was in the making. He had had two years experience in student work as a U.S.-2er in Florida. The feeling that he needed to be in a mission setting was what sent him on a trip to the Midwest to look at campuses which needed BSU work. It was in a "car prayer meeting" with two Nebraska pastors, Fred Garvin and Johnny Cox, on a cold December night that he felt God's call to Nebraska University. He confesses he did not like the idea—after all he was an OU graduate and shortly before had seen "the Big Red" team beat the Sooners soundly in the game of the century.

Max Barnett and the pastors from Nebraska set up an interview with Peck Lindsay in Wichita. Lindsay minced no words, "I don't know how you fellows want to do student ministry but if it involves buildings or a salary, forget it. We have got to find some creative and effective ways of doing it without the overhead that exists in the South." Yohn liked this man who saw things differently than any state staff person he had ever met.

In 1972 the letter of invitation came from the KNCSB to begin full-time work at the University of Nebraska, on faith, with responsibility of raising a large percentage of his salary. Yohn has felt God's leadership all through the years. When other calls came to leave, he heard God's voice saying, "Stay!"

Yohn was particularly pleased with Lindsay's emphasis on people, rather than numbers. At the first student retreat in his Kansas-Nebraska career, Lindsay called to ask the number of students who would attend. Yohn was fearful of the reaction when he could muster only five, and was delighted with Lindsay's commendation, "Five? That's great! Most years we have zero."

When Tri-Country Association found out they were not to have a person like Bob Anderson or Brett Yohn through the Oklahoma plan, they worked out a plan with Lindsay so that Dave and Sara Barteaux could be campus ministers at Pittsburg. The Barteauxs raised half of their own salary; the other half was paid by the KNCSB and Tri-County Association.

In 1977 Lindsay developed the plan of moving away from direct supervision of campus ministry by appointing Yvonne Keefer, Bob Anderson, and Brett Yohn as associate state directors. Their job was to coordinate state events for campus ministry and represent KNCSB on a board and agency level. Yohn saw this as another example of Lindsay's willingness to "color outside the lines."

Several years ago a committee from the KNCSB Executive Board studied the effectiveness of student ministry in Kansas-Nebraska. They found that between 1972 and 1989, BSU had produced the following fruit: twenty-four Missionary Journeymen or International Service Corps personnel, five U.S.-2 missionaries, fourteen career missionaries, seventy-two other full-time Christian workers, nine new churches in the Convention, and seven Student Ministries outside of Kansas-Nebraska. What a tribute to the service of the men and women who have served as campus ministers.

And the work continued to grow. The Student Work Committee continued to function. One report to the Convention included this main purpose of the BSU (*Annual*, 1972): "To relate the Gospel to the total person by assisting our campus directors and students in discovering and ministering to persons on the campuses of Kansas and Nebraska so they may see by our deeds, and know by our words that God loves them and wants to redeem them in Himself through their personal surrender to and growth in his son, Jesus Christ." Secondary objectives included assisting Baptist people in recognizing the campus as a mission field and challenging churches and associations to give "resourceful" support; to move toward a witness on every campus in Kansas and Nebraska; to provide freedom in which creative programming could be planned; and to provide training for directors and students to better equip them to do Christian campus ministry.

PROGRAMS

Through the years there have been helpful and inspiring meetings of various types for students: conventions, training sessions, and international retreats. Kansas and Nebraska students have regularly attended national student conferences at Glorieta.

At least two other activities must be highlighted. Thirty-six young men and women, representing ten campuses, participated in the Kansas-Nebraska Student Choir (*BD*, September 24, 1966). They sang at Glorieta, and also had a number of concert stops along the way. And, perhaps born before its time was the organization called Pilgrim 20 Singers (*BD*, September 16, 1967), which grew out of the vision of Ray Gilliland and Clint Dunagan, pastor of First Southern, Lawrence. The group was composed of six male and six female vocalists plus four instrumentalists from five campuses. The purpose of the group was to present a Christian witness on campuses in the twentieth century in a way that was acceptable to and heard by students. They used folk music, contemporary music in sound and tempo, a lively Christian witness, a bit of sharp repartee, and a little soft shoe. Also included was a talkback time to involve the audience. The purpose, according to Ray Gilliland, was to say hello to every campus. The name was chosen to speak of the Christian pilgrim in the twentieth century.

Keefer traveled with the group from time to time. "During one two-week period the group was on a different campus every night. This was during a school year. They would go back when they could to their classes and then go out again. They did about ten concerts in those two weeks" (Interview, Keefer). The money they raised was for summer missions. They were so popular that they began to book concerts over the summer and toured two or three years over the United States. They sang at the hemisphere at San Antonio with perhaps a thousand people listening to them. They cut two records.

Gilliland (Interview, 1994) recalled the first time Westmoreland heard the Pilgrim 20 Singers: "Dr. Westmoreland was just incensed with me—it was embarrassing to him—and did not do anything for Baptists, he said." Westmoreland stood at the back of the auditorium during one performance, and when it was over, he told Gilliland to see him in his office the following morning. Gilliland went in, wondering if he might be fired on the spot. But

Mrs. Westmoreland and their daughters had enjoyed the program; they suggested he was making too much of it. So he decided the group was not as off-line as he had supposed.

This was the first of the college singing groups and was recognized by the Sunday School Board as such. One of the tours in 1969 was to participate with 450 other Christians from fifty colleges and nineteen states and Canada in the two-week Easter vacation gathering of thirty thousand college students, which was becoming the "in" ritual for campus status-seekers *(BD,* April 26, 1969).

The demise of Pilgrim 20 came in 1970 when it "lost its purpose." It was never intended to be a money-making nor purely entertainment project, but it began to lean in that direction. The group decided that to have the practice time required, they needed to transfer to WSU. That took away leadership, and robbed the other campuses of ownership. Nevertheless, the Pilgrim 20 Singers made a mark. In the February and May 1970 issues of the *Baptist Digest,* there were brief reports of Pilgrim 20, which by that time was a WSU group. The group took a semester out of school and traveled for six months, through Oklahoma, Texas, back again to Daytona and Fort Lauderdale for Easter week activities, then to Atlanta, New York City, across the U.S. to southern California for an extended stay, and finished their tour at Glorieta, where they sang at Baptist Student Week. This was in celebration of the third anniversary of the group, which had made its first appearance in 1967 at the Baptist Student Week at Glorieta. In the three years the group had given three hundred concerts, reaching approximately three hundred thousand persons in twenty-six states. They had been featured in ten television programs and many radio programs. Two records were cut by the Southern Baptist Radio-TV Commission and one under the Klondike label *(BD,* February 28, 1970).

Gilliland stated that he did a lot of "growing up" in Kansas, which prepared him for the work he did later in New York as director of Student Work and as an appointee of the Home Mission Board in Christian Social Ministry.

Another emphasis of student work in Kansas and Nebraska is outreach to international students. Keefer shared an experience concerning her first involvement with an international student, a young man from Nigeria. In the personals in the campus paper was an ad placed by the student which stated that he would do yard work "if you will talk to me." She tracked him down and found that he had been in America for two years and had never sat down and had conversation with an American because he lived so much in the international community. This was the beginning of two programs at KU to deal with this problem, the Host Family Program and an organization named Operation Friendship. Rick Clock came to lead this program and became director when Keefer resigned. Staffing these programs for four years were U.S.-2ers. Other campuses began to pick up on this approach, and it is now done on almost all of them and done very well.

Outreach to international students had happened before this time, but not in an organized fashion. In 1958 *(BD,* December 13, 1958), KU hosted a

Thanksgiving banquet with the theme "International Symphony" for 142 international students from twenty-nine countries. Charles Beck, who was at that time "BSU Director," stated that this was the third year for the Thanksgiving get-together. Local churches in the association helped with the affair.

KU also has a special organization for black Baptist students, because the students wanted it. Throughout the South, there were black BSUs, which were organized into a national convention, which drew thousands to its meetings. In 1978 there was a black associate campus minister, Leo Barbee, at KU who wanted this separate organization (Interview, Keefer, 1994). Keefer was not entirely sold on the idea, for she wanted total integration of student work on the campus. She talked with a black pastor in Lawrence about the students' request for a separate organization. He was opposed because of his fear that black students would be patronized in such an arrangement. Keefer responded, "As long as I'm here, they will not be patronized." So he agreed that it was okay to try it. Six or seven students had a brainstorming session and came to Keefer with a suggestion, "You have a dinner, and we'll get the students to come." Keefer cut up chicken—it was cheaper to buy them whole!—until her fingers nearly fell off. Seventy-five students showed up for dinner and organization. So Harambee, a Swahili word meaning "let's pull together," was born. The organization continues to this day on the KU campus. There is continuing cooperation between the groups, black and white; one meets on Tuesday, the other on Thursday, with many joint activities. That same pastor, who is a past president of the National Black Student Union, directs the group. Gene Glenn helped to organize a Harambee on the campus at Pittsburg.

Bob Anderson (Interview, 1994) believes the key to the growth of campus ministry in Kansas-Nebraska was Peck Lindsay's openness to see it as a strategic mission field. "He was open to try and do things. The whole business of fund raising was totally new; he was willing to take some risks with that. The normal way campus ministries were supported was through strong churches in the area, but Kansas-Nebraska just didn't have those resources to support full-time student workers. Student work was really Peck's baby. He stayed very close to it. He was willing to put his neck on the line."

In the 1991 *Annual*, Roy Moody gave the following statistics concerning students and student programs: Total number involved 1,460, including Bible Study, 585; Evangelism Projects, 27; Evangelism Training, 122; Student-led Revivals, 5; Summer Missions, 22; New Students Reached, 818; Students Witnessed to, 710; Students Accepting Christ, 89; Career Mission Volunteers, 4; plus Summer Missions, $14,000. According to Moody, "Our campus ministry program focuses on reaching students for Christ, equipping them to serve Him, and involving them in mission service."

Every student director recalls a number of wonderful encounters with students. Keefer has seen "her students" on foreign and home mission fields, and in many places of vocational Christian service. But even more delightful is to "walk into a church somewhere on a speaking engagement and have somebody walk up who was one of my students. Many of them are serving in Kansas-Nebraska churches today. Of course, many are in other states as well because we had so many out-of-state students at KU. So all over the world they are serving in Christ's name in large and small places, in countless ways."

In 1994 there were full-time, part-time, or volunteer BSU directors on the following campuses: Emporia State University, University of Nebraska at Kearney, Haskell Indian Nations University, KU, UNL, KSU, Pittsburg State University, Pratt Community College, WSU, Coffeyville Community College, Dodge City Community College, Fort Hays State University, Hutchinson Community College, and Kansas Wesleyan University. From time to time, there have been either employed or volunteer directors on these additional campuses: Baker University, Central Community College at Hastings, Chadron State College, Colby Community College, Cowley County Community College, Creighton University, Garden City Junior College, Hastings College, Johnson County Community College, Kansas City, Kansas, Community College, Omaha-Metropolitan, Ottawa University, Peru State University, Sterling College, University of Nebraska at Omaha, and Washburn University.

Much could be said about campus ministry, and still the whole story could not be told. There are ever-widening circles of influence of students who have been equipped and enriched and have gone away from college campuses in Kansas and Nebraska to do the work of the church in communities everywhere.

As part of their focus, both Yohn and Anderson emphasize getting students involved in a local church (*BD*, May 20, 1991). "If we cannot help our kids plug into a local church, when they leave they won't be equipped to be laborers in the kingdom," Yohn said.

Anderson agreed, "I'm after kids who will walk with God 20 and 30 years down the road. We try to build convictions into their lives about what the Bible says and about sharing the gospel. This is not just a performance thing while they're here."

A statement Billy Graham made almost thirty years ago (*BD*, July 29, 1967) is apropos today. He called the American college campus the greatest single mission field in America. "The philosophy or idea that captures the minds of these youth will tell the tale as far as the future of America is concerned. To step up our ministry among these special people is imperative."

6

Christian Social Ministries

THE VERY ESSENCE OF CHRISTIAN SOCIAL MINISTRIES MAY BE "Seventy-nine haircuts provided"—meeting the needs of people where they are, and doing it in the name of Jesus. A haircut is different from a cup of cold water, but not very. This ministry was noted—along with 7,500 articles of clothing distributed and 240 requests met for food, medicine, and rent—in the report of the Omaha Baptist Center in January 1965, at the seventh annual session of the Eastern Nebraska Association.

A thoughtful editorial by Ross Coggins in the *Digest* (June 20, 1964) spoke forcefully to the issue of Christian social ministries among Southern Baptists. The central questions were: Is Christian social action scripturally defensible? Are Christians justified in attempting more than the conversion of individuals? What is the church's role in relation to the problems of modern society?

Coggins noted that in the SBC sermon that year, Enoch Clayton Brown had pointed out that first-century Christians had not dealt with outlawing great wrongs, nor with injustice, or slavery, or other societal and cultural problems. They took this position, "'not because they were indifferent to those wrongs but that they were engaged in a much more fundamental work. Because they recognized that the roots of all wrongs are in the hearts of men, their efforts were directed toward the regeneration of those hearts.'"

"Other Christians," said Coggins, "equally dedicated to winning individuals to Christ, believe that it is a gross over-simplification to reduce Christian responsibility to such dimensions. These contend that as the salt of the earth and the light of the world, Christians should . . . create a society where justice, mercy, and freedom reign. They have an impressive array of supporters from the Bible—Amos, Micah, Isaiah, Paul, James."

Coggins' "bottom line" in this editorial was the statement of a spiritual principle: "New possibilities create new responsibilities." We have action possibilities far beyond the early church, which was conceived and grew in a culture which made some social actions foolhardy. "When Christian truth has gained enough influence [as it has in our day] to make it possible to eradicate a social evil, Christian action is not only defensible, it is mandatory. . . . The heart of the matter is the relationship between evangelism and conduct." If we are to be salt, light, water, then our walk must match our talk. If we would be truly dedicated to taking the news of Jesus Christ to people far away, then we must be aware, and involved in the physical needs, as well as spiritual needs, of people whom we see and know. Baptists in Kansas and Nebraska have chosen to do this in a number of ways.

MISSION CENTER BEGINNINGS

The Omaha Baptist Center was born in 1963 as a Vacation Bible School on Chicago Street, with Quentin Lockwood, the associational superintendent of missions, as principal, the First Southern Baptist (Hillcrest) Church as sponsor, and Woman's Missionary Union as the midwife. The rented meeting space was in the Swedish Auditorium on Chicago Street, above the Avalon Bar. The report from the Lockwoods was glowing, "We started with seven the first day, with only two children from the area. We soon had 14, then 40, and now we have an enrollment of 110." Alene Lockwood (*BD*, August 22, 1988) recalled that at the first meeting, in addition to the two children, there were "twelve women, two preachers, and gallons of Kool-Aid."

By July the Chicago Street Vacation Bible School Mission had become a branch Sunday School under the direction of Hillcrest, but the whole association supported the work. Then the Home Mission Board began to see the possibility of a center in this area of the city. From these "mustard seed" beginnings came the Omaha Baptist Center as we know it today (Huddlestun).

By 1965, with Home Mission Board funds, there was the Gray House (504 No. 22nd), the White House (2212 Cass Street), and a nine-passenger Chevrolet Station Wagon. That year fifty thousand dollars from the Annie Armstrong Offering were allocated to build an auditorium.

Alene Lockwood served as director of the center, a service she rejoiced in and wanted to continue, even when her husband was offered a position with the Home Mission Board. She smiled as she told about that, "I didn't want to go, I was so happy at Omaha Baptist Center, and our children certainly did not want to leave Omaha. But Quentin wanted to go. I knew that if we got a divorce, neither one of us would have a job; so we all went to Atlanta" (Taped Communication, Alene Lockwood).

Duane and Betty McCormick became directors of Omaha Baptist Center September 1, 1968, after the Lockwoods left on June 1. For medical reasons Duane resigned in June 1992; Betty remained through August of that year, rounding out twenty-three years of service at the center. Since her retirement and after Duane's death in 1993, Betty continues to work with preschool children two days a week in a homeless shelter which is run by the Christ Child Society, where she worked in the morning day care program for thirteen years. She has been a short-term mission volunteer in Ecuador and Australia, working with preschoolers in both locations.

A brief resume of the center's progress in June 1967 (*BD*, June 16) noted that construction of a new building had been delayed because of "drastic changes in the area due to urban renewal and the building of a 4-lane freeway." Because of this, the Gray House and the White House were renovated and redecorated, which, according to the *Digest*, was not without merit, since rare and beautiful woodwork was discovered in the process, giving the buildings unusual attractiveness.

Betty McCormick described those houses (*BD*, September 25, 1989), "The center is located in two turn-of-the-century houses just north of downtown, in the shadow of Interstate 480 and Creighton University." The three-story house was originally built by a banker for his bride; the house was also an apartment building in the past. Betty continued, "Its ceilings are at least ten feet tall, and as for windows, you can't buy a curtain anywhere in the world. A stairway leads to the house next door. Collectors covet the pink marble stairway and the leaded glass windows in the house."

Albert Huckaby was pastor of the church that met in the center until he received an overseas assignment. George Sanders then was called as pastor of the group. Omaha Baptist Center is unique in this respect. It has a week-day program, but also is a church program. The Good Neighbor Center in Wichita and Pineridge Center in Topeka had tie-ins with nearby churches.

DIRECTORS OF ASSOCIATIONAL MISSIONS AS STARTERS

In this discussion we deal with "Christian social ministries" in a broader way than the responsibilities assigned to John Hopkins, who was named state-wide consultant for Christian Social Ministries Department of the KNCSB in 1974. This department has particular, well-defined tasks: mission centers, week-day ministries, youth and family services, literacy and migrant ministries, disaster relief, drug and alcohol abuse, and work in the criminal justice system.

Many current CSM programs grew out of the work and knowledge of superintendents of missions or directors of associational missions, as they were later called. The first man to stand in this line was Eugene Strahan who was called a state missionary and served in 1948 and 1949. He was followed closely by the second person to have this title, Ray Hart, who served in the western part of the state. One of Strahan's major concerns was student work.

Long before John Hopkins came to the state convention as consultant for CSM, one of the mission ventures in meeting needs of Kansas churches was summer missionaries appointed by the Home Mission Board. The first to serve in Kansas in this capacity were Keith Hamm and Charles Coleman. They later served as state missionaries; Keith Hamm served as a pastor in Kansas, also. When Strahan resigned as state missionary, in 1949, Ray Hart and George Walker were appointed. In 1951 (*Annual*) Orbie Clem was asked, in addition to his duties as editor of *Kansas Southern Baptist Beams*, to give half his time to the task of serving as superintendent of city missions for Wichita. This title was later changed to "Co-ordinator of the City Missions Committee." He was paid a salary of twenty-five dollars per month plus travel expense of twenty-five dollars per month.

Other early directors of associational missions closely connected with the development of CSM were Paul Elledge in Kansas City, Sam Russell in Sedgwick, George Roberts in Kaw Valley, and of course, Quentin Lockwood, Tom Wenig, and Harold Manahan in Nebraska.

George Roberts served as associational missionary in Kaw Valley from 1957 to 1969. He was followed by Frank Claiborne, Ken Townsend, Tom Sykes, and Randal Cowling, who has just begun his work in the association. Roberts came to Kansas from Louisiana, by way of the army. He served as a chaplain at Fort Riley, and remained in the Army Reserve and National Guard until his death in 1982.

He was the first pastor of the First Southern Baptist Church in Junction City, and served other churches in Kansas as well. After he became associational missionary, his son remembers that many times they drove two or three hours to get to church on Sunday morning, because of helping a new church get started or because his father was filling in for a pastor somewhere in the association. There were six children plus a younger sister of Mrs. Roberts, who grew up as a family member. When Roberts left Kansas, he returned to Louisiana to accept a position as missionary in Central Louisiana Association.

Paul Elledge served as associational missionary in Kansas City, Kansas, from 1962 to 1975, when he retired, and then served for a number of years as interim and supply pastor. Now he is enjoying service as a layman. He teaches a Sunday School class for senior citizens at Emmanuel Baptist Church in Overland Park. He started this church with twelve people in a prayer meeting in his home. In 1990 (*BD*, November 26, 1990), the church was holding three worship services and two Sunday Schools on Sunday morning. Elledge is "pastor emeritus," but prefers being called "founding pastor."

During the tenure of Elledge in the association in Kansas City, campus ministries at local junior colleges were begun, a deaf ministry was instituted, and work with juvenile delinquents was staffed. When he was there, ethnic churches seemed "clear out on the other side of possibility." Quite a change has taken place in this kind of outreach.

After Paul Elledge came James Griffin, an appointee of the Metropolitan Missions Department of the Home Mission Board, who served until 1987. Don

Reed, the present director of missions, has been in Kansas City since 1988.

Griffin was perhaps the first associational missionary without a pastoral background, but was an astute businessman. Griffin was instrumental in beginning thirty-seven churches, among them the first three predominantly black churches, and including a number of language groups. He paid high tribute to the associational staff and to the pastors and others in the churches. He listed a great number of people who moved up from the "ranks" into places of denominational leadership and on to home and foreign mission fields. After retirement, he worked for two years with several associations in associational strategy planning. He and his wife, Bootsie, are active in their church, regularly holding services in a nursing home and teaching "55 Alive," a driving course for senior adults.

Loren Belt was associational missionary in Sedgwick County Association from 1956 to 1958. He and his wife were instrumental in beginning the BSU at Wichita State. He left to join the state staff in Missouri.

Sam Russell followed Belt as associational missionary in Sedgwick County Association from 1959 to 1964, at which time he accepted the position of director of Missions Department and associate to the executive-secretary treasurer of the KCSB. During the seven years he was in Sedgwick Association, it experienced "fantastic growth" (*BD*, February 12, 1966). During his tenure and with his leadership, student ministry at Wichita was strengthened, the Good Neighbor Center was opened, a program of juvenile rehabilitation was staffed by Harry Moratto, property was bought for an associational camp, and the first building was completed in 1966. In addition, churches and missions increased from twenty-eight to thirty-six; from 8,849 members to 16,121 members. During this time, he preached eighty-eight revivals, almost one every month he was in Wichita.

Sam Russell was from Oklahoma, where he pastored a number of churches and served as superintendent of missions in Union Baptist Association. Less than a year after coming to the new position in the convention, Russell was killed in an automobile collision with a freight train near his office (*BD*, January 14, 1967).

Russell was followed by Paul Davis, who served from 1966 to 1968, and Don Beall, associational missionary from 1990 to 1995. When Davis retired in 1988, after twenty-two and one half years as director of missions in Sedgwick Baptist Association, hundreds of persons attended a banquet in his honor. One of the gifts to him and his wife was a quilt which featured embroidered pictures of each church in the association (*BD*, December 26, 1988).

Quentin Lockwood was the only missionary for the whole state of Nebraska until 1966, when Peck Lindsay was appointed to this position. Lockwood went to Atlanta in the Department of Pioneer Missions of the Home Mission Board, as administrator in the Western United States. Lindsay served as area missionary until 1971, when he went to a position with the KCSB.

C. Burt Potter held this position for three years, then Harold Manahan became DOAM for Eastern Nebraska, and Tom Wenig was appointed to that position in Western Nebraska. Manahan is still in Eastern Nebraska Association; Wenig retired in 1994.

Eastern Nebraska contains forty-one counties, covers great distances, and exhibits widely varying needs. In order to deal with this, the association is divided into zones: the Northeast Zone, made up of sixteen counties; the Metro Omaha Zone, made up of three counties; and the Metro Lincoln Zone, with about nine counties. There are two other groupings of churches in the southern part of the area which make up the South Central Zone and Southeastern Zone.

Manahan, in an interview, talked about what he called the "hodgepodge" of responsibilities that are his. The largest church in the Kansas-Nebraska Convention is located in ENBA: Westside, Omaha. Most of the churches, however, have less than one hundred. In Omaha, a city of five hundred thousand people, there are only nineteen congregations, which points up the great need for new church starts. In addition to the needs in the metropolitan areas, there are rural and ranch territories to be considered, language ministry, campus ministry, CSM, and ministry to the military.

Manahan grew up in Houston, Texas. While he was in high school, he and a great friend of his dreamed dreams: his friend aspired to be a newscaster, and he was going to be a sportscaster. Dan Rather's plans fell into place; but God took Manahan in other directions. After high school, he had a stint in the Marine Corps, and then went to Baylor, where he majored in journalism. During college years, he was called to preach, and pastored a church in Houston for eight years. Afterwards, there was Southwestern Seminary, where he met J. L. Williams, who accepted the pastorate at Raven Oaks Church in Omaha. The day Manahan graduated he had a call from the Search Committee at Chandler Acres in Bellevue who had heard about him from Williams. This was another example of God's "hand on a shoulder." After his work in that church and a short term in Alaska, he became the DOAM for Eastern Nebraska.

Manahan says one of the finest things that has happened in the association was the appointment, in 1993, of Eddie Smith as church starter strategist. Dennis Hampton "found" him in Southern California, and told Manahan about his fine work. So Smith accepted the invitation to Nebraska. Many new starts have been made under his leadership. The goal now in Eastern Nebraska is twenty-one new church starts in the next three years. Each of the forty-four congregations in the association is being encouraged to "Start Something New" in their own church and beyond their own church, working alone or with another congregation.

After twenty years as director of associational missions of WNBA (BD, October 31, 1994), Tom Wenig was honored in a meeting at Iglesia Bautista Hispana in Scottsbluff. At this same meeting WNBA was dissolved, with the formation of two associations. During his tenure as DOAM, Wenig traveled 38,000 to 40,000 miles a year. His association was a big one, covering about 60,000 square miles. While he served as DOAM, seven churches grew to sixteen and three missions, pastoral tenure increased, and language work was begun at Scottsbluff.

Through the years, the number of associations and DOAMs has increased and become more organized. By 1957 there were area missionaries, the forerunners of DOAMs, in Wichita (Loren Belt), Central (Cecil Adams), Western (A. L. Busbee), Kansas City (I. H. Lanier), Northeastern (George Roberts, Jr.), and Southeastern (Avery Wooderson). By 1958 there were three area missionaries, a city missionary in Wichita (Sam Russell), pastoral missionaries in Lincoln, Omaha, and Grand Island, Nebraska, and associational missionaries in Kansas City, Kansas, and Tri-County (Roy Walker).

By 1963 James Shope had begun to work as the DOAM in Tri-County. He served in this capacity for twenty-three years, which he believes is probably a record for such service in the Kansas-Nebraska Convention. The last eleven years, he served as DOAM for Twin Valley as well. Part of the time, he also pastored a church. None of the men who hold the position of DOAM works eight-hour days; there is too much to be done.

There continued to be an increase in associational missionaries, until there was such a person in every association. In "hard times" two associations were served by one person. Distances were great; resources were small. But the work went on, and by 1965, Meeler Markham, appointed in 1960 as secretary of the Department of Missions, made this statement as part of his report (*Annual*, 1965): "Several years ago, our program of area missions was terminated, and plans have been made and are succeeding in enabling the associations to develop full-time ministries by their missionaries. Only a few of the associations yet have a program requiring the missionary to give part of his time to pastoring a church."

By 1994 there were fourteen associations, plus a fellowship in the Panhandle, in the two-state area. The newest were Sandhills Association and Platte Valley Association, which took the name of the early WNBA, originally part of the Baptist General Convention of Colorado. Each, in 1995, except the two newest, had a full-time DOAM. The Convention looks to these directors and supports them in the mission ministries their associations pursue.

The Convention looks to the DOAMs to find the heartbeat of Kansas and Nebraska Baptists and equip them to reach out to others who do now know God, and to share their faith with them. The DOAMs look for places where new missions or Bible studies are needed, they encourage the pastors, and they train the laity for leadership roles. It is not possible to tell every story, but we can rejoice in every victory, and share in every sacrifice and heartache. We can pray for God's leadership for those who fill this role.

EARLY PLANS FOR MEETING NEEDS

One of the early dreams of N. J. Westmoreland was that the Convention establish a Baptist children's home in Kansas. "Are there not as many orphan children in Kansas as in Oklahoma?" he asked. A fund was begun for this "cherished project for orphan children" (*Annual*, 1949). It was nourished through birthday gifts given through the Sunday School, and supplemented by one or two years of Christmas Stocking dime collections, and in 1950 by a Thanksgiving Offering. "Not a few people," Westmoreland reported, "gave 'One Day's Pay' to this offering" (*Annual*, 1951). By 1952 it had grown to $3,300. The $370 earnings of the Baptist Book Store were added to the fund that year. In addition, the foundation held a will which named the children's home as beneficiary, amounting to between ten and fifteen thousand dollars, along with insurance policies in which the children's home was named as second beneficiary. Every Kansas Baptist was encouraged to have a part in bringing this dream to reality by making birthday offerings and giving to the Annual Thanksgiving Offering for the children's home fund.

By 1958 it was accepted that we would not be able to build a children's home in the near future for two reasons. First, there was not enough money, and the concept of a children's home was being replaced by other methods of caring for children. All the money allocated to this project was redesignated to the Child Care Program, which was to include Mothers' Aid, Foster Homes, Adoption Agency, and institutions, defined as cottages housing not more than twelve children. These cottages were to be put into operation at such a time as the cost could be absorbed by Cooperative Program funds. The Executive Board noted that a social worker would be a necessary staff addition before this plan could be in operation. Gifts from the State Mission Offering, which had been designated for the children's home, were postponed until the erection of the first cottage for child care.

The 1952 *Annual* reported serious consideration being given to the possibility of a Baptist hospital in Kansas. The president was authorized to appoint a committee to investigate the invitation of interested citizens in Garden City to the KCSB to lead in the establishment of a Baptist Hospital at Garden City, Kansas. The committee was to report to the Executive Board, which would make no decisions that affected the Convention budget. Any such action was to come before the Convention. Evidently, nothing could be done without funds, so the Convention did not go into the hospital business.

Institutions such as these did not come to be the way Kansas and Nebraska Baptists dealt with needs of people around them. The costs were too great; the resources, both financial and human, were too small. Instead, four Baptist centers were in operation over the years: Omaha Baptist Center since 1963; Baptist Good Neighbor Center in Wichita, since 1964; Pine Ridge Baptist Center in Topeka, from 1963 to 1991; and a program in Kansas City, which now operates as Wyandotte Ministries in space shared with the New Horizons Missionary Baptist Church in Kansas City, Kansas. In addition, Juvenile Rehabilitation Programs were begun, later called Youth and Family Services Programs. All these approaches provided valuable ministries.

CENTERS WITH WEEKDAY PROGRAMS

Omaha Baptist Center—The first director of the Omaha Baptist Center was Alene Lockwood. Next came Duane and Betty McCormick, who served from 1968 to 1992. Viola Webb opened the door for the McCormicks to go to the Omaha Center (*BD*, July 26, 1993). McCormick was pastor of Westview Baptist Church in Wichita where Webb was a member. When the director's position at the Omaha Center became available, she asked McCormick if he knew anyone who would be interested in it. McCormick answered, "Viola, I have felt for some time that the Lord was leading us in the direction of an inner-city ministry." And so they went, and ministered for twenty-three years.

Betty McCormick (Taped Communication) paid high tribute to the many, many volunteers who gave time and money to the center. One day a young lawyer, who had been transferred from New York City to Omaha, appeared at the mission. He had contacted the Home Mission Board and asked if there were a mission-type church he could be a part of while he was in Omaha. He volunteered at the center as long as he was there. The Glovers worked at the center for seventeen years. It began when Duane asked Mrs. Glover to teach a primary class "until Easter," and she agreed. Later, much later, Mrs. Glover said, "But he didn't say which year." One Wednesday evening, Betty presented the needs of the center at a church, then Duane preached. At the close of the service, a woman asked, "How many volunteered?" "Well, no one," Betty answered. So the Sharratts came and stayed for ten years. And these were only a few. Ruby Trujillo, now seventy-three years old, has been the janitor ever since the center has employed a janitor.

Classes were taught, transportation provided, clothes sorted and distributed, and visits made. When she was leaving, McCormick recalled Calvin Miller's telling her that "the only good thing about [her] leaving was that for the first time he could just tell somebody that he couldn't work at the Center any longer," which he had never had the heart to say to Betty.

Betty McCormick must have been quite a "persuader." On one occasion she "thought about" trying to learn sign language. When she mentioned this to Wendell Belew, he laughed and said, "I have no doubt about your learning it, but as fast as you talk I think you'd break your arms trying to speak it."

Upon the retirement of the McCormicks, Alpha and Ron Goombi, who were already Home Mission Board appointees working with Native Americans, were given this responsibility. They began a full-time ministry in 1991 (*BD*, December 19, 1991). Before that time, they commuted to the area for a part-time ministry while they were attending Midwestern Seminary. They also work on the Santee, Winnebago, and Omaha Reservations. Both are full-blooded Native Americans. Alpha is from the Kiowa Tribal Nation and Choctaw; Ron from the Kiowa Tribal Nation and Apache.

The Omaha Baptist Center through the years has made "multifaceted efforts" (*BD*, September 25, 1989) to meet people's needs "with the underlying goal of sharing Christ." The ministries include food pantry, clothing closet (open every other Thursday), Bible Clubs for children and youth which include games and projects, Ladies' Club which includes crafts and Bible study, summertime recreation, Vacation Bible School, and pastoral ministries. Meeting physical needs unlocks the door for ministry to other needs of the people. Volunteers from the churches are invaluable; Jo Criser, a member of Hillcrest Baptist Church, has helped with the Ladies' Club for fifteen years. Programs the McCormicks wanted to begin were tutoring, a reading clinic, and parenting classes. The majority of people who attend the Sunday services were reached through the helping ministries.

In 1991 (*BD*, December, 19, 1991), a new building was dedicated at 1030 South 24th Place. The old property was sold to Creighton University. Interstate 480 had cut the Baptist Center out of the community it served and forced the McCormicks to use vans to bring people to the center programs. The new building is in the heart of an inner-city housing area, next to an elementary school which was converted into low income apartments and is home to fifty children. Construction was done by dozens of volunteer groups from the local association, Kansas, Missouri, and Texas. Betty McCormick (Personal Communication) said many were surprised the building went up so quickly, since it was begun in May and occupied in October. One man stopped one day to say he had never seen a building go up so fast. Duane's answer was classic, "Well, you have to be a Southern Baptist."

Texas Retiree Baptist Builders was the first team to participate. They came in their travel trailers and mobile homes and stayed two weeks. It was not an altogether happy time. On Friday four and a half inches of rain fell, so before any construction could begin, mud had to be scooped out of the basement. That did not stop the Texans, whose average age was seventy-two. They kept on the job. And when they left, the building was in place.

It was a little threatening to the people to give up the old familiar center buildings and move to a new place, but everyone adjusted quite well, according to Duane McCormick. One "results" story Betty McCormick shared was a phone call from a young man who had "grown up" in the center. He called when he learned of the death of McCormick and asked for permission to speak at the Memorial Service. "If it were not for you," he said, "I'd be making this call from jail." As it was, he had become a Christian, learned a trade, and moved away from the inner-city.

Today, three congregations meet in the center for services. Ron Goombi pastors two of these: The All Nations Church, which is made up largely of Native Americans, and the Omaha Baptist Center Church, made up largely of Anglos. The Primera Iglesia Bautista, a work with Spanish-speaking people, is pastored by Isaias Martinez.

Baptist Good Neighbor Center, Wichita—The Baptist Good Neighbor Center in Wichita began operation in 1964. Dorothy Milam served as the director,

1964-1976; then Cheryl Sorrels, 1977-1984; followed by Bruce and Marianne Bass, who came to the center in 1988. Milam, a native of Kansas City, came to Wichita from North Carolina where she began the Dan Valley Mission Center and worked four years. Wichita was her fourth experience with a new weekday program (*BD*, January 8, 1965). From the 1966 *Annual* comes this word of commendation for the first director: "The Baptist Good Neighbor Center, Wichita, has been guided into a very good and thorough program by its director, Dorothy Ruth Milam. Miss Milam's dedication and experience mean much to a new center like this. A new building now means added facilities and multiplied opportunities." Ground was broken in 1966 (*BD*, June 6, 1966) for a new $78,500 building planned right next door to the old center building on 11th and Emporia. It was a two-story structure, with a small assembly room with a stage for programs and room to seat around eighty people. There were seven large classrooms; recreational, crafts, and sewing rooms; a kitchen and dining area; a laundry and clothing room; and offices for the Good Neighbor Center staff.

By 1969 (*BD*, June 7, 1969), the center in Wichita was ministering to Mexican, Chinese, African-American, and Anglo youth. Activities included ping pong, a weekly Bible study for senior citizens, and other events. More than sixty volunteers were regular helpers each month. A picture story in 1969 (*BD*, June 7, 1969) showed first graders in their weekday activity time, a Mother's Club which met regularly, and a Boys' Club.

In 1977 Dorothy Milam Bledsoe submitted her resignation. She had served as a home missionary for twenty years, "12 faithful years of which were spent in our convention" (*Annual* 1976). It was at this center that our first U.S.-2 worker, Diana Smith, was on staff.

The center continues to function as a point of food and clothing distribution and offers a variety of programs for children. It is open at least part of every day. The staff position for this center was terminated in 1994 by the Home Mission Board; therefore, it depends on volunteers. Associational leadership is searching for a Mission Service Corps couple to take up the ministry. In the meantime, Harry Moratto is overseeing the work.

Pine Ridge Baptist Center, Topeka—Pine Ridge Baptist Center had its beginning in 1963 as a Spanish mission. The work changed to a weekday ministry in 1967 and continued until 1991, because of the change in the community. Charles A. Rankin and his wife, Gladys, were appointed language missionaries. Rankin was from Louisiana, knew George Roberts at seminary, and came to Kansas at his invitation. He became the first director of the weekday program. They served until Rankin's death in 1972. After the Rankins, Eugene and Karion Krieger were the directors. They left in 1978 when Krieger accepted a position as chaplain in the U.S. Air Force. After a period of vacancy, Coy Webb was appointed director, followed by Tommy Goode and Larry Irwin. Lee and Ellen Martin came in 1991 and assumed the duties of Church and Community Ministry director (new Home Mission Board name for CSM) of Kaw Valley Association. The Topeka Center was phased out before Martin came, the building sold, and operations of the total Christian ministries program moved to the associational office and New Hope Baptist Church, in the inner city.

Construction of the first unit of the three-phase building plan for the Pine Ridge Baptist Center began in September 1964. Dedication Day was May 9, 1965. Sunday School enrollment was sixty-six and Training Union was forty-five. The chapel had a Girls' Auxiliary, a Sunbeam Band, and a Royal Ambassador Chapter, all of which remained active. One facet of the Pine Ridge Center was the ministry of music. Free piano lessons were offered to children and adults in the community by Gladys Rankin and Robert Hupe, assistant to Charles Rankin (*BD*, January 4, 1969). Music was an important part of the programs presented at a rest home and the Topeka Rescue Mission.

At the Pine Ridge Center, a ceramics class proved to be the means of winning a number to Christ. The woman teaching the class first came to the center because of her interest in ceramics. The center was ministering to over 150 persons each week (*BD*, June 7, 1969).

In 1995 Lee and Ellen Martin were at work in Kaw Valley. Although Pine Ridge Center is no longer in operation, Christian social ministries continue, all staffed by volunteers. Food pantries are in operation at New Hope Baptist Church and at other sites in the city. Shirley Inman directs a roving literacy program, set up wherever it is needed. There is a truck-stop ministry, regular ministry at nursing homes, and the Senior Center, where meals are served twice a month. Lee Martin coordinates chaplains who work with the police; Bryan Jones, pastor of the Wanamaker Baptist Church, serves as chaplain of the Sheriff's Department.

Another program is headed by Jeff Pile, who directs an activity program in Whispering Pines, a large housing unit. He "sold" this program to the management, who furnish an apartment for the Piles and a clubhouse for the program. Pile is minister with children, music, and missions at Wanamaker Road Baptist Church. The start was an after-school, latch-key program for children in grades one to six. This was such a success that Pile is now on the staff of Whispering Pines as activities director, and with the help of volunteers plans activities for residents "across the board" (*BD*, July 27, 1992).

Kansas City, Kansas—Elledge wrote (Personal Communication, Paul Elledge, 1994) that the CLA crisis was a "heartbreaker" for him and the Missions Committee of the Kansas City, Kansas, Association. For several years there had been efforts to establish a Goodwill Center in Kansas City. The first efforts really never got very far, but the third effort was underwritten by the Home Mission Board.

According to the report of the director of the Department of Missions of the Convention (*Annual*, 1968), plans were underway for a Mission Center in Kansas City. The site was located in the 1100 block of Central Avenue with a frontage of 180 feet, just across the street southwest of Bethany Park and Bethany Hospital. "Like much of the terrain in Kansas, this is a part of a steep incline, but should not hinder development of an excellent facility for the Christian Social Ministry" (*BD*, October 7, 1967). There are, of course, many around the country who do not believe there are any "steep" places in Kansas! In 1969 plans for a center operation were still not completed.

In 1967 (*Annual*) the Home Mission Board bought land, at a cost of twenty-four thousand dollars, on which to build a center in Kansas City. According to Elledge, they had also agreed to put the building project (seventy-five thousand dollars) into the Annie Armstrong Offering alloca- tions. Then came the crash of the CLA. When that happened, the Home Mission Board was no longer in the mood to put building money into Kansas. Elledge reported, however, that the Home Mission Board deeded the prop- erty to the association which was later sold for twenty-five thousand. These circumstances caused CSM to abandon the "center" plan in Kansas City and pursue a different route for meeting needs.

During Griffin's tenure money was used to buy and renovate property for an associational office, which up to that point had been housed in the First Southern Baptist Church in Kansas City. It was a filling station which he got for a good price because the owner was using it for a tax write-off. In 1979 the associational office moved to a very fine old house on four and a half acres in Olathe, which Griffin also acquired at a good price. This turned out to be quite valuable, since part of the land was needed for the construction of the inter- state. The association sold an acre of ground, and bought an office building in Overland Park. In 1994, after Don Reed came, the rest of the Olathe land was sold, the building in Overland Park paid off, and the residue placed in the Baptist Laymen's New Work Foundation, which will be used to acquire land in strategic locations for new churches in the Kansas City, Kansas, Association.

CHURCHES MINISTERING LIKE CENTERS

The centers described are all part of the CSM Department of KNCSB. There are, however, churches in the convention that operate almost like a center. Take First Baptist Church at Sutton, Nebraska, for instance. "It's the story of the five loaves and two fishes all over again, except it's happening here under the leadership of Eddy Smith and his associate pastor, Bill Speake" (*BD*, October 22, 1990). Brother Eddy, as he is known, likes the church to be called First Baptist Church Ministries. It is not a large church, but people in a fifty-five-mile radius are aware of the influence of this "small band of disciples." They maintain a clothes closet, a room in the church is equipped for overnight transients, canned goods are donated to feed about ten families a month, a garden on a vacant lot behind the building produced five hundred pounds of potatoes to feed the hungry, an Alcoholics Anonymous group meets in the church, and special ministries are conducted in Harvard, a neighboring town plagued with drug abuse, suicide, and domestic violence. Brother Eddy's parish "is a low-income farming area that leads down gravel roads in every direction. The days are long, and the budget is small enough to figure with pencil and paper. Yet the zeal in the pastor's eyes doesn't fade. He leads his small band to minister to the sick, hungry and hurting in the name of Jesus" (*BD*, October 22, 1991).

Forest Park Baptist Church in Lenexa (*BD*, November 23, 1992), using the interest from the money they had saved to build a new church building, provided a HUD house for a homeless family. The church leased the HUD house for a dollar a year, and agreed to pay property taxes and utilities. Volunteers cleaned, painted, carpeted, and furnished the house. A father and mother and their three children moved in from a house in which they had no refrigerator and the stove was not connected. The utility bill, because the house was so poorly insulated, had required about forty percent of the take-home pay of the working father. The work of ministry did not end with a move into a "new" house; the mother did not know how to do many things. None of the children was immunized, the three-year old was not toilet trained, and neither parent had a high school diploma. The whole church got involved: arranging child care so parents could get a G.E.D., providing transportation, giving hair cuts, celebrating the children's birthdays, making household repairs, and sharing "how-to" with the parents. By the end of the year, the mother had a job, the oldest child was in kindergarten, and both the mother and father were being discipled.

When the people in First Baptist Church in Coffeyville became aware of the unemployment situation in their town (*BD*, December 27, 1982), they decided to do something to help. Two major sources of employment, companies involved in oil production and heavy equipment manufacturing, had gone out of business; fifteen families in the church were out of work. So volunteers set up a "job swap." It is a way of putting people who want odd jobs done in touch with people who need jobs. Many of the jobs involved vouchers instead of cash payment for the work so as not to jeopardize unemployment benefits. Beyond the effect on the persons involved, the ministry spoke to the community, as evidenced by "those who stop Mitchell [the pastor] in restaurants and on the street to ask about the project or say thanks for what he and First Southern are doing for Coffeyville."

One Sunday in the early 1980s, Owen Dahlor, pastor of Nall Avenue Baptist Church in Prairie Village, preached a particularly moving sermon based on Matthew 25. As he stood at the door greeting people who had been in the worship service, a man said to him, "Well, Pastor, what are we going to do about it?"

"Do about what?" was the response Dahlor remembers. "The things you preached about this morning," replied this forever nameless Christian who listened seriously to the words of Jesus. And so was born the "Matthew 25 Club" at Nall Avenue, which still remains in action today. Ministry groups formed. Several Sundays each autumn were designated as coat, sweater, and blanket collection times. They weather-stripped homes of shut-ins; visited the lonely and those in prison; and distributed food and clothing (*Missions USA*, January-February 1989). The church continues to designate Peanut Butter, Coat, Toy, Mitten, Sweater, and Fan Sundays. They remember that whatever they do for others, the least of these others, they also do for Jesus. This is the mandate for social ministry; and it is endorsed by Jesus Christ Himself.

MINISTRY OF INDIVIDUALS AND GROUPS

In the ministry of caring, "the power of one" makes a difference. One day in October 1992, Jane Grayson, wife of the pastor of Southview Baptist Church in Lincoln, came across a brochure called "Carelift '93," which was a Campus Crusade Project (*BD*, April 26, 1993). The goal was to send shoes, boots, socks, food parcels, and Russian New Testaments to needy Russian children. Grayson got excited, and enlisted as her right-hand helper Cammy Hutchenson. They brought the project to their church and to other churches and businesses in Lincoln (Personal Communication). And the shoes came in. A trucker in Omaha agreed to take the donations to the shipping point. People offered storage places, pick-up help, publicity, time, and shoes and socks. In less than one month, 3,770 pairs of shoes and 3,535 pairs of socks were shipped to Russia from Western Nebraska, Lincoln, Omaha, and Council Bluffs. And then the two women joined four hundred volunteers from across the U.S. and went to Moscow to deliver the packages. They delivered New Testaments at a Greek Orthodox seminary, as well as at the underground railroad. They took vitamins to George and Veda Rae Lozuk who were the liaisons for new missionaries and volunteers. They reported a visit to a Russian family in their home. Not ten minutes into the visit, the mother said, "Tell me about God. I have so many questions." Likely, the church will never be quite the same again because of this ministry. And as a bit of serendipity, Grayson wrote, "I think we expanded people's view of Southern Baptists in our community." In July of that year, the Graysons were appointed by the Foreign Mission Board to serve in the Philippines, where Bob teaches Bible and Jane teaches music in the seminary.

Then there was the church in Manhattan, New Hope Community Church, which had an old fashioned barn-raising; only the barn was a garage (*BD*, May 20, 1991). The garage was built for the Golden family while Roby, a lieutenant in the 1st Infantry Division at Fort Riley, was in Saudi Arabia. They did this not because he needed it, but to show their care and concern for him and his family during the awful days of the Persian Gulf War.

One hundred ninety-one Southern Baptist chaplains served during the Gulf War period; one was Les Arnold, DOAM in Smoky Hill Association (*BD*, March 25, 1991). The Church Music Department of the KNCSB sent with him a hymn player, which turned out to be a valuable ministry tool. Arnold said,

"That was fantastic. All the chaplains were standing in line to use it."

Arnold held Bible studies, finally fourteen per week in seven different places; had counseling sessions at all times of the day and night, with colonels as well as airmen; set up a Kansas Country Store to deliver items addressed to "Any Soldier" (where Charmin toilet tissue proved to be a prize, due to the rough Saudi Arabian variety); helped soldiers deal with the possibility of death; and shared Jesus Christ with many, baptizing six of them in the Red Sea.

Churches near Fort Riley generated efforts to support families while husbands/fathers and mothers/wives were away. Churches teamed together under the leadership of John Lucas in a ministry called B-FOODS: Baptist Friends of Operation Desert Shield/Storm. The Korean Baptist Church of Central Kansas in Junction City was headquarters, and the ministry operated on Tuesday and Thursday afternoons to provide as much assistance as possible in the form of food and daily maintenance to whoever was in need. The VanBebbers at Crossroads Baptist Church set up a special service. Cheryl led a support group for wives whose husbands were away. There were about eight women and nineteen children in regular attendance. David VanBebber, the pastor of the church, took on the job of child care, which he said was not as taxing as taking a dozen Royal Ambassadors to a baseball game in Kansas City. College Heights in Manhattan offered "Wonderful Wednesdays" for respite child care. Churches most affected developed a family-to-family plan in which military families were adopted by non-military families.

These were dreadful days, and church families reached out to military members and to the whole community in marvelous ways: offering comfort and companionship, meeting physical needs, providing respite child care, and finding answers to questions. It was a time for loving neighbors in the way Jesus commanded, and church members rose to the occasion.

Ministry knows no geographical boundaries. Mary E. Speidel narrated a delightful incident, which was published in the *Digest* (February 26, 1990). Al Fraser, member of the Messiah Baptist Church in Leawood and a tractor salesman for a farm equipment company, traveled across western Kansas, displaying his wares in a great red-and-white tent. Putting up the tent was a hard job, and Fraser wondered why he was "breaking his back" learning how to do it. He found the answer when he went to Maracaibo for a week as a volunteer to work in an evangelistic crusade at the Capernaum Baptist Church.

One day, visiting in the home of the pastor of the church, he saw a great pile of red-and-white canvas. When he asked about it, he found it was a tent, bought by the church members, for a meeting place. Nobody knew how to put the thing up. When he examined it, he found it to be exactly like the old tent he had struggled with in Kansas. He knew, then, why he was in Maracaibo.

The story ended with these words, "Five years later, the tent Fraser installed is frayed and faded. But the 130-member Capernaum Church still worships under its shelter."

JUVENILE REHABILITATION PROGRAMS
(YOUTH AND FAMILY SERVICES)

A little later than the centers, another type of ministry was developed: Juvenile Rehabilitation Programs, later called Family and Youth Services. These programs today are part of the CSM Department of the KNCSB. The first program started in 1966 when Harry Moratto, pastor of the King's Highway Baptist Church in Wichita, accepted a part-time position jointly supported by Sedgwick Association and the Home Mission Board.

At the same time, Charles Vincent, pastor of First Southern in Kansas City, was doing an "unselfish and most successful volunteer work." By the end of his first year of ministry, Vincent and the church examined their ministry to deaf and to Cuban refugees and noted that these were factors in the growth of the church. Together they looked for other ways to extend the witness of the church beyond its walls. The pastor was asked to be chaplain for 350 police force personnel and their families, which led to other opportunities to work with the police department.

His work with the police and the Juvenile Court was quite successful. On Easter Sunday of 1967, of the 480 people in the First Southern Baptist Church service, sixty-two of them had been contacted through these programs. At that time he had thirty-five juvenile delinquent cases paroled to him by the courts. So successful was Vincent in his work with juvenile offenders and their families that he was named Kansas City's Outstanding Young Man of the Year by the Junior Chamber of Commerce.

By that time, the association was trying to get help from the Home Mission Board to continue and enlarge this work. Kaw Valley Association had voted to project such a program for 1967. John Cromer, pastor of Highland Park Baptist Church, was employed part-time as director of the program in Topeka during 1967. He was involved with the police in Kaw Valley Association through his work as a chaplain. His ministry touched youth and their families and included ex-prisoners and alcoholics. In 1970 he resigned his pastorate to give full-time to the work, by this time called Youth and Family Services.

Sedgwick Association—In 1966 (*BD*, January 29, 1966), Sam D. Russell, Sedgwick County associational missionary, announced that H. V. Moratto had been engaged as Juvenile Rehabilitation Director to establish a program in Wichita, which would utilize the laity of the churches in assisting young people in trouble with the law. These sponsors were to work in cooperation with and in support of the Juvenile Courts.

Moratto, as director, served mainly as a liaison between the home, court, and church. He attended court hearings, gathered pertinent facts about the child and his history, then enlisted a cooperating church closest to the youngster's home to furnish a sponsor.

Marjorie and Harry Moratto came from California to Wichita in 1959. When Meeler Markham, mission director for the state convention, and Sam

Russell came to him with the idea for a juvenile rehabilitation program, he said no. He was a pastor and to do anything else would be outside God's will for his life. Markam and Russell kept "badgering" him. So finally, Moratto agreed he would take on the job on a part-time basis to get it started, then he would go back to full-time pastoring. By the time summer came, he was "hooked." He resigned his church at the end of the year to take over the work full-time, and stayed with the program until his retirement in 1990, at which time, he kept at it in a part-time position.

The first meeting with the judge of the Juvenile Court was not terribly auspicious; the court did not need any more "bleeding hearts," he was told. Not daunted, Harry asked for permission to attend court sessions and talk with court personnel to learn about procedures and needs. This the judge allowed.

What he found were needy people, both children and their families. He enlisted churches to gather food and clothing and reading materials. On both the ninth floor of the county jail, where the boys were held, and in Friendly Gables, across town, where girls were held, he set up bookcases stocked with Bibles, magazines, and Christian "funny books." He found an old piano and had it refurbished for the first chapel service (BD, November 28, 1988).

He became a liaison between the children and Southern Baptist churches in the association and churches of other denominations—Methodist, Christian, Pentecostal; "everybody and every congregation that had any kind of kid that might have ended up being in the juvenile system."

Although he had a seminary degree, Moratto felt inadequate to deal with the situations he faced in this new job; he took courses in sociology and psychology at Friends University, enrolled in the pastoral counseling program at Wesley Medical Center, and then stayed on as chaplain. During this time he worked in the pediatric and teen areas of the hospital with critically ill children. This equipped him to help parents who were facing hard times with their youngsters.

By 1975 legislation was passed to close Friendly Gables and build a coed facility for juvenile offenders. Moratto designed a program for the position of chaplain and was given that post. In addition to being available to the youngsters every day, he began a Sunday School class and enlisted churches in the area to be responsible for this service. In the summer time he led "Serendipity," a six-week program for kids not in school, including crafts, music, and Vacation Bible School (BD, November 29, 1988).

Holidays are bad times for the children. By Christmas of 1976, the Morattos began a Christmas ritual which they continued through the years and which involved the whole Moratto family. It began with breakfast, a special one. On the menu were things the children liked: eggs, sausage, and pancakes, all cooked to order. There were gifts for everyone, given by the churches in Wichita. After their own children were grown and away from home, the Morattos enlisted other young adults, college students, and retired folks to share this time with them. Even after retirement in 1990, Moratto continued the Christmas Event. They also helped the children celebrate Thanksgiving and birthdays. Some children had their first birthday cake because of the Morattos.

One day an Hispanic child asked Moratto who he was, since he looked and dressed a bit differently from others working there. He told the boy he was a chaplain, and then explained that he was a kind of preacher or priest. The child was familiar with this and stated, "Then you know about God." Moratto said yes, he did know about God, and asked, "Do you know anything about Him?" The child answered, "Nope, but I need to know."

With a *Good News for Modern Man* New Testament in hand, Moratto and the boy walked down the Roman Road together. Moratto explained about Jesus and His way; the boy accepted Christ as his Savior. Later in the week, as Moratto sat around talking to children during the noon hour, as was his custom, he heard a voice call, "Hey, preacher man. This is my friend, Fred. He needs to know about Jesus just like you told me. Come tell him about Jesus." It was the young Mexican boy. Such experiences came again and again.

Moratto ministered to the children and to their families in hard times, sad times, and joyous times. He has performed weddings and funerals, and given support. Someone asked him how many baptisms he had out of the center. Not a one, was his answer. "That wasn't the role that God called me to do; He called me to sow seed."

From time to time he meets boys and girls, now grown up, to whom he ministered: a receptionist in a television station who remembered him; a young contractor who did some work on his house; a young man working in a service station; and others in the hospital and in the mall.

In 1988 (*BD*, November 28, 1988), Moratto was given the Citizen Recognition Award by the Kansas Correctional Association in honor of his thirteen years as a volunteer chaplain for the Youth Residence Hall. In the nomination letter, Marla Sutton, administrative officer of the Youth Residence Hall, wrote, "Every facility in the state of Kansas should have a Harry Moratto."

Moratto ended his taped interview, "Christian Social Ministries was not a social gospel, but was meeting people in a social relationship, sharing with them the claims of Jesus Christ on their lives. There have been hundreds and hundreds and hundreds of people from our Southern Baptist churches, from the Methodist church, the Christian church, Black congregations, Seventh Day Adventists, Pentecostal church. Men who came as a Bible study group out of Boeing had chapel services. The Christian Motorcycle Association is still passing out New Testaments to these boys and girls and sharing Christ. The work was begun; is still going on."

Kansas City, Kansas—John Hopkins began his work with juvenile rehabilitation in a quite different way. Hopkins, a retired Army officer and native of Texas, came to the Midwest in August 1968 (*BD*, May 31, 1969). He had served in the army as a criminal investigator focusing on deviant behavior and crime causation. He was trained as a sociologist. When he was ready to retire, quite early in his life, and looking for another area of work, his wife read an article in *Royal Service* about the board's interest in juvenile delinquency programs. Because of his training, he applied for a job with the Home Mission Board. While Hopkins was in school in Omaha, he met Peck Lindsay, who put him touch with Paul Elledge, DOAM in the Kansas City, Kansas, Association. Elledge was looking for a CSM director for Youth and Family Services. The Juvenile Rehabilitation Program had been broadened to include the concept of families as well as youth in trouble. Thus, Hopkins was assigned to CSM in the Kansas Convention in 1968.

Paul Elledge remembers this contact, too. He said, "Let me tell you a little known admirable fact about John Hopkins. Since we could do nothing for him in support of his work, I suggested that he try to find something he could do without monetary support from the association. He did just that.

"One day John walked into my office with an arrangement that amazed me. He had made an agreement with the Wyandotte County Court to set up a work with the Juvenile Department. It was free of charge and staffed by volunteers. He did an outstanding job, but because of the nature of his work, little was ever known about it and he got little credit for a job well done." Elledge considers the work which Hopkins put in motion without funds one of the "blessings" of the CLA crisis.

Hopkins began by contacting Judge Francis J. Donnelly, of the Wyandotte County Probate and Juvenile Court, and Patrick J. Finley, director of the county's juvenile court services, to recommend a denominational volunteer youth program with, of course, the enthusiastic backing of Kansas City, Kansas, Baptist congregations. Both Donnelly and Finley had felt for a long time that a volunteer program was the only way to go, and then along came Hopkins. He was welcomed with open arms and named director of volunteer services. He immediately enlisted and trained volunteers who worked with the youngsters in a one-to-one relationship. At the time, Hopkins was working on a doctorate at Midwestern Seminary, and he and a student from KU wrote a grant and received funds through the Law Enforcement Act for the administrative needs of the program.

The volunteers were everyperson: night watchmen, railroad workers, school teachers, ministers, motor car mechanics, carpenters, utility workers, nurses, housewives, architects, graduate students, and county employees. Each one was expected to spend an hour a week with a juvenile in trouble. Almost always, the time spent was much more than that. They broke up neighborhood feuds, found employment for those thought to be unemployable, and served as advocates for youngsters in need of a friend at school or at home or in court. They showed kids how to fish, take pictures, and bake bread. Many became "the inspiring other" in a child's life.

A quite important "first step," which was accomplished by Shirley Hopkins and her Sunday School class, was revamping the court's records system. This was before the days of computers, so getting the files in order was a great help to everyone and impressed the "higher powers" in the court.

John Hopkins continued to work with the court through a corps of volunteers until 1974, when he was appointed as the CSM consultant for the KNCSB. Later on, the court saw the value of this support program, set up a department, and employed personnel to do the work. Hopkins thinks it has probably lost some of its effectiveness because, even though paid staff may be quite competent people, they do not have the same "mandate for ministry" as those who volunteered from the churches.

This "mandate" led to the establishment of a number of services for the children and families in the area. For example, literacy was a problem. There was a need for tutoring and remedial school work. One of the real pay-off programs Hopkins established was a ten-week reading program in a church not far from a school. It was staffed for the most part by volunteers, but was formatted by a Home Mission Board missionary who was in Kansas City on temporary assignment. An educator by training, she set up the program and trained the volunteers. The program was a great hit with the children and their families; it was so popular there had to be a door tender to keep out those who had not enrolled and for whom there was no room. At the end of ten weeks, reading proficiency had increased by a full grade level.

Hopkins planned a special worship service on Sunday mornings. It was not only for the children in the detention center, but also for the church people who planned the service. In order to make it real, everybody was invited to come on Saturday night for a party. It was a time when the church kids found out the kids in the center were not gangsters and the kids in the center discovered the church kids were not too bad.

Another service in the Kansas City, Kansas, area is food distribution through the Wyandotte Ministries, begun about 1980. In 1993 the association distributed about 39,000 pounds of food to 4,400 families in the commodity program. In addition, there was distribution of emergency food baskets, 40,000 pounds to 647 families with 2,500 children. Shirley Hopkins works with this program which is now located in the basement of the New Horizons Missionary Baptist Church. John Hopkins suggested it is a good witness for the church to be the place where distribution of commodity foods is done. It brings people into the church where they can see available literature, resources, and smiling faces of Christian volunteers.

Steve Aycock described Wyandotte Ministries (*BD*, August 9, 1982) as "truly a broad-based community-wide project of caring." Working within a coalition of helping agencies, this program has distributed about three-quarters of a ton of United States Department of Agriculture surplus cheese to families who met government guidelines. Through contact with these families volunteers discovered many other family needs. A food closet was set up in First Baptist Church of Bethel, Kansas City. Food donations came from churches of all denominations throughout the city. One of the volunteers confessed that it was "hard" to work in the program. As she finished filling a box of groceries, she shook her head in disbelief, "Their utilities had been cut off. I had to give her stuff she could cook over an open fire in the backyard. Right here in Kansas City!"

Wyandotte Ministries was incorporated as Southern Baptist Ministries under the non-profit laws of the State of Kansas. It is a subordinate corporation to the KNCSB. John Hopkins serves as executive director, Shirley Hopkins serves as director of family services, and C. T. Cunningham serves as director of pastoral care and programs coordinator. T. R. and Reba Henry have served with the program as full-time Mission Service Corps Volunteers for thirteen years. About eighty volunteers serve in various aspects of the program during the year; a number have served in excess of ten years.

The main objective of Wyandotte Ministries is to "break the cycle of poverty and dependency by providing assistance and council in the areas of employment, education, child care and nutrition, money management, food preparation, drug and alcohol abuse, health, family enrichment, and Christian living" (*BD,* March 26, 1990).

Smoky Hill—John and Patty Lucas came to Smoky Hill Association because Charlie Russell, pastor of First Southern, Junction City, got an idea and dreamed a dream. At a Kiwanis Club meeting, Russell was introduced to the Court Appointed Special Advocate (CASA) program, which is designed to help abused or neglected children through the court system. This was a new route for Southern Baptists. Les Arnold, DOAM in Smoky Hill, bought into the dream, and contacted John Hopkins, who was by this time CSM consultant for KNCSB. Hopkins contacted John Lucas, who was serving with Wyandotte Ministries in Kansas City, Kansas, Baptist Association. The Lucases visited Junction City, saw the need, and began the process of being appointed through the Home Mission Board. They went to Junction City in 1988.

Junction City is located at the edge of Fort Riley, with a large ethnic population, including African Americans, Koreans, and Spanish-speaking. It is in a county (Geary) often in the upper five percent of Kansas counties in cases of child abuse and neglect.

The program, which began in 1989, operated with volunteers, carefully selected and extensively trained, and finally sworn in through the court system. Southern Baptists were not the only volunteers. In Junction City, local Presbyterians were committed to CASA as a long-term missions project. Christians of other faiths were also involved.

There are about 390 CASA programs in the United States, but this may be the only one that was organized on Christian principles and which looked for Christians to serve on the board and as volunteers. The program's aim was to focus on the needs of the child and on the child's family. The volunteers were to get to know the children, then write reports including recommendations for best treatment of each child. Because of the work of CASA volunteers, a child's case might well be processed in as little as eighteen months with a positive ending benefitting the child. Otherwise, the child might be shuffled though the juvenile court system until the age of eighteen.

When John and Patty Lucas began this program, they were supported through the Cooperative Program and the Annie Armstrong Home Missions Offering. Other program costs were supported through the United Way and other funding from the community. From the very first, John Lucas wanted this program to develop into a community-based program with leadership from the community. This would free him and his wife to move into other services.

KNCSB DISASTER ASSISTANCE PROGRAM

When the time was right, John and Patty Lucas moved out of the CASA program and began other programs in the association. Hopkins described John as "up to his eyeballs in disaster relief." He has taken all the Red Cross training and all the FEMA training available, conducts disaster training for groups over the Convention, and is fully involved with agencies outside the church that are doing Disaster Relief. This community involvement is what Hopkins calls "the genius of the Christian Social Ministries program."

Early in our history, this visible CSM action appeared as a brief report in the 1951 *Annual*: "Due to the emergency brought into the experience of some of our churches by the July floods, August 19 was designated as Flood Relief Day. An appeal for $4,000 with which to rehabilitate damaged churches was authorized." There is no record of whether or not this goal was met. Baptists in Kansas and Nebraska have always been able and willing to stand in the breach, to help make things right when a crisis occurs.

An item in the *Digest* in 1960 (June 28) also highlighted this kind of care and concern. The Glen Gottula family, who lived in the Indian village area near Salina, lost everything when a tornado struck. The family took refuge in the bathtub, as the fury of the storm rose. When it was over, the bathroom was the only room in the house left standing. Their home and possessions gone, First Southern Baptist Church stood in the breach. Out of their limited resources the church shared with this family.

In 1969 Kansas City, Kansas, Association joined with Baptists in Kansas City, Missouri, and took part in "Operation Camille," a crash program to aid those left destitute by the fury of the hurricane which struck Florida in 1967 (*BD*, September 6, 1967). In a matter of hours, seventeen Baptist churches became collection stations, handing out instructions and answering scores of questions on constantly ringing telephones. Responses came from people of every denomination and racial background, rich and poor, laborer and executive. The appeal reached other towns through television, radio stations, and newspapers. Needed items were brought from the area surrounding Kansas City. Volunteers worked "around the clock" receiving, packing, and moving out the supplies that were brought. In seventy-two hours literally tons of canned foods, baby diapers and formula, children's underwear, sheets, pillows, and blankets poured into collection stations. Local firms donated supplies and transportation. The project, coordinated by the Red Cross, was indeed a wonderful example of people reaching out to people.

Concern for people in this sort of distress led in 1978 to a major focus, the development of the KNCSB Disaster Assistance Program under the direction of Hopkins, designed to minister to individuals suffering from the results of natural disasters. By 1983 a variety of projects had been carried out with the disaster team's mobile ministries unit, a tractor-trailer vehicle which was used as a rest and information station at state, county, and regional fairs. It also has been used in ministry to truckers, holiday travelers, and to haul tons of food donated to the needy. This first disaster relief unit was the responsibility of a Mission Service Corps couple, T. R. and Reba Henry. They have worked with Wyandotte Southern Baptist Ministries for twelve years (*Baptist History and Heritage*, July 1994). Henry designed the first disaster unit by building a compartment in the trailer to store equipment, and adding a small kitchen and a bathroom area that took care of the crew. A little over half the trailer was open, which he carpeted, paneled, and dropped the ceiling. This made a comfortable room which is used in many ways: nurse's station, interview area, command post, and sanctuary for a little church on Sunday morning.

The eighteen-wheeler was disposed of in favor of a small twenty-foot trailer with a box truck, sort of like a car hauler for transport of automobiles. Again, the unit was designed and built by Henry. In it there is cooking equipment, an awning that spreads out, propane gas system, hot and cold water and, as Hopkins put it, "the whole nine yards."

"At the relief shelters they try to make people comfortable and secure. We have devotions and singing until they fall asleep," Reba Henry explained (*Baptist History and Heritage*, July 1994). The 1983 report (*Annual*) concluded, "The prayerful support of Christian Ministries personnel and their ministry efforts is encouraged. They are deeply committed to the task of carrying the message of Christian love and concern to all people. Their ministry caused them to drive 98,000 miles and has resulted in 70 professions of faith and 31 baptisms this year."

In 1988 (*BD*, November 28, 1988), a tornado swept through Topeka at the time of the annual meeting of the Convention. On-the-spot members of the disaster relief team joined with local agencies in recovery operations, and were able to minister to the psychological as well as physical needs of people in the area. The tornado's path came within a mile of First Southern Baptist Church and heavily damaged a section where messengers had been having lunch just an hour earlier.

All disaster assistance is not delivered by an official team. In March 1990 (*BD*, March 26, 1990), a major tornado touched down in Hesston. The pastor and members of Immanuel Baptist Church in Newton were on the job within fifteen minutes; volunteers from seven churches in Wichita plus students involved in the Baptist Student Union at WSU assisted with recovery efforts. John Hopkins commended the people for their caring response.

The KNCSB disaster relief team went to Wichita in 1991 (*BD*, May 20, 1991) in the wake of a tornado. The seven-member team, assisted by dozens of volunteers, prepared about 4,500 meals a day: breakfast, a hot evening meal, and sandwiches and beverages throughout the day. When Harry Moratto sent out a call for food, Wichitans responded; in four or five days, the people made about fifteen thousand sandwiches. Church buildings were opened for refuge, showers, and food. Just as important was the comfort and caring exhibited by people all around the destroyed area.

And then came the 1993 flood. Again the disaster team went to work, beginning in mid-July in Kansas City, Kansas, and very soon hundreds of volunteers were involved in providing food and manning a shelter for displaced families from July to August 14. There were so many volunteers at the very beginning, Hopkins said (*BD*, August 23, 1993), that they had to "wait." After the flood waters receded, everyone was needed to help with cleanup and repair.

The relief team also worked at Junction City, where Milford Reservoir reached capacity and thousands of acres were flooded, forcing about two thousand people to move to shelters. John Lucas, director of church and community missions in Smoky Hill Association, was coordinator of the shelter which was open from July 19 to August 2.

The team went to Wathena, Kansas, to work with volunteers who were sandbagging dikes along the west bank of the Missouri River. They distributed five hundred sandwiches an hour to workers. Then they went to Auburn, Nebraska, where volunteers from the community and from Fort Worth, Texas, were on the job. They worked also in Peru, Nebraska, about twelve miles from Auburn, as a clean-up crew. The children and staff enrolled in Vacation Bible School in the Baptist church at Papillion gave an offering of more than a thousand dollars for flood relief at Peru. These flood-relief efforts, according to Floyd Butts, pastor of Auburn Baptist Church, established credibility for Southern Baptists in Peru, where he had not been able to even begin a Bible study group.

By October 1993 (*BD*, October 29, 1993), Southern Baptists from Kansas-Nebraska and across the country had given about $8,100 to the KNCSB Flood Relief Fund; of that, $2,686 came from Nevada Baptists. This was their first "partnership" act with our two-state convention.

TRUCK-STOP MINISTRY

John and Patty Lucas began a truck-stop ministry in which volunteers from many churches in Smoky Hill Association are involved. At Bosselman's

Truck Stop at Exit 253 on I-70, the managers gave space for a service each Sunday. At 9:00 A.M., through the loud speaker, over the roar of eighteen-wheelers, comes the call to worship. Truckers from more than forty-three states have heeded the call. Two miles away, at the crossing of I-70 and US-81, twenty thousand cars and trucks go by daily. To the truck stop, groups come from various communities from time to time to share music and testimonies. Also, "care bags," including Christian tracts and personal items, are prepared for the drivers, possible in part because of Christmas in August and Gideons International. At least once, John has received a letter from the wife of a trucker who had stopped by, expressing her thanks for this kind of care and concern for her husband. In addition to the regular services, there is opportunity to work with truckers on a one-to-one basis, and to offer comfort and support along the road. John had a prayer time with one trucker whose brother was dying of cancer, and the driver was able to go on his way with renewed strength because of a shared burden.

Much earlier than this, James Griffin, who came to Kansas from Fort Smith, Arkansas, to serve as DOAM in Kansas City, Kansas, Baptist Association, along with Les Arnold, who now holds this position in Smoky Hill Association, began a ministry at the Mid-America Truck Stop on I-35. The associational offices were located in Olathe in a beautiful old home which included a swimming pool, a gym, and an area suitable for soft ball, volleyball, and other recreational activities.

The truckers came to this place for swimming and exercise, and stayed for a time of Bible study. While swim shorts were provided for the men, nothing was kept on hand for women truckers. One afternoon, a woman came who was equal to the situation. She peeled off down to her underwear and enjoyed the pool along with the men.

The ministry was the "target" of WMU Christmas in August one year. Packages were received from more than five hundred churches, including one or two from Hawaii and Germany. The items received were packed into convenient kits by women and children and passed along to the truckers.

Since that time, this property has been sold. The money was placed in a foundation which is used for church growth in Kansas City.

WITH THE NATIONAL BAPTIST CONVENTION (BLACK)

By 1966 money was available for organized aid and fellowship to the National Baptist Convention. Sedgwick Association was the main thrust; there was money to help to send a group of black children from the Baptist Neighborhood Center to camp; and a number of WSU football players were given scholarships to attend the National Fellowship of Christian Athletes Camp in Colorado.

Another ministry was in relation to the Prayer Movement sponsored by David Gray of the Pleasant Green Baptist Church in Kansas City. Gray was presented with a check for one thousand dollars from the Convention and Home Mission Board to apply to the sixty-thousand-dollar cost of building a "prayer house" for youth in the northeast section of Kansas City. This was an effort to reach youth on the streets late at night in the nightclub area of Kansas City by providing a coffee house operation along the same street where many of the night spots existed. Gray said, "It bothers me to pass along the streets and see all these kids milling around with no place to go." He had lived in the area when he was growing up and returned to minister as an adult. He continued, "In order to really appreciate what goes on, you would have to be down in that area at 2:00 or 3:00 in the morning during the summer to see the throngs. Because they are too young to get in the key clubs located in the area, they just mill around with no place to go." Gray saw the "prayer house" as a place where there would be food, entertainment, religious services, counselors for the kids with problems, and the services of a full-time staff.

Joint meetings between African American and Anglo ministers were conducted through the United Prayer Movement, which began in March 1968. Both races took part in a worship service and in a prayer workshop and rally. The purpose of these meetings was "to enable Christians to find deeper levels of mutual understanding, and to let God bring a true appreciation and love for one another."

For two years, a scholarship was awarded to Chuck Alexander, enrolled at KU, who worked among several SBC and National Baptist churches to strengthen relationships and increase understanding. On several occasions, a bus was chartered to help black students attend the National Black Student Conference. A student from KU, Timothy Sims, was elected president of the National Black Student Union. In 1983 (*Annual*) as a result of the work done with these students, at least one black Baptist church, Victory Bible Church in Lawrence, petitioned the local association to become a cooperating Southern Baptist Church. It was also out of these meetings that Harambee was organized on the KU campus, an organization especially for black students.

Existing centers and programs were given special help to reach black children and families in their areas. For example, Kansas City Association was able to bring a black Associational Sunday School Improvement Team (ASSIST) from Chicago to work in the Kansas City area.

REFUGEES

"Southern Baptists have resettled only 101 Cuban refugees" was the lead sentence in an article in *Digest* (September 15, 1962). "Just think, ten million born-again Christians, dedicated to showing Christ to the world, and emulating His love and compassion, have resettled only . . . 27 families in all." A note at the end of article stated, "Since this was written, First Southern of Kansas City, Kansas (John McBain, pastor), has begun plans for resettling a

Cuban family." Every experience cannot be recounted, but it really happened. Time and again, churches held out their hands and opened their hearts to displaced persons from outside the United States.

The words spoken by a young Cuban woman (*BD*, November 3, 1962), who with her family was greeted in the Kansas City airport by more than a hundred members of the First Southern Baptist Church of that city, were heartwarming, "In Cuba they told us there was a country like this, but I didn't believe it." It was truly a new beginning for this family.

"Fresh from the oppression of Cuba, and the worries of refugee-crowded Miami, Florida, Mrs. Othoniel Castro wept openly when she and her family were given a warm welcome as they arrived in Kansas City in October." And it went on and on (*BD*, March 27, 1965). Once the Castros were settled, they sponsored two of her cousins; next came the parents of one of the cousins, sponsored by First Nazarene Church. The total was up to eight. Then two more relatives of the cousins came, then Mrs. Castor's brother; the total was eleven. Nearby Leawood sponsored the next group of three, also relatives of the Castros. The Berean Baptist Church sponsored the next group of four, who were related to the original Otheniel Castro—his brother and wife and their daughter, and the mother of Otheniel and Miguel. It was a grand family reunion.

In January 1963 (*BD*, January 5, 1963), Olivet Baptist Church of Wichita welcomed another Cuban family, the Bustamentes, to a neat, white frame house on West 9th Street in Wichita. Mr. Bustamante was a college graduate and an experienced bookkeeper-office manager. When they left Cuba, they were allowed to bring almost nothing with them. Even Mrs. Bustamante's wedding ring had to be surrendered.

At that time, Southern Baptists were providing on-the-spot relief for the refugees; the Home Mission Board was appealing to Baptist churches to sponsor refugees so they could move out of Miami into places where they could be self-supporting. The Wichita church responded to this, and the process began. The church rented a two-bedroom house; members and friends donated "good substantial furniture," said Gordon Dorian, pastor of the church. "We didn't want any junk for these people."

Church members cleaned and polished the whole house and everything in it. All things were ready, even curtains at the windows, when the family arrived. There was money for groceries; Steffen Dairy Foods provided milk for a month; and Ark Valley Bakery supplied a month's bread for the family.

"This has been a wonderful thing for our church," Dorian reported. "It has opened our eyes to the needs of other people. We read about them in the newspapers, but when we see people like this, hear from them what Cubans are suffering, it makes us realize how little we have been doing."

At times such ministries to people from other countries were not nearly so formal. An item in the *Digest* (January 13, 1962) related a heart-warming Christmas experience of members of Ellinwood, Calvary, as they played host to two international students, seniors at North High in Wichita, one from Japan, the other from El Salvador. "The boys spent the holidays in the homes of several different members of the church and were entertained with real Western Kansas hospitality. Among new experiences for them were ice-skating and eating pheasant and deer."

First Southern Baptist Church at Lawrence adopted two families, one from Vietnam, in 1975, and one from Russia, in 1992. The Vietnamese family included the parents, children, and an orphaned niece they brought with them. The wife told how frightened they were as they dashed to the plane to leave, with bullets flying around them. She took off her shoes in order to run faster, and so arrived shoeless at a refugee camp, which was their first stop.

The whole church had a part in planning for this family. Committees were organized to take care of various needs: housing, furnishings, financial planning and banking, and employment. It was a good experience for everyone. As soon as the family was able to do so, they left Lawrence and joined family members in California.

The other family was a young couple who wanted to come to the United States to study; they were friends of a couple already in the church, one of whom came from Russia. There was already a Russian congregation in Lawrence, and since the young man was an ordained minister and wanted an opportunity to preach, they very quickly moved to a Russian settlement.

INTERNATIONALS—LITERACY

In 1979 Viola Webb served as international consultant as well as WMU director of the KNCSB. She reported on an International Student Conference held in 1981, at Camp Shiloh in Wichita, beginning on Wednesday and closing at noon on Sunday. There were thirty-seven international students from sixteen countries, and students from four campuses.

There were fifteen Muslims from Tunisia, the first time any Muslims had attended. Mrs. Webb wrote, "I could sense the spirit of suspicion or concern about the Christian atmosphere, but the Lord was with us all the way through."

On Thursday there was a traditional American Thanksgiving dinner; another day there was a tour of the Cosmosphere in Hutchinson. There was entertainment from a music group from Wichita, ball games in the gym, and dinners at various churches.

This was not the first International Conference held; the first ones had been held under the direction of Ray Gilliland when the students and their international guests gathered in the late 1960s. Webb revived this practice because of her deep concern for and interest in internationals.

Another way churches have ministered to internationals is through literacy missions ministries—conversational English, adult reading and writing, and after-school tutoring. Carol Ann Holcomb worked as a summer missionary in 1964 in Alaska with Louise Yarbrough. Yarbrough, who was WMU director of Alaska and later full-time literacy worker, sees this as an open door for ministry to internationals. Holcomb caught the vision of what this kind of teaching and friendship could mean to a person far away from home. When she came to College Heights Baptist Church, Manhattan, she found her ministry in literacy missions, a way to do foreign missions at home (*BD*, April 27, 1992).

The ministry began in 1982 when four women from College Heights, after meeting with Peter Hong, at that time pastor of the Junction City Korean Church, began to teach English to forty-one Korean adults. In 1983 the ministry was moved to Manhattan. In 1991 a class was added to assist with preparing for the U.S. Naturalization Examination. In 1987 an International Sunday School class was begun; more than one hundred bilingual Bibles have been distributed through this class. In 1988 a special class for international adults was provided during the Vacation Bible School program. By 1992 the conversational English program had ministered to 345 persons from forty-four countries, about three-fourths of whom are women. Since most of them are in the program only one year, there is only a brief time for impact. These women are bright, many with careers of their own which they have interrupted to come to the U.S. so that their husbands can earn degrees. Many will go back to their own countries into places of leadership. It is important that among the things they take back will be knowledge of and commitment to Jesus Christ. A number of churches in Kansas and Nebraska have begun such programs.

Jim and Ruth Fuller worked with Southeast Asia people in Wichita. As they shared with the students at Midwestern Seminary's World Missions Day (*BD*, October 24, 1988), they touched on a vital facet of working with internationals as they told about their work with just one woman. One must be willing to be involved with all parts of the lives of those to whom they would minister. When the woman's husband divorced her, the Fullers helped her find a job to support herself and her young daughter; they taught her to speak English. They were her friends. When she discovered she had cancer, she asked the Fullers to take care of her daughter after she died. They agreed and are raising the child as their own. Jim Fuller said, "Being a missionary is not a job, it's a lifestyle." All ministry is a lifestyle, not just an activity.

INTERFAITH WITNESS

A new emphasis, Interfaith Witness, was added to the work of the KNCSB in 1982 under the direction of Dewey Hickey. This is not a responsibility of the CSM Department, but it seems to continue the outreach to ethnics and prepare people for the important task of sharing the Good News with them. The purposes of Interfaith Witness are two-fold: (1) To make Baptists aware of persons of other religious persuasions in their midst; and (2) to encourage, enable, and equip Baptists to bear an effective witness to implement Bold Mission Thrust.

In 1983 eight people received training as Interfaith Witness associates with the Home Mission Board in the area of Mormonism; later, Interfaith Witness Awareness Conferences were conducted in various parts of the Convention. In 1987 Ken James, now regional director of Midwest-Great Plains Area with the Home Mission Board, became the coordinator of this program. Other areas of training included Judaism, Jehovah's Witness, New Age, and Islam. Roy Moody now is coordinator of this program for KNCSB.

In an insightful article in the *Digest* (May 22, 1989), Interfaith Witness was named as one of the most important mission programs in the SBC because of the growth of religious pluralism in the country. The world has literally come to our door. By the year 2,000 there could be more Muslims in American than Jews, and hundreds of short-lived millennial religions. We must understand other religious systems in order to be able to witness effectively.

CHRISTIAN SOCIAL MINISTRIES

In 1976 (*Annual*) CSM were reported through Baptist Centers, church community weekday ministries, youth and family services, literacy ministries, rehabilitation work with drug abusers and prisoners, and ministries to senior citizens. At that time there were six couples and two other individuals either full-time or part-time in this work. "These missionaries have dedicated themselves to the task of leading Christians to demonstrate their Christ-likeness just as Jesus demonstrated that he was the Christ. Matthew tells us that Jesus offered as proof his ministry to those individuals normally ignored and forgotten by the mainstream of society."

Areas of ministry covered by CSM include working with troubled youth and their families, prisoners, the elderly, and those suffering the consequences of drug and alcohol abuse. Programs have been developed to assist the economically disadvantaged, providing food, clothing, and rent and utility assistance.

What a difference comes because of the choice we make—the high road of servanthood or the low road of self-indulgence. The high road is seeing the needs of people around us as Jesus sees needs and people. The low road is the "me-ism" of self-gratification, comfortable churches, and unconcern. Inasmuch as we reach out to these, the ones far from home, the ones in poverty and distress, the ones in trouble, the ones in prison, the illiterate, the homeless, the hungry, those who cry and have none to comfort them . . . inasmuch as we reach out to these, we serve the Lord we love.

Women with a Mission

PAUL ONLY ONCE IN A WHILE ALLUDED TO THE ACTIVITY OF women in the early church: "Help those women who have contended at my side in the cause of the gospel" (Phil. 4:3). Not much detail is given about women, even about those who were first to the tomb, or about Sapphira and Lydia in whose homes churches were begun. So it is with the *Annuals* of the KNSCB. With few exceptions, we must read between the lines to discover the mighty role of women in the early days of the beginning and growth of the Convention. We might well borrow the approach Catherine Allen took (*Laborers Together With God*, WMU, 1987), when she presented the stories of twenty-two great women in Baptist life. She paraphrased the words of Jesus: "Let her alone . . . she hath done what she couldn't" (Mark 14:6-8). For Allen, these words characterized the untiring energy and distinguished accomplishments of women against extreme odds. So it was—and to a great extent, still is—in Kansas and Nebraska.

According to a report published in the *Beams* (November 1946), "a goodly number of Kansas Southern Baptist women met together, Monday, October 14, at Burden a short time before the opening session of the First Annual Convention of Kansas Southern Baptist Convention for the purpose of organizing Woman's Missionary Union, Auxiliary to Kansas Convention of Southern Baptist Churches." Likely Orbie Clem, the editor, was referring to the formal designation of the status of "auxiliary" by the Convention. According to a brief review of history, which Lois Bondurant Clem included in her 1951 report to the Convention, WMU had been officially set in place by the women on March 20, 1946 (*Annual*, 1951).

On October 14, 1946, between sessions of the first annual meeting of the Convention, the constitution and by-laws were adopted and officers for the

194

next year elected. The officers included the president, Mrs. J. D. Williamson of Burden Church; vice-presidents from Cherryvale and Wichita (representing the two Zones); and a young people's secretary, Mrs. R. W. Preboth. Also, committee chairs were named for community missions, Margaret Fund, mission study, stewardship, white cross, and nominations. Mrs. Orbie Clem, who was elected executive secretary-treasurer, served without pay until 1950, and then with salary, albeit a small one, until 1953, when she left Kansas with her husband, who had taken another position.

At the Convention meeting in 1949, a motion passed: "Funds for the salary of the WMU Executive Secretary-Treasurer are to be derived from the State Mission offerings and they are to start receiving the money monthly when they have secured the full-time service of a reliable person to fill this office. By their request all of their funds for State Missions are to be included and paid out of the general budget of our Convention."

In 1952, when the Executive Board met on July 15, there was an announcement that the Home Mission Board had allocated $2,100 for the current year to be applied toward the salary of the WMU executive secretary-treasurer. This was the result of a special designation for Kansas through the Annie Armstrong Offering by the Texas WMU (*Annual*, 1952). Such an allocation from the Home Mission Board for WMU continues to this day.

In the November 1946 *BEAMS*, Mrs. Clem gave general direction for first steps in organizing the WMU family in the local church. She suggested ordering a number of materials, including the 1947 WMU *Yearbook* at a cost of ten cents, for each officer, and asking for free literature, sending along enough money for postage. The women were encouraged to order *Royal Service* at fifty cents a year, *World Comrades*, *Ambassador Life*, and *The Window of YWA*, each one dollar a year. Materials for the leaders of Sunbeam Bands, which included boys and girls from birth to age eight, were included in *World Comrades*. The women were urged to observe the Week of Prayer with the Lottie Moon Christmas Offering for Foreign Missions in December.

This was not the beginning of WMU in Kansas; women had been active in their churches and in the formation of the fellowship from the very beginning. In a meeting on November 26 and 27, 1945, at the time of the organization of the KSBF, Mrs. J. D. Williamson, Burden Baptist Church, was elected chair of women's work, which was called the "Women's Assembly." An interesting insight to this action comes from the minutes (typed) of the fellowship meeting. Clem moved that the body elect a director of publicity for the WMU. After discussion, the motion was amended to read: "that we change the name of Director of Publicity of WMU to Chairman of Women's Assembly." The amendment and motion were passed. Mrs. Ethel Coleman and Mrs. J. D. Williamson were nominated; Mrs. Williamson was elected.

At that time the state was divided into Eastern and Western Zones. A meeting in the Eastern Zone was held in January in Baxter Springs, where Mrs. Williamson made her first presentation on "WMU Objectives." A WMU president was elected for the Eastern Zone, and a month later at a Western Zone meeting, at Calvary Church in Ellinwood, a president for that zone was elected. Things moved quickly; on March 19, 1946, in the basement of the Chetopa Church, an organization was formed which was called KCSBC. On March 20 the women met and organized Kansas WMU, electing Mrs. J. D. Williamson as president. Mrs. Clem was asked to serve as executive secretary-treasurer. At the Chetopa organization meeting, a scheduled program item was the WMU Board gathering at 1:00 P.M.

The second meeting of the state WMU took place three months later at Airlane Baptist Church in Wichita with twenty-two women present from five churches. The third WMU meeting took place the same year at the First Baptist Church, Burden. On that occasion, Mrs. Berta K. Spooner, who was secretary-treasurer of Oklahoma WMU, was guest speaker. She stayed after the meeting to help draft the first constitution and by-laws. There were forty-three women present from four churches.

Based on the work the women began in March and continued through the year, Article VI of the By-Laws of the KCSBC read as follows: "Section I: This Convention shall recognize the W.M.U. as an Auxiliary of the Convention. Section 2: The W.M.U., Auxiliary, shall write its own Constitution and By-Laws, outline its own programs, and elect its own officers and Board. The Convention shall have no voice except in case the above action of W.M.U. shall violate the Constitution and By-laws of the Convention or its purpose and spirit in any manner." This auxiliary relationship remained intact until 1957, when WMU became a department of the state Convention.

At the first annual meeting of the Convention at the First Baptist Church of Burden in October 1946 there was a scheduled report from WMU, Auxiliary to the KCSB. Very early the women went to work on their own projects. In the report of the 1946 annual meeting of the Convention, this piece of business was transacted: "October 27 designated as State Missions Day in all of our churches. This will follow the inspiring emphasis placed on the Day of Prayer for State Missions by the WMU earlier this month."

In 1951 Kansas WMU, for the first time, was responsible for program preparation and follow-up for the State Missions Day of Prayer. Up to that time, N. J. Westmoreland had prepared the material; it was a Convention undertaking.

In March 1956, the first Woman's Missionary Society was organized in Nebraska at First Southern (Southview) in Lincoln. Mission groups for children were organized in October. All met in homes, since there was no church building at the time.

In 1957 Ethmer Kordis, chair of the Nominating Committee of the state WMU, wrote to Mrs. Jack Adkisson, wife of the pastor at Hillcrest in Omaha: "The women of Kansas would particularly like to have a representative from Nebraska on our State Board and wondered whether it would be possible for you to serve as a two-year Board member, 1957-58 and 1958-59? It is our sincere prayer that this will be possible for you" (Huddlestun, 1966). Mrs. Adkisson evidently agreed to this, for Viola Webb "informed" her that she had been placed on the Young People's Committee and on the YWA subcommittee.

In 1957 Nebraska women attended the "Leadership Tour" meeting held at First Southern Baptist, Topeka. It was no small matter for the women from Nebraska to get to associational meetings; they had to drive about 140 miles to each one. Even so, two Nebraska women served as associational chairs in 1957: Mrs. Tom Hodgin, community missions, and Mrs. Bill Prevatt, prayer. The year 1957 marked two other "firsts" for Nebraska: GAs went to Camp Bide-A-Wee for camp; and a Smoky Hill associational rally was held in Lincoln, at the pastor's home. Betty Freeman, young people's secretary of Kansas WMU, attended this meeting, as did Mrs. Collins Webb, who taught the *WMU Yearbook*.

In the 1957 report of the secretary to the Convention, the following appeared: "We have completed the first of five yearly emphases, setting a goal of $5,000 for a New Church Sites Fund. All departments of our Convention life were invited by the WMU to participate in the promotion of the offering. To that end, cooperation has been excellent. The final totals are not in, but many churches sought to reach goals equaling 33 1/2 cents per member and were successful. In 1958, the offering will [again] be directed to the Church Sites Fund and the goal is $7,500. It is believed that this is one of the most challenging phases of our Five Year Expansion Crusade."

In 1958 (*Annual*), again the State Missions offering was designated for the New Church Sites Loan Fund, with a goal of $7,500. The WMU sponsored the offering with the help of Assistant Secretary Paul Allison. Westmoreland's opinion was that the people thought the state missions offering "one of the most thrilling events of our Convention life." In 1959 the offering for state missions, with a goal of ten thousand dollars, was designated for the development of the state assembly. By this time, a calendar change to bring the Week of Prayer for State Missions and the Sunday School emphasis on state missions to the same week in September had been made and was working out well.

An interesting item in the Convention minutes for 1950 concerning the Tuesday evening joint session with WMU (*Annual*, 1950) follows: "Mrs. J. D. Williamson [president of state WMU] accepted a quilt from the TEL class of Emmanuel Baptist Church of Coffeyville and presented it to Brother W. A. Burkey for the future Children's Home." J. Ivaloy Bishop [Royal Ambassador leader of WMU, SBC] was the evening speaker. His topic was "Men for Tomorrow's Tasks."

In the early years, the annual meeting of Kansas WMU was held just prior to the state Convention. This plan continued until 1967 when the Convention Committee on Order of Business asked all groups meeting prior to the Convention to move their meeting time to the spring of the year. It was too confusing to have one meeting on top of the other; many people could not take that much time away from home and so left the Convention before it was over.

The first spring meeting of WMU was held in 1967 at the Metropolitan Baptist Church in Wichita. Westmoreland wrote about this decision (*BD*, May 6, 1967). He thought the change would not be made until after the November meeting of the Convention, but WMU in its spring board meeting voted to reschedule that year's annual meeting. The Brotherhood rescheduled their meeting also. Only the pastors continued to have a meeting prior to the Convention meeting.

Westmoreland commented about WMU (*BD*, May 6, 1967):

> The WMU has a wide range of important ministries with the main focus on missionary education. In addition to the ministry to women, Sunbeams, Girls' Auxiliary, and Young Women's Auxiliary organizations round out the panorama of WMU personnel emphases. The stress on missionary education does not neglect soul-winning and stewardship. When the girls of GA have completed each step through the Queen Regent, they will have encountered Bible-based and factual information regarding the current missionary needs of the world and actions by Southern Baptists that may well compare with any Freshman college Bible course. Dr. Herschell Hobbs said that he had never known a girl to finish all of those steps who did not conduct herself as a lady. This type of self-confidence and poise and dedication is an objective to be coveted by each of our churches. Surely, in all of our Southern Baptist life, we could never properly calculate the reservoir of missionary knowledge possessed by women and girls which serves as an undergirding factor in all phases of our work. The KCSB voted at its annual meeting to allocate $12,509 in 1967 for the WMU Department, and the Home Mission Board will be contributing $4,500 also for the Department.

Mrs. Orbie Clem, an unusual woman, was well equipped to be the first secretary-treasurer of Kansas WMU. Her name was Lois Maurine Bondurant Clem, but she was always referred to as Mrs. Orbie Clem. Her husband was pastor of churches in California, Oklahoma, and Kansas, and was the first editor of *Kansas Southern Baptist Beams*, which later was named *Baptist Digest*. She was one of four daughters of a pioneer western Kansas family. Her maternal grandfather had been born in Ireland on St. Patrick's Day and settled in Kansas in 1878. Lois Bondurant graduated from Ness County High School, from Hills Business College in Oklahoma City, and from Southwest Baptist College in Bolivar, Missouri. All this in the late 1920s and early 1930s. Mrs. Clem recalled that Dr. Courts Redford had inspired her to enroll at Southwest College. She left the business world after being a legal secretary for seven years when she married Orbie Clem.

From 1926 to 1930, she was employed in the law firm of Peters and Schoeppel in Ness City. The firm was dissolved when Loren Peters became Judge of the Thirty-third Judicial District of Kansas, and Andrew F. Schoeppel went to Topeka as Governor. This circumstance she credits with moving her back to Kansas in 1940.

Much of the following information comes from her obituary; the rest comes from the scrapbook/notebook history which Mrs. Clem compiled. While working as a secretary for the president of OBU in 1935, Miss Bondurant corresponded with Rev. Orbie R. Clem, pastor of the Sunland, California, Baptist Church. It is not certain whether this was "business" correspondence, or some other sort. In November 1935 Orbie Clem came by train to Shawnee, proposed at first sight, and they were married almost immediately. After living in California for a time, they came back to Oklahoma, where Clem was pastor of Capitol Baptist Church in Oklahoma City.

One day in August 1940, Mrs. Clem received a call from Judge Peters asking her to come to Ness City to work again as his court reporter. In her scrapbook, she reported, "On September 5, 1940, Orbie was called as pastor of First Baptist Church in Ness City (a Northern Baptist church). My husband resigned his pastorate at Capitol Baptist Church on the 8th of September and we both moved to Ness City."

Clem preached for three Sundays, but then trouble came to Ness City, trouble with a capital T! Opposition began to build against having a Southern Baptist pastor in the First Baptist Church of Ness City. After much debate and heated argument, a deacon who had been leading the opposition asked the pastor to resign, which he did, and immediately began holding prayer services in the home of a pioneer Baptist preacher, C. B. Coleman. The group was pitifully small at the start, two couples and Mrs. Clem's mother. Then another family joined. Very soon they were searching for a regular place to meet, which turned out to be a large room in the Haag building, a grocery store owned by Mrs. Haag and her son. The Haags used only the north end; the south end was perfect for Sunday services. They rented a piano for a dollar a month. The little mission continued through 1943. During 1943, Clem began to check on other Southern Baptist churches in the area which might be affiliated with the Missouri or Oklahoma Conventions. He contacted N. J. Westmoreland, pastor of the Emmanuel Baptist Church in Coffeyville. Both men were great letter writers, as was Lois Clem. After much correspondence they decided on the first fellowship breakfast, during the Oklahoma Convention, with three other pastors in southern Kansas. From this beginning the KNCSB grew. Trinity Southern Baptist Church, in Ness City, which began with only five members because of controversy over doctrine, was one of the four churches which formed what is today known as the Kansas-Nebraska Convention of Southern Baptists.

Lois Clem was as involved as her husband. If her husband was out of town when a letter from Westmoreland arrived, she opened it, put into motion things he requested, and sent him whatever materials he needed.

Then she wrote him with suggestions about next steps.

Mrs. Clem served as secretary-treasurer of the Kansas WMU until 1957, when Rev. Clem was named editorial assistant of the Dallas-based *Baptist Standard*; she became the director of advertising. Both remained active in mission work at the First Baptist Church, Dallas, and at the Grove Temple Baptist Church. They moved to Houston in 1971. After her husband's death in 1978, Lois Clem set out to secure a secretarial job and was hired at the age of seventy-three by the Parks and Recreation Department of the city of Houston. She worked until 1985. She continued to be an active member of the Tallowood Baptist Church and served in many areas of WMU there.

The Clems had one son and one granddaughter. At Mrs. Clem's death, in 1990, there was a memorial service in Houston, and true to her standards, she had asked that, rather than flowers, contributions be made to the Southern Baptist Cooperative Program.

In 1988 she wrote a letter to her dear friends, Ray and Anne Gilliland. She reminded them she was praying for them on their birthdays listed in the *Royal Service* prayer calendar, and told them of her activities: living in a duplex, attending Sunday School and church, involved in WMU, leading a Current Missions Group once a month, and preparing the *Tallowood Bugle*, a newsletter handed out at the Baptist Women's meeting on the second Tuesday of each month. At eighty-one she was still driving her car. She ended her letter fondly, "When you have the time I would love to hear about you and your work there. I often think of our beginning days in the Lord's work in Kansas. I am so thankful for having the privilege of knowing you and Anne."

In 1989 she sent to the Gillilands, to the SBC Historical Commission, to WMU Archives, and to the KNCSB a notebook/scrapbook on the history of early Southern Baptist work in Kansas. According to the preface, she was inspired by an article in the March 1989 issue of *Royal Service* entitled "Follow the Leaders in Kansas-Nebraska." She wrote, "Since only one short paragraph was written pertaining to Kansas, I decided to get busy and prepare more about the beginnings of Southern Baptist work in Kansas. My husband and I were in it from the very beginning. The material I have included in this history was taken from my library of loose-leaf scrapbooks I have kept for each year of my life." The history she shared through notes, copies of letters, articles from *KSBB*, and programs from various meetings begins in 1940 and goes through 1953.

Many things were begun during Clem's tenure that have marked Kansas-Nebraska WMU through the years. Great use was made of lay leadership, with state officers and committee chairs attending WMU, SBC, training sessions and then coming home to tour Kansas and Nebraska and hold training institutes.

The first GA House Party was held in December 1947 at the Airlane Church in Wichita, where, by that time, Orbie Clem was pastor. The following announcement appeared in the church bulletin on the Sunday before the event: "We are expecting 50 or more girls from about 10 of our churches in this activity. *All* girls of GA age are urged to attend. The girls are to sleep in the basement of our church so a call goes out to our ladies for plenty of bedding. Old quilts or blankets are welcome too as padding for the cots. . . . We will also be asking for food donations. Each church is supplying part of the food. Money will also be accepted. Each girl is only paying 25 cents for the entire House Party" (History, Clem).

The House Party began at 5:30 on Monday, and closed at 11:30 on Wednesday. No time was noted for "recreation" or "crafts." There was a bit of free time after 4:00 on Tuesday; bedtime was 10:00. There was a formal banquet on Tuesday night. Mrs. Worthington, "one of our Indian missionaries," was the speaker on Monday night.

A second Royal Ambassador Conclave was reported in 1951. In 1953 Orbie Clem drove to Atlanta with five boys to attend the first RA Congress ever. Clem reported (*KSBB*, September 24, 1953): "If you feel that you are growing old, all you have to do to become rejuvenated is to take a load of boys on a long trip. You will not experience a dull moment but you may wish you could. . . . Our experiences on the way included spending a night in Paige Seats' grandparents' home; stopping on a mountain drive to take pictures and throw rocks; fighting the battle of Lookout Mountain in Tennessee over, winning a decisive victory over the Union forces; ferrying the Ohio River where it is a mile wide; pillow fighting at night while the writer called the signals; learning whether waitresses can take the kidding boys give. . . . What an exhilarating experience to spend three days among 5,000 boys and not hear a word of profanity, but rather singing and praying attended by the enthusiasm and hope of youth. Atlanta was permeated with the influence of boys who are truly Ambassadors for Christ."

The only camps reported by Mrs. Clem were those held at Camp Cedar Bluff, near Coffeyville, which were not designated for GAs or RAs, and those held at the statewide camp, Camp Fellowship near Goddard. In 1950 Mrs. Clem included this paragraph in her report to the Convention (*Annual*, 1950): "We have had associational houseparties and conclaves for our young people, but we are not satisfied with this. We are looking forward to the day when Woman's Missionary Union shall be able to use the State Camp we are to have in the future for the various weeks of camp we hope to plan for our young people." It was during these years that we bought an assembly site, 130 acres near Quenemo, about twenty-five miles west of Ottawa and thirty miles south of Topeka. This site was never developed, although there was a plan to lease plots to individuals, local churches, and associations, for cottages, cabins, and dormitories on the land. It was sold in 1967 (*Annual*, 1967).

Women were involved in many kinds of ministry and witnessing. In June 1949, Irene Chambers, a field worker with the Home Mission Board, visited Kansas and shared the needs of the B. I. Carpenters, new missionaries in Alaska. Out of this came the project, "Linens to Alaska." Boxes of linens were sent from the women of Kansas to Ketchikan, Alaska. Perhaps this was the forerunner of the Partnership Plan we now enjoy.

A letter of thanks came from Helen Carpenter, which she asked be printed in the paper since some of her notes had been returned to her because of insufficient addresses: "Believe me, there has never been a time when we had a more timely gift. My last sheets had turned up with holes in them and could stand only a few more launderings. I have had someone extra in my home now for six straight weeks. A young boy from Canada came here with his school track team and his parents were very anxious for him to be in a Christian home. We kept him for a week. An expectant mother from Annette Island was with us for three weeks waiting for the arrival of her baby. A young Coast Guardsman could not find housing for his wife and baby so we took them in for a couple of weeks. And so it goes from week to week, someone who needs help. Yes, physically it is a burden, but the joy we get from helping someone in need compensates for the physical handicap."

In 1951 the First Baptist Church of Claflin was organized with twenty-seven members. "A factor in beginning the work at Claflin was the organization of a WMS Circle among women members of Trinity who live in Claflin. This was done by the Hoisington WMS" (*KSBB*, May 31, 1951). WMU has continued this emphasis on "new starts" and the part that women can play.

Ruby Turner, charter member of Hillcrest Baptist Church in Omaha, talked about the early days of that church. In addition to Sunday School and Training Union, she mentioned Brotherhood and WMU and particularly, GAs and RAs. She said, "When we stopped having GAs and RAs, the kids sort of drifted away."

In these early days, there was emphasis on church-wide participation in the Lottie Moon Christmas Offering for Foreign Missions and the Annie Armstrong Offering for Home Missions. Clem included an item from the Sharon Baptist Church in Wichita in her report in the *Beams* (January 8, 1952). "In contrast to the practice of many churches, the Lottie Moon Christmas Offering was not just 'left up to the women' of the Sharon WMS and its organizations; it was made a church-wide affair, with much being said about it from the pulpit by the pastor; thus, giving every church member, Sunday School member, BTU member, and visitor, an opportunity to have a part in this most important of all special offerings." A brief biography of Lottie Moon was given in the opening assembly of Sunday school; Mrs. Carter Wright's story of "The Unexpected Christmas Guest," which emphasized the importance of giving, was read at the closing assembly of Training Union; and the theme "Lovest Thou Me . . . Feed My Sheep" was displayed in the sanctuary.

Furniture for the state WMU office was given by the women of Kansas through their associational organizations. In April 1953, Clem was presented checks, with a promise of more to come, for the purchase of new office furniture. With the first gifts she bought a large oak desk and a green typewriter posture chair "which matches the color scheme in the room" (*KSBB*, April 9, 1953).

In 1953 (*KSBB*, June 11, 1953), Clem wrote about plans for a Day of Prayer for Christian Education. The goal was three hundred dollars with the following designations: State Scholarship Fund, one hundred dollars; Burney

Gifts (Margaret Fund), seventy-seven dollars; Carver School of Missions and Social Work (formerly WMU Training School), fifty dollars; and Baptist Chair of Bible, Pittsburg, seventy-five dollars. Z. Linston Brister, who occupied the Chair of Bible, wrote the program and was commended for a fine job.

Clem and four other Kansas Baptist women were present for the first WMU conference held at the brand new Baptist Assembly in Glorieta, New Mexico, in July 1953. She gave a full report of the conference which included Bible study, mission study, manual study, missionary addresses, vespers, and every afternoon free for recreation and sight-seeing tours. YWA week, just the week previous, had been attended by two YWAs and Ida Polk, WMU secretary-treasurer elect. Polk was also at the WMU conference.

Again and again Clem attended SBC meetings. In 1949 the Convention met in Oklahoma City. She, along with "a number of our people," was there. Robert G. Lee was president. "This was a historic Convention because for the first time in the Convention's history, a Black man from outside its fellowship was invited to preach. He was E. W. Perry, for over half-century pastor of the Tabernacle Baptist church, Oklahoma City. When Lee presented him, he put his arm about Perry and said, 'Brethren, you are looking at a portrait of black and white painted in red.' The Convention stood and cheered" (Clem, Scrapbook History).

The Clems resigned their work in Kansas in 1953, she in August and he in December. In regard to Mrs. Clem's resignation, Westmoreland wrote *(KSBB, August 14, 1953)*:

> She has been identified with all of the missionary endeavors of Kansas Southern Baptist women from the very start of our organized missionary advance. From the first fellowship meeting of Kansas Southern Baptists at Burden, Kansas, November 26, 1945, to the time of the organization of the Woman's Missionary Union in 1946, and until today, she has participated in the planning of each phase of its work, cared for many routine duties, and attended every state and many associational meetings that the women have sponsored. . . . During these years, Kansas Woman's Missionary Union has grown from only a vision in the hearts of our faithful women to an aggressive organism which is busy at the task of missionary education and service, and of enlistment in missionary giving. The task is well begun. The future promises astonishing gains. Through the years ahead the memory of the beginnings of Kansas WMU will be associated with that of the labors of Mrs. Clem. . . . In gratitude, all will remember that Mrs. Clem was "first" in executive leadership of Kansas Southern Baptist missionary women.

Ida Polk, the second secretary-treasurer, served from 1953 until 1956. She was a native of Texas and a graduate of Southwestern Baptist Theological Seminary. She was preparing for the foreign mission field, but the way was blocked. There is no indication as to why this happened. During the year prior to her selection, she had been living with a sister in Sedgwick, Kansas, and teaching school.

Her first report appeared at the end of August 1953 (*KSBB*, August 27, 1953), titled "Not There, But Here." "Eight years ago I dedicated my life to the Lord for foreign mission service; today by His grace I am serving in the home mission field of Kansas. I have prepared to be there, but by His grace I serve here. Looking at the work after one week of routine in the office and one week profitably spent at the State Assembly getting acquainted with the people and the work, it falls my responsibility to prepare the material for this page. One year ago, I had no idea that the Lord would lead in this way. I had prepared for foreign missions, but He has led the way into a vital home missions program. I am new in this field of work and it will take time to learn the people, the way the work is being done, and the steps the Lord would have us take. Your suggestions will be greatly appreciated."

By that time, Betty Freeman was young people's secretary of Kansas WMU. She was not the first; after Mrs. Preboth, Mrs. Fred Hansen, Coffeyville, was elected to this position, as a volunteer, with the first roster of officers. Soon after, no later than 1949, Mrs. Miles Cowden was elected young people's secretary. Betty Freeman was the first salaried young people's secretary of Kansas. In Ida Polk's first report to the Convention, in 1953, she stated, "Woman's Missionary Union has two full-time workers; the Secretary-Treasurer and the Young People's Secretary. Mrs. Miles Cowden has served four years in the capacity of Young People's Secretary giving full time for free. We extend our deepest appreciation to her."

During Polk's tenure, the number of Woman's Missionary Societies increased from sixty-four to 129; we had our first RA and GA camps, under the direction of Betty Freeman. In those days, reports included many items we no longer keep track of: number of tithers, number attending mission study class, number engaged in directed community service, and number receiving mission magazines. We also reported the number of family altars, the number of Missionary Round Tables, and the number of organizations reaching the Standard of Excellence.

When Viola Webb (Interview, 1994) was asked if she thought these kinds of reports were helpful, her reply was emphatically affirmative. She also thought that their discontinuation was "one of the biggest mistakes Birmingham ever made." During those years, she said, "we kept up with our members. We don't do that anymore. We don't have any idea what's going on here and what's going on there. When the reporting stopped, there was a bit of falling off here and a bit of falling off there."

By 1956 the report for WMU for the Convention *Annual* was written by Mrs. Collins Webb. Polk had resigned to go to the North Fort Worth Baptist Church. Webb was interim secretary-treasurer.

In 1956 (*Annual*, 1956), Kansas WMU was recognized by WMU, SBC, in a number of instances: Kansas was third in percent of churches having a WMS;

third in average number of mission study books taught per society; fourth in percent of A-1 Young Woman's Auxiliaries; first in percent of members subscribing to the *Window of YWA*; first with 166 percent increase in mission study books taught in societies; second in percent of increase in Woman's Missionary Societies participating in directed community missions; third in percent of increase in number of societies observing Week of Prayer for Home Missions; and first in increase of youth organizations participating in directed community missions. In those early days we talked about Full-Graded WMUs (a Woman's Missionary Society, and at least one of each of the youth organizations). In 1956 Mrs. Webb reported seven such unions: First, Baxter Springs; Shawnee Southern, Topeka; and Midway, Pershing Avenue, Immanuel, First Southern, and Indian Southern, all of Wichita.

In 1957 we were using Aims for Advancement to recognize superior work. The Berean Baptist Church in Kansas City was an Honor Society; five societies had advanced standing, and two were approved.

Eva Berry was elected secretary-treasurer of Kansas WMU in January 1957. Mrs. Webb wrote (*Annual*, 1957), "Miss Berry did a splendid work in the state, going from association to association holding enlargement campaigns in WMU work, but she finished her work, June 2, 1957. The Lord took her home to be with Him."

The 1957 annual *Book of Reports* was dedicated to Berry, including a brief memorial statement. She grew up in Alabama, went to Howard College in Birmingham and WMU Training School in Louisville, Kentucky. She did secretarial work before beginning WMU work. She served nine years as WMU young people's secretary in Alabama. For four years she was WMU field worker in Missouri, and then was WMU secretary-treasurer of Missouri for six years. Six months was her allotted time in Kansas; she was killed in a car accident on her way home from the WMU, SBC, annual meeting. In that same accident, Jack Adkisson, pastor at Hillcrest in Omaha, Nebraska, was seriously injured.

In July 1957, Mrs. Collins Webb was elected secretary-treasurer of Kansas WMU, where she served for a quarter of a century, retiring in 1982. Viola Webb grew up in Texas, the oldest of eight in a close, loving Christian family; "poor but we didn't know it then; we were rich in so many ways," she said (*BD*, August 22, 1988). It was also a strict, conservative family, and when at fifteen she felt called to go to Africa as a missionary nurse, her father said that life was entirely unsuitable for a girl. When it was time to go to college, her father "could not part with his little girl." When they were able, he told her, they would move to a college town and she could go to school then.

Collins Webb, who grew up in the same community, had gone away, and when he returned, he began to court Viola. One thing led to another; they shared their dreams, fell in love, were married, and, over her father's protests, moved away and enrolled in school. Collins had been called to preach, and that required education. He had an eye difficulty; Viola became his eyes, reading to him, explaining what she saw under the microscope, and typing his papers. He graduated from Howard Payne College, and she had learned a lot in the process, although she did not have a degree.

Collins served churches in Texas and New Mexico. Viola served as WMU president in her church, associational young people's secretary for six years, as church secretary for three years, educational director for three years, and was an elementary school teacher, in addition to having a good background in bookkeeping.

As an associational young people's leader in New Mexico, Viola's concern was to plan a camp for the young people. She was discouraged by the women: no place to meet, never been done before, who would come? Her first attempt was grandly successful and sealed for always her love for camping programs.

Collins was called as pastor at New Home, Texas. In order to show their love and care for their new young pastor and his wife, the women in the church presented Viola with a new outfit, from the top of her head down to shoes, including matching "ear screws." Now, in Viola's experience, ear screws were not very short of the work of the Devil. All her pastors had warned against such things, including fingernail polish and make-up. Collins was different. Come Sunday, when Viola dressed in her new outfit, he insisted that she wear the ear screws, too. She said, "I don't know where Collins got the idea that 'any old barn looks good with a little paint on it.' That's what he would say when the people came to talk to him about the way women were doing." At any rate, Viola wore the ear screws and fell in love with them. They became sort of a trade mark for her. She confessed that if she ever left home on the way to a meeting without her ear screws, she stopped somewhere along the way and bought a pair.

The Webbs came to Kansas in 1954 when Collins was called from Pampa, Texas, to pastor the Pershing Avenue Baptist Church in Wichita. Viola got into WMU work straightway and became benevolent chairman of Kansas WMU. She had not been here more than two months when she was asked to chair the Youth Committee, working with Betty Freeman who was young people's secretary. Freeman asked her to head this committee because of the experience Viola had in camp work in Texas and New Mexico.

Webb remembers great experiences as she and Betty drove all over Kansas and parts of Nebraska trying to find campgrounds suitable for girls and boys. They had to schedule dates on the state calendar, then find places that were open for camps on the dates which had been chosen. The first camp used was Bide-A-Wee near Wichita, which would accommodate only ninety campers. Camps were also held at Camp Fellowship and at Camp Webster.

When she first began to work with Freeman, in her volunteer capacity, she remembers Freeman would say, "Now, Viola this is a state camp, not an associational camp." Her general comeback was, "I know that Betty, but we had 500 kids in our associational camp (this was Texas), and you don't have that many in all of the Kansas state camps." The GA Coronation Services were also big associational events. She remembers one in particular when many of the girls fainted." Collins was behind the stage taking care of that part of it. I don't know if it was the heat, the strain they were going through, or what. Those were the days! It's so different now."

Webb was asked to serve as interim after Ida Polk left and before Eva Berry came to Kansas. When the committee came to her, she thought she would be filling Betty Freeman's place as interim, since Freeman resigned about the same time. She did not know, until she was escorted into Polk's office, that she was to be interim secretary-treasurer of Kansas WMU. She said, "I was so embarrassed. I thought, good grief, I don't know what I'm doing. I have no idea what's going to happen." It turned out, however, that she enjoyed it; the people were understanding of her mistakes as she learned; she liked working with the pastors.

After the untimely death of Eva Berry, the committee went back to Webb with the invitation to lead the Kansas WMU. By this time she was working at Montgomery Ward, where she had just been offered a promotion to Credit Department director with a salary of one hundred dollars per week, which was no small money in 1957, and twice as much as the Convention job offered.

She talked with Collins who put it right back in her court, "It's your decision," he said. Webb confided that Collins was no help at all, since every time she leaned in the direction of Montgomery Ward, he would point out the difficulties she would face in that job; and when she leaned toward the Convention job, he pointed out advantages the Montgomery Ward job offered. She finally chose WMU, and was confident and happy in that decision all through the years.

Until Pat McDaniel came, her salary was always lower than the salaries of her male counterparts in the Convention office because she was married and had a husband to support her. When McDaniel came, that changed. He gave instructions that Webb's salary should be the same as other department heads.

When Webb came to her position, the first concern was the changing of the status of WMU from auxiliary to the Convention to a department of the Convention. She admitted she was pretty upset about this to begin with. All she knew was an "auxiliary" relationship. WMU did not have much input into this change; although a joint committee worked on some of the details. This dual committee, one appointed by the Convention and one by WMU, began work on July 16, 1957, to recommend changes in the WMU by-laws so there would be full harmony with the Convention's constitution. After the re-write and corrections, the new WMU by-laws were adopted at a called meeting of the WMU board.

Discussion of this change had begun during the tenure of Eva Berry, who also had not liked the idea. Webb recalled that Berry had trouble with this because "she was a dyed-in-the-wool Southerner." Through the years, Webb had a bit of difficulty with presidents who had grown up in the deep South, which she called "auxiliary states." After department status had been established, these presidents were still prone to recall the way it was done "down home" and Webb would answer, "But we do it this way. Now we are under the Board in Kansas-Nebraska and we cooperate with other departments." Working with some of these die-hard presidents was not easy. Later on, there was written into the WMU by-laws the provision that a woman must have served for four years as an associational director or a state consultant before she could be nominated as president of the Kansas-Nebraska WMU.

After it all "shook down," Webb liked the new situation, because it made her feel more a part of the Convention. Before this change she felt sort of "out-of-it." With the change budgeting became easier. No longer did Woman's Missionary Society members have to pay dues, which were called "apportionments," of twenty-five cents per month per member to support the work of WMU. Rather, the new department shared with other departments in Cooperative Program funds.

According to the *Digest* for August 31, 1957, "Mrs. Collins Webb, the new executive secretary for the department of WMU, believes the most important thing in the new by-laws is that there will be three youth directors—YWA, GA, and Sunbeam—instead of just one. These will be in both the local and associational organizations." Another change was that the "Board" was renamed "Council."

Webb is a many-faceted person. She is a strong woman, but also gentle, a steel magnolia, if you please. In 1962 she was elected president of all the state WMU secretaries in the SBC (*BD*, June 30, 1963).

Opal Bates, state WMU president from 1971 to 1976, had this tribute: "Viola is a lovable, sincere, and dedicated person. She has given her life to the Lord's work. She helped me tremendously. We spent many days together. Viola was so well known in Wichita that when Internationals arrived at the airport, airport officials would instruct them to call Viola Webb. 'She can help you' was their assurance to these strangers. She housed many of them for days or weeks until they could get enrolled in school or find a job. She also gave them the Gospel message."

According to Webb, her interest in internationals flowered after her trip to Berne to the Baptist World Alliance. She experienced firsthand the difficulties and frustrations faced when it was not possible to speak the language. She purposed to make transition easier for those coming from distant places to Wichita. And she did it.

In the 1957 report (her first one), and in most subsequent ones, Webb gave emphasis to a part of the work that was near her heart—camping experiences for youth, and other youth meetings. Betty Freeman directed three weeks and one weekend of camps, with 165 campers and forty-four staffers on the campgrounds during that year. Two cars loaded with thirteen girls went to Glorieta for YWA Week. "Educating Youth in Missions" meant camps to Webb. In 1959 the "best ever" GA camp was held, with 264 in attendance. Also, mention was made of the Queen's Court and the YWA Houseparty.

In the 1959 report (*Annual*, 1959), Webb called attention to the only Ann Hasseltine YWA in Kansas or Nebraska, located at Kansas State Teachers' College, with a membership of ten. In the area of benevolence (there was a state chairman), "One hundred thirteen boxes were sent to foreign fields, home fields, and retired ministers during the past year. Mrs. Daisy Wilcox is doing a good work leading the women to 'do beyond the association' what they do in the association."

Beverly Hammack came to Kansas-Nebraska August 17, 1959, as young people's secretary, with salary provided by the Home Mission Board. She grew up in Missouri, and graduated from OBU and Southwestern Seminary. She had already served with the Home Mission Board at Rachel Sims Mission in New Orleans, and in Arkansas for a summer of Vacation Bible Schools, and felt Kansas was just another place for home missions service.

She had responsibility for all youth work plus the summer camps sponsored by WMU. Hammack remained in this position until July 1961 when she took a position with the Home Mission Board. She wrote, "Kansas-Nebraska Convention gave me the experience I would need in the years of home mission service. It was here I learned of the struggles of a smaller Convention, short on finances, and yet productive in starting churches and growing its youth. I will ever be grateful for the responsibility given me by this Convention." Hammack was the last paid young people's secretary of the KNSCB. Since that time, the work of missions education and camping experiences for youth have been under the direction of the volunteer age-level consultants.

Hammack shared memories of her time in Kansas. One concerned associational training events: "We rented a U-Haul type of trailer and pulled it on the back of Mrs. Webb's car. It contained the multitude of boxes of materials that we carried everywhere. We crossed and re-crossed train tracks all over Kansas and Nebraska! I told Mrs. Webb that if we were ever hit by a train, WMU literature would be scattered all over the cow pastures, and the cows would give purple milk. Those boxes of materials that had to be lifted and unlifted by all of us women will always remain in my memory and will always be evidenced by my bowed back."

Camps were special times for Hammack. The cost of GA camp in 1961 was $12.50, including twenty-five cents for insurance and twenty-five cents for handicraft materials. Kansas and Nebraska girls went to YWA weeks at Ridgecrest and Glorieta, where far-reaching decisions were made concerning life plans. She recalled the camaraderie in the office, the humor and team spirit that got everyone over lots of rough spots; the annual trips to Birmingham for WMU Board meetings; the winter wonderland of snow on blue spruce trees in Nebraska; and relationships with pastors, state staff, WMU women, and youth that have lasted through the years.

A major lesson she learned from Webb was never to cancel a meeting—no matter what! "I was overwhelmed when a blizzard hit; I would confront Mrs. Webb with the need to cancel whatever state meeting was scheduled. She taught me that if we once canceled, no one would know what we would do when the next snow came. She was a determined, dependable leader who was a wonderful mentor for me."

Hammack was not the only one who learned that Webb operated in this fashion. Bernice Elliot, from the Birmingham office, was to come to Kansas for one of these associational tours, and a snow storm developed ("I mean a deep snow," Webb said). Elliot called to assure herself there was no need to come given the weather conditions in Kansas. Webb would have none of it. "Bernie, the people would come," she insisted. Elliot was still skeptical on Monday morning when they drove to the meeting; she did not think anyone would be present. Webb answered, "Okay, we'll see." A hundred women were there for the meeting that snowy, blustery morning.

Many times, Hammack recalled, she drove alone across the state in her red Valiant. She wore jeans in case she had car trouble. When she got to the city where she was to speak or preside over a GA coronation service, she pulled into a service station, changed into the special green satin dress, did her "thing" at the church, and then stopped again at the service station and got back into jeans for the drive home. She commented, "I often wondered what the guys at the station thought I was doing."

The greatest disappointment that came to the department during 1961 was the resignation of Hammack when she left to go to the Home Mission Board. Webb wrote, "Certainly we were pleased for her to get the promotion but it has hurt our department. She did an outstanding work in the short time she was with us" (Annual, 1961).

The first weeks of the 1960 and 1961 years were marked by leadership training tours of the associations, with the state chairmen participating. Rev. Loren Turnage, missionary to Colombia, was the missionary guest in 1961. That year, 306 women attended: fifty-two local presidents, thirty prayer chairmen, forty-two community missions chairmen, fifty-one mission study chairmen, and thirty-seven stewardship chairmen.

An "aside" to this incident was that Loren Turnage married Cherry Kincheloe. Her father, C. A. Kincheloe, was an early Kansas pastor; she was office secretary, for a time, for the KCSB. Turnage was pastor of Kansas Baptist churches before their appointment in 1959. Westmoreland wrote about their appointment in light of the "Two Plus" plan, which was to encourage churches to increase gifts to the Cooperative Program by two percent (BD, September 19, 1959): "It put foreign missions on wings. They [Turnages] went by plane and very likely reached their destination [Costa Rica for language study] in the span of one day's sunshine. Flying is not new to missionaries, but with adequate funds it may mean that they will do more and more flying to and from their assignments and provide more frequent furloughs and vacation opportunities." Cherry Turnage, serving with her husband in Portugal, was one of the missionaries listed on the WMU Prayer Calendar during the WMU Council meeting in January 1995.

John Hopkins went along on some of those leadership tours, since he had responsibility for the Brotherhood, and therefore Royal Ambassadors, in his early days with the Convention. He met with the men and boys while the others met with the women of the association.

In 1963 the emphasis was on enlistment; the goal for the next year was 707 units with 8,500 members. Several suggestions were made for increasing the number of units: "Check existing auxiliaries for size. When an organization reaches a maximum it should be divided to form a new organization. Plan to start new organizations in churches where there are none. In churches where the auxiliaries meet at night, begin an organization for those who cannot attend night meetings. Be sure to consult your pastor before changing meeting time" (*Annual*, 1963). This goal was not quite reached. At the end of the "One Great Year of Advance," there were 631 organization with 7,133 members.

That same year, the Girls' Auxiliary Convention in Memphis was "a real success" (*Annual*, 1963). Webb was asked if she could have fifty girls from Kansas present for the meetings. She nodded her head in agreement, albeit a bit fearfully. When the meeting times rolled around, there was a total of 158 girls and counselors. Among this group were two carloads from Nebraska.

The celebration of the seventy-fifth anniversary of WMU came in 1963. One of the recommendations was a seventy-five-day period of prayer, July 18 to October 1, preceding the year of celebration. Webb wrote (*BD*, June 30, 1962), "We feel that one of the great needs of our time is a calling back to God of our people. Let's make this a real season of prayer in each local church, making it a time of Bible study, of soul searching, and of rededication of our lives." Many "75" goals were set for this special year.

GA Camp in 1963 was held at Camp Webster in Salina. The theme was "World Missions USA." Webb wrote (*Annual*, 1963), "We wanted the girls to be more aware of the many nationalities in the Convention to whom they could witness, many of these living in the same neighborhood with them. The following nationalities were represented: Japanese, Lebanese, Chinese, Indian, Spanish, and Bohemian. This was an experience many of the girls will never forget."

In 1966 three regional YWA Houseparties were reported: Great Bend, First Southern in Topeka, and Cedar Bluff Campsite in Independence, with 102 in attendance.

In 1968 preparation for change began in Kansas that would culminate in a new look for WMU in 1970. Willingness to change when necessary, when in the best interests of the purposes of the organization, has been a hallmark of WMU. The headline in the January 4, 1969, issue of the *Digest* was "WMU Gets New Names for 1970." Since 1888 WMU had done the work of missions awareness, participation, and education under a rubric that had remained fairly much the same. The 1970 changes involved new names, new periodicals, and new programs. Gone were Woman's Missionary Society, YWA, GAs, and Sunbeam Band. The decision came in part in order to cooperate with changes in age- and group-grading in other organizations in the church. The umbrella term of WMU was retained. The new names adopted were: Baptist Women (adult division, ages eighteen and up); Baptist Young Women (adult division, ages eighteen to twenty-nine); Acteens (youth division, ages twelve to seventeen); Girls in Action (children's division, ages six to eleven); and Mission Friends (preschool division, ages birth through five). The name Woman's Missionary Society, with its circles to denote various groupings of women, was replaced by Baptist Women and Baptist Young Women. The new names suggested a more "action-oriented" approach.

New periodicals were announced in keeping with the 1970s organization plan for WMU: *Dimension* for WMU leadership; *Royal Service* was continued for Baptist Women; *Contempo* was new for BYW; for Acteens, there was *Accent* plus *Accent Leader's Edition; Aware* was prepared for Girl's in Action leadership, and *Discovery* for the girls; *Start* became the new piece, published quarterly, for Mission Friends leadership.

There were also program changes in 1970: An individual achievement plan was developed for Acteens called Studiact; the old GA standby, Forward Steps, was replaced with Missions Adventures. Another change was the transfer of missions education of six- to eight-year-old boys to the Brotherhood. Up to this time, boys and girls up to age eight were enrolled in World Friends. In 1970 boys became part of the Crusader Division, which included boys through eleven. The Pioneer Division of Royal Ambassadors was for boys from twelve to seventeen. This in itself was not a new action for WMU, for a number of things begun through the years by the organization had been delegated to other groups in the Convention. Responsibility for Royal Ambassadors (boys twelve to sixteen) had been turned over to the Brotherhood in 1954. Seven years later, plans were initiated by the Brotherhood to include seventeen-year-old boys in this organization.

Change never comes easily; it is an easy time to drop out of programs. Many women in Kansas, as well as in other places, were not pleased with the new ways proposed and adopted by Birmingham. Webb said women missed the "circles"; organizations were lost. Of course, in many places things went on pretty much as usual, particularly with the adult women: circles became groups; there was still a *Royal Service* program; and mission action was still referred to by many as community missions. The modifications came, and were assimilated. Societal changes affected WMU: more women were at work away from home; and there were a great many more opportunities for involvement in the community as well as in church. These made alterations in the WMU format imperative, but also difficult.

In 1994 other changes were introduced, for many of the same reasons. Again, the general umbrella term to denote the organization was kept: WMU. The only name change was in the grouping for adult women, no longer Baptist Women and BYW, but Women on Mission. Program changes were a bit more far-reaching than in 1970, but the basic tasks of WMU remained the same: to be responsible for missions education and activity. It is the purpose of the local WMU to help a church involve all its members, especially women, girls, and preschoolers, in missions. To be involved in missions means that persons will be committed to and will carry out the missions mandate of the Bible.

With the new plan, there will be more emphasis on missions projects, church-wide activities and co-ed organizations. These changes were made in order to "speak to" Christians as we move into the twenty-first century. They are meant to give more choices and opportunities for self-direction based on the needs in the community and interests of the women, particularly among small churches.

In September 1995, after eighty years of publication, *Royal Service* ceased to be, replaced by *Missions Mosaic,* a smart, snappy periodical conceived for today's woman. Program plans are presented in *Missions Mosaic Executive.* The curriculum pieces for Acteens are *Accent* and *Accent Leadership Edition;* for younger GAs, *Discovery,* for older GAs, *GA WORLD,* and for GA leadership, *AWARE,* a quarterly publication. *Start* continues as the quarterly publication for Mission Friends leadership.

In the 1970 report (the 1969 and 70 reports dealt with changes in WMU), Viola Webb wrote, "In *Choices and Changes* one title is 'Can You Be Trusted With Today?' and another is 'Are You Ready For Tomorrow?' We trust that all of our churches are ready for tomorrow with new organization, with new materials, with a new zeal for winning lost people with the same gospel. In the book, *Don't Park Here,* C. William Fisher wrote: 'Life is a Way, a Road, a Thoroughfare; not a Parking Lot. Life is a School, not a Cemetery; Life is an arena, not a feature seat; Life is for growth, for movement, for development, for struggle, for progress. The life that becomes static becomes stagnant and this is very true in the world in which we live today. We must keep moving.' Dr. Robert J. Hastings, editor of the *Illinois Baptist,* said: 'No enemy is deadlier than complacency.' To be satisfied with yesterday is to pull the rug out from under tomorrow. We must not be satisfied with yesterday and its accomplishments, but we must look forward to tomorrow."

As we talked with her, Webb recalled the sad days of the difficulties with the bonds, and the good days when Baptists lived up to their commitments. She was one of the two who remained on the staff after 1968. She did not consider herself very involved in the situation. There were a lot of things the staff was not aware of at the time. She was even less aware than the male members of the staff; the men talked at coffee breaks and over lunch, but because she was a woman she was not included in this informal information network. She recalls that when Pat McDaniel arrived on the scene, first as Home Mission Board administrator and then as secretary, a new day dawned. Many of the old binding restrictions were lifted. For example, Westmoreland thought it not a good idea for a man and a woman to travel together, or even two men and two women. It was okay for one man and two women, but not the other way around. This was changed. Travel money was made available. All staff were invited to attend board meetings and to give more input than simply reports of work accomplished. McDaniel wanted and valued the contributions of the professional staff.

When the move was made from Wichita to Topeka, Webb did not plan to go. She was sixty-three years old; she did not think it would be a good use of Cooperative Program funds to move her when she was so near retirement. McDaniel came to her office and asked, "What's this I hear about your not moving to Topeka." When she gave him her reason, he continued his questions: Is that the only reason? You mean you do not mind moving out of Wichita? It does not make any difference that Collins and you lived together in that house and that you are going to Topeka without him? She answered all his questions, and concluded, "I just had not planned to go, but if that's what the Lord wants, then I'm ready to go."

According to Webb, McDaniel put his hands on his hips and looked at her: "You're going. Understood?" And so Webb moved to Topeka and served another six years.

In 1981 the state mission offering was named the Viola Webb Offering for State Missions. Webb spoke publicly against this: "It is not smart to name an offering after someone who is alive because that person might just go and embarrass you." The will of the Convention prevailed. The following resolution was presented and passed during the 1981 session:

WHEREAS Mrs. Viola Webb has given twenty-five years of sacrificial service to the Kingdom of God in the Kansas-Nebraska Convention of Southern Baptists; and,

WHEREAS Mrs. Webb has made a most significant contribution to missions education in our two-state Convention; and,

WHEREAS Mrs. Webb's life has exemplified Christian character and a missionary spirit; and,

WHEREAS we have come to love and appreciate her as a sister in Christ;

BE IT THEREFORE RESOLVED that the prayers of this Convention be for God's blessings of good health, love, and peace to continue with Mrs. Webb in her retirement; and,

BE IT FURTHER RESOLVED that the churches of this Convention continue to consult with her in mission education and support; and,

BE IT FURTHER RESOLVED that the Viola Webb Offering for State Missions be given all enthusiastic support and promotion possible as an appropriate expression of our appreciation for her services.

On recommendation of the Council of Kansas-Nebraska WMU, this offering was renamed in 1995 The Viola Webb Missions Offering.

In 1993 the whole Convention celebrated Webb's eightieth birthday as a kick-off to the special offering for Webster Conference Center. That year, sixty-five thousand dollars of the Viola Webb Offering for State Missions was earmarked for Field Missions, and the rest for Webster. A total of $155,000 was given for these causes. While we did not reach our ambitious goal, the offering was forty-nine percent greater than it had been the year before. The offering was in commemoration of this fine, strong woman, who believed in the camping experience and what it does for youth in our state.

Webb recalled many people with whom she had worked, presidents, committee chairs, associational officers, consultants, and pastors. She referred to women as Mrs. so and so, never by their given names. When she was asked about this, she said it was the custom; women just did not call each other by first names in formal situations. She said, "If anyone ever called me Viola, Collins gave them a look and they just didn't do it again. He thought that women who were married ought to be respected. You see that's what it was like in the old days." But finally, she came to be known as "Viola"; and then she added, "But, gee, they didn't do it for a long time." Although it did not "sound right" at first, it came to please her very much.

We asked Webb if she thought having WMU in the two-state Convention had made any difference over the years. Her answer was classic, "I'd hate to live here if it hadn't have been for WMU. There would not have been the caring, loving, spirit. It is WMU who keeps before the church the importance of missions, which is what the Lord intended the churches to do. One of our mandates is to see that the Word is spread, and that's what WMU is about. Not just here at home, but throughout the world. Woman's Missionary Union leads the church to a world view."

At the 1982 meeting of the KNCSB, Webb was given a royal farewell. The state mission offering was named in her honor; she received a new car and money for a trip to Nigeria. Her plans were to serve in Nigeria four or five weeks, spend Christmas in Kenya with some national friends, and then go to India for three weeks to serve in various areas. Kansas-Nebraska WMU also celebrated Webb's years of service. Carolyn Weatherford, director of national WMU, was the surprise banquet speaker. Webb's final report contained these words (*Annual*, 1982): "A new day dawns with the election of Yvonne Keefer as Director of Woman's Missionary Union. Welcome, Yvonne, to the best group in the United States. You will need to pray for Yvonne as she continues the missions education program. No two people are going to do it alike. She will have her way, perhaps much better, bring new ideas, new concepts, and you will be praying for her as the work continues to grow in missions education in Kansas-Nebraska."

When Webb retired in 1982, Keefer was elected to the position of director of the WMU Department. She brought a vastly different experience and point of view than that of the women who preceded her. Yvonne Kelsoe had been born in the midst of the depression on an Oklahoma farm, but before she was two years of age, her family moved to Oklahoma City. She characterized her parents as people who "knew how to love." They loved each other, their children, "grandparents, aunts, uncles, cousins, and everyone else who came around."

At eight years of age, Keefer attended a Sunday School class and fell in love with her teacher. "She was attractive, kind—a real class act." But when she was nine she was promoted to a class with another teacher; so she did not go back, although she remained on the Sunday School roll. Then along came another teacher, three years later, who brought her back. She engineered parties, wonderful ones, but Keefer's mother would not allow her to attend the parties unless she went to Sunday School. Keefer reported, "It was love at first sight. This time it was not just with my teacher, but with the church, and with Jesus." A year later she made a profession of faith. Her mother thought she was too young to know what she was doing, but allowed her to make her own decision. She has been making her own decisions ever since. Since that time, the church has been the center of her life.

She met Jim Keefer when she was a sophomore in high school and he was a senior. They dated through high school and continued through college days at Oklahoma A & M (now Oklahoma State), where both were active in BSU. Yvonne called this BSU experience a "hands on course in ministry."

They were married in June 1956, when he was on military leave and she was fifteen hours short of her degree. Later on, she finished her degree with hours from WSU and two summers back on campus at Oklahoma State.

Their first church home as a couple was the Central Baptist Church (now College Heights) in Manhattan. The church was without a pastor, but had a rented parsonage, which they were glad to rent to the newly married young couple. The young church took the Keefers in and put them to work; they fell in love with the Kansas brand of Baptists. When they left to go back to Oklahoma, she remembers, laughing through her tears at a farewell party the church planned, "We are going back to God's country and you have to stay in Kansas." She thinks now that she and Jim are the only ones of that group who are still in Kansas.

After discharge from the army, Jim went back to work for Southwestern Bell, a company he continued with until his retirement. This meant moving from time to time, and after a short stay in Oklahoma, they were back in Wichita, where the Keefers met Ray and Anne Gilliland, who helped them get settled in Southern Baptist work. Yvonne worked part-time for the Convention and for the associational missionary as secretary, took classes at WSU, worked with WSU Baptist Student Union, and "taught more study courses than I knew existed." When they moved across town, they also moved to North Hillside Church.

Then, "Ma Bell" moved them to Parsons, and from there, in 1959, to Topeka, where they remained until 1964. These were the Vietnam War years, so Forbes Air Force Base was in full swing; the Keefers were up to their eyes in work with "young people," who were defined at that time by Southern Baptists as people from seventeen to twenty-four. By this time, their two sons, Steve and Brian, had joined the family.

Then they went back to Parsons for two years, and in 1966, returned to Topeka. Ray Gilliland invited Yvonne to begin Baptist Student Union work at Washburn; they jumped in with "all eight feet." It was a family affair that included the boys.

On an occasion when Jim was squiring Gerald Locke around to speaking engagements, Locke introduced Jim by telling the people that God had called Yvonne into full-time Christian service in a place where there were no funds. He went on, "Yvonne doesn't need to have a salary because God gave Jim the ability to earn enough to support their family." This was their ministry together.

When Yvonne recalled this incident, she said, "For the first time in our lives it all made sense. God had indeed called us to Kansas-Nebraska missions—on His own terms."

Two years later the telephone company demanded another move, this time to Lawrence. Keefer reported that after nine moves in twelve years she said to Jim and to God, "This is it. The next move will have to be to an institution." She chuckled as she continued, "I assume they both believed me, because we are still in the same house."

They became deeply involved in the church in a score of ways. Then came November 1968 and the Bond Crisis. Two dear friends, Ray Gilliland and Garth Pybas, lost their jobs, the campus ministry program fell apart, and campus centers were sold. They felt cheated by those who had rubber-stamped plans presented to them, rather than questioning, researching, and making responsible decisions.

At this time Keefer began to juggle two full-time jobs: educational director for the church, when the pastor took a sabbatical to continue his studies, and campus minister for KU, when Bill Marshall had to leave in the aftermath of the financial crunch. In 1969 she became the full-time, almost volunteer campus minister at KU, where she remained until the end of 1982.

When Viola Webb's retirement drew near, Peck Lindsay approached Keefer about the position of WMU director for the KNCSB. At first she laughed; she was where she planned to stay. But each time he mentioned it, she "laughed less and got a little more hooked." After all, missions had been her life "forever."

Carolyn Weatherford, at that time director of WMU, SBC, came to Kansas to interview three candidates. Afterwards, Lindsay invited Keefer to interview with the committee and board. She said, "My respect for him and his leadership would not allow me to say no." Even after the invitation by the board to fill this position, it was two or three days before she could decide to accept it. KNCSB can be thankful that she felt God's leadership in this direction and accepted that appointment which became effective on January 1, 1983.

When Keefer came before the committee, in 1982, for a final interview concerning the position of WMU director, N. J. Westmoreland, by that time quite feeble, got the attention of the chair. Through the years, he and Keefer had had differences, but things had changed for both of them. He wanted the privilege of making the motion for her employment. His motion carried unanimously.

Her degree from Oklahoma State University is in family relations and child development. She has traveled extensively, and enjoys traveling, reading, games, and needlework. What she also likes is lots of ice in anything that is supposed to be cold.

She began her first report to the Convention with these words (*Annual*, 1983), "This year has been an exciting one for me as I have grown to appreciate even more the people in our Convention who love missions and act on that love." A hallmark of Keefer's work is action. Do something!

During the thirteen years Keefer has been director of WMU, there have been a number of "first time evers." In 1983, at the regular leadership training time in August for associational leadership, there was a class for Spanish women taught in Spanish. A consultant for ethnics became a part of the state WMU committee. Keefer initiated the State Prayer Calendar for missionaries, Convention employees and officers, and their families, printed in the *Digest*.

Specialized weekend retreats for women, at Webster Conference Center, have been inaugurated, planned and led by volunteer state consultants, supported and encouraged by Keefer. They have been outstanding achievements: Baptist Women's Retreat, Baptist Young Women's Retreat, Acteens Retreat (which had been in place before Keefer became), Girls in Action Retreat, and in 1992, a GA Mother-Daughter Retreat for younger GAs.

Prior to this, the plan was a GA-RA camp and an adult missions-weekend. The coed adult weekend had served its day; attendance and interest were dwindling. A decision was made to have, instead, a Baptist Women's Retreat, which was instituted by Millie Stengl, Baptist Women's consultant, which has been well received by women over the Convention. This was followed by a separate retreat for BYW, begun by Mary Jo Troughton when she served as BYW's consultant.

Consultants have come from both Kansas and Nebraska. While Wendy Whaley, from LaVista Baptist Church in LaVista, Nebraska, served as Baptist Young Women's consultant, she was one of those chosen to be a BYW Enterpriser. With a group of BYWs from over the SBC, she went to Russia in 1991 to deliver Bibles to thousands of people. Since that time, Whaley and her family have returned to Russia on two other mission tours.

In 1984 there was an orientation conference for the writers of state mission study materials. This was a time to meet and dialogue with the missionaries across Kansas and Nebraska who were to be featured in that year's materials. This has been continued each year.

In 1984, at the National Acteens Conference (NAC) in Fort Worth, Kansas and Nebraska had 214 girls. The first NAC was held in 1972 at Glorieta with nine hundred girls present. Since that time, such conferences have been held in Memphis (1975), Kansas City (1979), Fort Worth (1984), San Antonio (1989), and Birmingham (1994). All have been successful.

During the NAC in Fort Worth, Martha Mitchell, of First Baptist Church, Bellevue, Nebraska, was chosen for the National Acteens Advisory Panel. In that role, she served as a page at the national WMU annual meeting and at the SBC in Las Vegas, and helped in a number of ways with the NAC meeting in San Antonio. One of her jobs was to "star" in a video made by WMU, SBC, to promote Acteens. She was at that time working on the State Citation, the highest level of achievement in Studiact. Lori Arnold Chambers, member of First Southern Baptist Church in Beloit, is the only other young woman in the Kansas-Nebraska Convention to have received that citation.

The Acteens National Advisory Panel, for which six girls are chosen each year from hundreds of applicants, was inaugurated in 1977, by WMU, SBC. Acteens accomplishments, Christian maturity, school and community excellence are all taken into account in making these choices.

The first Kansas-Nebraska Acteen Advisory Panel was elected in 1978 at the retreat at Rock Springs (*Annual*, 1978). There were other important things at that retreat, as well. It was well attended with representation from seven associations. For the first time there were ten girls from Haskell Institute and ten deaf girls at the gathering.

The newest member of the WMU retreat family is the weekend for younger GAs and their mothers, planned for girls in grades one through three. It was the brain-child of Beverly Hilton, Girls in Action consultant. The first Mother-Daughter Weekend was held in 1991, when a time-slot became available because of a cancellation of an associational retreat. It has grown each year, with the favorite activities being things that mothers and daughters do together. At the first retreat there was a three-generation family of mothers and daughters: Linda Bowie, a missionary to Peru, her mother, and her twin daughters, who were adopted in Peru.

In 1984 WMU, SBC, moved from downtown Birmingham to the beautiful new building at 100 Missionary Ridge. Each state was given the opportunity of furnishing an area as a state memorial. The Kansas-Nebraska space is the reception area. Gifts were received from over our two-state Convention to make this possible. Right now, Mary Jo Troughton is making a doll, which is one of her skills, which will be dressed by Alpha Goombi, in a replica of her husband's great-aunt's beautiful beaded buckskin robe. The doll will have a place of honor in the Kansas-Nebraska area.

As another 1984 "first-ever" event, Ken and Linda Bowie were appointed as missionaries in residence for Kansas-Nebraska. The churches were delighted with this couple and the added missions emphasis they gave.

In 1987 there was a time of rejoicing when the Viola Webb Offering for State Missions was all in. With a goal of ninety thousand dollars, receipts totaled $90,066.41, which was a twelve percent increase over the year before (*Annual*, 1987).

For the first time ever, the annual meeting was held at Webster Conference Center in 1988. In addition, all the events planned by WMU are now scheduled on weekends, rather than at a mid-week time, in deference to working women.

In 1989 Keefer did a stewardship survey of churches in the KNCSB based on information in 1987-88 Church Letters. What she found was startling: ninety-seven percent of churches with WMU made gifts to the Cooperative Program, while only sixty-four percent of churches without WMU made such an offering; eighty-five percent of churches with WMU gave through the Viola Webb Offering for State Missions, while only thirty-six percent of those without this organization made an offering. The same differences were seen in regard to the of Annie Armstrong Offering for Home Missions and Lottie Moon Offering for Foreign Missions: ninety-four percent to forty-eight percent and ninety-four percent to fifty-four percent. It looks as though good stewardship can be increased by organizing a WMU. Churches and missions with a WMU gave 123 percent more per member (based on resident membership only) to the Cooperative Program, thirty-one percent more to the State Missions Offering, eighty-three percent more to Annie Armstrong Offering and 123 percent more to the Lottie Moon Christmas Offering (*Annual*, 1989).

The "get ready" year for the celebration of a hundred years of WMU, SBC, was 1987. The anniversary celebration, with the theme, "A Century to Celebrate; A Future to Fulfill," was held in Richmond Virginia, in 1988. In associations all over Kansas and Nebraska, there were "at-home" birthday parties for this grand and glorious event.

Of the eleven thousand persons gathered in Richmond, thirty were from Kansas and Nebraska, a delegation dwarfed by those from the southern states. Nevertheless, Kansans and Nebraskans played a significant role in the celebration. Mike and Pam O'Donnell from Topeka were among the home missionaries commissioned. Mike had just become a part of the state staff in our Convention, and Pam was one of the featured singers for the festival in the park on Friday evening. Also commissioned as home missionaries were Doug and Brenda Lee. Lee is a former pastor of First Baptist Church, Chetopa, Kansas, one of the founding churches of the KNCSB. In addition, earlier in his career, he had started churches in Nebraska, his home state. Don and Sue Gardner were commissioned as foreign missionaries; they were appointed to serve in Hong Kong. Gardner was the former pastor of Emmanuel Chinese Mission in Overland Park. Jon and Priscilla Sapp, on furlough from Zambia, were featured speakers at two separate banquets. Mary Crumpton played the piano for the banquet at the Ramada Renaissance Hotel. Yvonne Keefer, Viola Webb, and Jeanie Nolan rode in the beginning processional. Kansas-Nebraska had six official delegates, representing the following associations: Twin Valley, Tri-County, Kansas City, Kansas, Sedgwick, Smoky Hill, and Kaw Valley. The celebration was marked by exciting sessions, gala events, nifty favors, laughter, remembering, and planning ahead.

Inaugurated at that time was the Second Century Fund whereby it is possible to touch the future of missions with gifts made now and at the time of death. This may have been the inspiration for a similar fund set in place by the Kansas-Nebraska WMU: Strengthening Missions Beyond My Lifetime.

The Kansas-Nebraska Nursing Fellowship became a reality in October 1988. The group has regular meetings, but, more importantly, has planned missions projects. In 1992 (*BD*, September 28, 1992), eleven nurses, one emergency technician, and three Spanish interpreters went into Mexico where they visited Baptist churches, did health assessments, provided health education, and checked medication for the Rio Grande River Ministry's clinic. The group worked with Betty Callaway, a Mission Service Corps missionary with the Home Mission Board and the Rio Grande River Ministry.

Maxine Thorne from Twin Valley Association served as the first president of the fellowship, followed by Donna Swindle from Sedgwick Association and Murle White from Kansas City, Kansas, Baptist Association.

Since her appointment, Yvonne Keefer has worn more than one hat. In addition to being director of the WMU Department of the Convention, she also works with Terry McIlvain in the Family Ministry area. McIlvain's responsibility is with senior adults; Keefer's responsibility is with marriage enrichment and parent education, chiefly promoting and training trainers to use "Covenant Marriage" and "Parenting by Grace." She is responsible for the Jordan Partnership and for work with short-term foreign mission volunteers. Mark Clifton is responsible for the Nevada Partnership; McIlvain works with Home Mission Board volunteers. In her "spare" time, Keefer serves as general overseer of the building in order to keep it in good repair, which provides a comfortable and efficient place to work, and a beautiful place for all of us to visit.

What shall we say of women who served as presidents of Kansas-Nebraska WMU? All have been volunteers; all have given freely of their time and gifts, from the first one, Nellie Williamson, to the current president, Mary Jo Troughton. To tell the story of each one is not possible, so we have chosen ones who have served in "auspicious" ways or times.

Elizabeth Lobaugh, president from 1957 to 1962, is the only person from Kansas or Nebraska who has served as a national officer of WMU. She was recording secretary from 1963 to 1969. She grew up in Miami, Missouri, attended business college, and graduated from William Jewell College. She also attended the WMU Training School in Louisville, Kentucky. She served on the Convention's Executive Committee in 1957-1960. In 1953 she was a member of First Southern Baptist Church in Kansas City, Kansas, where she was employed as church visitor. A long-time friend remembers that Elizabeth Casebolt was a "great soul-winner, adept at sharing the Gospel." She was WMU director of Kansas City, Kansas, Baptist Association, in the late 1950s. She married J. R. Lobaugh in the early 1960s. After his death in 1975, she moved to Johnson County. Today she is a member of the Leawood Baptist Church in Overland Park.

Mrs. James Zeltner, whose husband was pastor in Plainville, came to Kansas in 1955. She had this to say about Elizabeth Lobaugh. "I will never forget the first time I saw Elizabeth. I couldn't believe that a laywoman would be willing to give so much of her time and so much of her energies and so much of her income to help in the work. There was no doubt in my mind that Elizabeth Lobaugh loved missions. She was a very outstanding person in her local church in Kansas City, Kansas. She loved WMU and did many things to help us grow and promote the work."

Opal Bates was president of Kansas-Nebraska WMU from 1971 through 1976. She was a member of the Executive Board of the Convention, in 1967-1969, during the years of the bond fiasco.

Bates wrote that she is "not a native of Kansas—but very close!" She is from Missouri, but has lived for forty-three years in the same house, in Galena, Kansas, where her husband came to work in 1951. She began her association with Kansas WMU by taking GAs to camp at Webster. She served as Tri-County Association WMU director, and had various tasks during the time she was a member of the State WMU Council.

Bates shared about the leadership and training tours which Viola Webb engineered each year, "She scheduled with various churches in each association a time to bring all age level directors to present a training session to their churches. Can you imagine the tight fit when six people got into Viola's car and took off. Each person had her own props and posters. We were packed We had serious moments of prayer, but we also had fun. We did a lot of planning along the way, also." Even in those days there was a shop-aholic along. Mrs. Bates confessed to this obsession. "If we had any extra time before the meeting, which we seldom did, everyone knew I loved to shop."

Millie Stengl, president from 1991 to 1995, was chosen to serve on the WMU, SBC, Long-Range Planning Committee which recommended the goals of WMU going into the twenty-first century. This was an "exciting, stressful, and rewarding" time for her. She could see God at work as the committee, made up of women from all parts of the Convention, sought direction for WMU. As the hard work came to a close, she was able to say, "As the Core Values and the Mission Statement were adopted by the Board at the meeting January 1993, I felt the Holy Spirit was there to place His seal of affirmation on the decisions that were made."

She was born in Oklahoma and grew up in the church: "If the doors were open, we were there." After she and Jack were married in 1958, they moved a number of times because of work and education opportunities. Everywhere she went, she organized a Women's Missionary Soceity and a GA group.

In 1962 the Stengl family, then with two sons, moved to Wichita, where they found a wonderful church family at Pleasantview Baptist Church in Derby. When her daughter was only two weeks old, Millie was asked to be WMU director of Sedgwick Association. She served from 1964 to 1969, years of change for WMU.

In 1971, after a short time in St. Louis, Millie was back in Kansas where she became involved at state and national levels. She served two terms as Baptist Women consultant, began to write for *Royal Service*, led conferences at Glorieta and Ridgecrest, and then was elected president of Kansas-Nebraska WMU.

While she was in high school, Millie attended a summer conference at Falls Creek and felt God's call to missions. She is now able to look back at that experience and say, "I know that God called me to a missions lifestyle and gifted me to lead out in missions education, support, prayer. As an added bonus He allowed me to make four trips to Africa as a partner in missions, working alongside some of our foreign missionaries. He has also given me a special ministry through my professional career in nursing."

Mary Jo Troughton is the current president of Kansas-Nebraska WMU. She grew up in a family with a "missions lifestyle" where she learned the importance of missions in action. "Excited" is a word which describes Troughton. She is excited about serving God, about reaching out to all people and helping them to grow, about the educational and growth possibilities of WMU, and about using her skill in a great many crafts. She is not a "business-as-usual" person; she is enthusiastic about new directions and about broader outreach to women in the community, inclusion of everyone, not just the "regulars," in missions education and participation.

She became a Christian early in her life. She was a member of missionary organizations off and on as she grew up, but did not consider herself a WMU person. As a young mother she was invited to attend WMU "circle meetings." The older women offered to come by for her; child care was provided; and she got "hooked." They asked her to fill an office. When she said she did not know how, they answered, "No problem; we'll help you." They did and she did! When the Troughton family began to attend Nall Avenue Baptist, she took her children to the music program on Wednesday nights. She volunteered to work with Acteens, so she would not be wasting her time while she waited for the children. On her birthday that year she went to a training session for Acteen leaders, and came home determined to have a real Acteens organization. By the end of the year there were two organizations with twenty girls enrolled. She reached out to other Acteen groups in the association, and was invited to become associational Acteens director. Because of her outstanding work in that position, she was invited to become the state Acteens consultant, where she served five years. During the year she did not serve on the state WMU Council, she was elected to the KNCSB Executive Board. Then it was back to the State WMU Council as BYW's consultant where she served five years, even though she thought she was not the "right age" for this job when she took it. In 1994 she completed five years as WMU director of Kansas City, Kansas, Baptist Association.

She and her husband, Kent, helped start the Quivira Road Baptist Church in Shawnee and also were a part of the beginning of Emmanuel's (Overland Park) satellite church, Westside, now Lenexa Baptist Church. She was local WMU director at Quivira for ten years, at Westside for four years, and now holds the position of WMU/Women's Ministry Director at Nall Avenue. She has done a great deal of writing for *Dimension*, prepared the promotional materials for the Viola Webb State Missions Day of Prayer programs, and has led conferences for BYW at Glorieta, as well as training sessions all over

Kansas and Nebraska. Briefly, she was on the staff at Nall Avenue Baptist Church as minister of missions.

Then came the council meeting of 1994. She and her husband were on vacation in California. It was the first time Troughton had not been part of the council meeting in ten years. When she called home, her daughter told her Yvonne Keefer was eager to get in touch with her. So, in the middle of the San Diego Zoo, next to the monkey enclosure, Troughton called Keefer. The Nominating Committee wanted her to consider becoming president-elect of Kansas-Nebraska WMU, an office that had not existed prior to that time. She wrote, "Somehow God had prepared my heart and mind to accept." Her election to this place of service at the annual WMU meeting in 1994 was greeted with joy and appreciation by the participants.

In our history we have had fourteen WMU presidents. This is not an easy task, for these women must assume responsibilities not only to Kansas-Nebraska WMU, but they also serve as vice-presidents (trustees) of WMU, SBC. They have served well, setting the pace for those, in the paraphrased words of Ethlene Boone Cox, "who follow in their train!"

We have talked so far about women who have served professionally as paid or volunteer staff of WMU in Kansas, who have made an indelible mark upon what has happened in Kansas-Nebraska churches. However, there are other women, who also have made great impact: pastors' wives, approved workers, members of the board of WMU and of the board of the Convention, and women across the state who have taken on tasks of leadership in their local churches and associations—all volunteers. Their name is Legion.

In 1990 Mrs. Ed Falconbridge was asked to give a testimony at the annual meeting of the Convention on what the church had meant to her family. She was a member of Olivet Baptist Church in Wichita. This is a lengthy journey for this church. When Gordon Dorian was called to Olivet, he was serving in a church in Texas where he thought the women talked entirely too much, especially during business meetings. So at Olivet he set a policy that no woman could make a motion; she could speak to any motion, but her husband, or another man, had to present the business to the group. Gordon Dorian had the grace to say in 1994, "Wasn't that awful!" He has mellowed with the years.

Wanda Westmoreland was one of those pastor's wives who "stood by the stuff" while her husband was busy about many other things. She lived in spaces too small and moved too much. Even so, she seemed always able to make room for one more.

She had great responsibility for their two sons and three daughters. She was an excellent pianist, but there is little reference to her filling other "church" or denominational responsibilities. This is easy enough to understand since she was looking after her husband, who had but one concern—building Southern Baptist churches in Kansas and Nebraska to proclaim the Word to the lost, while encouraging the brethren. She does not consider herself to have "looked after N. J. " Her comment was, "N. J. looked after himself."

In the eyes of other people, however, she came across as a woman whose great contribution was support for her husband. Strahan, the first state missionary said, "She was a strong supporter and encourager of N. J. and in a way allowed him to give so much to the work."

In a tribute to Westmoreland by Orbie Clem in 1953 (*KSBB*, March 19), he pointed to Westmoreland as a man of faith, "a faith strong enough to face the opposition of pagan and other un-scriptural religious orders, surmount seemingly immovable obstacles, endure the taunts and scorns of the faithless, and lead on to victory."

In the same piece, he had this to say about Wanda Westmoreland, "This story would not be complete without pointing out that a companion has shared willingly in the many sacrifices experienced by her husband in a labor of love on this great mission field. . . . Mrs. N. J. (Wanda) Westmoreland has been found ready to go when and wherever her companion felt led of the Spirit. Hers has been an unselfish spirit in suffering inconveniences and loneliness as she stayed at home and cared for the children. In addition to her home duties, she has been active in church life. Yes, she shares and will share with him in the rewards for the faithful."

Marjorie Moratto shared an insight into the family, as she recalled things she learned from Mrs. Westmoreland in the early years. During simultaneous revivals in the Topeka area, six preacher families were living together in a sorority house near the university. The women were cooking for the whole group. One day Mrs. Westmoreland made the grocery list and asked N. J. to pick up the supplies, which he did. As the women were putting things away, Mrs. Westmoreland found a jar of honey. "Why did you get honey?" she asked. "It's so expensive." He replied, "Because it was on the list." And out came the list to prove his point. Sure enough, right in the middle of bread, potatoes, and rice were the words, "Honey, I love you. But," he continued, "I got the smallest jar I could find."

Wanda Westmoreland explained to young Marjorie Moore that she often wrote tiny love notes to her husband and tucked them away for him to find. He was on the road so much, and there was so little time together, she had chosen this little scheme to "keep in touch." Sometimes the note would be in the toe of his sock, or the front of his shirt, or in his Bible.

In 1967 Wanda Westmoreland completed a B.S. degree; in 1981, an M.S. degree. During these years, she has taught off and on in various capacities. She has through the years been active in her local church, through music and various organizations. During one period she served as state WMU GA consultant. Since her husband's death she has had two periods of service in Japan as a volunteer. She was in Kyoto for almost a year in 1989, then home for about six months. When she went back to Japan, she was in Niigata, a more remote area "on the backside of Japan," where she taught English and Bible for about fifteen months. She is a member of First Baptist Church in Corsicana, Texas, where she works with international students, and teaches piano.

Another lesson from Mrs. Westmoreland, Moratto shared, tells much of her philosophy. One day Moore was complaining about something or other, and perhaps thinking that all the difficulties were just not worth it. Mrs. Westmoreland answered, "I'd be terribly disappointed if your being in Kansas didn't make a difference."

And what a difference it has made: the presence of Marjorie Moore Moratto; the Westmorelands; countless pastor-families from Oklahoma, Arkansas, Texas, and Missouri; and laymen and women who came from the uttermost parts of the SBC and even the world, along with, more recently, native sons and daughters, to proclaim the Word and minister to the people. So many have felt called to minister in a pioneer area. In 1995 we celebrate together beneath the banner, "50 Years . . . Making a Difference."

Barbara Noble is another pastor-wife who has helped her husband make a difference. Noble, called to the pastoral ministry during World Word II (*BD*, January 27, 1992), enrolled in Southwest College at Bolivar as soon as he was out of the service. Westmoreland went to Bolivar, visited with the ministerial students, and told them about Kansas; Noble accepted the challenge to serve in a truly pioneer situation.

Noble came in July 1948 to hold Vacation Bible Schools in and around Burden, Kansas (Personal Communication, 1994). He stayed to become pastor of First Baptist Church at Arma. In September, sixteen-year-old Barbara came to Kansas to become Mrs. Wilbur Noble. They stayed in Arma a year, then went to Pleasant Hill Baptist Church, "which is out in the country nine miles southwest of Columbus, Kansas." In 1950 they bought a small trailer, parked it at Charley Camp's house, and started a mission in that house. It is now Mission Creek Baptist Church. For six months there were just Camp and the Nobles; finally, through "soft-ball game ministry" (Wilbur was a great ball player and organized a team wherever he went), Charlie Folsom began to attend the services. He brought others and they brought others until finally there was an enrollment of 130 in Sunday School. Sunday School was in Camp's two-bedroom home. Barbara reminisced, "We sat on beds, floors, chairs, make-shift benches. I believe I led more people to know the Lord using the bathroom as a conference room in that home than in any other place since."

One of the ministries was a pick-up service, sometimes as many as twenty to thirty people. One of these was a youngster who was twelve or thirteen years old. His name was Forest Tuter; he became pastor of the Whitechurch Baptist Church in Kansas City, Kansas.

The Nobles committed themselves, and it was as truly a commitment on the part of Barbara as much as on the part of Wilbur, to a bivocational ministry to small, struggling churches in Kansas. Noble has worked at secular jobs, along with pastoring, since 1946.

In 1952 they moved to Eudora and had a meeting on Sunday in the home of Myrtle and Clifton Long with a nucleus of families from Arkansas. During the week, the landlord banned any church services in that house, so the group moved to another house, and finally rented a theater building. Barbara laughs as she says, "Wilbur always said that's where he got his loud mouth. The theater seated way over a hundred people and everyone sat in the back row. He had to yell for all of us to hear."

They stayed until a church building was underway at Eudora and moved on to Eureka, with a larger trailer, which seemed like "heaven, after living in a 25-foot trailer." A church was organized there, and like Paul, they moved again, this time to Antioch in Lawrence, where they started East Heights Church, which merged with Faith Baptist to become what is now Cornerstone Baptist Church.

During this time (1952) Noble formed his own drywall construction company based on the experience he got while building and repairing church buildings for congregations he had pastored. Barbara must get a good deal of the credit for this. She tells it this way, "We lived in a little trailer park, and a man came next door and offered our neighbor a sheet-rocking job in Kansas City. When the man to whom the job was offered said he already had a job, I called out and said, 'Can my husband have that job?'" He got the job and learned a trade.

He began buying, repairing, and reselling houses. He has bought more than forty houses in Topeka, plus several in Kansas City. Some of those houses, when repaired, were used as church buildings and were deeded to the congregations when they became churches.

From East Heights they went to Trinity in Topeka to revive the church, which had dwindled to four members. For the first time they bought a "place to be their own" and lived in the basement while they built on top of it. They remodeled the garage and used that and the house for classes. Barbara continued, "Let me tell you folks, you've not lived until you've had church in your home; until you've had all the young boys to the bathroom at the same time." Finally, a building was completed at Trinity, all with volunteer labor.

From Trinity they went to Kansas City and began Hillside Baptist Church in 1965, which was a mission of Metropolitan Baptist Church in Kansas City. Hillside Church bought property, and they built a home. Again, there was "church in the house" until the church building was completed.

From Hillside, which is now New Hope Baptist Church, they went back to Trinity, where attendance was down to thirteen people. The church was about to go under and a brewery was to be built next to the church property. "We couldn't see that which belonged to the Lord become something that belonged to the devil," said Barbara. So back they went to Trinity. The church grew, and the debt was paid.

From Trinity in the fall of 1985, they went to Carbondale to "fill in" for one Sunday, and the fill-in grew and grew until Wilbur became pastor. Again there was building to be done, and a church was organized. This was an old church, but had evidently come upon hard times.

The Nobles then went from Carbondale to Eskridge and from Eskridge in 1990 to Berryton. A group from Alabama came in 1991 and put up the building which was finished by other volunteer labor and dedicated in the summer of 1992. In 1993 they went to Silver Lake, to Lakeside Baptist Church, again to help them get started on their building.

In January 1992, the Nobles established a charitable annuity trust with the foundation consisting of real estate and insurance holdings valued at $1.2 million. The bivocational church builder and his wife will reach into the future and continue to touch the lives and hearts of Kansas and Nebraska people, building churches and sharing in the advance of the Kingdom.

When the Convention was very young, women were called upon and appointed to be "approved workers" whose job it was to train Sunday School and Training Union leadership in the local church. In 1950 (*Annual*) Mrs. C. O. Little, member of the First Baptist Church, Sedgwick, was named an approved general worker to serve in cooperation with the Department of Religious Education. In this capacity she has served churches in Sunday School enlargement campaigns, in the promotion of Vacation Bible Schools, and in the improvement of Training Unions.

According to a report in the 1952 *Annual*, three more approved workers were named: Mrs. George McClelland, Intermediate worker; Mrs. Forest Reed, Young People's worker; and Mrs. Ray Gilliland, Elementary worker. Mrs. James Zeltner wrote that the thing which meant most to her during her time in Kansas-Nebraska was being a state-approved worker, training leadership throughout the church in early childhood education. She was the Sunbeam Band director for the state, from 1958 to 1961 (Written Communication). These volunteer trainers were available for study courses and enlargement campaigns. Local churches were asked to pay their expenses except when on assignments for the Department of Religious Education. By and large the system was continued, with volunteers from the Convention trained by SBC leadership and then reaching out to associations and local churches.

Women have been engaged in many "unsung" ministries. Women have found ways in which to minister to others in unusual ways. For example, Ethel Herrick, in her retirement years, is pen pal to the police force in Topeka (*BD*, April 24, 1993). She sent birthday cards to show her appreciation for the services of the police officers. During one three-month period, she sent 150 cards. She said, "Life's fairly short and you have to appreciate the chances you get to help other people."

Joe Novak, editor of the *Digest* (March 7, 1959), paid tribute to a Kansas Baptist (American Baptist Convention) woman, Mrs. M. B. Hodge, a native of Arkansas City, who grew up in Wichita and attended high school there. He reviewed her service and closed his article by saying, "It shows what people can do who are dedicated to their calling, that of 'measuring up to the needs of the hour.'"

Mrs. Hodge at that time (1959) was serving as president of the ABC, the fourth woman to fill the position. She was also serving as the first woman president of the Oregon ABC, and had just been reelected as president of the North American Woman's Union of the Baptist World Alliance. Mrs. Hodge had been in Wichita to speak at the tenth Evangelistic Conference for the Kansas ABC.

Through the years there have been many other dedicated servant women in Kansas who belonged to Southern Baptist churches. None of these, however, were tapped for the kind of service that Mrs. Hodge was allowed to render through the ABC. That seems a terrible waste of God-given gifts, as well as energy and creative ideas.

At the organization of the KCSBC in 1946, Mrs. Orbie Clem was elected recording secretary. Before the first meeting of the Convention in the fall, she became secretary of Kansas WMU, and so was not able to continue to serve as an officer of the Convention. Mrs. George Mitchel was elected recording secretary at the first annual meeting in 1946, and served two years. Since that time, no woman served as an officer until 1956, when Mrs. Miles Cowden was elected historical secretary. She was elected again in 1957, and served through 1961. Her 1961 election made real news, for the Convention constitution had just been amended to include the historical secretary of the body as a member of the committee, so Mrs. Miles Cowden became the first woman to serve on the committee by virtue of her office.

After Mrs. Cowden finished her six-year stint as historian, no woman was selected again until Mary Jo Robertson was elected as recording secretary of the Convention, from 1980 through 1989. She was also appointed parliamentarian for 1988 and 1989. Marie Clark served as assistant recording secretary in 1987 and 1988 and again in 1994 and 1995. In 1992 and 1993, Mary Wolfington was elected assistant recording secretary.

To have utilized Kansas and Nebraska women in only twenty-four slots out of approximately 250 "officer years" in our fifty years of Convention existence seems a dreadful loss. Perhaps we need to remind ourselves that there are Southern Baptist women, who, like Mrs. Hodge, are dedicated to their calling and ready to "measure up to the needs of the hour."

Through the years a number of women have served on the KNCSB Executive Board. Mrs. Miles Cowden was the first; Mrs. Lyn Dungey, Mrs. J. D. Williamson, Mrs. Roger Knapton, Gertrude Mitchell, Margaret Reedy, and Elizabeth Lobaugh were others in the early days. Today nine women serve on the board of the Convention representing seven associations: Kay Lacy, Valley Center, Sedgwick; RoyLynn Pameticky, Severy, Blue Stem; Cloie Brevik, Salina, Smoky Hill; Beverly Simon, Sidney, Nebraska, Platte Valley; Judi Freemyer, Kansas City, Kansas City, Kansas; Karen Williams, Garden City, Western Kansas; Beverly Wood, El Dorado, South Central; and Annette Aldape, El Dorado, an at-large representative. In addition, Marie Clark, assistant recording secretary of the Convention, fills that duty on the Executive Board and Committee. Three other women also serve on the Executive Committee: Lacy, Freemyer, and Williams.

The 1994-95 theme for WMU was "A Time to Grow." "Grow" referred to both numerical and spiritual concerns: more organizations, greater offerings, and more people involved in prayer and giving and service. It also referred to development of skills in witnessing and ministry, nurturing of the pioneer spirit, and development of a missions lifestyle. There is a sense of urgency in these words which lead into the current WMU theme, "Risk the Journey." Certainly women in Kansas and Nebraska will continue to step into places of servant-leadership, to risk the journey. With bright hope they look forward to God's tomorrows and their places in His great plan.

8

First the Seed . . . Then the Blade . . . Then the Fruit

PAT MCDANIEL PRESENTED HIS RESIGNATION AS EXECUTIVE director-treasurer to the Executive Committee of the KNCSB at a special meeting on June 10, 1977. It was to be effective July 31. He had accepted a position as executive vice president of the Annuity Board, SBC. His letter read in part, "Kansas-Nebraska Southern Baptists have given me a unique opportunity to serve them in our Lord's work for nearly eight years. I personally feel that it is time for new leadership and direction for this great Convention. I know the Lord will give direction as you and the Executive Committee seek out that person who will lead out in the exciting years ahead" (*Annual*, 1977).

At the same Executive Board meeting, a motion was made that R. Rex "Peck" Lindsay be asked to serve as the Convention staff and office coordinator. He was already in place as director of missions, evangelism, and student work.

At a subsequent meeting of the Executive Board, Lindsay was elected executive director-treasurer of the Convention and was presented to the 1977 Convention in his new role. He recognized the staff and introduced the new business administrator-comptroller, Harold Conley. Yvonne Keefer remembered that in a short speech to the Convention he reminded them that "a peck is, after all, only quarter of a bushel!" Both Lindsay and Conley still serve the Convention.

There were several changes in personnel at the 1977 Convention due to the move to Topeka. One of these was Robert Powell, who for several years had worked as administrative assistant with fiscal responsibilities. These duties were assumed by Harold Conley.

Conley, a native Kansan, grew up in the Wichita area, graduated from the University of Kansas with a degree in business, and worked in Wichita, Leoti,

231

and Great Bend. He was an active layman about 1970 when he felt the pull of vocational full-time Christian service, resigned his position, and went looking for work. Finding a church-related position was not easy. An interview with Peck Lindsay at that time left him traumatized, since he had no seminary training and was not disposed to accept the youth work jobs that were offered through the Home Mission Board. He found other work and kept "at it" in the local church and at the associational level. He was good at his job, so when one position folded up, another door always opened. He waited, and God turned the calendar pages in His own manner. In 1977, when Lindsay became executive director of the Convention, he sought out Conley to come to Topeka to fill the job of business administrator/comptroller.

By 1977 our debts were paid; Cooperative Program giving was up forty thousand dollars over the previous year. The State Missions Offering reached a record high and was designated for literacy, language, CSM, church pastoral aid, and student work. Both the Annie Armstrong Offering and Lottie Moon Offering showed increases over the year before. Circulation of the *Digest* had reached seven thousand. The move from Wichita to Topeka had necessitated new publishing arrangements which had slowed the subscription growth rate. One result of this was permission to purchase a typesetting machine which gave the Convention greater control and versatility in the publication of the *Digest*.

Ten full-time DOAMs were at work in twelve associations. There were four pastor directors at work in Pratt and Garden City, Kansas; and South Sioux City and Scottsbluff, Nebraska. There were student directors, all paid except one (Lila Martin at Fort Hays), on nine campuses; Wichita was without a director at the time. There were eleven language missions in five associations, work with National Baptists, and active CSM programs in five associations, with seven appointed missionaries listed. There were forty-one church-type missions in the Convention and 236 churches.

In addition, the Convention authorized, that year, a committee to work with the new executive director to ascertain the personnel needs of the Convention. This was to be with particular attention to the employment of a Brotherhood director, who was to have the same status and rights as the WMU director. Things were looking up. It was time to lengthen the cords, strengthen the stakes, and enlarge the place of our dwelling.

The pathway had not been easy to this point, but wonderful stories can be told of the beginning of churches, and of the people who were responsible for this growth. When the Convention was organized, one of the first official acts was the inauguration of the "Five-Year Plan" and the "100 Club." This was a plan to organize one hundred Southern Baptist churches in Kansas by 1951 (five years). The "100 Club" was a plan for subsidizing the support of pastors in these one hundred new churches with regular "extra" gifts. That goal was not quite reached. In 1951 there were fifty-six churches and missions affiliated with the Convention, with a membership of 5,047. That the goal was not reached in no way dampened the ardor of the leadership in Kansas. The second "Five Year Plan" was inaugurated in 1951.

The ambitious goals of the Second Five Year Plan were to organize two hundred additional churches; increase total membership to twenty-five thousand; realize a creditable beginning in establishing Bible chairs and a Bible institute; achieve the goal of fifty thousand dollars in a Revolving Building Loan Fund; establish a sinking fund for purchasing permanent headquarters property; and work toward the establishing of the Children's Home Project (*Annual*, 1950). In his report, Westmoreland continued, "Should anyone be of the opinion that our goals are not practical and are visionary, we would remind him that what has happened during the past five years, would have appeared visionary if these statistics had been listed as goals. During the past three years, we have made an average gain of 35 percent in membership. If this average is kept up, we should have 30,276 members by August 1, 1956. We must remember that Kansas has about 1,000 communities without a Baptist witness, and more than 1,200,000 people who have no connection with any evangelical church body. So long as there are such fantastic numbers of lost people surround us, we must at least attempt great things for God" (*Annual*, 1950).

Passing the century mark, with the organization of the Convention's one hundredth church (at El Dorado), and right on its heels, the 101st church (at Douglass), was reason for celebration (*BD*, July 10, 1954). The Convention was eight years old and had increased tenfold. "In that period, [the Convention] can report that for every 31 days, it has gained one church, 150 members, and church property valued at $21,000" (*BD*, July 10, 1954).

Church number one hundred at El Dorado (which was named Immanuel Southern Baptist) was organized with twenty-four members, and called R. H. Maultsby to be pastor. This "typical" church began as a mission of the Burden Baptist Church, which had been cooperating with the SBC for thirty-five years. Burden Baptist Church was the sponsor of the first church to affiliate with the Kansas Convention after its organization, the First Baptist Church of Winfield, organized June 20, 1946. Through that church, Burden Baptist Church was, by 1954, grandmother to five other churches, including the one at Douglass.

Finances for the El Dorado church show up like a beautiful patchwork quilt made of pieces of love from many sources: Burden invested $1,200 in the mission; $1,500 came from Immanuel Baptist Church in Wichita; the Home Mission Board had given the mission one hundred dollars per month for six months; and First Baptist Church, Henderson, Texas, voted to underwrite a loan of fifteen thousand dollars for a new building. And, of course, there were contributions from members of the church. The church bought an acre of land and planned a building with a 250-seat capacity auditorium and education space. A new brick parsonage was purchased at a cost of $13,500.

The pastor, R. H. Maultsby, was a product of Southern Baptist missionary advance in Kansas. He was one of the first two persons baptized into the fellowship of the Emmanuel Baptist Church, Coffeyville, and became its second pastor, the first one ordained by the church. He and Eleanor Hanson were the first couple married in the church.

His colorful history was recounted in the *Digest* (October 22, 1966) when he left the state to pioneer in Ohio. He was called the "dean of Kansas Convention of Southern Baptists pastors," since he had been in (and out of) the state for thirty years. He went from Coffeyville to Chautauqua, and organized a church; and then back to Oklahoma for several years. He returned in 1946 at the invitation of N. J. Westmoreland to conduct one of several revivals in Wichita. From this effort, Southside, Wichita, was born, on the front lawn of a home. He became pastor, in his words, of "two vacant lots." The Maultsbys moved from a seven-room parsonage in Oklahoma to a two-car garage, and he found a job to supplement his salary from the church.

The first building of the Southside Church was in a welding shop. On Sunday morning, chairs were crammed in everywhere, and children sat on newspapers spread over greasy benches. Many times, Maultsby and the song leader shared the same chair, since one of them was always standing. No member of the church will forget the only wedding; the bride and groom entered the "sanctuary," which was decorated with welding irons, anvils, and other tools, from an attached chicken house. Perhaps all weddings should be performed in "welding" shops!

From Southside, after he had helped build a building, Maultsby went to Burden for four years, then to Wichita to organize and pastor Olivet. He stayed until the first unit of the building was up, then he was off to El Dorado for the formation of church number one hundred of the Convention. His next call was to Derby where he led the entire construction program and saw the church grow to a membership of more than three hundred with $165,000 worth of property and buildings.

Maltsby likes to joke, "I organized four churches and built five, before I found out you just can't do that without a seminary education." His joy was starting churches and watching them grow. On one occasion, one of his children, after their fifth move in nine years, asked, "Daddy, why is it that just when things get comfortable, we have to move on?" Out of his love for pioneer work came his answer, "I wouldn't trade places with any man. There is something about pioneer work that you get nowhere else" (*BD*, October 22, 1966).

The story of the 101st church, at Douglass, also has a miracle glow about it. Henry Cox became the pastor of the mission of First Southern Baptist, Winfield, in August 1953. This was after a summer of revival meetings under the direction of the Winfield pastor and W. A. Burkey, secretary of missions for the Convention. Handbills were distributed and advertisements placed: "'Baptist revival in the American Legion Building in Douglass, Kansas, April 27-May 10.' . . . However, the closing sentence read: 'Keep watching each week as we announce the time and place of our services until a permanent place is secured'" (*Brief History of First Baptist Church of Douglass*, 1991).

Under the trees in the backyard of the house where the group was meeting, the church at Douglass was constituted on August 16, 1955, with sixty-one charter members. Cox continued as pastor until 1959, when he went to Midwestern Seminary. During his tenure a building was erected, and a mission at Rose Hill was begun. In 1955 an article and picture appeared (Douglass newspaper): "The new church building will be used next Sunday, April 1. . . . It was erected largely by members of the congregation, is a modernistic structure . . . and is one of the finest looking church structures around here."

In the summer of 1983, the church voted to build a new sanctuary and contacted the Home Mission Board concerning building crews (*Brief History of First Baptist Church of Douglass*, 1991). Edgewood Baptist Church of Columbus, Georgia, had planned to put a prefabricated building in place for a mission group in South Dakota. Construction materials were on the parking lot, ready to be transported to South Dakota, when the Georgians received word that the mission in South Dakota was not ready. No doubt you can guess the rest. The Home Mission Board put Edgewood Baptist Church in touch with the people in Douglass. As the result, "A miracle building in which First Baptist Church now worships was constructed and dedicated in seven days." In 1990 the church needed more educational space, which was built, again with volunteer working crews.

Lois Cox wrote a story, titled "A Cold Cup of Water," published in *Home Missions* (June 1960), that tells the next miracle story in her husband's ministry. Ray Bond, from Turner, left his just-poured cup of coffee when he had an urge to talk to another layman from Westport Baptist Church in Kansas City about the possibility of a Baptist church in Turner. Starting a mission in the area surrounding Kansas City, in 1959, with its lack of building sites or even meeting places, and because of the heavy debt load of most Southern Baptist churches in the area at that time, was uncertain at best. Tommy Williams promised to pray with Bond about it.

In the meantime, Henry Cox resigned from Douglass to attend the seminary in Kansas City, and was looking for a mission area in which to work. The Coxes were house hunting, hoping to find something that would be suitable for a home and for a new mission. About 8:30 one night, the realtor with whom they had been working reported that a house in Turner had just gone on sale—within the hour. It had an attached double garage, and the price was reasonable. The Coxes bought the house the next day.

When the Coxes moved to the area, they joined the First Baptist Church of Bethel, where Roger Knapton, who was chair of the associational missions committee, was pastor. As they began to talk about a good spot for a mission, the two parts of the story came together: the layman with a cold cup of coffee and the pastor with a house in Turner. A fellowship meeting with seventeen present was held in Ray Bond's home. The first Sunday worship service was held in the Cox home, and the Southern Baptist Chapel of Turner, mission of the First Baptist Church of Bethel, came to be. After only a few weeks, plans were made to buy three acres of land and a ten-room house on the corner of 55th and Metropolitan, a "cross-roads" area. It was a piece of property that had not been for sale in more than a hundred years, "having been in the same family since it was purchased from a Shawnee Indian." Since it was to be used for a church, the owners agreed to sell the property, at a price of thirty-five thousand dollars, with a down payment of five thousand dollars. In just eight months, the mission had been dreamed of, organized, a down payment made on a building, plans for remodeling completed, and revival dates set. In 1962 (*BD*, March 24, 1963), Turner Chapel in Kansas City was constituted into the Metropolitan Baptist Church. It was the 163rd church in the Kansas Convention and the forty-ninth church constituted in Kansas since the 1956 beginning of the Southern Baptist Convention's 30,000 Movement. So the Lord works with people of vision.

The 30,000 Movement was called "one of the most exciting projects Southern Baptists had ever undertaken—to establish thirty thousand new missions and churches across our Convention between 1956 and 1964" (*BD*, May 26, 1962). It was part of the Baptist Jubilee Advance, a brainchild of C. C. Warren, who was president of the SBC when the plan was adopted: "Every Church with a Mission." The First Baptist Church of Omaha was the first church started in Nebraska after the 30,000 Movement began.

A mission was defined as "anywhere one or more members are sent from the local church or churches at regular intervals to preach or teach the Word of God" (*BD*, May 9, 1962). Such groups included home fellowships; institutional missions, such as jails, homes for the aged, and hospitals; extension Sunday Schools; and "regular or church type missions," which frequently grew into churches.

A Kansas goal set in 1957, as part of the 30,000 Movement, was the organization of fifty-seven new missions, and featured the catchy slogan, "57 in '57." The results were disappointing, as only eleven new missions saw the light of day during the year. This brought the total number of missions in operation to twenty-four. The leadership suggested that our difficulties had to do with the large turnover of pastors. Pastors were urged to continue their efforts to set up mission points.

Burkey's report read in part: "Preliminary work has been done in about 12 places. Surveys reveal that there are at least 8 immediate possibilities for establishing Home Fellowship Hour programs and that at least 14 churches could begin immediately to sponsor one or more missions" (*Annual*, 1957). The goal was not fully realized; but great strides were made in Kansas and across the Convention. In 1962 the goal for Kansas was sixty-five new churches and missions, which Meeler Markham, Secretary of Department of Missions of Kansas Convention, called "still within our reach."

During the period, 1956-1964, 65 new churches and 233 missions of various types were established. At the beginning of 1964 (*BD*, February 6, 1965), there were thirty-seven church-type missions in existence, "the largest number ever at one time within the Kansas Convention of Southern Baptists." It is true that in order to do our best, our reach must exceed our grasp.

The story of Mulvane was unusual in that it may have been the only time when N. J. Westmoreland thought "another church" was not a good course of action. William McKean was born in Kansas, migrated to Oklahoma, but after he was married, moved back to Kansas in 1953. After he had pastored a couple of churches in Oklahoma, he came back to Kansas because he "began to feel God's call to come to my native state of Kansas to minister." He contacted Burkey who sent him to Mulvane to supply one Sunday in July 1953. On Monday the church had a business meeting and extended a call, which he accepted.

The church at Mulvane had begun some years before, but while the pastor was on vacation, the mission voted to leave the SBC and join the General Association of Regular Baptists. By 1952 a group in the church decided this was not for them and started another Southern Baptist mission. A bit later, the main body of the original church realized they had made a mistake, and called N. J. Westmoreland to ask what they needed to do to affiliate again with the SBC. His answer is worth remembering, for it may be the only time that Westmoreland felt there were "too many Baptist churches" anywhere!

There was just not enough room in Mulvane for two Southern Baptist churches, Westmoreland counseled, so the two groups would have to get together, work out their differences, and form a new church. This is what happened. As usual, a revival was planned and by the end of the summer there were forty-one members. McKean came as pastor. Every Sunday there were additions; in six months, the membership had reached sixty.

The following summer, a team of summer missionaries, working with McKean, got interested in Udall, and one was so "burdened" for this town, that he extracted a promise from McKean to begin a mission. In January, a preaching service was started; a young linotype operator at Mulvane became the mission pastor. The church was meeting in a rented building downtown when a tornado destroyed the town. After the storm, a man who had suffered great loss donated five lots to be used as a mission site. Another man, member of an Independent Baptist church in Wichita, donated a tent which was pitched on the empty lots, where the church in Udall now stands.

The congregation received money "from all over everywhere" from people who wanted to help this devastated church and town. Some mail was simply addressed "Baptist Church, Udall, Kansas" with a check in it. With the money, the church bought (at one hundred dollars per running foot) a portion of an old building that was being abandoned by the college in Winfield. It was cut into two fifty-foot pieces and moved onto the lot, and forms the basis for the present church in Udall. It has been remodeled since that time, but McKean says he often talks about the "church that a tornado built."

McKean remained in Kansas, getting a degree from Friends University, serving at First Southern Wichita, Indian Baptist in Wichita, Southside

Wichita, Fort Scott, Edwardsville, and in Edgerton. For forty-one years, the McKeans have been part of church growth in Kansas. One important memory is that on a hot summer day, he attended the organization of the church at Douglass, the 101st organized in Kansas.

CHURCH STARTS—AND STOPS—AND RESTARTS

Churches have "come to be" in Kansas and Nebraska through many channels. Southern Baptist laypersons have moved into Kansas and Nebraska, found no Southern Baptist church, and started one. This has been accomplished in various ways, sometimes by their own efforts, sometimes by "agitating" until someone got stirred up about it. Not a few times, those called to preach have felt moved to come into a pioneer area, because friends "laid hands on their shoulders" and helped them see the need in Kansas and Nebraska. So they came, and formed congregations, time and again beginning with a handful, in a front room of somebody's house or in some make-shift building.

In the case of some church starts, "mother" and "grandmother" churches have "purposed" to grow a church in a needy spot. So it was at Nall Avenue in Prairie Village, under the leadership of Owen Dahlor, who encouraged the members to multiply their ministry through starting missions. At one period the members covenanted to start ten missions, one per year. So in 1977 an Hispanic ministry was begun in what had been the Westport Baptist Church property, with Ben Ortiz as pastor. Next came a mission in DeSoto, which became the Clear Creek Baptist Church, which later became the First Southern Baptist Church of Lenexa. The Laotian ministry was recognized as a mission in 1983. Next came a mission in Louisburg and then a ministry to East Asian Indians. Parkway Baptist Mission, now constituted as a church, was started in 1987. A satellite church on Turtle Mountain Indian reservation in South Dakota grew out of a youth mission trip (Personal Communication, Owen Dahlor). So from 1977 to 1989, ten missions grew, reaching people who probably could not have been reached if Nall Avenue had followed its first desire to build a larger church. These were not the only missions started by Nall Avenue. The first one was begun in 1957, just four years after Nall Avenue was founded by four Southern Baptist families because there was no Baptist church in Johnson County.

A further word about the Turtle Creek outreach must be written. Pete Zaste and his wife went to the reservation after he hurt his arm and could not work as a carpenter in California. He is an enrolled member of the tribe, "looks like a burly biker and acts like the Apostle Paul." At the invitation of the pastor of the Dakota Baptist Church in Fort Totten, North Dakota, a group from Florida came to help. Since they arrived in 1989 (*BD*, July 23, 1990), Zaste has been the lay pastor of a group of twenty-nine who gather six times a week for Bible study. He also visits at the jail, nursing home and in private homes, not only on the reservation, but in nearby towns. The Nall Avenue youth group made three summer trips to this area for Backyard Bible Clubs, a week-long crusade led by Cloyd Harjo, and worship services in a camp.

Gossip was the starting point of the Hillsboro Church (*BD*, November 12, 1966). Gaylon Wiley, superintendent of missions for Blue Stem Association, followed up on fourth-hand information and found a "nest of Baptist families." It seems a pastor's wife from a neighboring association had taken her mother to the doctor in Hillsboro, and was asked by the doctor why there was no Baptist work in Hillsboro. He told her there were about thirty families there. She told the missionary in her association, Weldon Barnett, who passed the information along to Wiley, who went immediately to visit the doctor. It turned out the doctor had only "heard" about these Baptist families, but called his pastor who put Wiley in touch with one Baptist family, the Bill Stoneciphers. That very day Wiley and Stonecipher contacted eight other families who were interested, set up a meeting for the following Friday, and had fifteen in attendance. More Baptists were discovered; in a month the group was having Sunday services.

All church starts have not been unqualified successes. There have been churches which closed their doors or just faded away, for various reasons. Sometimes the location was wrong, sometimes the population shifted, and sometimes proper support could not be provided when it was needed. But little or much, long or short, each of these efforts has paid dividends in new Christians, community awareness, and Christian obedience.

Some of the churches have been begun again—and again. A few examples will suffice. Claflin Baptist Church was one of these (*BD*, May 28, 1990). When the oil industry was at its peak in Kansas, so was the church in Claflin; classrooms were overflowing in the cinder-block building. With the collapse of the oil industry, people moved away, and finally dwindling attendance closed the doors of the church for five years. During part of that time, there was a lay preacher-school teacher who came on Sundays to lead a service.

In the late 1980s, Norval and Edith Maness went to Claflin, appointed by the Home Mission Board as "church re-starters" through the Mission Service Corps. They were really supposed to go to Ellsworth, but the work was not quite ready, so they were diverted to Claflin. The Manesses had lived in Wichita; he worked at Boeing, she at the Coleman Company. Both were active in the Sharon Baptist Church, and helped start Cedar Pointe Baptist Church, a mission of Sharon.

After Norval Maness's recovery from a dreadful illness, they began to sense God's leadership to full-time Christian service. They had heard Doyle Smith, pastor of Great Bend Baptist Church, speak about the closed doors at Claflin. They volunteered, through the DOAM of Central Association, to rent a part-time home in Claflin, and try to open those doors again. They began services in the little church just ten days after their arrival. The community is small; most of the residents claim allegiance to a church; and about half are Catholic, while the others are Lutheran and Methodist. The people came back; the Manneses remained for two years.

Howard Click had filled in at Claflin from time to time, so when Maness left, Click became the interim, and continued the ministry. It is not large; about ten attend worship service; and there are two Sunday School classes, one for adults, most of whom are older, and one for a small group of youth. There are three other churches in the town, but Ruby Smith, a long-time member, says she just would not be comfortable in any other church but her own.

The church at Florence, Kansas, a small community about forty miles from Emporia, has had a rocky up-and-down time. Ray Hart, an early state missionary, had a hand in its reorganization in 1949. The church went about its work quietly for eighteen years. In 1967, when membership had dwindled to nineteen and Sunday School enrollment was only four, the doors of the church were closed. The church did not "disband"; it just quit meeting. In 1970 two summer missionaries, Jean Wilson and Cheryl Bassett, went to Florence for a week. They did a telephone survey, conducted a Vacation Bible School, and engineered a revival with Wayne Hett as preacher. Some of the old members were still interested in a Baptist church in Florence, a few prospects were found, and the spark of interest burst into flame. Gerald Locke, DOAM in Blue Stem, began Sunday morning services and within three Sundays, five were baptized and five were received by letter. Wayne Hett began serving as pastor, along with his work at Cottonwood Falls. He preached at Florence at 9:30 A.M., then drove to Cottonwood Falls. The Florence people had their Sunday School hour at the 11:00 "preaching hour." Midweek prayer service was held on Thursday instead of the "traditional" Wednesday night schedule. And so the church was alive again.

Again, hard times came. First Baptist in El Dorado, South Central Association, took the group under its wing as a mission. The church transferred to South Central.

In 1990 Ellen and Bud Noeller went to Florence. Their experience is typical of scores of bivocational "preacher families" in the Convention. Bud Noeller, who began to preach in middle-adult years, is a foreman for KPL, where he puts in long hours. Along with his job, he had been preaching here and there as he was needed. When the Florence Church returned to mission status, the Missions Committee of the El Dorado Church asked the Noellers to go there in view of a call. They sold their house in Augusta and moved to the field. He said, "A bivocational pastor must be dedicated and have a definite call from God." He also emphasized the need for his wife's support for this ministry. Ellen Noeller was the only Sunday School teacher in the church and also was WMU director in South Central Association. They worked together, even in their kitchen.

The Noellers remained in Florence through 1991, when his company transferred him to Derby, where he continued his KPL work and pastored the church in Sedgwick, Kansas. During his pastorate at Florence, Noeller was enrolled in extension courses in Wichita. If he had to be away on a Sunday, he enlisted another student from the class to fill in for him. One of these was Larry Zimmerman, who now continues the ministry at Florence. He is a layman from Tyler Road Baptist Church in Wichita and a mechanic by trade. Each church in Florence (there are four) is responsible, once a month, for a service at Regency Health Care Center. Zimmerman travels from Goddard to Florence, when it is the Baptist Sunday to go to Regency. On that Sunday, according to member Helen Graves, Zimmerman preaches at the church. The church makes a contribution to the Cooperative Program, pays Zimmerman a small stipend, has Bible study every Sunday, and most Sundays plans something else, such as a singing service. Some months Zimmerman comes to the church more than once (Personal Communications with Helen Graves and Ellen Noeller). Adult Bible study attendance ranges from five to eleven; there are no children's classes. Sometimes there are as many as twenty in the preaching service. Helen Graves just would not feel right, she says, going to any other church as long as "we can keep our church going."

Because Noeller and Zimmerman were both enrolled in extension classes at Tyler Road Baptist Church in Wichita, this church has taken an interest in the Florence group, which has constituted as a church once more. A group from the Wichita church has helped to get the church building in "meeting order" again.

A wonderful story from the December 1992 issue of *Missions USA* (reprinted in *BD*, February 22, 1993) concerns the Missions Service Corps tentmaker-pastor of York Baptist Church in Nebraska, Jim Ellis. The little white church-house was empty for a long time; it had not been completed, and what was there had fallen into disrepair. Over its thirty-year history, there had been a pastor for only ten years. But at least somebody, the Englands, in York prayed that something would happen so there would be services in the church again. One Sunday that something happened. Jim Ellis went to York, and there was "preaching" in the little church. The Englands were among the first to attend the revived church.

In 1992 Ellis was working part-time as a research and development engineer. He spent mornings studying in a tiny partitioned-off triangle near the baptistry. There are no windows in the office; it is lined with full bookshelves that reach from floor to ceiling; the desk is covered with commentaries and Bibles; and on the walls are a calendar, a to-do list, and a homemade Father's Day card from Karen and Jed. After a morning of study, with no telephone to interrupt, he pedals home for lunch (the bicycle saves gas money). From one to five he works at his shop job. Each evening he finds time to read to Karen and Jed, then it is off to church where he and one of the members do construction work for an hour before Latzel, the helpful layman, goes to the 11:00 to 7:00 shift at his job. The two men call this "the Baptist Hour."

Sunday School attendance grew from eleven to twenty-six; monthly offerings have tripled; there was a kitchen in the basement; and bathrooms were almost completed when the story was written in 1992. Ellis wanted to see York become a "stepping off" point for missions in the seven counties surrounding York where there are no Baptist churches. People drove to York from as far as thirty miles away.

Even then he feared the job with the Oklahoma-based company would not last. They live on Jim's half salary, and Melody admits it is not easy. "People ask how she feeds a family of four on $15 a week. She doesn't know. Somehow it works."

A "post-script" to the story in the *Digest* article was headed: "Pastor Loses Secular Job." By 1993 what Ellis feared had happened. His department was eliminated, and he was looking for another job. According to Harold Manahan, director of missions for Eastern Nebraska Association, "Various sources of income have come through for the Ellis family, and they are still 'tiding over.'"

In 1995 the going was still tough for this church. Ellis, six months after his bivocational job played out, found a job as a machinist in a town twenty-five miles away. His wife says the Lord took care of them through that period, by way of their mailbox. There is no "core group" in York; there has been little growth. Two years ago, however, a mission beginning was made in Seward, in an adjoining county where there was no Baptist witness.

The Westview Church in Chanute, Kansas, different from Trinity, Chanute, which was one of the early churches, was constituted in 1970, after eight years as a mission. Ten years earlier, Gerald Locke, DOAM in Twin Valley Association, discovered there was no Southern Baptist work in Neosho County. In 1961 two summer missionaries found prospects through a telephone survey, which led to the discovery a bit later of a "sufficient interest" to begin services in Chanute. Emmanuel, Coffeyville, sponsored the mission. In 1962 Wednesday night and Sunday Services were held in the Seventh Day Adventist Church building (*BD*, November 21, 1970). It has continued to function and grow.

Sometimes the shoe was on the other foot. In the 1963 *Annual*, in the report of the Executive Board, the Executive Committee recommended, and the board affirmed, the withdrawal of fellowship from the Madison Avenue Baptist Church, Iola, Kansas, and its Hutchinson mission. That was all; there was no word of explanation.

In 1966, when Keith Hamm was leaving the state, N. J. Westmoreland gave details about this action (*BD*, July 9, 1966). Hamm resigned as the pastor of Grace Baptist Church in Iola, after a two-and-a-half-year tenure, to become pastor of Webster Street Baptist Church in Springfield, Missouri. Westmoreland wrote, "This closed an important era in our work at Iola. It fell to Brother Hamm to lead in rebuilding our work there and rehabilitating public opinion after our loss of a church to heresy and fanaticism."

Madison Avenue was the original Baptist church in Iola, begun as a mission in 1957, and organized as a church in 1958. It was the biggest and among the most prosperous churches in Blue Stem Association, and one of the most missionary-minded churches in the SBC. In 1961 an eighty-thousand-dollar church plant was built, with a loan from the CLA. The following year the pastor began to lead the congregation into "heretical and fanatical practices," counseled the church to drop out of associational ministries, and to default on its loan. This brought disgrace on the name of Baptists in the town, and in 1963 some of their actions attracted the attention of national news media, "who played up sensational elements to the embarrassment of our Convention." So fellowship was withdrawn from the congregation, the loan was foreclosed (after eighteen months of no payments), and the building was repossessed.

Soon after this, Grace Baptist Church was organized and met in the building repossessed by the A. B. Culbertson Bond Company. It was not a good situation. "Citizens of Iola confronted the new congregation with bitterness and contempt, identifying them with the old church because they were worshipping in the repossessed building. One school teacher was threatened with the loss of her job because the identity of the new church was not clear. Pastor Hamm confronted sullen prejudice from outsiders everywhere. Ordinary gestures of good will by the average man-of-the-street were absent. News media were closed to the church, because of the cloud of suspicion surrounding any 'Southern Baptist' church member. Southern Baptists who moved to Iola were often prejudiced against the church by irate citizens eager to help the Grace Baptist Church fail."

Keith Hamm prevailed. The church grew and gradually rebuilt its place in the town. Grace was the fifth church Hamm had pastored in the state, four of which he started: Cambridge Baptist Church, Calvary Baptist of Columbus, First Baptist of Arcadia, and First Baptist of Cherokee. He stayed with each one until the first unit of a building was complete, each with only a modest debt which never endangered programs.

In 1967 the church at Larned lost about half of its members due to a split over doctrine and practices. One group withdrew to form a congregation which practiced speaking in tongues (*BD*, September 13, 1969). The group that was left found it difficult to make a comeback. N. J. Westmoreland came to the rescue, and with his preaching gave hope and support to the discouraged group. Other groups of youth and adults came from Calvary Baptist in Ellinwood and Olivet in Wichita. The DOAM, L. N. Stamper, gave time and attention to the church. A turning point came when, in 1969, the Rutledge family, with two teenaged sons, came from Louisiana. Rutledge took a job at Larned State Hospital in order to be of help to this church. Soon after, Charles Pipes came to be pastor, again with teenaged sons. With this influx of freshness, the church became enthused and began to grow again.

In 1972, when Doyle Smith came to Kansas, both Larned and Great Bend were without pastors, so these two were yoked together, with Smith as pastor. The church at Great Bend was pretty well known as one of the two most in-debt churches in the Convention. The church was sixteen thousand dollars behind in its payments and was facing possible foreclosure. In three years, the debt was caught up and finances in such condition that the church could plan on getting a loan to enlarge Sunday School space. Smith pastored both churches for about four and a half years. By that time, Larned was again strong enough to call a full-time pastor, and Smith became full-time pastor of Great Bend.

The Sandhills area of Nebraska presents a different picture—sparsely populated, large ranches, and few towns. Home missionary Dennis Hampton described it this way, "When we talk about 'rural' in Nebraska . . . we're talking about thousands of head of livestock on tens of thousands of acres. . . . We're not talking about 'good ole boys,' we're talking about agribusiness-men with degrees in agriculture and veterinary science. We're talking remote and we're talking sparse" (*BD*, October 24, 1988). These ranchers work fourteen to sixteen hours a day, so Bible study cannot begin until about 9:00 P.M. January, February, and June are the "down months" when these people can get more involved in Bible study.

A ranch ministry has developed in response to these needs. The work began in the 1960s (*BD*, October 31, 1994) when Dewey Hickey was pastor of First Baptist Church at Valentine, Nebraska, but it has changed a great deal since that time in location and program model. Currently Hampton heads this work.

Hampton, a Kentuckian, went to New England as a church planter under the influence of Wendell Belew. In 1974 Charles Hawley, the pastor of First Baptist in Bellevue, who had been a classmate of Hampton's, invited him to come to Bellevue as educational director, and, he was assured, he could church-plant to his heart's content. After a year and a half, Hampton decided there was not enough time to do educational work in a large Baptist church, and church-plant, too. So he left this position, and at the invitation of the people, went to Sutton, Nebraska, and started a church. From there he went to Hastings, and Keystone Baptist Church was born, followed by Shepherd's Way in Grand Island, and a Baptist chapel in O'Neal.

He became interested in ranch ministry because of a call from a young woman who, with her cowboy husband, had a ranch in the Sandhills area, there was no church nearby. She had been a twelve-year-old girl in Sutton when her parents had helped Hampton with the formation of the church there. So she called and told him she could get a group of families together if he could come for a Bible study. So this unconventional ministry began.

He went into an area, stayed for a couple of days, living in the homes of ranch families, teaching and preaching, then on to another area. After about a year and a half of this sort of work, the Home Mission Board and the KNCSB employed him to do ranch ministry and develop lay leadership.

During the summer time there are Vacation Bible Schools which are held in one-room school houses (of which there are 125) in the area. In order to follow-up on these summertime studies, Mail Box Clubs came into being. Materials are sent to the children with "assignments," which they mail back. In 1991 Jeff and Karen Elliott, U.S.-2 missionaries, were appointed to serve in the Nebraska Sandhills. The Elliotts reached out to children through a "Party-a-Month" Club with games and decorations, refreshments, choruses, and a Bible story (*BD*, August 26, 1991).

Out of the weekday Bible studies which Hampton led grew Sunday meetings called Sunday School. The lay leaders are not comfortable with talking about being pastors and preaching, but they are willing to be Sunday School directors, have a devotional in an opening assembly, and then teach Bible study classes. They also make contacts, deal with visitors, and care for the needs of people who attend.

In most of these Sunday Schools, there are not many adults, only one or two teenagers, a couple of children, and little leadership. Three of these groups, at Green Valley, Dorset, and Center, about fifty-five miles apart, "went together" to form a non-geographic church called Country Side Baptist Fellowship. They meet together for fellowship and training, once a month on Sunday afternoon, in different places: a school, a vacant building, or someone's home. The group has called a pastoral missionary, Joel Wentworth, a rancher who had some training at Calvary Bible College. Hampton calls this a "church of fields" (*BD*, October 31, 1994) to highlight the difference between this ministry and that of a "church field."

Another method of reaching people is through Bible correspondence courses. In 1988 Hampton reported people in twenty-three towns and twelve counties involved in this program (*BD*, October 24, 1988).

Hampton (Personal Communication) cites two key factors in the necessity for and success of the ranch ministry. First, due to dwindling population, the mainstream Protestant churches closed their doors in the small towns and villages and expected folks to attend the "county seat church." By the time chores were done, this was too long a drive for scattered ranchers. The second factor was the farm crisis, which left in its wake hurting people who had nowhere to turn and needed the support and direction of the church. So Bible study fellowships have flourished, for where two or three are gathered together in the name of Jesus, there is He in their midst. Variations of this system are being set in place in areas of Kansas and Nebraska as a viable way to reach people who live in isolated areas.

Sometimes it is hard to measure the result of this sort of ministry. Dewey Hickey shared one heartwarming experience. He and Tom Wenig were returning to Kearney from Scottsbluff one night and stopped at a gas station to get a "can of pop." There was a big fellow in the shop with a great black beard. "You guys going to Valentine?" he asked. No, they answered, they were not. Then the man asked, "Are you a minister?" And Hickey answered, "Yes I am, and I used to live in Valentine." As the conversation went on, Hickey found the man had been stuck one night on the sand trail near the Minor Jorgenson Ranch. Hickey had stopped to help, then took the man home. "I became a Christian that night," he said. "You had a little baby," said Hickey. The "baby" was sixteen, and the man was active in the Presbyterian

Church. "I told you I'd never forget you," said the rancher, "and I haven't."

Not all churches in Kansas and Nebraska are small or struggling. For example, in Nebraska there is First Baptist Bellevue, which was the most influential church in Nebraska during its first twenty years. Westside, Omaha, is the largest church in the two-state Convention. In Kansas there are Emmanuel, Overland Park; Nall Avenue, Prairie Village; and Metropolitan and Immanuel in Wichita.

John Click is pastor of Immanuel Baptist Church, the largest Baptist church, and the third largest church, of any denomination, in Wichita. It was organized in 1916 and affiliated with the NBC.

In view of the fact that all the records of the church were destroyed by a "torrential rain which fell about the 20th of June, 1923, which filled the basement of the home of the clerk of the church, with water, in which the records were kept," G. A. Creekmore, first pastor of the church, wrote a "brief and fragmentary history of the early years."

The church, called the South Lawrence Avenue Mission, was established by the First Baptist Church of Wichita. The building, about 26 X 30 feet, faced the alley behind a residence, was constructed of plain boards, and lined with a layer of brown paper "tacked on the inside to keep out as much of the cold winter wind as possible, and which was almost unbearably hot during the summer months.

In 1916 fifty-two members of the mission requested their letters in order to organize a new church. The first thing the congregation did was to authorize the construction of a ten-thousand-dollar building, although the church, "with one exception, was made up of families of limited means, and with a wage of twelve dollars a week." The men of the mission had little time for outside work, nor did the women, who were rolling bandages and involved in other war-related jobs.

Nevertheless, "the design for the building, as it is seen today, was decided upon, and a man with horsedrawn plows, scrapers and dump wagons was employed to excavate for the basement of the building." When the basement was completed, it was roofed over and became the first home for the new church in 1917. Work on the "super structure" was begun in 1918 and "carried to its present height." Doors and windows were boarded up, and the space was put into use. During that year, more than a hundred members came into the church, sixty-five by baptism.

The church became a part of the KCSB in 1949, when George McClelland was the pastor. There was no abrupt departure from one Convention to the other. The church simply began to cooperate with the KCSB, even as it continued to cooperate with the ABC.

Additions were made to the original structure. Now, in addition to the eighty-five thousand square feet in the worship-education building, Immanuel also has seventy-two thousand square feet in a Family Life Building that was completed in 1992, and used for recreation and education. Yvonne Keefer reported a conversation with a pastor who was looking around that church for the first time. She asked if she could help him, for he seemed a bit bewildered. "No," he said. "I was just looking. There are more square feet of space in this hallway than in my entire church."

Immanuel has five "satellite" congregations, including the main group at Immanuel: Vietnamese, which meets in a building across the street from the church; Chinese, which meets in the Immanuel chapel on Sunday afternoon; and two other Anglo groups which meet in other parts of the city, one in a school and one in a building which Immanuel is buying. All have full-time pastors on staff at Immanuel. The people are all members of Immanuel Baptist Church.

John Click became pastor of this church in 1972, after pastoring in other places for several years. Since that time, he has been active at both the state and national Convention levels. He served as Kansas-Nebraska Convention president in 1986 and 1987. Even though he comes from Texas, perhaps after twenty-three years, he feels almost like a Kansan. There are twenty-five staff persons.

Roger Roberts has been pastor of Metropolitan Baptist Church in Wichita since 1983. He is from Ohio, his wife, Nancy, from Indiana. He wanted to be involved in a pioneer work in the Midwest; she had deep family roots in Kansas. Nancy's mother's family were charter members of the church at Chautauqua, one of the founding churches of the Convention.

Metropolitan Baptist Church was founded by members who withdrew from the First Baptist Church (ABC), in 1962, because of doctrinal differences. In 1993 this church was described as the ninth largest church in Wichita with a membership of 2,900, a budget of $1.1 million, and 80,000 square feet of space. There is a multiple staff with varied responsibilities: worship and music, outreach and education, youth ministry, and a Vietnamese mission. Other part-time staff do pastoral counseling and direct programs for children and preschoolers, including a Mother's Day Out program. In addition, there are an administrator and an administrative assistant. An outstanding Christian international group began when the church in 1981 voted to adopt a Southeast Asian family. In May 1985 the church began participating in the River Festival with the Sunday afternoon program "Down by the Riverside," which has become a major attraction.

Roberts characterized the church as a leader in mission support through the Cooperative Program and special offerings. Members are active in the Good Neighbor Center. Here again, there is emphasis on satellite congregations. For this effort to reach pockets of people in areas where probably a "regular" church cannot be organized, the church has agreed that fifty people are needed for this ministry, which will offer a worship service and a fully staffed Bible study hour for children and preschoolers. Forty people have already made this commitment for a satellite congregation in another section of Wichita.

Roger Fredrickson was pastor of the First Baptist Church, ABC, which still occupies the original site and has also continued to grow. In 1981, when Phil Linberger was pastor of Metropolitan, he and Linberger initiated a reconciliation for the two churches. There was a service at Metropolitan, and two weeks later one at First Baptist. Relationships improved.

The first meeting place of the Metropolitan congregation in 1962 was the Southeast High School, with 1,839 charter members. Sharon Baptist Church loaned its space for Vacation Bible School, baptisms, and weddings. The land for the present building at McLean and Douglas in downtown Wichita, across from Century II, was acquired after long negotiations. It was property occupied by the Midland Valley depot; negotiations were underway to sell it to Missouri Pacific Railway. Miraculously, the railroad decided to sell to the church, but the church would have to clear all the "reversionary rights since the property had been dedicated for railway use back in 1911. If ever that changed, it would revert back to the original owners" (Huston, 1987). This seemed impossible, but again, a miracle. All rights were held by only one heir, who lived in Wichita and was willing to sell those rights. So the railroad property, plus an adjacent used car lot, was purchased for less than two hundred thousand dollars. In 1962 Metropolitan Church voted to cooperate with the SBC, and two hundred members left the church to start an independent church (Huston, 1987).

In 1965 the congregation moved into the completed building, which was debt free, land and building, by 1979. Since that time, a million-dollar fellowship hall was planned and named in honor of Jesse Vardaman, who was on the staff from before the split, serving when F. B. Thorn was pastor, until 1974 when he retired. He was named associate pastor emeritus.

Carl Garrett is pastor of Emmanuel Baptist Church in Overland Park, and is in his second term as president of the KNCSB. An article in *Missions USA*, March-April 1995, begins with these words: "The hill where Emmanuel Baptist Church sits is surrounded by suburban development, shopping centers, office parks and high-rise hotels. Ten years ago, Carl Garrett could stand on this high point of land and watch farmers work their fields. Today, the farms are gone. Cars line four-lane Metcalf Avenue bumper-to-bumper two miles in either direction. Overland Park, Kansas, transformed from a sleepy, unincorporated village on the outskirts of Kansas City where Wild Bill Hickock once served as marshall, is now one of America's corporate centers."

Ten years ago, there were about 375 in worship service on Sunday morning. Today, there are 2,700 members, with averages of 800 in attendance at two morning services and 731 in two Sunday Schools. Garrett characterizes the ministry of the church as being to people in their mid-forties, upwardly mobile, executives in key corporate positions. Many will be in Kansas City less than two years before they are transferred to another place. One year thirty Sunday School teachers were lost in one month because of such transfers. The schedule of the church is "streamlined," and events usually last one hour. According to Garrett, people are called on for "three units of time a week," rather than the usual six or seven many others churches ask for.

Emmanuel, in thirty years, has sponsored four missions, three of which have become churches: Blue Valley Baptist Church, in 1978; Emmanuel

Chinese Baptist Church, in 1981; and Lenexa Baptist Church, in 1988. Friendship Baptist, begun in 1993, is still a mission. One hundred fifty members from Emmanuel moved to Lenexa to get it started. Garrett said, "The mission not only needed them, we needed to clear space here to grow."

Another ministry of the church is the Pastor's Retreat. The church invites ministers and their families from Kansas and Nebraska to spend three days after the Fourth of July holiday in Overland Park, at no expense, for rest and recreation. The guests stay in the homes of church members; all meals are provided; and wives are given twenty-five dollars to buy something for themselves. Fifteen families were guests of Emmanuel Church in the summer of 1994.

This is the church begun by Paul Elledge when he came to Kansas City and discovered the church nearest to where he lived was five miles away. In 1964 Emmanuel held its first service in the south tower of what is now K-Mart at 95th and Metcalf. Ken Combs served fourteen years as pastor. Both men are still members of this church.

Reynolds has been pastor of Nall Avenue Baptist Church in Prairie Village, Kansas, since 1990. He is the fourth pastor; Owen Dahlor served the church for thirty-two years; there were two short-term pastors before that, Raymond Collier and William O'Dell. The church was organized in 1953 by four families who had a dream of a Southern Baptist church in the community. The first meetings were held in the home of Stella Stock, grandmother of Paige Seats, son of Southern Baptist missionaries in Africa. In a month's time, there were fifty-three members. Their first building was completed in 1956; the sanctuary in 1962. In 1970 the educational-activities building was added, and in 1978, the Christian Life Center.

By 1993 there were 1,545 members, and the church had an annual budget of $602,660, with 14.5 percent designated to missions. In addition, the church supports gifts to the Lottie Moon Christmas Offering for Foreign Missions, Annie Armstrong Easter Offering for Home Missions, and the Viola Webb Missions Offering for work in Kansas and Nebraska.

There are many activities for members of the church and those who live in the community: day care ministry, Blood Bank program, Boy Scout Troop, summer recreation camp, and special programs for singles, seniors, young parents, men, women, and youth. Other outreach ministries include language ministry with Laotians, monthly "Feed the Hungry" offering, disaster relief, specialized conferences, and celebrations through the year. In addition, over the years this church has sponsored several missions which have become churches.

There is emphasis on the music program in this church. Harry Taylor was the first full-time music director. There are special choir presentations, a handbell choir, and youth choir trips.

Tony Lambert, only the second pastor Westside, Omaha, has ever had, came to Nebraska from Mississippi in 1992. Calvin Miller became mission pastor in 1966 and remained until 1991, when he went to the faculty of

Southwestern Seminary. The church was constituted in 1968. By 1970 the congregation bought property and built; they expanded their building in 1973 and again in 1979. By that time there were one thousand members. In 1987 the church built on a new ten-acre site, and have since added an educational wing to that building.

This church is the largest in the KNCSB with about 3,300 members; it has two worship services and three Sunday Schools. A survey a few years ago showed the average age of members to be thirty-five years.

There are six ordained ministers on staff, plus staff for children's and preschool programs, secretarial and custodial staff. The church operates a day-care facility in the building and has a Mom's Day Out program two days a week. There is an emphasis on pageantry in the church as an outreach tool: Easter, Fourth of July, Christmas, and a "drive-through" pageant in the fall. There are special ministries for youth, singles, seniors, as well as inter-generational events. The latest staff addition is a college minister to reach college students all over Omaha. Church members are involved in various services in the community: Open Door Mission, Omaha Baptist Center, and the Santee Reservation.

200 BY 2000

In 1980 the KNCSB adopted five broad objectives as a program of work to lead us into the twenty-first century, each with major goals, support goals, and action events. Objectives were: (1) To help alert Kansas-Nebraska Southern Baptists to mission needs in our communities, homeland and world, and to challenge our people to mission study-support action; (2) to assist Kansas-Nebraska churches and associations in establishing new units of work; (3) to help Kansas-Nebraska Southern Baptists explore, understand, and achieve their biblical role in family and church relationships; (4) to help provide learning opportunities whereby Kansas-Nebraska Southern Baptists can become better equipped to do the work of the ministry; and (5) to help Kansas-Nebraska Southern Baptists come to a biblical understanding of the role of persons serving in church and associational staff positions and to lead churches and associations in providing adequate spiritual, emotional, and physical support for these ministers and staff.

The lead goal in Objective 2 was "to establish 200 new churches, and church-type missions, by 2,000." In 1980 the Convention passed the following resolution:

"*We are convinced* that the bold vision of beginning 200 new church-type missions by the year 2000 in our two-state Convention is not merely a noble goal but it is definitely an attainable goal.

"*We are convinced* our Lord is more excited about His church and her purpose than we often are. The capacity to begin these new churches in the power of the Spirit of God is available to those willing to pledge themselves to the task.

"Therefore, we, the 35th session of the Kansas-Nebraska Convention of Southern Baptists resolve to reaffirm our commitment to beginning 200 new churches by the year 2000."

This goal was not "pulled out of the air." Doyle Smith was president of the Convention at that time. Both he and Peck Lindsay were committed to church growth, and they dreamed together about what could be done. Lindsay worked closely with the DOAMs. At one session with them, he asked that they list the places in their associations where a new work start seemed necessary, and likely. When the lists were made, there were 214 places where DOAMs thought work could and should be started. Smith's sermon that year articulated the basis for this new-start thrust. Then he and Lindsay went on the "fried chicken circuit"; one or the other went into every association to help pastors and other church leadership "own" this plan. They succeeded even beyond their dreams.

Five years ahead of the target date, in 1995, this goal was reached. Between 1980 and 1995, two hundred new church and church-type mission starts have been made. Not all of them have lasted, but through the efforts of these "new starts," whether they were long-lasting or quick-flowering and gone, progress has been made. Things have happened that would not have happened if they had not been born. Mark Clifton, director of extension missions, reported to the 1994 annual meeting: "The churches established since 1980 in KNCSB are contributing greatly to the growth in our Convention. For the year 1993 alone, those churches started since 1980 baptized five hundred people and gave nearly one half million dollars to mission causes. There have been more groups studying the Bible, because Sunday School classes were organized. There are people who know more and care more about missions because WMU units have been started in these churches. Children and youth have been touched forever."

In order to reach "New Starts" goal of "200 by 2,000," the following targets were set: fifty-five by 1985, which was exceeded when sixty new starts were reported in that period; thirty-nine by 1989, which was exceeded with forty-three new starts; and fifty-five by 1995, a goal reached in October of that year. We will go far beyond 200 by 2,000. We have done exceedingly well.

Clifton included this information in his report: "Lyle Schaller states that any denomination which begins less than three new works per 100 churches a year is in decline. . . . In 1994, with 340 churches and missions, KNCSB began 21 new works." This was a ratio of almost seven to one hundred, more than double the figure Schaller stated is needed for a growing denomination. Schaller's criteria would suggest we are in a period of radical growth.

ETHNIC AND LANGUAGE MISSIONS

While ministry to ethnic and language groups is not the oldest concern of the Convention, it has been part of our ministry for a long time. Our first outreach was to Native Americans, then to Spanish speaking who came to work, next to Southeast Asians who came as refugees, and then to other groups. In the early 1960s, in addition to the work with Indians at Haskell, under the direction of James Goodner, and the Spanish Chapel, which was the forerunner of the Baptist Center in Topeka, there was only one other language group, an Indian Southern Baptist church in Wichita. Today, however, outreach to language and ethic groups is one of the fastest growing areas of our work.

James Goodner, a native Oklahoman who had been a home missionary working with the American Indians in the San Francisco Bay area (*BD*, February 16, 1963), came to be pastor of Wichita's First Indian Southern Baptist Church. He worked with the Pueblo Indians in New Mexico for three years, then pastored a church in Raton for a year. He left New Mexico to study at Golden Gate Seminary; when he completed his work there, he felt called to serve Indians who were coming off the reservations into the cities. So for six years he worked in the Bay area.

He was asked why Indians needed all-Indian churches. Why could not they just worship and serve in already existing churches? Goodner explained that Christian Indians felt a strong call to minister to their own people. It was easier for them to get their friends to come to all-Indian churches than to others. The First Indian Southern in Wichita at this time had members representing twelve tribes, most of them from Oklahoma. Goodner went to Haskell Institute in 1965.

On October 16, 1960 (*BD*, September 23, 1961), the Latin American Mission of First Southern Baptist Church in Topeka, had its first meeting. At the end of a year, there were nineteen enrolled in Sunday School, and two people had been baptized. A Midwestern Seminary student, B. E. Benitez, began the work and served as first pastor. This church was one of the "30,000 Movement."

In 1967 Jerry Moore was listed as pastor of Templo Bautista in Garden City. The following year, Albert Smith was leading Spanish work in Ulysses. This mission had an unusual beginning (*BD*, September 5, 1964). The First Southern Baptist Church in Ulysses bought the vacated Roman Catholic Church, with the idea of organizing a Spanish Baptist mission. Initial leadership was provided by two preachers from Argentina, members of the sponsoring church. A revival was held, with a Wayland Baptist College student from Argentina preaching. The work grew; when the two Argentina preachers moved away, Albert Smith, a member of the sponsoring church, began to serve as pastor. There were classes in English and Spanish, songs in English and Spanish, and preaching in English.

By 1970 Spanish work was also reported in Leoti. In 1976 work in Dodge City and Emporia were added. The first Spanish work in Nebraska was reported at Omaha with Mike DeLuna as the leader. In 1975 a Spanish-speaking congregation was formed in South Sioux City, Nebraska.

Pablo Jimenez, pastor of the Iglesia Bautista Hispano in Scottsbluff, Nebraska, believes he was in "the right place at the right time" (*BD*, August 23, 1993). About twenty percent of Scottsbluff and Gering, a sister city, is

Hispanic. They come from Mexico for farming jobs and to work in the packing plants.

Jimenez, when he became a Christian following the witness of a Cuban Baptist living in El Paso, was disowned by his family. So he brought his wife and two sons to the States from Mexico in 1982. He went first to Phoenix, then to Guymon, Oklahoma, to work in beef processing plants. When the job ended, he went in 1987, to Garden City, to another meat-packing plant. Along the way he worked in missions of the churches and in discipleship training. When he was assistant pastor in Garden City, he went to Webster Conference Center, where he heard of the need for a pastor in Scottsbluff. He talked with the DOAM; one thing led to another, and in April 1991, Jimenez moved to Scottsbluff. The church, which started as a mission of Bethel Church and met in the church basement, rented an office building, and then bought it.

Jimenez met the Martinez family at a Glorieta conference and persuaded them to move to Scottsbluff, find jobs, and minister in the Spanish-speaking church. Because of Martinez's skill, the church's counseling services could be expanded. Jimenez does not want to limit his work to only Spanish-speaking people, but to extend it to Native Americans and to Anglos, as well.

In other areas and from time to time, churches have reached out to small groups of non-English speaking people in much less formal ways than beginning a mission. A report from the pastor of College Heights Baptist Church, Manhattan, Kansas (*BD*, September 23, 1967), details one such effort. One day "someone" indignantly addressed a member of the church: "Why aren't you Southern Baptists ministering to those Spanish-speaking Baptists out at Britt's farm?" That member talked with the pastor, who with two laymen went to the truck farm and found three Mexican Baptist families, among whom were seventeen children. At the time, there was no one in the church who spoke Spanish, but soon a woman who did speak Spanish appeared in Manhattan for summer school. So a class was begun on Sunday evening. By the close of summer school, one of the members of the church, who had been attending the class, and had some Spanish background, felt competent enough to continue it. The ministry continued with the small group as long as there was someone who could speak Spanish.

By 1966 Donald D. Otwell had a ministry to the deaf in Olathe, Kansas. Work among the deaf had begun much earlier. In 1962 Glen Wood was pastor of the Ridgeview Church in Olathe, when, because of a throat ailment, one doctor bluntly told him he needed to give up preaching altogether. He commented, "It may not be as hard as you think." Wood had been in Olathe since 1958 and had felt a growing pull to service with the deaf in this town, which is the location of the State School for the Deaf. At the time he arrived, there was a flourishing ministry under the direction of Mr. and Mrs. Robert Hunt, whose son was deaf. They had begun a class in 1958.

Wood was so interested in communicating with the deaf that he enrolled in the Beginners Sign Language course, then in an Advanced Signing course.

When the Hunts had to leave Olathe, Wood felt called to take over their work with the deaf; at the same time, he was overburdened with the many responsibilities of the pastorate. So when the doctor said, "no more preaching," even as he heard a door close, he heard another open. He took a job in insurance to support his family and gave his ministry time to the deaf.

Otwell and his wife, Yvonne, had worked in a deaf ministry in a church in Atlanta, Georgia, and came to Kansas to attend Midwestern Seminary. He was employed by two associations in two states: Kansas City, Kansas, and Kansas City, Missouri. Paul Elledge, associational missionary in Kansas City, (*BD*, February 5, 1966), wrote, "In a very real sense Mr. Otwell's ministry will be state-wide, since the Kansas School for the Deaf is in Olathe. It is said that there are more deaf people in Olathe than in any other city its size in the United States."

Pat Heriford was a teacher in the Kansas State School for the Deaf. She used her skills in many ways in the Kansas City, Kansas, Baptist Association: taught sign classes in churches; prepared materials for medical professionals to use in working with deaf patients; took deaf children to camp; and worked with deaf choir presentations in shopping malls for several years.

Korean work began about 1970 in South Sioux City, Nebraska; in 1979 in Junction City, Kansas; in 1981 in Topeka; in 1982 in Wichita; in 1983 in Lawrence; and in 1984 in Salina and Overland Park. Vietnamese work began in 1982 in Wichita; Laotian work in 1983 in Prairie Village and in 1987 in Wichita; Chinese work in 1977 in Overland Park; Filipino work in Bellevue, Nebraska, in 1988; East Indian work in Prairie Village in 1986; and Hmong and an India mission in 1988 in Kansas City.

Every work among language groups has a marvelous beginning story. The First Southern Korean Church in Olathe (*BD*, June 24, 1991) in 1991 launched a fund-raising drive to finance their own building; they planned a craft show, used clothing sale, and a car wash, along with plenty of Korean food. While this was an unusual procedure for a Baptist church, this is not a typical Baptist church. The church at that time met in the same building as the First Southern Baptist Church. While the Anglo church had Sunday School, the Korean church used the sanctuary for worship; then the groups swapped places. Both congregations benefitted from this sharing together.

The Korean Baptist Church of Central Kansas in Junction City (*BD*, April 23, 1990) began as a mission of First Southern in Junction City in 1979, with Peter Moon Hong as pastor. The church building, a Lutheran school, was bought in 1987, and a few months later the church began an English-speaking mission. The mission is made up mostly of American servicemen married to Korean women; Ken Edmiston, a retired Army chaplain, now a marriage and family counselor, is the pastor.

Every morning at 5:30, Hong and a dozen or so people came to the church for prayer. This early morning prayer time is a tradition among Korean Christians. At this time there were fourteen home Bible study groups for adults and Sunday School classes for children and youth at the church. In the eleven years of Hong's ministry, 1,300 Koreans were part of this church; 1,100 have accepted Christ. Hong was followed by Paul Kim. The new pastor is Sand Sun Lim.

Harrison Street Baptist in Omaha sponsors a Korean mission where Chang Choi is pastor. Choi was a student a Midwestern Seminary; he pastored a group in Lawrence, Kansas. He went to Omaha because of the large number of Koreans there, and began a mission in the front room of his home. Soon, this space was too small, so he approached Harrison Street Baptist Church, the church nearest the Korean community and made a covenant agreement with them to sponsor this mission, which meets on Sunday afternoon. This was the third attempt to start Baptist work in this area. The first was led by a Korean doctor, who was a Presbyterian. There is now a "neat" Presbyterian Church in the area (Telephone Communication, Harold Manahan). The second attempt, under the sponsorship of Chandler Acres, disbanded when there was a problem between the Korean pastor and the people.

Mark Zerger and his wife were foreign mission volunteers, but when Rhoda developed severe rheumatoid arthritis, they could not continue with these plans. Mark had pastored a Cambodian Baptist Church in Mineral Wells, Texas, while he was in the seminary. Dewey Hickey, who was director of the Department of Missions for the KNCSB, was looking for a catalytic missionary to work with Southeast Asian people around Omaha (*BD*, April 11, 1988).

This became an "open window" for the Zergers, after they faced the closed door to foreign mission appointment. They were appointed as home missionaries and went to Omaha in 1987. Zerger found Southeast Asians in a number of ways, although he reported it was a little like "looking for a needle in a haystack." He visited Oriental businesses of various kinds, and sent letters to people with Asian sounding names from telephone book listings. At that time there were more than three thousand South Asians in Omaha, including Vietnamese, Lao-Hmong, Cambodians, Filipinos, Japanese, Chinese, and Korean, which was the largest group. He considered one of the most successful parts of his ministry to be the Filipino fellowship at Chandler Acres Baptist Church in Bellevue, Nebraska, which was begun by Frankie Aquino.

Zerger's ministry included teaching English, leading a Bible study for Chinese doctors and their spouses, working with the Filipino fellowship at Chandler Acres Baptist Church in Bellevue, and finding and talking with Southeast Asians whenever and however he could. He left this work after a short time to go into the service as a chaplain.

Frankie Aquino was an answer to prayer; it seemed he just "fell out of the woodwork on us," said the pastor of Chandler Acres Baptist Church. He is a product of Southern Baptist missions in the Philippines, was a pastor there for thirteen years, but he wanted to come to the United States. Aquino's uncle was the first convert of Southern Baptist missionaries in the Philippines. The uncle heard a Southern Baptist broadcast from China, and wrote a letter asking for more information (*BD*, March 28, 1988). Missionaries went to Dagupon City in answer; a church was begun. So Aquino grew up in a Baptist church.

He had a sister in Omaha, so he arrived there in 1987. He attended the First Baptist Church in Bellevue and noted on his visitor's card that he was a Filipino pastor. Someone gave his name to Mark Zerger who introduced him to another Filipino family, and a Bible study was begun in Tagalog, the national Filipino dialect. The Bible study, started in the home of the man who became pastor of the group, moved into one of the Chandler Acres buildings.

Aquino had a job as a meat boner, and worked hard there, beginning at 4:00 A.M. His goal was to make money so he could return to his country with equipment to begin an evangelistic association. This work, like many other language starts with particular ethnic groups, is no longer viable due to population shifts. Aquino is at work with the youth in Chandler Acres Church.

Binh Than Nguyen (*BD*, August 24, 1992), thousands of miles from his native country of Vietnam, is pastor of the Vietnamese Congregation, a satellite of Immanuel Baptist Church in Wichita. He escaped from Vietnam in 1980 after five years in a "re-education camp." He was arrested and tortured when he refused to close his church. He left Vietnam with other escapees on a fishing boat. It was a difficult time; food and water ran out, but they finally washed up on the Chinese shore, and from there made their way to Hong Kong. He had a sister in Wichita, so was allowed to come to the U.S. as a refugee.

The sister-in-law of Glen Zumwalt, a member of Immanuel Baptist, worked for World Relief, and met Nguyen in Hong Kong. When she found he was being sent to Wichita, she called Zumwalt, made contact with Nguyen, and took him to Immanuel Church; and so the ministry was begun. It is "very hard" to reach the people, Nguyen said, because of their Buddhist tradition. His method is friendship. In their parking lot, Immanuel had two houses, which became refugee houses. As Vietnamese refugees came and went, Nguyen helped them in many ways.

Vicki Caddell (*BD*, August 27, 1990) began to work as Vietnamese coordinator for Western Kansas Baptist Association in 1990. Her husband is pastor of the First Southern Baptist Church in Garden City. Vicki finished her college degree in Garden City and got a job in a bilingual school. Her class consisted of seventeen Vietnamese, two Laotians, one Korean, four Hispanics, and four Caucasian children, which brought her to see her mission as work with internationals. She talked with Andy St. Andre, who at that time was DOAM in Western Kansas, and who also desired to enlarge the ministry to this population group. Meat-packing plant jobs, in part because they require no English, attracted this group to Garden City, Liberal, and Dodge City. Vicki met every plane when Vietnamese were arriving. She presented them with a fruit basket, helped them get into the low-income housing provided by the city, and then took them around to the clothes closet provided by the association.

Her first goal was to provide English classes for parents, then help churches be aware of and meet the physical needs for food and clothing among the people. Her big goal was to present the gospel, which she did through Backyard Bible Clubs.

Vicki no longer coordinates the work; this is done by Thomas Tran, a Vietnamese (*BD*, December 28, 1992) who literally bought his way to freedom across Cambodia and into Thailand. He had almost reached freedom, but turned back to find his wife and son and daughter. They paid five ounces in gold per person to be guided across to the Cambodian border, only to be captured by the Khmer Rouge. A Red Cross doctor came to their rescue, first because their son was ill, and then in order to negotiate the rescue of Tran and his daughter. This time the ransom was paid in rice. Tran wanted to go to Australia, but this was not to be. Instead, his destination was to be the United States. After months in a Thailand refugee camp and then in the Philippines, he wandered by a Baptist church, an experience which brought him finally to true freedom. He heard singing, and wondered why people were happy when he was so burdened. Because of the witness of a Vietnamese Christian, and through the Word of God, Tran became a Christian. Through his witness, his wife and daughter also accepted Christ. Tran lost track of the friend who had led him to Christ, who had come to the states ahead of him.

The Tran family first lived in Wichita but heard of jobs in the packing plant in Garden City and went there. Soon after their arrival, a Vietnamese revival was held; Vinh Le, who was a pastor in Colorado, was the evangelist. It was a joyous reunion between the two old friends. As a result of the revival, a Sunday School class and English-as-a-Second-Language groups were started. Later, Tran was ordained by the Garden City Church and became pastor of the mission. At the beginning, he was also working six days a week in the packing plant on the night shift. He and his wife had a big garden in the summertime, from which they shared produce with the community. Now Tran also preaches in Liberal and conducts a Bible study in Dodge City.

The work with Laotians at Nall Avenue Baptist in Prairie Village began in 1975 after Laos fell to the communists and the first Laotian refugee attended the church. Three couples, with the help of the church, began to sponsor some of these refugees, and then began a special Sunday School class for them. Thira Siengsukon became the pastor of the Laotian mission congregation in July 1983 (*BD*, February 24, 1992).

Siengsukon, of Chinese descent and born in Thailand, became a Christian through the influence of American Baptist missionaries and was studying at the Southern Baptist Seminary in Bangkok (*BD*, February 24, 1992). When he and his wife, Montira, came to the United States, he enrolled at Central Seminary, where he was approached by Nall Avenue. The work has not been easy since cultural differences must be taken into account. The youth do not speak Laotian, and there are few trained leaders or Laotian pastors. Siengsukon, with the aid of Midwestern Seminary, KNCSB, and the Home Mission Board, began a Laotian School of Theology. In 1991, on the eighth anniversary of the mission (*BD*, August 26, 1991), a celebration began with the baptism of five recent converts, and the licensing of three Laotian men to the gospel ministry. These men had been leading Bible studies in three areas, each with the potential of becoming a mission. Another breakthrough in 1991 (*BD*, February 24, 1991) was the In-D.E.P.T.H. Conference attended by twelve Laotian youth, which gave them a better understanding about what it means to be a Christian and a Southern Baptist.

At the end of December 1994, Siengsukon resigned as pastor of the mission church in order to devote full time to training Laotian pastors. The extension program through Midwestern Seminary has become more and more widely known and fruitful. He not only has taught, but has translated textbooks and other teaching materials into the Lao language. By the time he resigned as pastor, he had study groups in Wichita, Kansas; St. Louis, Missouri; Little Rock, Arkansas; Texas, Oklahoma, and Minnesota. His plan in 1994 was to put the courses on videotapes so pastors could study at home. His role will be a "circuit rider," visiting the training points as often as he can. His support comes from Kansas City, Kansas, Baptist Association, KNCSB, and through the Mission Service Corps program (Personal Communication from James Reynolds, pastor of Nall Avenue).

Prablhakar Nemili, who accepted the position in 1986, was Nall Avenue's first "missionary" to internationals (*BD*, July 24, 1989). He accepted Christ in India through the ministry of American Baptist missionaries, and came to the United States and then to Midwestern Seminary through the influence of a pastor in Missouri. He had wanted to become a doctor, but doors to medical school were closed. After graduation, he wanted to continue to work with internationals as he had during seminary years. Thira Siengsukon suggested he talk with Nall Avenue's pastor, Owen Dahlor, who himself had been burdened for the Indian community in the Kansas City area. A deal was struck, and Nemili joined the Nall Avenue staff. He did not hold regular worship services, but ministered in other ways as a volunteer chaplain at the University of Kansas Medical Center and Western Missouri Mental Health Center, and through home Bible studies and recreation programs. He left in 1990.

The Russian work in Lincoln (Telephone Communication, Dan Cate, pastor) began when a handful of members of the Southview Church became involved in helping to resettle refugees in Lincoln, where there were already a number of Russian families. As more and more arrived, the whole church became involved in meeting the needs of these newcomers. A number of those who came to Lincoln were already Baptists; some spoke English and began to attend the services at Southview. Then an interpreter was found, and Russian-speaking people came and wore earphones during the service, listening to the translator from the sound booth. Finally, a request was made to Southview that the group be allowed to have their own meeting in the church on Sunday afternoons. The request was granted. The lay pastor of the group, Vitaly Solkan, who speaks five languages, leads the group in many activities. At the evening service of the forty-ninth annual session of the KNCSB, music was presented by the Russian orchestra and choir. When they first began to meet, they did not wish to be "tied" to Southview Church; there was basic distrust of "organizations" in connection with church. Through the years, they have come to trust Southview Church, and in late 1994 approached the church and asked for mission status, which was granted on December 11. There are approximately a hundred regular attenders, counting the children, who are often not counted by Russian churches.

It is well to remember that, although we are not on either coast, and most of us do not live in teeming cities, we nevertheless have the world in our midst: wives of servicemen, migrant workers, students, refugees, and immigrants. Many of these will go back to their own countries, and those with Christ in their hearts and lives, because of our ministries, will be missionaries where we cannot go.

Language groups are among the most responsive of all groups to the gospel, according to Mark Clifton, director of Extension Missions and Brotherhood for the KNCSB (*Annual*, 1993). He calls the growth of language missions in Kansas and Nebraska over the past ten years "astounding." In 1993 eighteen new missions and churches were begun among language groups, with two new groups added to the list: Russian and Japanese. In 1993 there were thirty-six churches and missions representing ten different language groups.

NATIONAL BAPTIST CONVENTION

N. J. Westmoreland reported in 1960 (*Annual*) that Loren Belt, former DOAM in Sedgwick, director of work with the National Baptist Convention (African-American) in the state of Missouri, asked for the privilege of working with National Baptist churches in Kansas. In 1960 the Missouri and Kansas organization of National Baptists worked closely together. There was no money for the Kansas Convention to participate in this work of the Home Mission Board, but the ministry of Belt paved the way for our future participation. The Executive Board asked if work begun by Belt's department would be continued by that department until Kansas was able to assume it as a budget item. Evidently the answer was affirmative, for by the next year, preliminary plans were underway for what Kansas could do to support and cooperate with the National Baptist Convention. The 1962 *Annual* mentioned work among National Baptists, which was initiated early in 1961.

By 1966 there was money available for joint social ministry projects. Next came joint meetings between Afro-American and white ministers conducted through the United Prayer Movement, which began in March 1968. The purpose of the meetings was to "enable Christians to find deeper levels of mutual understanding and to let God bring true appreciation and love for one another."

Currently, Mark Clifton is responsible for Black Church Extension. In the report for 1991 (*Annual*), he wrote, "The Black Church Extension program works with churches and associations in our Convention to reach lost and unchurched who live in predominately black communities. Two of the churches started in 1991 were begun in such communities.

"Eight pastors of predominately black churches attended a one-day workshop in Topeka. The conference was designed to assist these pastors in understanding how Southern Baptist programs can positively impact on the predominately black church. The conference was led by Willie McPherson, Associate Director of the Black Church Extension Division of the Home Mission Board."

In 1993 (*BD*, October 29, 1993), this item appeared, from a report by McPherson: "By the end of 1995, we'll have over 300 new black congregations a year. In 1992, Southern Baptists gained 117 new black congregations, a 48 percent increase compared to 1991 when they had only 79 new works. Currently, 1,353 predominately black Southern Baptist congregations exist." He predicted more than three thousand such congregations by the year 2000.

Mark Clifton reported to the 1993 Convention (*Annual*) that there were nine predominantly black churches affiliated with the KNCSB. Three were reported as new church starts for that year.

CHURCH BUILDINGS

People, not buildings, are the churches. People are churches. Nevertheless, a place to get together for worship, praise, confession, study, and fellowship is necessary for a congregation to move along the pathway of "becoming" and to really build a faith family. There are heroic stories behind church buildings in Kansas and Nebraska. The stories concern land, money, sharing, borrowing, volunteers, enlarging, and recycling. Church buildings are made of more than brick and mortar and stone, more than footings and pilings, and shingles and doors and windows. They are also filled with tears and laughter, joy and pathos, and humor and even, at times, conflict. Many of them in Kansas and Nebraska have been "made with loving hands at home."

A two-page review, pictures and text, of volunteer labor in church construction appeared in the *Digest* in 1990 (September 24). One group, made up of volunteers from Kansas, Missouri, Illinois, Oklahoma, and Louisiana, participates in a church building project every year. It is not organized, and it has no name; they just build churches efficiently and professionally. George Owens, pastor of a Missouri church, finds a location; his father Glen Owens, a contractor in Liberty, Kansas, is the on-site coordinator. This kind of volunteer work saves thousands of dollars in church construction every year. In addition to the money saved, such volunteer groups also give a real spiritual lift to the congregation with whom they serve.

For the church at Garden City, volunteer teams came from Angus Acres Baptist in Tulsa, Oklahoma, from Loxley and Mobile in Alabama, and from Texas. Many volunteers and members of the churches being built donated their professional skills in electrical wiring, bricklaying, and installing heating and air conditioning equipment. In Cherryvale, a team of sixty-eight persons from Centre, Alabama, and Meridian, Mississippi, worked on the addition. Another crew came from Mississippi to help; one couple had just been married, and left the next day to spend their honeymoon working on the church in Cherryvale. Volunteers from Kansas and Nebraska churches help other churches in Kansas and Nebraska. This volunteer construction has a way of uniting Christians across denominational lines. Wayne Hett, the pastor at Cherryvale, reported they had two Presbyterians on the roof one day. These are only examples of the kind of thing happening all over our Convention—people helping people in a thousand ways.

Many churches are adding and changing current facilities in order to provide more meaningful ministries for a changing population or to meet the need of new growth patterns of the community. This is what happened to the First Southern Baptist Church in Salina. The church was located in the 600 block of South Santa Fe Street, a few blocks from downtown. There was no way to add the desperately needed space without eliminating the also necessary parking area. So the church sold the downtown property, moved out in mid-October of 1987, and held services at Webster Conference Center and later at Kansas Wesleyan University. Property was purchased for sixteen thousand dollars at the corner of Ohio and Magnolia Streets, an area in south Salina, the direction in which the city is growing.

Building began in June 1988 with Delbert and Juanita Klassen of Phoenix, Arizona, camping at the building site and serving as general overseers of the work. Both are Christian Service Corps Volunteers. Juanita considered herself a "real good gofer." One day she made six trips to the local lumberyards.

The Klassens (*BD*, July 11, 1988) got involved with this kind of volunteer work when they helped Immanuel Baptist Church, Newton, build an educational addition. Klassen said, "We were just messing around, and I didn't know what I was going to do with the rest of my life."

An interesting sidelight was an observation from Mrs. Klassen. It may be one of the unanticipated advantages of building a church with volunteer labor: "First Southern's building is attracting attention in Salina. It is a conversation topic in the local lumberyards. Curious local residents stop by the building site just to watch."

Even before the first unit was finished, more space was needed for this growing church. Since the first unit was completed, two more have been added, all according to a master plan that moves toward meeting needs in the growing community. A third unit was completed in 1991. On the dedication program, November 17, 1991, were these words: "Many hours, sore fingers, sweat, blood, and tears have been poured into this building that the Lord has given us today."

A mission in Seneca, organized almost twenty years ago, became New Hope Baptist Church in 1981. Because the congregation had no building, and they met in various places, they "were a bit of a mystery" to their German Catholic neighbors (*BD*, August 23, 1993). They were looked on as "outsiders and foreigners." In 1992 four volunteer work groups helped construct a five thousand-square-foot building. In April 1993, New Hope was "invited to participate in the Seneca Chamber of Commerce annual spring homes tour."

Nearly two hundred persons came. Some thought the church had a hot tub, until they listened to members tell about the baptistry. There were questions and comments, which gave New Hope members an opportunity to talk about their faith. The pastor, Jimmy Hedrick, who grew up in College Heights Church in Manhattan, concluded, "New Hope's new building is giving the church a long-awaited sense of credibility and acceptance in our community."

There is a church in Kansas which can say with conviction, "Silver and gold have we none, but we do have something to give you—even better." It is a church that meets in a bank building in Kiowa, Kansas (*BD*, February 8, 1988). The mission was begun in 1984 by Ron Klingsick, pastor of the Medicine Lodge Church. Ray Hart came to the chapel when Klingsick left and the group was meeting in an agricultural chemical building, which had no space for Sunday School rooms. In 1989 Roy Moody came by for a visit and suggested they rent the vacant bank, one of the farm crisis casualties, on the east end of the downtown district. An offer was sent to the bank officials, a ridiculous figure of two hundred dollars per month. Bank officials not only accepted this offer, but suggested the people buy the building. The chapel was the only bidder and bought the building, worth about five hundred thousand dollars, for forty thousand dollars. With minor changes, the building was ready for occupancy in August 1987. An added bonus was the sale of a good many bank fixtures such as the vault door and four tellers' windows.

When Hart left, Jimmie Pitson became pastor. Attendance in Sunday School is up to an average of forty-nine; there is a strong youth program. In January 1994, the Kiowa Chapel became Kiowa Baptist Church, with much more to offer than silver and gold as it reaches out into the community.

Some churches are just lucky with buildings! Take the First Southern Baptist Church at South Sioux City in Nebraska, for example. In 1989 (*BD*, June 26, 1989), "a charismatic congregation that disbanded in the summer of 1988, gave its building to First Southern Baptist. It is just two blocks from where the church was meeting, in a building that was almost too small for the congregation, and is now being used for the community food bank. The congregation did some remodeling and now have more than twice the space they had before." Perhaps this was not "luck," but rather all in God's plan.

Southview Baptist in Lincoln was one of those churches which had a great debt in 1968. They lettered out 105 people in one week; they had about fifty or sixty members left, and a weekly debt payment of $234. But then people began to move in again for one reason or another. The debt was refinanced and then paid. Time came when the congregation bought a seventy-one-acre tract of land on Highway 2 and 84th Street. The plan was to build a complex with a retirement center, nursing home, radio station, and school, as well as a church.

One thing led to another, and a decision was made not to move, but they could not seem to get rid of the property on the highway. Some members thought it would be a good idea just to quit making payments, default on the debt. That suggestion was not accepted. Then the city built a street right through the parking lot, leaving a small piece of land on the other side, which the church tried to sell and could not.

Finally, a decision was made to rebuild right where the church was located. Suddenly, the property on the highway was sold at a good price, and the land across the street was sold at almost three times the original asking price. To make a long story short, when the million-dollar building was complete, three-quarters of the debt was already paid.

Then there are churches that cannot seem to find a permanent building. Abraham Aldape did not want to go to Madison, Nebraska, to pastor Calvary Church. His wife needed and wanted to work, and there was no job available, and they could not find a house. But then, things changed; a house became available, and Annette found a position as principal of an elementary school in a town not too far away. Aldape became pastor of an eleven-year-old church that met for ten years in nine different places. With volunteers from Texas, a church building of their very own was constructed, and now more educational space is needed because of the growth that has taken place. Aldape is now a church starter in Sedgwick Association.

Three different congregations share the Omaha Baptist Center building: the All Nations Church, made up largely of Native Americans, and the Omaha Baptist Center congregation, which is Anglo, both pastored by Ron Goombi, along with the Primera Iglesia Bautista, a Spanish work, pastored by Isais Martinez. The Spanish church was meeting in another building, but found it could not meet payments. They rented the building to a congregation of another denomination and moved into the center.

In the Sandhills of Nebraska (*BD*, December 24, 1990), churches meet where they can. Dorsey Community Church meets in a one-room schoolhouse. Burwell Baptist Church in Burwell, Nebraska, met at Jensen Irrigation for five years, before it had a building. It was called the "Steel Cathedral."

A new building may give a whole new pattern and direction for a church. Take McPherson, for example. In its heyday, according to the pastor, Dave McNeal, there were several hundred members. Vera Gardner, who serves in Thailand, was sent out by this church (*BD*, August 23, 1993). It was located in a building on Highway 56, and the Methodists moved in right next door. There was no way to expand. It came to the point of almost dying.

By the time Les Arnold came to Smoky Hill, the church was operating in the "survival mode": pay the preacher, keep the doors open, and fear trying anything new. The building, besides being located poorly, was a World War II barracks building, not very attractive. Then Dave McNeal, retired from the Army and a member of Junction City Baptist Church, came as pastor. He pushed them to sell the property, and with the money buy a more suitable site and build. They did this, but had to meet for awhile in a school building before their own building was available.

When McNeal came to McPherson, there were only thirteen people on hand that first day, and the McNeal family made up half the crowd. Things began to happen, including lots of visitation, lots of training for the leadership, and new community involvement. This brought about a change in the attitude of the community toward the Baptist church.

Paul and Susan Feltman, from Odessa, Texas, moved to McPherson, and Calvary members got them involved. The couple knew a volunteer church builder in Texas, who put them in touch with T. O. Upshaw, who leads a group known as Church Builders, an organization begun in 1978. The group has built thirty-eight buildings, from Mexico to Montana. Along with volunteer labor, the Church Builders also bring strong financial support to a building project. A gift of fifty thousand dollars was presented to the McPherson church, thirty thousand dollars came from the First Baptist Church in Midland, Texas, and the rest from the volunteers and other interested persons. Upshaw also inspired the members to bring an offering, which totaled about forty thousand dollars. Even so, they needed to borrow money, so the association cosigned the loan guaranteeing $150 per month, if needed.

The guarantee was never needed; the church has doubled up on its payments, and has paid the note to a point that it can borrow again for a much needed addition.

The building crew began work at 7:00 A.M., Monday, July 12, on a bare concrete slab. By the end of the week the building was ready for the finish work. A team came the next week from Euless, Texas, to do this. During the week, storms came, and the builders sloshed around in mud up to their knees because they had only a limited time to get the work done.

The Abilene building is another hard-to-believe tale. The church was bought from a Presbyterian congregation when population was booming. Then came the time when this was much more building than was needed; it was expensive to heat and keep in repair. The congregation was ready to sell it for twenty thousand dollars, but a buyer came forward and paid forty thousand dollars for it, giving the church the privilege of remaining in the building until their new structure was complete, and also footing the tab for utilities during this period.

There was an announcement in the *Digest* (July 23, 1990) of the formation of a volunteer construction team that would work only with churches in Kansas and Nebraska. It was headed by Herman and Mary Jo Robertson. They are Mission Service Corps Volunteers of the Home Mission Board. Robertson retired from the Owens-Corning Fiberglass Company, after forty-two years. During the summer of 1990, he worked with the church at Ogden, Kansas. He parked his trailer at the building site and was at work every morning by 6:00 A.M. Mary Jo handles the paper work of putting the teams together. For a number of years she was recording secretary of the KNCSB.

CONVENTION PERSONNEL

The first state missionary of the Kansas Convention was Eugene Strahan, who served in 1948 and 1949. He was followed closely by Ray Hart, who served in the "unreached areas of Western Kansas." One of Strahan's major concerns was with student work. He had a hand in the Pittsburg student-work ministry. Hart was instrumental in organizing the churches in Hoisington, Chase, and Cunningham. As the associational missionary, he helped the church at Florence to organize. Under his leadership they pledged $2,010 to build an auditorium and pastor's home (*KSBB*, October, 1949).

Another of the early associational or area directors of missions was Cecil Finfrock. He thought "Kansas City, Kansas" were ugly words! He had no idea of ever going to that region for any reason. "But," he said, "don't ever tell the Lord you'll not serve in a certain place because that's probably where you'll end up." So it was with Finfrock who came to Kansas in 1953 as super-intendent of missions in the Eastern Area, at the urging of good friends of his already at work in Kansas: W. A Burkey and Jack Stanton. When the offer was made, he laughed at it. He had a happy pastorate; the Kansas area was impossibly large, and the salary and expense funds impossibly small. He remembered that "the work operated on a shoestring which had been broken and tied back together with a knot." At that time there were three associa-tions in the area: George W. Truett Memorial, Twin Valley, and Tri County. During his tenure Kansas City, Kansas, Kaw Valley, and Blue Stem Associations were organized.

Finfrock covered a third of the state, and during one ninety-day period was away from home seventy-eight days and nights. There was no equip-ment; he bought his own typewriter and a mimeograph machine, which were pretty basic necessities, and set up an associational office in his rented home. When any mention was made of the shortage of funds, N. J. Westmoreland answered, "These are the days of missionary opportunity," which came to be an in-house joke, when things did not move along smoothly. Finfrock com-mented in this regard, "Great man that he was, [Westmoreland's] philosophy of missions was the more that you did without and the more you sacrificed and suffered, the better job you were doing as a missionary. Everybody didn't agree with that, but that was the way business was conducted."

One Sunday night, when the family had gone to Haskell Institute for the worship service, their three-year-old daughter, rummaging in her mother's purse, found a dollar bill and put it in the collection plate when it was passed. That was exactly how much money they had, which they planned to use for food on the way back to Wichita. "Talk about sacrificial giving," he said. "But it was an accident." They drove home dinnerless that night.

Cecil Finfrock stayed in Kansas until 1957. He left for the same reason many others left pioneer areas; he had to survive. The money ran out. They spent all they had saved and had to go somewhere else to earn enough to live on. He went to First Baptist Church in Aurora, Colorado, still in pioneer missions, then to Miami Beach. In 1966 he became director of missions in the Valdosta Baptist Association in Georgia where he served for more than twenty-three years under a variety of titles.

The story of Kansas-Nebraska pastors is one of personal enlistment. Chester Stotts, a pastor in Wichita, gave Strahan's name to the committee looking for a state missionary. Strahan recruited Stanley Gasswint to lead the BSU at Pittsburg State Teachers College and Allan Morris from Oklahoma to lead the Baptist Student ministry at Haskell. This has happened over and over.

In 1951 the Executive Board of the Convention authorized positions for superintendents of cooperative missions and of evangelism. In 1951 the position of superintendent of evangelism was offered to A. A. Watson, from Long Beach, California. He accepted, then later declined. Jack Stanton, from Carpenter Street Baptist Church in Moberly, Missouri, accepted the position in 1952 and served until 1955. He went to the Colorado Convention after leaving Kansas, then to the Home Mission Board to develop evangelism materials, and then to Southwest Baptist University in Bolivar, Missouri.

Stanton was followed by John Havlik (1956-1961), J. Frank Davis (1962), and, after a period of vacancy, Garth Pybas (1965-1968). In 1968 this was another of the jobs taken over by Pat McDaniel, when personnel was cut to the bone. Peck Lindsay received this assignment when he joined the staff in 1971. The work was handled in different ways through the years. Roy Moody became director of the Department of Evangelism in 1986, and in addition is responsible for campus ministries and stewardship.

Moody is an Oklahoman. Both he and his wife, Sharon, graduated from Wayland Baptist College in Texas. Moody graduated from Southwestern Seminary; he has pastored a number of churches in Texas, Oklahoma, and Washington. Perhaps it was his summer as a Home Mission Board worker in Kansas that caused him to consider his present position. Before he came to Kansas, he served as associate director of evangelism with the Baptist General Convention of Oklahoma from 1981 to 1986.

Moody has been active at the state convention and SBC levels; he has done some writing. Two programs he has developed and written in Kansas are "Committed to Christ . . . Committed to Tithe," and "Sacrifice to Grow," a capital fund-raising program.

His forte is training people in personal evangelism to help them know how to share their faith. He feels a greater commitment to witness training events in the associations and the Convention than to evangelism conferences for pastors and other leadership. He feels there is a growing awareness among Christians of the impact of prayer. Both he and Andy St. Andre point to the widespread use of Henry Blackaby's "Experiencing God" as evidence of this.

In 1951 W. A. Burkey was elected by the Executive Board as superintendent of cooperative missions, later labeled in different ways with varying responsibilities. He served until 1959. From Kansas, Burkey went to California, served a couple of terms as president of the California

Convention, and was the first missionary in the Los Angeles and San Francisco areas. He settled in Fairfield, California. He was followed by Meeler Markham (1960-1964), F. Galen Irby (1966-1968), Pat McDaniel (1968-1971), and Peck Lindsay (1971-1982). Lindsay became executive director-treasurer in 1977, but retained responsibility for associational missions. Dewey Hickey was appointed in 1978 as director of the Extension Missions Department and later was given responsibility for the "200 by 2000" goals. He also was Brotherhood director. After he left in 1987 to become the executive-director of the Dakota Fellowship, the position was vacant for a time; then Mark Clifton was added to the staff to fill these two areas of responsibility. He is also director of the Nevada Partnership Program.

Clifton, born in Missouri, graduated from William Jewell College and Midwestern Seminary. He came to Kansas from a position with the Home Mission Board as director of the Project Development Office, in the New Church Extension Division. Earlier, he was associate director of the Church Starting Department at the Home Mission Board.

In the Roswell Baptist Association on the northeast edge of Atlanta, Clifton helped start six churches in less than two years. While he was in seminary, he started Castleview Baptist Church in Blue Springs, Missouri, through the PRAXIS program. In three year's time, the church was self-supporting, had two hundred enrolled in Sunday school, had a new building and five acres of land, and had a full-time pastor and a part-time music director *(BD,* February 26, 1990).

During his college years, Clifton was a disc jockey for KWXS Radio Station in Excelsior Springs, Missouri; later, he served as program director for KWPB in Liberty. During this time he was also pastor at Alta Vista and Independence in Missouri.

Rather than choosing "places" for new church starts, Clifton likes to talk about "people groups" who need to hear the Good News. Out of this emphasis, the Home Mission Board conceived the strategy of "satellite" churches, which are really congregations of a church meeting at different locations from the "main" church.

Andy St. Andre until April 1995 was director of teaching and training, a department that has undergone a number of name changes through the years but has always had a director or secretary. Ed Russell, in 1949, was the first secretary of the Department of Religious Education, which included Sunday School, Training Union, and Student Work. He was followed by Ray Gilliland, who stayed until the bond fiasco in 1968. During Gilliland's years of service, divisions were made in the workload; Hillary Brophy, Howard Halsell, Ray Conner, and Harold Inman all served as secretaries of the Department of Sunday School. After 1968 Inman continued as director of the Department of Religious Education, and he also had responsibility for church music and church architecture. He retired in 1991 but continued to be active on the Convention staff as architectural consultant, Volunteers in Missions coordinator, and the chair of the Fiftieth Anniversary Celebration of the KNCSB.

Inman's chief emphasis was training. His plan for Sunday School and Vacation Bible School was to bring a team from Kansas and Nebraska, to be trained by SBC staff, who would go back to associations to train church teams, who would go back to their churches to train people who would touch boys and girls and men and women. So ten would touch a hundred, who would touch seven hundred, who would touch upwards of twenty-one to twenty-two thousand. For twelve or thirteen years, a training team went to each association for Training Union work. Another emphasis was "Master Life Conference" and teaching people how to use these materials. This now has been largely replaced by "Experiencing God" materials. Ray Conner began the Music Festivals which Inman continued and upon which Taylor enlarged. In the early days, Inman worked with Gilliland in planning and conducting youth assemblies on college campuses. Interest gradually dropped, and other activities were set in place. When Harold Whatley left, church architectural concerns were added to Inman's responsibilities. Although Inman has officially retired, he really has not. He continues to work with churches in planning for the kind of space they need to meet needs for teaching and worship. He helps them to look down the road about ten years, and project probable needs and resources for necessary ministries.

Andy St. Andre became director of teaching and training when Inman retired. He was born in Louisiana, but has spent most of the years since 1961 in Nebraska and Kansas. He came to Nebraska in 1961 and was stationed at SAC Headquarters, where he spent eight years, with an overseas stint during the time. He and his wife, Jeanne, were members of First Baptist Church in Bellevue, and the first time this church reached out to the Chandler Hills-Acres area, a meeting was held in the St. Andre's home. This was not quite the right place, so the emphasis shifted to the home of another member of Bellevue who lived in Chandler Acres. From this Bible study group came the organization of the Chandler Acres Baptist Church.

In 1970 St. Andre went to Alamedo Hills Church in Denver; in 1972 he came back to Bellevue as associate pastor and minister of education. During this time he completed his seminary education at Midwestern. Then he moved to Louisiana and then to Alabama. In 1985 he met Peck Lindsay at the Convention in Dallas. Lindsay asked, "What in the world are you doing down in the Bible Belt?" Almost immediately afterwards, St. Andre had a call from Quentin Lockwood, who was at the Home Mission Board at that time, inviting him to make application to the board so he could accept a position as director of missions in Western Kansas Association. In April 1986 he went to Garden City and served the Western Kansas Association for six years.

During his tenure, the Vietnamese work was begun, now pastored by Thomas Tran. Mead and Moscow are examples of the church starts made under his leadership. The church at Mead had made two or three previous beginnings, but when the Christian Church in the town closed its doors, there was an even greater need for the Baptist church to try again. So the Baptist group rented the Christian Church building; Andy brought in a team of his

Bible Belt Alabama friends who repaired the church, held Bible school, and led a revival service. The Christian Church folk were so impressed with the investment the Baptists made in the building they deeded it to them. The Baptist church is not large, but it is a witness in the community.

The pastor at Hugoton, Larry Bradford, felt impressed to start a work at Moscow, sixteen miles away. He drove down, began knocking on doors, and found sixteen people interested in a Bible study group. Bradford finally resigned in Hugoton and became pastor at Moscow, which is now larger than the mother church.

St. Andre has emphasized discipleship at the KNCSB. He is concerned that seventy-seven percent of our churches give no training to new members. If we are to grow strong churches and reach out to people with the gospel, we must have members who understand who they are and what they believe.

Ray Conner served in Kansas in 1963 as state Sunday School and Church Music secretary. After he left Kansas, he worked one year in Missouri and then twenty-eight years at the Sunday School Board, SBC, first in the Church Music Department and then, for twenty-two years, as director of the Church Recreation Department. He is now on the staff of Belmont University in Nashville. Harold Inman served as Church Music secretary from 1964 to 1975. Harry Taylor came in 1975 as the director of the Department of Church Music. Taylor also has responsibility in the areas of Church Administration, Minister Relations, and Church Recreation. Another of his jobs is buying and leasing cars for Convention employee use.

An early dream of Harry Taylor's was to become an oral surgeon, but the love of church music and the call of the Lord won out, and he transferred from Phillips University to OBU. In 1956 he and Joela, his wife, went to Memorial Baptist Church in Tulsa, where he served for more than twelve years in music and administration. In 1968 he was called to Nall Avenue, where he served until January 1975, when he became director of Church Music and Church Administration for the KNCSB.

Taylor followed through with the Music Festivals which Conner had begun and Inman continued, which brought together children's and youth choirs from Kansas and Nebraska on two spring weekends for fellowship, training, and competition. In order to involve churches not big enough to have such choirs, Taylor instituted vocal and keyboard competitions.

In 1989 a junior high school student from Washington, Kansas, won first place in voice and second place in keyboard. Everyone knew Erin Syring, and everyone was delighted. The pastor invited Harry to come for the Sunday morning service and then stay for the afternoon reception and present the awards to Erin. The whole town turned out, and sitting on the front row, proud as punch, was the organist from the Methodist Church, who introduced herself as Erin's piano teacher.

A highlight of Taylor's ministry is with a project of the Sunday School Board: Musicians on Mission. The plan was to invite ministers of music to come to a state, be assigned to a church, and work in that church for a week.

About twenty locations were scheduled for each year. Taylor produced a training video and went to many meetings over the SBC enlisting musicians who came to Kansas. Our Musicians on Mission workshop was scheduled in April 1986. One hundred ninety-eight musicians came to Kansas, took part in the Friday-Saturday training sessions, and then went to churches all over our two-state Convention to work with music and worship committees, children, youth, and adult choirs, whatever the church wanted. These were talented men and women who came at their own expense to invest a week of their lives in our churches. It was a highly successful undertaking.

When the new *Baptist Hymnal* was published in 1991, a great celebration called PraiSing took place in Nashville, in which people came together for a week of music making, marking "the Baptist Sunday School Board's Centennial year, the church music department's 50th anniversary and the hymnal's publication" (*BD*, March 25, 1991). In Kansas, a PraiSing II was planned at the close of the State-wide Evangelistic Conference in September 1991 to introduce the new hymnal. A number of artists were on hand: Jeri Graham Edmonds, Max Lyall, Henrietta Davis, Dean Wilder, and a host of others. It was held at the Metropolitan Baptist Church in Wichita, and there was not room enough to hold the people who came. It was the largest gathering of Southern Baptists ever held in Kansas. Autographed copies of the new hymnal were given to the first six hundred who registered; the others received a copy of a special printing done for Kansas. Taylor served on the committee that developed the hymnal, which was a two-year task.

The Singing Men of Kansas-Nebraska was organized in 1981 and was open to all full-time ministers of music in the Convention. Later, it was opened to all full-time staff. The purpose was to present special music at state meetings, but the group soon received invitations to sing at SBC meetings as well. Singing Women of Kansas-Nebraska was organized in 1992, and is open to staff members and spouses of staff members. Setting practice times is a bit difficult, since getting together entails much planning. For the celebration of the fiftieth anniversary of KNCSB, all alumni were invited to come back for a grand presentation. Also for the celebration an anthem was commissioned: "Our Heritage, Our Destiny," with text by Calvin Miller, long-time pastor in Nebraska and professor at Southwestern Seminary; and music by A. L. Butler, professor of church music at Midwestern Seminary. The words and music for an anniversary chorus, "The Vision . . . Hand-in-Hand," were composed by Ray Hilderbrand and Helen Harrell Redmond.

Sue Lindsay is church media/library consultant. She has been involved in this outreach for more than thirty years, but really "stumbled" into it. In Omaha she attended an associational meeting where Glenn Hill, from the Sunday School Board, was conducting a library conference. She had no other pressing needs, so she went to that conference and was hooked. This became another tool in her work as educational director in Nebraska.

When the Lindsays first moved to Wichita, Sue did her work behind the scenes, but became increasingly more visible. When the move was made to

Topeka, space was designated for a library. The first concept for use of this space was as a study area for staff members and shelf space for books which the staff needed and shared. Harold Inman began to gather training materials, and placed them in the library for use by churches. Gradually, videotapes, which can be borrowed by the churches, have also been added.

Viola Webb wore the "library" hat when the move was first made to Topeka. She planned training conferences, and worked with library staff in local churches as she could. She reported 142 libraries in 1978. The next year, Jeanne Pendleton, Bellevue, Nebraska, was serving as KNCSB media center consultant. At the annual meeting in 1980, there was a special luncheon for church library/media center people, where Mancil Ezell from the Sunday School Board was the speaker. Through these years, Sue Lindsay led conferences and conducted training sessions for media center personnel. After Webb retired, Lindsay was officially listed as church media/library consultant, at first on a volunteer basis, and later underwritten part-time by the Sunday School Board.

She has three goals: to assist churches in training library staff to build libraries which assist and support the growth and work of people in the church; to plan for the best use of the physical library/media space in the Baptist building; and to set up a system for preservation of the history of the churches and Convention. She is trainer, supporter, and archivist.

Lindsay gives much of the credit for interest in library/media to Mrs. C. O. Little of Valley Center Church, who was one of the earliest appointed "approved workers" in the state. No doubt, Little recognized the value of a church library in "equipping the saints." Lindsay plans two conferences each year, one in the spring which moves from one section to another, and a two-day conference at Webster in the fall. At least two associations have organized TACMO: The Associational Church Media Organization. Twice, Nashville has chosen Kansas for regional library conferences at Metropolitan in Wichita and Liberal, to which all media people west of the Mississippi were invited. Both were well done and well attended.

Growth has marked the KNCSB throughout its fifty years: proclamation, ministry, outreach to new territories, and equipping of the saints. It is time to set new goals as we enter into the twenty-first century.

9

The House That Jack (the Baptist) Built

THE FIRST CONVENTION OFFICE WAS ONLY AN ADDRESS: Kansas Convention of Southern Baptist Churches, P. O. Box 729, Wichita Kansas. This was before the days of zip codes. Actually, a pivotal piece of work by the Executive Board, persuading N. J. Westmoreland to become the full-time executive secretary treasurer of the infant Convention, in June 1946, was accomplished on a bench in Linwood Park in Wichita. It was at this time that the Westmorelands left Coffeyville and moved to Wichita, which was a central location for the churches affiliated with the KCSB.

In the first months of the Fellowship and Convention, Westmoreland operated out of the Coffeyville Church where he was pastor. Office equipment, what little there was, and office space were furnished by this church.

When they came to Wichita, the Westmorelands moved into a mobile home that belonged to a family which was away for a period of time. There were few modern conveniences; on top of that, the family came back to Wichita much sooner than expected, so the Westmorelands moved into a basement apartment. The landlord lived upstairs, where the only bathroom was located.

At this time Bob Maultsby moved from Oklahoma to Kansas, where he became pastor of the Southside Baptist Church in Wichita. Little building had been done during the war years; rented housing was almost impossible to find. Finally, the Maultsbys located a garage apartment, and the family moved from a seven-room parsonage into the converted two-car garage. The apartment had one corner partitioned off for a toilet and sink, and the remainder of the space served as kitchen, living room, dining room, bedrooms, and whatever. The Westmoreland family lived in the basement of the house in front of the garage. The landlord's family, the Westmoreland

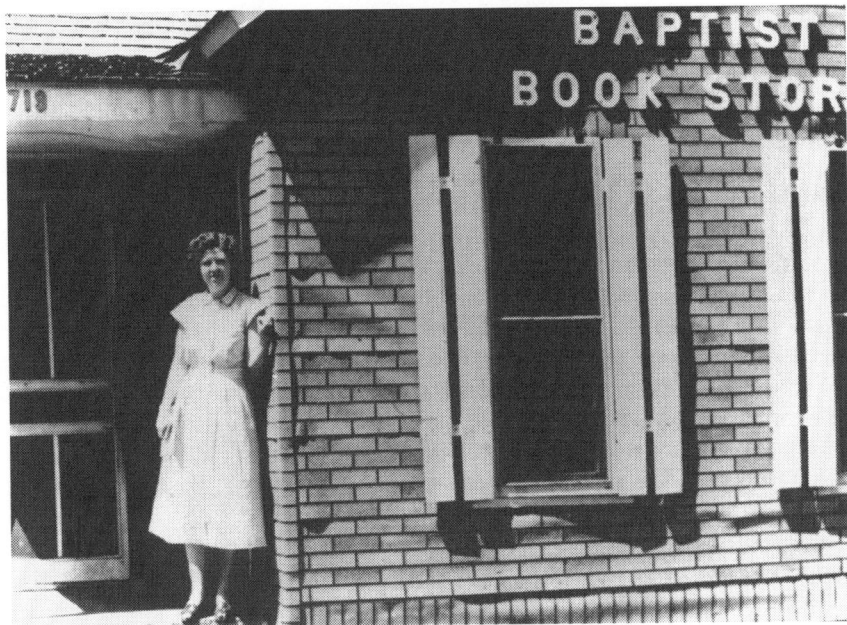

Marjorie Moore, now Marjorie Moore Moratto, stands in front of the Westmoreland home in Wichita, Kansas, which also served in the late 1940s as headquarters and Baptist Book Store for the Kansas Convention of Southern Baptists.

family, and the Maultsby family all used the bath tub in the landlord's upstairs bathroom.

The Westmoreland's place of residence in those first few months seemed to be wherever there was a church that needed strengthening or tending. For a while they lived in the student house in Pittsburg. They had the whole downstairs, students lived upstairs, and the house was also used for the meeting place for Trinity Baptist Church in Pittsburg. The house needed a great deal of work. Westmoreland and Keith Hamm spent many hours re-wiring and shoring up the floor; they stayed busy with whatever things needed doing. For a time the Westmorelands lived in Osawatamie. By then there were three children; there was no running water or bathroom in that house.

When they moved back to Wichita, in September 1948 (*BD*, May 4, 1963), they lived in a house on Hydraulic Avenue. This was the first "official " office space—if one can so designate a room in a house, which was at best hardly big enough for a growing family. When Marjorie Moore (now Marjorie Moratto) was hired in 1946 as office secretary, she lived in the "front bedroom" of that house. To make this possible, the Westmorelands and their three children moved to the dining room. There was only one bathroom in the house, which had to be entered through the room where the Westmorelands slept. The enterprising young just-graduated-from-college office secretary devised a way of climbing out the front-room window and in through the bathroom window, rather than disturb the Westmorelands. She did not tell what sort of a costume she wore for this adventure.

Mrs. Westmoreland remembers that when Ed Russell joined the staff, funds were made available for his salary by the Sunday School Board on condition that the Convention would make office space available for him. By that time, Moratto had moved into a room in another house, and the Westmorelands had reclaimed the bedroom. To meet the request of the Sunday School Board, they put a partition in that front bedroom which gave working space to the new secretary of religious education and the executive secretary-treasurer of the Convention.

In 1951 property was purchased by the Convention at 3420 W. 13th Street for $9,500, but at no cost to the Convention. This was home for the Westmorelands. The down payment was made by Richard Dumas, and the Westmorelands paid rent to the Convention of seventy-three dollars per month, which covered the loan payment. In 1954 the Executive Board authorized the sale of this house to Olivet Baptist Church for $9,700 (*Annual*, 1954). At the same time, a committee was appointed to select a new residence for the executive secretary-treasurer. The new residence, located at 3507 Pecos, was built at a cost of $13,400, and greatly added to the comfort of the Westmoreland family. A water-well and electric pump were authorized in May to aid in landscaping the new property.

When they moved from Pecos, the Westmorelands bought a house at 721 North Young. They remodeled the basement to provide room for their growing family. Later, they built a house on West Street. By this time there were six children, plus a live-in student from Alaska. From time to time, N. J.'s mother and Wanda's father lived with them, also.

The property at 719 Hydraulic was purchased in 1951 for $2,900. It was in need of repairs, according to the Executive Committee report (1951), which may have been the understatement of the year. It was obtained with no down payment and believed worth the cost of repairs. It was to be used as a residence for "Convention employees." It was sold the following year (1952) for $4,700 to First Baptist Church, Wichita. A house was purchased in 1952 at 1931 Madison as a residence for Jack Stanton, who joined the Convention staff as secretary of evangelism. This house was sold in 1956 on contract. This was the last residence provided to any Convention employee.

Westmoreland described office space used in the months before the Hydraulic house, from June 1946 to September 1948, as follows, "I literally operated from my brief case, often with the typewriter on my knees, sometimes from a table in our residence and sometimes from the back seat of the dilapidated 1937 Plymouth, or nearly-as-dilapidated 1939 Oldsmobile" (*BD*, May 4, 1963). In February 1947, the WMU bought a portable typewriter for his use.

The April 1947 issue of *SBB* pictured the "State Headquarters Established in Downtown Wichita." It was described as "a suite of rooms on North Broadway between Douglas and First Street in the heart of Wichita's busy business district, housing the Convention and State WMU offices, Editorial office of the *Southern Baptist Beams* and the Baptist Book Store." The address was 138 1/2 North Broadway.

Marjorie Moratto remembers that there was a liquor store and a sewing machine shop, Clark's Sewing Machine Exchange, on the ground floor. The KCSB and the Baptist Book Store were on the second floor. Her desk was in a large open area at the top of the stairs, where the book store was also located. Others shared offices in little rooms around this area. Many times, as she came to work in the morning, she had to lay liquor bottles and beer cans to one side in order to get up the steps. It was such an unsavory neighborhood that Westmoreland and Russell would not allow her to stay in the building after hours. She did not have a car, so she walked several blocks to a bus stop. In bad weather, she recalls, Westmoreland, whose rule was that a man and woman, not married to each other, should not ride in the same car unless there was another woman present, often walked with her to the bus stop. Sometimes he gave her the keys to his car to drive herself home, and then he walked downtown and took the bus home. Westmoreland commented on this building, "Although unattractive in many ways, it was a great improvement" (Filmstrip Script: *Kansas, 1955*).

Moratto has many memories of the generosity of the Westmorelands and others during the hard beginning days. When she lived at the Hydraulic residence address, she had all her meals with the Westmorelands. She paid no board and room; this was part of her salary. Even after she moved to another house, where there were no cooking privileges, these provisions continued. She "nibbled" in the morning. At noontime, she was at the Westmorelands, "looking hungry," so she was always invited to lunch. The same was true with the evening meal, which was ready about the time she was "getting off."

She also remembers attending meetings around the state. Nobody had money for motels, so they were housed in the homes of people in the community. One night there were so many in one house, that, because she was the youngest, she slept on the floor. On one occasion, when she went to a meeting without a penny in her pocket, a woman slipped two dollars into that empty pocket. "I thought I was the richest person at the Convention," she said.

Finally, in June 1949, a five-room building was rented at 244 1/2 North Main Street in Wichita. By this time Marjorie Moore Moratto had left, and Cherry Kincheloe was office secretary. There were many who frowned upon the Convention's choice of rental space—again, not in the choicest part of town. In the February 14, 1952, issue of *KSBB*, Orbie Clem included a group of pictures of the "dens of iniquity and stinking filth polluting the 200 block on North Main Street." However, it was space, and for the first time all of the staff, full-time and part-time, had a place of their own in the same building.

The Baptist Book Store was located downstairs at this site. There was a bar next door. In the same issue of the *KSBB* (Febrary 14, 1952), Westmoreland wrote in detail of a confrontation he had with a police officer who stopped him as he left the office one evening. He had received a complaint from the manager of the liquor store next to the entrance of the book store. It seemed that someone was moving the empty bottles from the stairway entrance to the book store and putting them in front of the liquor store. Westmoreland asked the officer what could be done about the problem. He continued, "It is dangerous for the ladies of our staff to work until their six o'clock quitting time. The drunks often are on the street three or four abreast and are entirely beyond courtesy." The officer agreed that North Main Street had become the "Skid Row" of Wichita, but he had no suggestions about the empty-bottle problem except to get an "adequate trash barrel into which you can put them." After all, he continued, this was a legitimate business, and if, what the manager might well have considered harassment, did not cease, he would swear out a complaint against the person doing it.

Westmoreland assured the officer that he wanted to cooperate with the law and would relate this report to the staff. In a "note" in her scrapbook, alongside this story, Lois Clem wrote, "If I remember correctly, I confessed to Bro. Westmoreland that I was the one who had perpetrated this deed!" This action was also "claimed" by other persons on the staff.

The Wichita headquarters building, located at 231 North Main, was purchased in June 1952 by the Convention, and occupied in October of that year. The building was 25' by 130', had two full floors with a basement under the back sixty feet and was located in the heart of Wichita's "Furniture Lane." The purchase price was twenty-four thousand dollars. The first floor and a basement were leased to the Sunday School Board for the Baptist Book Store on a ten-year contract at two hundred dollars per month. Of this twenty-four thousand dollars total, the Sunday School Board loaned the Convention fifteen thousand dollars at three percent interest, fourteen thousand dollars of which was used as a down payment. The balance needed was borrowed at four and one half percent interest from the Bankers Life Insurance Company of Wichita. The two hundred dollars per month from the Sunday School Board were used to retire both loans at one hundred dollars per month each; the building was to be paid for in ten years.

Transactions concerning this building were reported in detail to the 1952 Convention meeting (*Annual,* 1952): "The entire building has been in the process of being remodelled for the past three months. For approximately $6,500 we have been able to provide nine office rooms decorated after the latest trends and with air conditioning for both winter and summer, in the front half of the building. The remaining portion of the second floor will serve as storage space and, as needed, additional office rooms will be provided and an assembly room large enough to accommodate Executive Board meetings will be completed. A loan to cover the remodeling costs is being sought whereby that cost can be retired at $65.00 per month. Thus, our monthly payments will be $265 per month, with only $65 coming from our operating budget. This is a $5.00 per month increase over what we have been paying for less adequate and unattractive office quarters."

In addition, the Sunday School Board spent $6,500 in permanent improvements to the first floor and basement, which added to the value of the property. The Sunday School Board also installed "white birch fixtures in the book store costing $7,500." So, forty-five thousand dollars was the cost of opening the new headquarters at 231 North Main. Westmoreland concluded his report, "We face an opportunity without precedent to Baptists in Kansas and perhaps not before experienced by a new Southern Baptist constituency as young as ours. We praise our God from whom all blessings flow and express our gratitude for the timely aid from the Sunday School Board."

In the beginning only the east end of the upper floor was used for offices. The staff increased, so in 1957 (*Annual*) the west end of the building was remodeled for office space. At a cost of slightly more than six thousand dollars, four office rooms, one twice as large as existing offices, a second rest room, a hot water heater, and drinking fountain were added. The executive secretary-treasurer moved to the larger office, equipped with new furniture and completely air conditioned. In 1962 the stockroom was moved to the basement and that space claimed for offices.

In 1953 (*Annual*), an announcement was made of "construction totalling more than $6,000,000 within two and a half blocks of our building, and of $3,000,000 to $4,000,000 additional construction that is pending. The last project will include the removal of all the taverns in our block and the remodeling of the fronts of all the buildings in the same area. This will greatly increase the value of our property."

In 1953 substantial additions to Convention equipment were reported (*Annual*) at a cost of $1,505.17: a typewriter, three executive-type steel office desks, one Dictaphone dictating machine, a Speed-O-Print duplicator, and a Monroe Calculator. The installation of a dial type buzzer system for the operation of the intercommunication units, at a cost of $125, proved to be worth many times its cost in improved efficiency of the office staff (*Annual*, 1956).

In 1958 (*Annual*), more equipment ($1875 worth) was added: folding machine, postage meter, letter sealer, Verifax copy maker, two fire-proof safes, one executive desk, one secretarial desk, three work tables, three typewriters, one four-drawer filing cabinet, and five storage cabinets. All equipment fit in with the established objective of acquiring gray metal office furniture. Such details in reporting expenditures seem a bit strange, particularly in light of the CLA debacle.

In 1959 (*Annual*) Westmoreland reported to the Convention: "To say that we are over-crowded at the Baptist Building is the understatement of the year. Our office areas for secretaries have been over-crowded for the past year. To the mailing room, which was over-crowded for that function, was added the offset press which actually needs double the space of our ordinary office rooms. Storage space is no longer available in a convenient way. Should the occasion arise for the employment of another department head or an associate, we could not care for him at 231 1/2 North Main."

Just as a sideline to this report, it seems a foregone conclusion that any new employee would be male. It probably did not cross Westmoreland's mind that a new competent, qualified staff member could be female.

Because of the location, and lack of proper space, in 1959 a committee was appointed to study and do preliminary planning for a new office building. The contract for this edifice, located at 3000 West Kellogg, was signed in 1962. The total cost was $298,700, which included furnishings and landscaping. The building included 7,500 to 8000 square feet which could be rented at four dollars per square foot per year producing $30,000 to $32,000 rental income per year. The annual payments on the property totaled $31,800 for thirteen years. Roe Messner Construction Company, contractors, guaranteed the rental income of one-half of this floor space for the first three years. No payments were to be made until January 1964. This was a verbal agreement; no written contract was drawn, and Messner never delivered on his promised lease of offices

In May 1963, the beautiful new headquarters at 3000 West 54 Highway (3000 West Kellogg) was dedicated (*BD*, May 4, 1963). In that issue of the *Baptist Digest*, Westmoreland wrote, "The building has been designed as a service tool to implement our missionary advance. It will provide for present and anticipated needs in floor space for at least 15 years."

Unlike the others, this building was in a strategic location, with easy access near the intersection of U.S. 54 and Interstate 235. It was less than ten minutes driving time from downtown and from the municipal airport. The building was completely air conditioned and had parking spaces for 125 cars. There was an automatic elevator; a freight dock was in the rear. It was the largest denominational office building in Kansas and the only new office building on Wichita's west side. The building, the decorations, and the furnishings were first-class all the way. The building was appraised at four hundred thousand dollars, and Westmoreland believed it could be sold for a handsome profit, if we wished to do so.

Space not used by the Convention was to be rented with a potential income of thirty thousand dollars per year. Westmoreland saw the building as a contribution to missions: "If the area remains leased we will have free office space amounting to $30,000 per year." When the entire space was used by the Convention, "the building will contribute floor space valued at nearly $80,000 per year. Such contributions to missions should be realized by 1978. . . . The building alone will be worth nearly $2,000,000 to missions every 25 years" (*BD*, May 4, 1963).

He saw the building as a workshop for mission advance with department heads making plans from this "vantage point." He added, however, a word of caution, "Actually, department heads and field workers will spend only limited time in these offices, for our victories are won on the field." People from many states were expected at the dedication, as they made their way to Kansas City for the Southern Baptist Convention, "possibly [even] Texans."

The building was described in detail in the *Baptist Digest* (May 4, 1963):

The three-story Baptist Building in Wichita has exterior walls of cocoa-brown brick and beige-tone porcelain panels, with deep cocoa-brown trim. Panels of white solar screen accent each end of the front of the building.

Entrance to the building is through the foyer which reaches the entire height of the building. It has cinnamon-tone brick walls with warm walnut paneling, with the two outer walls of solar glass panels. Flooring is terrazzo.

From the entry, a half-flight of stairs leads to the floor which is occupied by the Kansas Convention of Southern Baptists. The secretarial suites which open on the corridor, are complimented with a terrazzo-tone tile flooring, fully draped plate glass walls on the corridor, and mahogany paneling for the other walls. The executive suites have mahogany paneled walls and cabinet work, with the exterior walls treated in beige-tone porcelain enamel panels, which also function as the outside window-walls. Executive offices are carpeted in Roman Gold Acrilon.

Furniture is all contemporary in style, with satin-finish walnut topped desks, and chairs upholstered in gold-tone Naugahyde. Secretarial desks are bamboo in color, with satin-finish walnut tops.

Main accents in the decoration are pictures chosen to remind us constantly that we are a world missions enterprise.

Statewide work is pictured in the full-color photographs of Kansas and Nebraska scenes, which are hung in the offices of the secretaries and associates. These pictures, obtained from the Kansas Industrial Commission and Nebraska Fish and Game Commission, show the capitols of the two states in Topeka and Lincoln; the sandstone bluffs of Scottsbluff, Nebraska; a Kansas wheat field; cattle in the Kansas Flint Hills; the Platte River in Nebraska; an old mill in Kansas; a waterfall in Nebraska; a sunflower, and other scenes typical of the two states.

In the executives' offices are pictures showing scenes from across America, to represent Southern Baptist home mission work. These range from the Cypress Gardens of Florida to the Grand Teton Mountains.

In the paneled conference room are scenes to represent the worldwide reach of the Southern Baptist program. Skyline photo-murals of San Francisco and New York City represent gateways to the world; and other pictures show scenes from Japan, Peru, Spain, Italy, Germany, and France, where Southern Baptists are at work, preaching the Gospel.

The new building was called a "made-in-Kansas" product. The architects were James H. Safely and Associates; the contractor was Roe Messner Construction Company. Both were Wichita firms.

In the May 18 issue of *Baptist Digest*, Westmoreland reported a gift of ten dollars from a former Kansan living in Arkansas, Mrs. Nora Winfred, who had been a member of Emmanuel Baptist Church, Coffeyville, from 1940 to 1950. He listed several items which were not a part of the contract, but were needed: directory to be placed in the foyer, nameplates for office doors, and appropriate outside signs. The item ended, "We hope that many other friends of our missionary cause will follow her noble example."

Even this building was not a very safe place to go alone at night. Collins Webb always accompanied Viola if she had to go back to her office at night, which she often did.

Keeping tenants happy so that all the additional space could be rented was a chief concern during the occupancy of the Kellogg building. Viola Webb recalled that every time a new tenant was found, there was an office shuffle in order to meet the needs and wishes of the paying guests. She wound up in the basement before the move to Topeka.

Although the building seemed picture perfect when it was dedicated in 1963, there were problems. Two years later (*Annual*, 1965), action was taken to complete and or improve features of the new office building, including the installation of parking curbs, trees and shrubs, an auxiliary driveway to Sheridan Street, and evergreens in the foyer, and the correction of the problems of heat and glare in the foyer. Pat McDaniel (Interview, 1994), who served as executive secretary at the time the building was sold, recalled that it was in an "unbelievable state of disrepair." When the rains came, the foundation on the north side absorbed moisture to the extent that you could stick your finger through the cement blocks. There were real concerns about the possibility of collapse.

At the 1974 (*Annual*) Convention, a far-reaching recommendation came from the Executive Board and was approved by the messengers: "To look with favor upon moving the state office to Topeka in approximately five years . . . and that authorization be given to the Executive Director in consultation with the Executive Committee for necessary planning preparatory to moving."

Also, at the 1974 annual meeting, messengers voted to follow through on the proposed sale of the Wichita headquarters building (*BD*, November 25, 1974). The offer of $325,000 was made only the Saturday before the Convention began on Tuesday, November 8, 1974. Just before the afternoon meeting, the Executive Board met, discussed the proposed sale, and approved it by a vote of twenty-two in favor with three abstentions. There was much discussion, some debate, and a great many questions, from board members and from visitors who attended the board meeting.

The plan was to sell the building about March 1, 1975. Edgar Dwire, attorney for the Convention, presented a number of considerations in favor of the sale of the Wichita property. The Convention's charter stated that it was to be a non-profit organization, but with changing laws, any group that was in competition on the open market, and made a profit, could be called upon to pay income tax on all its income. This would subject all gifts from the churches, as well as income from rental property, to the bite of income tax. While not in non-compliance at that time, Dwire suggested that the "laws seem to be gravitating in that direction."

He also pointed out that a great deal of administrative time that could be better spent in ministry projects in Kansas and Nebraska was being used in handling building affairs. An even more telling argument, perhaps, dealt with surveys of office space in Wichita which indicated that there would soon be more office space on the market than clients to rent it. Such a situation would make a higher vacancy rate in the headquarters building, resulting in greater overhead.

Dwire is one who merits special recognition as a consultant who "came aboard" as legal counsel during the CLA crisis. His commitment to the Convention speaks to his loyalty and concern for the affairs of Southern Baptist churches in Kansas and Nebraska. It also speaks to the integrity of the Convention through the years. The officers and leaders recognized the need for specialized expertise, found it, and have relied upon it.

The buyer, Roe Messner, the contractor who had built the complex, agreed to pay $342,00 for the property (*BD*, July 28, 1975). He assumed the mortgage which was owed to the Home Mission Board and paid the difference in cash to the Convention. The Convention planned to remain as tenants for five years and was to pay five dollars per square foot, or approximately $16,500 per year.

The sale was completed in July 1975. The final price meant a net gain to the Convention and the foundation of almost $108,000. The Convention owned the building; the foundation owned the land and several small houses surrounding the building, all of which were included in the package deal with Roe Messner. The foundation received $44,900 and the Convention almost $64,000. The money received by the Convention was earmarked for "site, building, and office and employee moving expense" connected with locating headquarters in Topeka (*BD*, July 28, 1975).

This move to Topeka may have been the cause for the debate about selling the building in Wichita. It certainly was not greeted with enthusiasm by all the churches in the two-state area. Nebraska churches were probably a great deal more in favor of this development than many churches in Kansas. Churches in Wichita, which felt they would be losing a great deal of their leadership if Convention employees moved to Topeka, were particularly upset by this possibility. The Topeka decision came because of a survey of the two-state Convention (*BD*, November 25, 1974) which showed that 81.7 percent of the churches affiliated with the Convention were within a 150-mile radius of Topeka, and 98.8 percent of the membership of the churches lived in that area. Further, 77.4 percent of the total population of the two-state area lived within a 150-mile radius around Topeka. Wichita could boast only 65.5 percent of the churches, 72.4 percent of the membership of these churches, and 46.2 percent of the total population of the two-state area within a 150-mile radius of the present state headquarters office. This survey was conducted by the statistical department of the Home Mission Board, at the request of the Executive Board.

By the time the Convention met in 1975, a great deal of progress had been made. William Kiene, of Kiene-Bradley Architects, was introduced and presented plans for the Topeka Office building. A site had been found and escrow payment made ($51,000). Pat McDaniel, executive director, introduced a plan for fund-raising: $8.50 per member over the next three years which would net approximately $520,000. The Southwest National Bank of Wichita was willing to lend the Convention four hundred thousand dollars by February 15. A motion was made to follow through on these suggestions, which carried with only twenty opposing votes. The target date for completion of planning was set for February 1976. A contract was let by the Executive Board in April 1976 for a new Baptist headquarters building in Topeka. By the time the Convention met in November, the building was underway with prospects of being completed by March 1977 (*Annual*, 1976). More than one hundred thousand dollars had been pledged in the fund-raising effort labeled "Debt Free in Three."

As it turned out, the building, at 5410 West 7th Street in Topeka, just off Interstate 70 at the Fairlawn Exit, was not ready for occupancy until August 1. Evidently the use of the Kellogg space in Wichita ended in mid-June. In the words of James Shope, historical secretary, "This caused considerable consternation and much inconvenience" (*Annual*, 1976).

The dedication service for the new building was held on Tuesday afternoon during the state Convention. Keefer remembered that there were so many people in the conference room that day she feared for the foundations. Doy Jones, president of the Convention, introduced five past presidents of the Convention in attendance: Paul Davis, Jimmie L. Martin, H. E. Alsup, Gordon D. Dorian, and Luther Berry (*Annual*, 1977). Forrest Robinson, secretary of the Kansas Department of Aging, brought greetings from the Governor of Kansas.

The program for the dedication carried this information about the building, written by William R. Kiene:

> The site for the new headquarters office building is a gently rolling one overlooking Interstate 70 and the Kansas Governor's Mansion, Cedar Crest, to the north. The general area around the building is zoned and used for light office purposes. The site is of sufficient size to allow expansion both to the east and the west, should that become necessary in the future. Ample parking is provided with two parking lots. The one to the west serves mainly the employees and gives access to the building through the lower level. The east parking lot is intended for visitors and provides access to the building through the main entrance.

The building itself was designed for general office usage with some specialized consideration to tailor it to the needs of the Kansas-Nebraska Convention of Southern Baptists. These special features include a large conference room with an adjoining lunchroom, both readily accessible from the main entrance lobby. The business offices carry special consideration for the computer and the provision of a fire resistive vault. Other special features include a media center library on the lower level, a large duplicating facility and a photographic darkroom. The balance of the lower area is devoted to storage and mechanical equipment.

The basic construction is a wood fame over a reinforced concrete foundation and footing system. The exterior finishes are primarily face brick with accent areas of wood siding. The roof is of cedar shake shingles.

Interior finishes are primarily painted gypsum board walls with accent areas of wood siding. The floors, generally, are carpeted. The entryway is brick tile and restroom walls and floors are ceramic tile.

Highlighting the main lobby is a brass sculpture of the KNCSB logo. This work was commissioned [by Pat McDaniel] and executed by Topeka artist John Whitfield.

The first floor contains 8,858 square feet, while the basement area totals 8,029 square feet for a total building area of 16,887 square feet. Final cost, subject to minor adjustments, is $493,881 or $19.25 per square foot.

In three years, rather than five, the Convention was established in Topeka. Pat McDaniel, who had served as the executive director for almost eight years, had accepted a position at the Annuity Board of the Southern Baptist Convention. R. Rex Lindsay had been named executive director of the KNCSB in October 1977. Kansas-Nebraska was out of the rental business. "God was in His heaven, and all was well with the world!"

10

KN℃SB

SERVING KANSAS/NEBRASKA SOUTHERN BAPTISTS

Camps and Conferences

DOYLE SMITH CAME TO KANSAS FROM SOUTHWESTERN Seminary in 1972. He had never really considered being a pastor in a pioneer area. He wanted to find his place in a small-town church, in an area that would be safe and good for raising a family, and in a situation where it would be possible to continue his independent study of Process Theology, which he had begun at the seminary. He did not consider himself a great pulpiteer; he felt his strength lay in working with small groups, in teaching, and in one-to-one consultation.

On Lynn Clayton's invitation, Smith came to Kansas to consider a situation. The first one did not work out, but then Pat McDaniel negotiated the linking of Great Bend and Larned, in order to get Home Mission Board support, and this looked right. The church in Great Bend was deeply in debt, but one of Smith's strengths was setting goals and planning ways to carry through. He was not one to become discouraged over problems. He was committed to staying in a spot long enough to win the confidence of the people and get something accomplished. He was able to do this in Great Bend, and in three years the church was on top of its financial problems. In four and a half years, the church in Larned was ready to call a full-time pastor. Smith remained in Great Bend.

During Smith's growing-up years, he had seen many bivocational pastors in Arkansas, Oklahoma, and Texas. They were men who had grown up in those states, were at home there, and felt called of God to bivocational ministry. In Kansas it was different. In Central Baptist Association, in eleven churches, there were only six pastors, and not one was born and raised in Kansas. They were all imports, and Smith wondered why.

Although he had not been involved in camping experiences in his youth, he was aware of the camping programs in southern states. He knew it was in such places that youngsters were brought face to face with God and His call, and many made life-changing decisions. There was no such place in Kansas-Nebraska. There were some associational camps, but no state camp. What was needed, Smith decided, was a first-rate state camping program. Kansas and Nebraska youth needed to hear God's call.

In the Larned Church there was only one young person; in order to grow, youth needed association with other youth. This same situation was true in many other small churches. So Smith began to dream about a place where young people could go for fellowship with their peers and could hear the call of God. Kansas-Nebraska needed native-born pastors, trained leadership, and called-out young people. A camping/conference place was the answer.

SMITH'S FIRST ATTEMPT

About 1977 Camp Aldrich, a Girl Scout Camp near Great Bend, became available through bankruptcy. Smith approached the Executive Board of the KNCSB with a proposition, "Let's buy Camp Aldrich." Nobody thought he had lost his mind; owning a camp was a good idea. But there was no money. He was given permission to send a letter to all the pastors in the KNCSB, asking them to present this project to the churches and then make a pledge to be paid over a period of three years. Many were interested; some, of course, were not. The pledges amounted to only twenty-five thousand dollars. The largest pledge of $4,130 came from the Great Bend Church; the smallest pledge, forty dollars, from the church at Larned. The project had to be shelved for a while.

Then in late 1980, Doyle Smith got a call from Peck Lindsay. O. K. Webster, a Salina businessman, had offered Camp Webster to the Convention. There were strings attached, but the Executive Board believed the Convention should look into the offer. Smith, who was president of the Convention, was the man for the hour.

CAMP WEBSTER

Many years earlier, Ila Belle and O. K. Webster had developed a vision for a camp (*BD*, August 23, 1993). They were members of the Brethren Church, which merged with the United Evangelical Church. That denomination merged with the Methodist Church to become the United Methodist denomination. The Websters followed each merger, and finally became Methodists.

Ila Belle was the active camping person. At a camp session in northern Kansas near Concordia, a flood occurred which made the leadership long for their own safe campsite. Mrs. Webster talked to her husband about this dream of the Brethren Church.

She must have been a good talker, because Webster bought a farm north of Salina and made the wooded area available to the Brethren Church for a camp. Webster had construction experience, so he began to build the camp himself. Then the Brethren came upon financial difficulties and could not operate the camp, so Webster bought the camp from them. Later, he gave the campsite to the United Evangelical Church with whom the Brethren had merged. Webster placed a lot of strings around his gift to assure himself that the land and buildings would be used as a camp, not for something else, or simply be stripped of its valuable timber and left.

For one reason or another, the facility fell into disuse, so Webster retrieved it from the United Evangelical Church and gave it to the United Methodists with whom the United Evangelicals had by that time merged. Somehow, he got wind of the idea that the United Methodists were sort of dragging their feet about the development of the camp, waiting for him to die so they could sell the property and do what they wanted with the proceeds. Because of the reversion clause in the contract with them, he threatened to take the group to court. Rather than face that, the campsite was returned to Webster.

During this interval, he had been doing more building. At that time, there was on the property a chapel, a boys' dormitory, and a combination girls' dormitory and dining room, all built according to Webster's rather economical specifications, with little attention to codes or a unified plan.

But what Webster really wanted was to see Camp Webster used as a church camp. Gale Pack, pastor of the First Southern Baptist Church in Salina, knew this, and one morning went to see Gerald Locke, who was director of missions for Smoky Hill and Blue Stem Associations, and had a heart for the camping program. He told Locke about the man in Salina who had a camp he might give to Smoky Hill Association. Locke knew the financial condition of the association; he remembers the visit with O. K. Webster as "awkward." His explanation to Webster was that "we would not able to pay the electric bill on the property let alone all the other things that would be involved" (Taped Interview). Locke persuaded Webster to allow him to set up a meeting with Peck Lindsay to see if the KNCSB might be interested. A meeting was arranged. Thus, it came to pass that Lindsay called Doyle Smith.

This was not the first time a camping program had been broached. The church in Coffeyville had a regular summer program of camping when N. J. Westmoreland was pastor of that church before the Convention was organized. In fact, one of the early meetings of the churches which preceded the formal formation of the Fellowship was at this summer camp. In July 1945, pastors and youth from three other churches attended the fifth annual session of this church camp: Burden, Ellinwood, and Chatauqua. It was a good time, and encouraged the pastors to keep on working toward closer cooperation.

In 1946 the first summer Youth Camp under the sponsorship of the Convention was held at Cedar Bluff, the Coffeyville Church camp, overlooking the River Verdigris. Young people from Treece, Chetopa, Coffeyville, Chatauqua, Burden, Winfield, Wichita, and Ness City were on hand, along with a group from Oklahoma. A camping program held high priority almost from the birth of the Convention, and its importance would continue.

EARLY CAMPS

The first land purchased by the Convention, in 1952, was a 130-acre tract southeast of Quenemo on the Marais des Cygne River for a state assembly. In 1951 a committee was appointed to investigate the possibilities of buying a site for the development of a state assembly. By October of that year, the land was found and the vote was affirmative. It was considered the highlight of that board meeting.

This site was located forty-one miles south of Topeka, southeast of Quenemo. The property was bought for thirty dollars an acre (thirty-nine hundred dollars) on contract, three hundred dollars down, with the deed to be given to the Convention when fifteen hundred dollars had been paid. The Convention was then to pay three hundred dollars per year until the debt was paid (*Annual*, 1952). The report finished with this sentence: "The way in which it has come into our possession has been considered as remarkable indeed."

In the *Annual* for 1957, there was a proposed calendar for the development of the site: By November 1957, retire the indebtedness of twelve hundred dollars; by March 1958, complete topographical survey at a cost of one thousand dollars; by May 1958, complete final plat of assembly grounds, which the Department of Church Architecture offered to do without charge; by December, 1958, enlist churches, associations, and a few individuals in leasing building sites on the grounds which would generate thirty-five thousand dollars; by June 1959, install water and sewer systems and roadways—enough to have a "pioneer assembly" in mid-summer 1959; by September 1959, receive ten thousand dollars in the State Mission Offering, designated for the assembly; and by June 1960, complete forty-five-thousand-dollar improvement project for maximum use of assembly facilities for all groups and all ages.

By this time, an easement across the western edge of the site had been granted to the Kansas City Power and Light Company for $167, which made possible the extension of electric service to the property at a reduced rate.

But this dream never was realized. In 1967 the land was sold for thirteen thousand dollars. About ten thousand dollars was applied to the Convention's operating deficit. About three thousand dollars of original designated money was deposited with the foundation, with other funds marked for a future assembly.

In the State Mission Day of Prayer material for 1947, Westmoreland extolled the value of camping programs. He mentioned one sponsored by Southeastern Association at Coffeyville, which resulted in eleven conversions and a week of wonderful fellowship. "Camp O' the West was held at Wichita under great handicaps." What the handicaps were, we can only guess. There are many tantalizing gaps in reports to and minutes of Convention meetings. "We will be wise," he said, "to place great emphasis on these camps as projects of evangelism and fellowship to be promoted by our state Convention. Others will be in session next year in other portions of the state."

In 1949 a state camp was reported (*Annual*) at Camp Fellowship, near Goddard, which was rented from another denomination. Westmoreland wrote, "We found the camp to be a very pleasant place with facilities more than adequate to take care of our people who attended." The camp was big enough for four hundred; registration for this week (August 1-6) was 140 "with many coming in just for one day or for the evening services." One feature of the camp was election of King and Queen. Good sportsmanship was reported to have prevailed in this contest. Two other camps were held that year, one at Camp Cedar Bluff at Coffeyville, with 110 enrolled and another at Topeka with approximately fifty registered.

In 1950 there was again a report of a state camp at Camp Fellowship with 155 full-time campers and 180 registrations. "The camp fire fellowship services under the direction of Stanley Gasswint were inspirational and a fitting climax each evening." Camp Cedar Bluff was again in use, by Tri-County and Twin Valley Associations, with 152 campers. The report noted, "There is no other place that people can find the fellowship and great spiritual influence as at a Baptist summer camp like we have at Camp Cedar Bluff" (*Annual*, 1950). In 1952 registration for the Kansas Southern Baptist Assembly was 247 full-time campers with representation from all seven associations.

In 1951 Glorieta Assembly was being developed as the "Ridgecrest of the West." Kansas Southern Baptists agreed to raise one thousand dollars to pay for construction of one room in the one-hundred-room main hotel. June 1, 1952 was designated as "Glorieta Day" (G-Day) in the churches.

By 1956 the Camp Committee, composed of three members, asked that the committee be increased to seven, each given three-year terms. The State Assembly was held at Forest Park, Topeka, and was owned by Kansas Conference of the Evangelical United Brethren. It was scheduled for the same place the following year. The report noted, "The recreation equipment and dish towels purchased this year are now stored in the Baptist building in Wichita for use in future State Assemblies."

At the 1957 State Assembly, for the first time, there was a conference on visual aids provided by the Baptist Book Store. There was also a short film each night before the camp pastor spoke. In 1958 a church library conference was added. The committee closed the report with good news and bad: "If our Assembly grows next year as much as it did this year, only those who pre-register will be permitted to attend. This will be because we will not have the space to care for them. We are praying that the Lord will give us vision and means for our own grounds in the very near future." We still had the land, but nothing had been done to make it usable for a campground.

In 1959 a recreation conference was added to the regular state assembly program. It was led by Grady Nutt, who was also recreation director for the assembly. There were 370 full-time campers, 35 of whom commuted, with 165 visitors, making this the largest attendance ever reached at the Kansas Assembly (*BD*, September 5, 1959). The State Assembly was reported to have "moved along smoothly" in 1960 with 404 campers and "scores of others coming in through the week." The State Assembly program was designed for the whole family, as well as the workers in the church. Paul Andrews, pastor of Emmanuel in Coffeyville and member of the KCSB assembly committee, claimed that, "many were planning to spend part of their vacation at the assembly."

The State Assembly was canceled in 1961 because the owners of the assembly failed to reserve the rental of the facilities in the name of the Kansas Convention. But, never daunted, ever hopeful, the committee reported, "This will affect in no way the plans for 1962."

This may not have worked as well as hoped. In the 1962 *Annual*, it was noted that the Youth Retreat and Pastors' Retreat were conducted in place of the regular State Assembly Camp. They were conducted simultaneously on the campus of Kansas University. "It has been suggested that these two Retreats be planned again for next year and be conducted in the same place. The Pastors' Retreat was a real time of fellowship, information, and inspiration. The Youth Retreat was considered one of the best youth activities ever to be sponsored by our State Convention."

Ray Gilliland gave direction to the youth assemblies until he left in 1968. Afterwards, Harold Inman conducted at least three such assemblies at Hillsboro and Emporia.

ASSOCIATIONAL CAMPS

According to James Shope (*ESB*, 1982), at least five associations in the KNCSB have owned and operated their own camps: Tri-County, Sedgwick, Twin Valley, Blue Stem, and Central.

In 1960 (Shope, 1982), Tri-County Association became the first to buy a camp for its own use: eighty acres near Weir, Kansas, at a cost of twelve hundred dollars (*BD*, September 8, 1962). Five acres were suitable for the camp and the remainder was to be "developed later for hiking, cookouts," and other such uses.

In 1961 and 1962, the land was fenced; water and sewer systems were installed; a tabernacle, temporary kitchen, and dining hall were built; and central showers and restroom facilities were installed. The first camps were in 1962 for GAs and RAs, and the site has been used for camp every year since. By 1980 ten churches had built cabins on land leased to them, with sleeping facilities for 120 persons. The association enlarged and improved the original facilities, and planned to put in a swimming pool and ultimately to have about twenty cabins. They have done what they planned except for the swimming pool. Campers are transported to nearby Columbus for this activity.

Tri-County Baptist Camp became Weir Baptist Camp in 1994. Twin Valley Association was made an equal partner in the camping program.

In 1962 Sedgwick Association had a report from an assembly committee that "about 50 acres of beautiful, wooded area on the north bank of the Arkansas River was available." The associational missions offering the following year was designated for this project. That plus an offering of twenty-five hundred dollars and a loan of seventy-five hundred dollars were used for the purchase of this tract. Sixty different groups used the assembly ground in 1964, with receipts of more than three thousand dollars. Two cabins and a swimming area were constructed in 1968. During 1969 a total of 1,155 persons from forty-nine groups used Russell Conference Center, as it was called prior to 1970. It was named in honor of Sam Russell, who had been director of missions in Sedgwick Association, and then associate executive secretary and director of missions of the Convention. It is now called Shilo Baptist Assembly.

For one thousand dollars, Central Association bought the old Mitchell School, including a little more than four acres of land, which was just across the street from Mitchell Baptist Chapel. On the property there was a gym, restrooms, showers, a kitchen, and five classrooms. The first year it was open, 1969, about one hundred persons camped there. Space in Mitchell Chapel was used for part of the activities. Extensive remodeling was done in 1974, using volunteer labor. After a study of the feasibility of ownership, the camp was sold in 1975 for twenty-five hundred dollars.

For the summer of 1970, Twin Valley Association scheduled RA and GA camps at Cedar Bluff, near Coffeyville, but before camp time, plans changed. In February of that year, Twin Valley joined with Blue Stem Association in accepting as a gift Virgil School in Virgil, Kansas. There was a three-story brick building which could accommodate one hundred campers, and a brick gym which needed lots of work. The dormitory had steam heat, so could be used year-round. It was officially known as Locke Hall, in honor of Gerald Locke, who was director of missions when the gift was made. There was also room for a ball field, archery range, and general playground space. In 1976, in four weeks of camp, there were 679 campers.

When Gerald Locke retired and Bill Kneisly became DOAM of Blue Stem Association, the camp was sold. It was simply too expensive to make renovations necessary to bring it up to code requirements.

WMU CAMPS

There had also been experience with Camp Webster through the years. Viola Webb reported that WMU scheduled many places for GA and RA camps: Bide-a-Wee, just north of Wichita, which finally was not large enough to accommodate all the campers; Camp Fellowship, near Goddard, where Viola wanted to live by the river and listen to the water splashing against the house; Rock Springs; and "early on," Camp Webster, which was a convenient place. At that time, Betty Freeman, WMU young people's secretary, planned a one-week camp for GAs and one week for RAs. According to Webb, "That was enough when you have to pay rent and take all the responsibility for that many." The children were transported to Salina for swimming, half the group at a time. Mrs. Opal Bates recalled taking four GA girls to Camp Webster. It make a great impression on her. For thirty years she remembered the speaker was Mrs. Aycox, a Japanese war bride who sang like an angel "in the cool of the evening."

YWA camp was held many years at Rock Springs. Since there were no camps for young men, Webb invited the men to come to the YWA camp. Webb remembered as quite an experience one of the last YWA camps held at Rock Springs. A storm began to brew on Sunday afternoon. She never left the camp until every one was gone and she had inspected all the cabins to be certain that everything was shipshape. So, the storm was well advanced by the time her group of fifteen started to Wichita. The snow came down, more and more of it. By the time they reached Herrington, the road was closed. Nobody was getting through. They went into a service station, and she began to make phone calls. A man, so impressed by the behavior of the youth in the group, invited them all to his house so that Webb could make the calls in more comfort. Some of the kids brought in their guitars, began to sing, and to have a wonderful time in general. Webb and her host went to the store and bought groceries, came back, and everyone helped with the cooking. When night came, the host was worried about beds and decided he would have to take part of the group somewhere else for the night. Webb said, "Who needs a bed. We've been sleeping in sleeping bags. We can stay here." So she got a big bedspread out of her luggage and hung it between the living room and dining room; the girls slept in one room, the boys in the other. The girls used the downstairs bathroom, and the boys used the one upstairs. They stayed in Herrington for three days. There must have been many hilarious tales about this experience that probably grew with the telling. As far as we know, all the other campers got home safely.

WEBSTER TRANSFER

When word came that acquiring Webster was a possibility, Webb was elated, but afraid that it would not come to pass, because "I knew Peck didn't like camps. He was just not for camps at all. I could not see him working for Webster at all." Of course, she kept these opinions under her hat.

It was not that Lindsay "didn't like camps." What he did not like and did not want to happen was using mission money for capital improvement. He wanted to protect Cooperative Program funds, both in the local church and at the state level. In this he succeeded very well.

At the time the Executive Board was having the crucial meeting to decide what to do about O. K. Webster's offer, Webb was in a meeting in

Albuquerque. She enlisted the women as a prayer group, and they spent most of the night in prayer. The next morning, just as soon as she could, Webb called to see what happened and found out the board had voted to take on the responsibility of the camp. There was great thanksgiving among the praying group of women.

Webb commented, "I don't think there's anything that can take the place of the camp, or get closer to boys and girls or women than a camp experience. I don't know about men, but for women, camp is a real bonding situation."

After the deal was struck, Webb went out to see the property. It had been a number of years since WMU had used Camp Webster, and what she saw must have made her shudder. "We could not go back out there; the weeds were almost as tall as I; it was awful; the porch had fallen off the dining hall."

Even so, she thought it could be put into shape for camping: "There was no place any prettier than Webster, in all the camps we went to. Water, forest, trees, everything you'd want."

But back to that day in late 1980 when Peck Lindsay called Doyle Smith to talk about Camp Webster. A special Executive Board meeting was held in Salina in February 1981; the group made a tour of the campground. There were approximately eighty acres of wooded area, with three buildings of sorts, and O. K. Webster.

Webster's proposition was that he would give the land to the Convention if the board would agree to finish the buildings according to his plans and directions, and dig a security ditch on the western edge. It had come to his attention that people had been wandering onto the property, cutting trees for firewood, as well as valuable lumber—poachers, if you please—and he wanted it stopped. He had planted many of the trees himself, and did not want them destroyed. He also wanted to change the course of Mulberry Creek, a natural waterway. This could not be done, legally, without the approval of the State Corps of Engineers. Webster had little time or love for anything governmental, or any restriction on his actions. His scheme was to dig the ditch, fill it with brush, cover it with dirt, then when the water flowed through it, the brush and dirt would be washed away and then the water would flow in a new way, not through any wrong doing on his part. He also suggested that he could park his truck at the Ohio Street exit and sit with a shotgun to stop whatever government agents might want to investigate any action connected with Mulberry Creek. The committee did not think the shotgun plan a good one, so Webster did not follow through.

There was another special meeting of the board in Wichita. One thing to keep in mind is that the Convention was not very long out of the worst financial debacle any Convention had ever seen. The board members were more than a little nervous about spending money, particularly mission money. Pastors did not want to endanger church resources. The Executive Board did not want to see Cooperative Program dollars flying out the window.

Doyle Smith invited a construction company from McPherson to look at the camp and make an estimate of what it would cost to put it into operation.

The estimate totaled over a million dollars. The buildings would have to be torn down, since they had been built in the 1940s and 1950s and were far below building codes for fire and health.

In addition, the board had to deal with Webster's conditions. He wanted the Convention to place in escrow a sum of money sufficient to complete the buildings according to his plans, finance the digging of the security ditch, and re-channel Mulberry Creek. After that was all done, he would give the Convention a clear deed to approximately eighty acres. This was intolerable.

The Executive Board simply would not go through with this. They did not like the estimated cost of renovation, nor the conditions under which Webster was making the gift, and they were a bit worried about Webster's pattern of giving away and taking back. So their answer concerning Camp Webster was, "No thank you."

After that July board meeting, Doyle Smith and Peck Lindsay went to see the Websters to explain the decision of the board. When the explanation for the negative answer had been given, Webster, a volatile man, was angry. He paced up and down, pointing out that it would not cost the kind of money the Powell Brothers had suggested, and there was no need to bother with codes. He would build it himself, using volunteer labor.

Doyle Smith related that he posed a case study for Webster. Suppose, he said, "I agreed to give you a piece of land on which you were to build a house that suited me. When the house was built, if it suited me, I would give you a deed to the land; if it did not, everything belonged to me including the house you had built." He assured Webster that he knew he was too smart to agree to any such deal. When he had completed the scenario, he said, "That's what you want our Convention to do, but we are too smart to do that, too." The only way the Convention could accept this land, he assured Webster, was free and clear, with no strings attached.

Webster is reported to have raged about the projected cost (he could do it all for much less), and about government interference through building permits and codes. "Because you can't afford to please the government, you can't take this land," he said. Whereupon Mrs. Webster, who was evidently much calmer than her husband, said, "No, dear. What they are saying is they can't afford to please you and the government."

But that is not the end of the story. The next morning between six and seven, Doyle Smith's phone rang. "This is O. K. I have been thinking about this all night. We'll take you up on that offer."

Doyle Smith had not been given any authority to act, if Webster offered another plan. His only instruction had been to tell Webster it was "no go." So the board was called together again.

An agreement was finally reached. The Convention's attorney, Edgar Dwire, carefully worked out the contract. The Convention would establish an escrow fund of twenty-five thousand dollars and would be responsible for clearing the land and completing a security ditch and purchase of materials for the chapel addition. Webster would do the work. When that was done and paid for, the eighty acres would be deeded to the Convention free and clear. There were a couple of other conditions: Webster wanted to remove from the grounds and buildings things that belonged to him; he also wanted an agreement that no tree would be cut without his consent. The Convention made this agreement go both ways. So any tree cut down on the property must be agreed to by both Webster and the Convention.

This transaction took almost a year, from the time of the original offer made sometime in the fall of 1980 to the final transaction in August 1981. John LaNoue of the Baptist Sunday School Board, widely recognized as one of the most knowledgeable camping program persons in the United States, did a feasibility study. He must have brought an affirmative report, although the only word in the *Annual* about the study is that it was presented in the February session of the board.

In May the discussion concerned cost estimates and how to bring the camp buildings up to code. In July the officers of the Convention along with the Convention's attorney, Ed Dwire, met with Webster and went over the contract. At the September 10 meeting, the Executive Board invited Webster to share his dreams and hopes for the camp if Southern Baptists should receive it. "After much discussion and prayer the Board voted to accept Camp Webster as a gift and place in escrow $25,000 to meet the conditions of the contract" (*Annual*, 1981). At the same Convention in which this decision was presented, the Executive Board also brought a recommendation that an additional two hundred acres bordering the camp on the east be purchased at two hundred thousand dollars, to be paid in yearly payments of twenty-five thousand dollars. Webster was to carry the papers; no interest would be charged. After payment of the first one hundred thousand dollars, the Convention was to receive the crop royalties from the land (*Annual*, 1981). This was completed in December 1989 (*Annual*, 1990). At that time, the Convention held clear title to 231 acres of Webster Conference Center.

In 1981 Doyle Smith was asked by the Executive Board to serve as chair of the Camp Webster Committee, which he agreed to do. The following year, James Shope, a member of the Webster Committee, brought a recommendation from the committee that the name be changed from Camp Webster to Webster Conference Center (*Annual*, 1982). Shope remembered that there was much discussion about whether or not to include the Webster name; but the motion passed.

BUILDING A CONFERENCE CENTER

An understanding reached by the board, strongly promoted by Peck Lindsay, was that no Cooperative Program money would be siphoned off for Webster. This was a real and constant concern of Lindsay's and likely for many pastors across the Convention. Gifts for Webster were to be above Cooperative

The dorm at Webster Conference Center in 1981 when the KNCSB received the facility.

Program gifts. This, of course, meant fund-raising. Some felt this ban was on all "missions" money, which caused misunderstanding, since part of the Viola Webb State Missions Offering frequently had been designated to WCC.

Smith set up a committee, including Faye Graves from Wichita. They had no experience in fund-raising, but together planned a one-time Camp Webster Day Offering, which was labeled "Prove Your Love" Campaign and which was set for Valentines Day. The committee knew the people across the two states did not know or "love" Webster, but they were depending on love for children and what a camp would mean for children and youth. From that campaign twenty-five thousand dollars was realized, about the same amount that had been pledged when a letter of inquiry had gone to the churches years before. The amount of the offering was remarkable, considering what Smith called the "amateurish effort" that was made. The money was used to hire an architect, Jim Williams, to start planning what was needed.

In order to share the planning, a letter was sent to pastors to ask how they saw the camp being used. What did they want? The answers indicated it would be used for church and associational retreats, Super Summer, mostly for groups of twenty to thirty, with the exception of Super Summer. At that time, no retreat had a larger enrollment than 150. So it was decided to get ready what buildings were needed to house about 150 people, to plan housing for couples, classrooms for conferences, and do these things quickly so the camp could be put to use as early as possible. What they did not realize was when there was a "camp of our own" on which we could depend and schedule as we chose, attendance would increase dramatically. For instance, RA camps had averaged about 150 when they met here and there. When the group started to come to Webster, even before it was finished, attendance grew, so the camp seemed inadequate for the four hundred in attendance before the first phase was even finished. There were those who criticized the committee for not planning "big enough."

The buildings on the ground were in disrepair, which may be the understatement of the year. There was a dormitory about two hundred feet long with an aisle down the middle between two rows of bunk beds on either side, and a bathroom at one end of the room with shower nozzles along one side and toilets along the other. At the other end was a kitchen which was probably as good as kitchen facilities in most of the camps that had been rented through the years. When Webster built the dormitory, he had laid a foundation for a porch that had never been built.

A new dormitory was built right over the barracks building, putting in baths and showers and partitioning the space into rooms designed for groups of campers. The porch was enclosed and made into meeting rooms. The whole was finally carpeted, painted, heated, and air conditioned. Wayne Hett, who had a construction background, was hired as manager. He did construction work himself, and supervised volunteers of all shapes and sizes and skills. The Webster committee planned to subcontract the work, and to use volunteer labor; the latter now and again proved a mixed blessing.

Volunteers sometimes did the work incorrectly, and it had to be done over. Volunteers only worked when they could, so progress came slowly. And there was always O. K. Webster looking over everyone's shoulder all the time. He thought there were not enough volunteers. The work did not go fast enough. Too much money was being spent. Finally, a contractor was hired who was able to use volunteer labor wisely.

In 1984 it was time to look at the money situation again. The firm, Cargill and Associates, was hired to do a feasibility study: how much money could we expect Kansas and Nebraska to put into this project? The answer was probably half a million dollars, with the top limit of a million to a million and a half. That was not enough, but it would be a start. The plan was to saturate the state with publicity, then hold banquets in various areas arranged by local people and to which local people would be invited. The cause of Webster would be presented; the group would be asked to give money and make pledges to be paid over a three-year period. Eighteen days were set aside for this. Peck Lindsay, Doyle Smith, and Terry McIlvain went to every banquet. Others accompanied them from time to time. One can only hope that the meals had variety—and were not all cream chicken and English peas.

Doyle Smith said he lost count of the number of times they ate and made presentations. He left Great Bend on Monday morning, came back on Wednesday for midweek service, left on Thursday morning, returned on Saturday night to preach on Sunday, and was off again on Monday morning.

Sometimes good plans had been made for the meeting, sometimes almost none. In one place, not even the restaurant manager knew there was to be a meeting, and the "leader" did not show up. Even so, the result was between three hundred thousand and four hundred thousand dollars in pledges and between fifty thousand and sixty thousand dollars in cash.

Up to that time, building was done only as the money came in, which had been the stipulation of the Executive Board from the very beginning. In 1984, however, the Convention approved a plan for borrowing $250,000 from the foundation against these pledges. People were getting eager for the WCC to become fully operational. Even though people had not seen it, they had caught the vision. They believed we needed this facility now! This was in the "good old times" of high interest, so a good deal of the money was used up in interest payments.

By this time people were asking, "When will Super Summer be at Webster." It was Hurry! Hurry! Hurry! Get it finished! So a second fund-raising campaign was planned. This time the target was not churches, but individuals. The strategy was about the same: publicity, advance contacts with people, banquets, and pledges.

In 1988 Mike O'Donnell was hired as the area consultant in youth evangelism, and the "Vision to Victory" Campaign director. Another feasibility study suggested half a million dollars possible, with tops of a million. What was needed was $2.5 million to complete the Conference Center as it should be, a first-class facility, with uniformity among the buildings.

VISION TO VICTORY

This "Vision to Victory" Campaign was approved by the Convention to run for a period of twenty months, beginning in November 1987 and concluding in June 1989, with the possibility of extending it six months, if necessary. The goal was set at $1,550,000 with a challenge goal of $2,200,000. Bill Holley was employed to be general counsel to assist the implementation of the campaign. He was to be paid three thousand dollars per month.

Doyle Smith outlined the improvements needed in order to bring Super Summer to WCC (*BD*, February 22, 1988). The chapel was to be remodeled, and an addition constructed on the north end to house meeting rooms, sleeping rooms, and bathrooms. The main lodge (dining room) was to be remodeled with the upstairs made into dormitory space. This would allow four hundred persons to be housed and would also allow three different church groups to use the conference center at one time.

In the first fund-raising campaign, 735 persons made pledges or gifts averaging sixteen dollars per month for three years. In the "Vision to Victory" campaign, the organizers were aiming for twelve hundred persons who would pledge sixteen dollars per month for five years.

MAKING A DIFFERENCE

All that was needed was to get about three times as much pledged at each banquet as had been done in the first campaign. This time the campaign had a director who made contacts and arrangements; there was not the utter dependence on the local folk. The banquet in Topeka went well, with about three times more pledges than the first time around. Salina was even better with four times more pledges. But by the time the group left Kansas City, the committee knew the campaign was in trouble; the pledges were only fifty percent of the first time around.

Part of the difficulty was that Mike O'Donnell had resigned and moved to Texas. With him, in his head, went the planning he had done and the contacts he had made. The bottom line was that the campaign was not nearly so successful as had been hoped.

Even so, worthwhile things came out of the effort. It raised awareness of people over the two states. When people saw Webster, they said, "Let's finish it." About this time, Wayne Hett retired. Jim Spence, with experience in construction, in food service, and in people skills, was hired, in 1987, as manager and caretaker, and moved onto the grounds.

The "Vision to Victory" Campaign through August 1989 had $451,110 in pledges and gifts. At the 1988 annual meeting, a motion was made to list the churches which had WCC in their budgets (*Annual*, 1989). Churches were contacted and 280 churches replied. Of that number, twenty-six churches replied affirmatively. During 1990, fifty churches made gifts to WCC.

Terry McIlvain joined the Convention staff in 1979 as evangelism intern, a title he kept until he finished his program of study at Midwestern Seminary, at which time he became area consultant in youth evangelism and special mission ministries. An Oklahoman, he attended OU and OBU, but received his degree from WSU after he came to Kansas in 1975 to become youth minister at Immanuel Church in Wichita. McIlvain remained on the KNCSB staff until 1986, when he accepted the position of associate pastor of the North Phoenix Baptist Church. His heart, however, was in Kansas and Nebraska, particularly with youth and Webster, so God allowed him to return in 1990.

When he left the Convention in 1986, he said in a letter of resignation, "This Center [Webster Conference Center] is a vital part of future ministries in KNCSB and the world. We want it to succeed." At the time he left, the McIlvains were completing a five-thousand-dollar pledge they had made to Webster, and even though they were going to Arizona, they were ready to make another pledge to this cause in Kansas. He is now a Home Mission Board area consultant in youth evangelism, with responsibility for volunteer missions, Webster Conference Center, and family ministry.

McIlvain's first Kansas activity in 1978 was Super Summer. No sooner had he gotten into Kansas than Lynn Clayton, KNCSB director of evangelism, called to ask him to help put together a week of camping for junior and senior high school youth at Emporia State University. His answer was "sure," even though, he confessed, he did not know who Lynn was or the location of Emporia. He continued to be a part of this project.

At that first week of Super Summer, there were 194 youth and sponsors. By 1981 campers were turned away because of limited facilities at Rock Springs Ranch. Two weeks were planned in 1982, with 796 campers attending. In 1987 another week was added with a total of 1,290 campers. In 1989 one of the three weeks was scheduled at Camp Maranatha in Nebraska; the other two remained at Rock Springs. In 1990 there were four weeks of Super Summer with two weeks in each place and 1,314 campers registered. For the first time, in 1991, two weeks of Super Summer were scheduled at WCC. In 1993 there were five weeks of Super Summer: one at Rock Springs, one at Maranatha, one at WCC, and two at Pratt Community College. The Pratt Community College weeks were scheduled for Webster—but that was the year of the flood. Even with this change, there were 1,932 campers.

It would be impossible to record all the wonderful things that have happened because of this emphasis on the youth camping program. Joe Stiles, presently minister of youth and education at First Southern Lawrence, attended the first Super Summer in 1975 as a new Christian in the First Southern Baptist Church in Wichita. At the assembly in Falls Creek the following year, he heard God's call to the ministry. Since that time, he has been at Super Summer every summer either as a camper, a staff person, or a counselor with the youth from his church. In 1981 he met the girl he married at Super Summer. He is a Kansas native, nurtured through Kansas ministries, and serving in God's place for him in Kansas. This is the fulfillment of Doyle Smith's dream so many years before.

In the summer of 1995, Bethany Harrison, from Prairie Hills Baptist Church in Augusta, Kansas, was scheduled to serve as a summer missionary with KNCSB. She is in school at Southwest Baptist University in Bolivar, enrolled in the counseling curriculum. She says, "Super Summer has meant so much to me; I need to return some of what I have received. I want to give back to those who have given to me." She will serve as a staff member at WCC. Again, a native Kansan serves native Kansans and Nebraskans.

Already, a "second generation" is committed to Super Summer. Linda Meyer, member of Parkview Baptist Church in Lexington, Nebraska, for more than six years, has been taking youth to Super Summer and remaining with them as a counselor. Gia Adelson, now living in Stromsburg, Nebraska, was a member of the first youth group Meyer took to camp at Rock Springs. Adelson went back three more times. Two summers ago, she stepped into a new role; she returned to Super Summer, held at Camp Maranatha, as counselor. She confessed it was difficult to put one's finger on the thing that was most important and most meaningful about camp. It was everything: the friendships, conversations, conferences, messages, music, pranks, fun, fellowship, role models, and much more. It was something she and others in her group looked forward to, planned toward, and worked for. The intangible something that marked her life as she came back to her own community was difficult to define. Perhaps it was a new awareness of God and His leadership. Maybe it was the ability to lift eyes to the hills and plains and lakes, and know that all help comes from God. At any rate, it made a difference in her life and in the lives of other youth whom she knew.

A December youth evangelism conference was begun in 1983, a winter conference for seventh to twelfth graders. In 1984 the name was changed to "Acts 1:8." In 1990, when McIlvain returned, the winter conference name was changed to "In-D.E.P.T.H." which means "Involved in Discipleship, Evangelism, Personal Training Helps." Attendance has grown each year, from 176 in 1984 to more than a thousand in both 1993 and 1994.

"Let's Have a Party . . . Share Jesus Now" was the theme for the 1995 two-day conference, in which 1,171 youth and sponsors participated.

IMPROVEMENTS AT WEBSTER

Kent Troughton, a Southern Baptist layman, owner of the Holiday Pools of Kansas City, made a proposal to the WCC board and the KNCSB. He would build a pool twenty-six feet wide and fifty-three feet long (one-third the size of an Olympic pool) with a depth of three and a half to five and a half feet (a deeper construction would be more expensive to build and operate, and insurance rates would increase substantially (*BD*, February 25, 1991). It was to be of vinyl construction (which is superior to concrete, with a life expectancy of ten to fifteen years), including a cover, pool deck and lights, at a cost to Webster Conference Center of nineteen thousand dollars. This represented a gift from Troughton's company of more than thirty thousand dollars. The Convention agreed to be responsible for a bathhouse and fencing, which brought the "pool project" to about thirty-five thousand dollars.

Swimming has always been a concern in the camping program. Part of Ray Gilliland's early responsibilities included directing Camp Fellowship near Goddard. There were a lot of camp "rules" in those days, particularly concerning swimming. "Mixed swimming" was not allowed. He tells of one occasion when a pastor from Chase was upset about the lifeguard, who was quite a handsome lad. The pastor was afraid he might try to kiss some of the girls. The lifeguard had to "turn his head" until all the girls were in the water.

Most of the camps that were rented had no pool; campers were transported in shifts to nearby city pools, with separate swimming times for boys and girls. Webster Conference Center has solved this problem; the pool was completed in 1992. It is located between the chapel and the manager's house.

In the 1990 report, heating and air conditioning units had been installed in the first floor of the main lodge, which made it usable the year round. Cosmetic improvements had been made in the chapel. The following year, a concrete basketball court was added, and two sand-pit volleyball courts and grass areas for baseball and soccer were prepared. The back wall separating the chapel from the sleeping and meeting rooms had been constructed, and two outdoor meeting pavilions had been built.

The recreational area was a special gift from Kansas-Nebraska WMU in celebration of the centennial of WMU, SBC. Gifts were sent from organizations all over Kansas and Nebraska. In 1988 Albert Smith, long-time Kansas pastor, presented an American flag to Webster Conference Center, along with a commitment for money to install a flagpole.

In 1991, for the first time, a week of Super Summer was held at WCC with a registration of 232. The youth who came to Super Summer dedicated their offering of more than thiry-four hundred dollars to the pool at Webster. This brought the pool fund to over six thousand dollars.

By 1992 a great many improvements were made at the Conference Center. Partitioning and showers were added in the chapel addition. Lights were added to the two outdoor pavilions. Somewhere along the way, the amphitheater in the area across the bridge was refurbished, and a lighted brick walkway was added. In 1992 two weeks of Super Summer were held at Webster Conference Center with 496 campers and a total registration of 541. That year the Super Summer offering, $2,446, was designated for chapel improvements. The profit of fifteen hundred dollars from T-shirt sales also went into the chapel fund.

In order to house the larger groups who were coming to Webster for various meetings, a line of credit was approved for up to $175,000 to add more bed space. The chapel addition was finished into a large barracks style room, with bathrooms and showers. Later, this space was partitioned into smaller sleeping areas, and classrooms were added to the second floor.

1993 DEVELOPMENTS

The Executive Board and Kansas-Nebraska WMU designated the major portion of the 1993 State Missions Offering for WCC. WMU tied the offering plan to a great celebration of Viola Webb's eightieth birthday. The goal was set at $280,000, with the first sixty-five thousand dollars earmarked for Kansas-Nebraska field missions and field missionaries (*BD*, March 23, 1992). There was much discussion of this decision to use "mission" money for the Conference Center. Lindsay assured the board that designating the State Missions Offering in this manner did not in any way compromise Cooperative Program funds. Even so, while twenty board members voted for the plan, nine voted "no."

And in the meantime, O. K. Webster was still at work here and there. In 1992 he leveled the floor in the upstairs of the main lodge so it would be suitable for future construction. McIlvain called this a "major contribution, since it would have cost the Convention about $50,000 if a contractor had been hired to do the work" (*BD*, March 23, 1992). Webster also built new bunk beds.

Webster is "his own man" when it comes to building. His philosophy is "waste not, want not." Now and again through the years, he found lumber on sale and bought it. The length of the lumber determined the size of whatever building he was working on. He would not have dreamed of cutting off two feet of a good oak or mahogany four by six in order to make the size of an addition conform to the building already in place. A story is told of the manner in which he renovated his house in order to make it more enjoyable for his wife. She was in a wheelchair and could not see out of the windows. Webster fixed that. He cut the wall, moved the windows down, and used the pieces he cut out below the windows to close the openings left above the windows.

This also can be said of Webster. He appreciates what a camping program can do for children, youth, and adults, a proposition he likely learned from his wife. He has put his strength, time, and energy into this project he cares about so passionately. Baptists in Kansas and Nebraska are the richer for it. It is good for us that the Websters had a vision, and let us in on the dream.

GA and RA weekends are regulars on the Webster schedule. There are missionaries, crafts, fun, and serious times for the kids and their counselors.

At the RA Congress, the Pinewood Derby is a special event. Boys build cars according to strict specifications before the big weekend. For more than fifteen years, Harold and Hazel Pape have supervised this event, set up the track, weighed in the cars, and timed the heats. Even after they moved to Arkansas, in 1980, they continued to return to Kansas each year for the RA Congress at Webster Conference Center. Hazel registers the contestants and weighs in the cars, while Harold sets up the tracks. Pape began his participation at the invitation of Earl Barrager, when they were both members of the West Haven Baptist Church in Tonganoxie. Now Barrager is at the Tyler Road Church in Wichita. Pape has not only worked out a computer-controlled system of timing the racers and determining Derby winners in each age group, but also a computerized data-management program to keep up with scores for each camper for all events. The Papes also furnish all the trophies for the Derby winners. It is one way they try to keep men and boys interested in the Royal Ambassador program.

Another mark of greatness in the RA camp is the small use of hot water for showers. There are tales of boys who return to their home with their never unpacked suitcases holding their never disturbed clean clothes.

In 1990 the scheduled Royal Ambassador Congress had to be canceled because of a measles epidemic in Salina. John Hopkins, who was in charge of Brotherhood at that time, decreed that all boys who attended the 1991 Congress would receive badges for the 1990 Congress, as well.

As more facilities were available and amenities added, camper days increased. In 1989 there were fifty-one hundred camper days; in 1992 there were 9,993 camper days. And then came 1993 and the "500-year flood." Water came up into some of the buildings and over the fields. Two weeks of Super Summer were moved to Pratt Community College in Pratt, Kansas.

According to the report in the 1993 *Annual*, the flood produced some good news as well as bad. In 1951, when the "100-year flood" came, all three buildings had water in them. In 1993, during a much worse flood, only two buildings, the dining room (ten inches) and the dormitory (three inches), got water. The damage in both buildings was minor; thorough cleaning and a little paint made them shipshape. Also, information was gained which will help in future landscaping design, road construction, and placement of recreational areas to better serve the safety needs of conference center people. Special appreciation was given to Jim and Darlene Spence, and to faithful volunteers, who worked countless hours in fighting the flood water and in the cleanup that came afterwards. The facility was restored to a useable condition in an incredibly short period of time.

The greatest damage to Webster was not physical, but the loss of revenue from cancellations of scheduled meetings. While the buildings were ready for campers, the grounds, according to Jim Spence, were a sorry sight. However, when the cancellations left vacant space, Spence worked with John Hopkins to convert the lodge into a mass feeding center to prepare food for flood victims. This was not needed; yet it is good to know it was available and could be so used in another emergency.

On June 26, 1993, Webster Conference Center was the host place for the celebration of Viola Webb's eightieth birthday party. What a glorious day it was: people all over the place, balloons, games and activities for children, tournaments, face painting, a dunking tank, entertainment by groups and individuals from all over the Convention, a pig roast, a huge and beautiful birthday cake with real candles, and a moving worship service to climax the festivities. And in and through it all was Viola Webb, Kansas-Nebraska WMU director emeritus, gracious and charming, and a bit overwhelmed. She kept wondering if anybody would really come. And they did, over a thousand. This was the kick-off day for the Viola Webb Offering for State Missions that was dedicated to Webster Conference Center. "Webster: Making a World of Difference" was the offering theme. It was fitting in every way. Webb is every bit as committed to the camping program as O. K. Webster. "There isn't anything that can take the place of camping for young people," she said to Kansas-Nebraska WMU members (*BD*, April 26, 1993). During the morning there was a "Mission Fest," featuring Kansas and Nebraska missionaries at work in the states and abroad. The afternoon worship service was opened with a parade of the flags of the 128 nations where Southern Baptists minister. Leading the parade, right behind the U.S. flag, were flags from Kansas and Nebraska. Then came the flags from our partnerships, Jordan and Nevada. Next were the flags from Malawi and Zambia, the former Kansas-Nebraska Convention partnership countries (*BD*, June 30, 1993).

Doyle Smith, who served as chair of the Webster Conference Center board of directors for ten years, reminded the group of the ways in which Webster is "making a world of difference." When children and youth make decisions to follow Christ at Webster Conference Center, Webster is impacting the world, for these are the ones who will "go and tell." Richard Jackson, pastor emeritus of the North Phoenix Baptist Church, Arizona, was the keynote speaker. Kansas-Nebraska Singing Men and Singing Women, and Pawnee and Mitch Camp, from Metropolitan Baptist Church in Wichita, made the rafters ring with their beautiful music.

The service was brought to a glorious close as Alpha Goombi, a Choctaw from the Kiowah Tribal Nation, wearing a beaded buckskin dress made by her husband's father's great-aunt, presented "The Lord's Prayer" in Native American sign language. It was truly a birthday celebration for all seasons!

The offering and celebration were wonderful salutes to Viola Webb and to WCC, and to the men and women, who through their gifts of labor, love, money, and prayers, have made it all possible.

In the near future, there will be space and time for five weeks of Super Summer at Webster Conference Center. When this happens, a great milestone will be passed. This was one of the early objectives of the Baptists of Kansas and Nebraska.

At least one quite unusual event has taken place at Webster: a wedding in the Chapel. Kent Canady and Vicki Holmgren-Canady were married in Lake Tahoe, but really wanted a formal wedding in Webster Chapel. They met in the summer of 1984 while Kent was a summer missionary helping to build the camp and Vicki was an active member of the Bel Air Baptist Church youth group. Bel Air youth group always invited the summer missionaries to their activities. When the summer was over, Kent went back to Texas to school and Vicki went to the University of Kansas. "Seven years and several romances later, their old flame was rekindled while they were both living and working in southern California" (BD, 1992). After their marriage in Tahoe, they came back to Texas, and from there made the sentimental journey back to Webster.

In 1993 Dana and Sherri Wood, Mission Service Corps volunteers, joined the staff as assistant managers. They live at Bennington, where Wood is a school counselor for kindergarten through twelfth grades, and Sherri is a substitute teacher. They served as Southern Baptist missionaries for five years in Zambia, in Southern Africa, and have pastored churches in Kansas both before and after this service.

The board of directors is investigating avenues of making Webster more useable and inviting: preparing for wilderness camping, building a lake, and landscaping. According to Terry McIlvain, administrator for Webster Conference Center, in the summer of 1995, the KNCSB Campers on Mission Chapter will build a recreational vehicle area on a slab of concrete on the east side of Ohio Street that formerly was a service station. The Campers on Mission plan to come each year and volunteer a week's work to Webster, doing whatever needs to be done. Plans soon to be completed include more recreational facilities, a restroom addition in the dining hall, and sleeping and meeting space on the second floor of the dining room.

The dreaming, begun almost fifty years ago with Quenemo, goes on. Webster Conference Center is a legacy of love and hope, joy and beauty, we leave to future generations of Kansas-Nebraska Southern Baptists.

Epilogue

THE KNCSB MET AT THE SOUTHVIEW BAPTIST CHURCH IN Lincoln in October 1994 for its forty-ninth meeting. Southview was the first Southern Baptist church organized in Nebraska, so it was a fitting site to begin the year of celebration for the KNCSB's year of Jubilee.

Ray Conner, state music secretary for the Convention in 1963, led the praise time. One could feel the joy and expectation upon entering the beautiful sanctuary—a far cry from the abandoned garages, store fronts, and living rooms of the early churches, and from the half-finished church in Chetopa in which the first Convention had been held in 1946. In that church, even the basement was not fully completed. A plumber was working on the bathroom that day. He is said to have commented to someone later, "I didn't know anything important was going on, so I just went on plumbing."

There was a spirit of banter as President Carl Garrett excused himself for failure to remember names because he had been on medication during the week. There was amusement as he confessed, "I'll be using that excuse all week." Garrett, who is presiding officer for the Fiftieth Anniversary of the KNCSB, was also the presiding officer for the 150th Anniversary of the Missouri Baptist Convention in 1984.

There was the usual seating of the delegates; petitions for recognition by the State Convention from four new churches were received. Those churches represented both "traditional" and "non-traditional" congregations, and both English and non-English speaking groups. The chair of the Committee on Order of Business reported that the Russian Choir was not coming as planned; later, he reported that the choir was coming, but on Tuesday evening, not Monday. Since this was all formally presented and approved by the body, it will show up in the minutes, but not the reason. This was not caused by an international incident; the program committee and the choir did not have clear communication about the time the group was expected.

Peck Lindsay, who has guided the Convention through almost a third of its history, presented the budget, the Executive Committee report, and the state of the Convention address. While it was necessary to tighten the economic belt, there was no whining and no fear of the future. Adjustments had been made, and the marching orders were to move ahead.

As Lindsay left the platform, there was a bit of joking about the Fiftieth Anniversary banners hanging in the room. Lindsay was reported to have said that he could not go to Big Red Country with purple banners, the original color chosen. So the banners for the Convention were done in official Corn Husker Red. The president concluded, "Peck was sensitive enough to see the problem, and resourceful enough to do something about it."

Then came the first vignette, written by Calvin Miller, long-time pastor of the Westside Church in Omaha, writer of novels and poetry, painter of no small renown, and now professor at Southwestern Seminary. He was supposed to have presented them, but at the last minute found he could not get away from the seminary. So the vignettes were presented wonderfully by Pawnee and Mitch Camp, ministers of music, Metropolitan Baptist Church in Wichita.

We listened to a simulated tape of the grand and glorious occasion when Kansas was admitted to the SBC after the thunderous affirmation of a motion made by a preacher from Lakeland, Florida. His motion overturned the negative report of the committee which had been appointed the year before to investigate the Kansas petition. We were caught up in the applause, the joy, the wonder of it all.

Then magically the Camps took us back to those early days of the Triennial Convention when Baptists met only once every three years—before we thought we needed a meeting every whip stitch—and the beginning of the work with Indians in Kansas, the days of the beginning of the SBC, and the transfer of Indian mission work to the newly formed Home Mission Board. Baptists in those days did their work in the same way we do it today; they appointed a committee to lay the plans.

We smiled and chuckled and chortled and guffawed at the references to honorariums paid by the Sunday School Board, the resemblance of Harry Truman and some Baptist church choir directors, and church business meetings referred to as the "combat zone."

Ray Hilderbrand, recording artist/composer, from Metropolitan in Wichita, had been commissioned to write a chorus for this year of celebration. With guitar accompaniment and a bit of joshing and soft shoe, he led the group in learning and enjoying his creation, complete with a few well-placed, rhythmical clap-claps.

Music highlighted the inclusive ethnicity of our Convention: a children's choir of Native Americans and Anglos from All Nations Church in Omaha; a choir from God's Missionary Baptist Church in Omaha; a predominately black church; the sanctuary choir from Westside Church in Omaha; and an orchestra and choir from the Russian Church in Lincoln.

James Reynolds, pastor of Nall Avenue Baptist Church in Prairie Village spoke; "Paradoxes of the Christian Faith" was his topic. The final paradox was, "I must be doing things, for everything I do is important; on the other hand, nothing I can do really makes any difference."

He continued, "If I hang on to the one part of the paradox that only what I do matters, then in my expression of strength, I become weak—accomplish nothing eternal. On the other hand, if I think that what I do does not matter, then in my expression of weakness, I do experience defeat. So it is important that I hang on to both ends of the paradox. The reality of the matter is through the work that one does, empowered by the Holy Spirit of God, the programming of human beings can be changed."

"When God," he continued, "puts his arms around us, what we do becomes important. For God adds the base chords on one side, and the treble chords on the other side, and our tiny melody joins with His to become the music of the Kingdom, the music of the Universe."

Bible studies from Colossians were led by Russell Dilday, former president of Southwestern Seminary. He is now special assistant to the president at Baylor University and interim dean of the George W. Truett Theological Seminary. Jimmy Draper, president of the Sunday School Board, brought a keynote address in which he emphasized the need for servant-hood. "The essence of the Christian life," he said, "is a ministering life" (*BD*, October 31, 1994).

President Carl Garrett brought the sessions to a close with a fitting sermon on the Year of Jubilee. The Jubilee Year, as outlined in Leviticus, was to be a time of "rest and celebration." It was a time for canceling debts, for new beginnings. Garrett urged Kansas-Nebraska Baptists to get out of the "too busy" cycle, and to stop for a time of celebration over who we are, where we have come from, and what we can yet accomplish in God's timing. He urged us to be forgiving and offer healing to each other, and during this year of celebration to really "cancel debts."

And so our Year of Celebration has begun. Perhaps it is only in looking back that we can see the clear marks of God's leadership. At this time, and in the years to come, let us continue to remember that as He has led us hitherto, so He is able to lead us henceforth, to finish a good work in us.

THIS 'N THAT

It's your turn now. This blank page is for you. Record what is important to you, from yesterday and today, so your children and their children may know and appreciate their heritage.

Appendices

Appendix I

Historical Table of Convention Meetings

Year	Dates	Place	President	Recording Secretary	Executive Director	Sermon
1946	March 19-20	Chetopa, KS	Ray Walker	Mrs. Orbie Clem	N. J. Westmoreland	Ray Walker
1946	Oct. 14-16	Burden, KS	Ray Walker	Mrs. G. Mitchell	N. J. Westmoreland	Orbie R. Clem
1947	Oct. 13-15	Wichita, KS	Clifford Wells	Mrs. G. Mitchell	N. J. Westmoreland	N. J. Westmoreland
1948	Oct. 12-14	Coffeyville, KS	Clifford Wells	E. L. Whitaker	N. J. Westmoreland	Clifford Wells
1949	Nov. 1-4	Wichita, KS	W. A. Burkey	E. L. Whitaker	N. J. Westmoreland	G. W. Morrison
1950	Oct. 31-Nov. 2	Pittsburg, KS	W. A. Burkey	Travis Piland	N. J. Westmoreland	E. J. Price
1951	Oct. 30-Nov. 1	Salina, KS	Geo. McClelland	W. T. Coston	N. J. Westmoreland	C. A. Kincheloe
1952	Nov. 11-13	Wichita, KS	Geo. McClelland	W. T. Coston	N. J. Westmoreland	G. E. Caskey
1953	Nov. 10-12	Wichita, KS	Geo. McClelland	William O'Dell	N. J. Westmoreland	William O'Dell
1954	Nov. 9-11	Hutchinson, KS	Howard Whatley	William O'Dell	N. J. Westmoreland	Raymond Collier
1955	Nov. 8-10	Bethel, KS	Howard Whatley	William O'Dell	N. J. Westmoreland	David King
1956	Nov. 6-8	Coffeyville, KS	Jack Hall	William O'Dell	N. J. Westmoreland	Alvin Harms
1957	Nov. 12-14	Wichita, KS	Rang Morgan	Roger Knapton	N. J. Westmoreland	Garth Pybas
1958	Nov. 4-6	Topeka, KS	Rang Morgan	Roger Knapton	N. J. Westmoreland	Paul Davis
1959	Nov. 3-5	Wichita, KS	Gordon Dorian	William O'Dell	N. J. Westmoreland	Lawrence Kennon
1960	Nov. 8-10	Salina, KS	Gordon Dorian	George Vogt	N. J. Westmoreland	James Zeltner
1961	Oct. 31-Nov. 2	Bethel, KS	Garth Pybas	George Vogt	N. J. Westmoreland	George Boston
1962	Nov. 13-15	Wichita, KS	Garth Pybas	George Vogt	N. J. Westmoreland	John McBain
1963	Nov. 12-14	Omaha, NE	Forrest Siler	George Vogt	N. J. Westmoreland	Roy Brown
1964	Nov. 17-19	Hutchinson, KS	Forrest Siler	George Vogt	N. J. Westmoreland	Stanley Nelson
1965	Nov. 9-11	Great Bend, KS	Paul Davis	Fred Hollomon	N. J. Westmoreland	Andy Hornbaker
1966	Nov. 15-17	Coffeyville, KS	T. R. Grozier	O. L. Patterson	N. J. Westmoreland	Cecil Smallwood
1967	Nov. 14-16	Kansas City, KS	T. R. Grozier	O. L. Patterson	N. J. Westmoreland	Fred Hollomon
1968	Nov. 12-14	Topeka, KS	W. E. Thorn	O. L. Patterson	N. J. Westmoreland	Eugene Skelton
1969	Nov. 11-13	Wichita, KS	W. E. Thorn	Tom Riddle		Gordon Dorian
1970	Nov. 10-12	Wichita, KS	H. E. Alsup	Tom Riddle	Pat McDaniel	H. E. Alsup
1971	Nov. 9-11	Kansas City, KS	H. E. Alsup	Tom Riddle	Pat McDaniel	Doy L. Jones
1972	Nov. 7-9	Wichita, KS	J. L. Martin	Doy L. Jones	Pat McDaniel	Edward Wooten
1973	Nov. 6-8	Bellevue, NE	J. L. Martin	Doy L. Jones	Pat McDaniel	Tom Riddle
1974	Nov. 12-14	Overland Park, KS	Luther M. Berry	J. W. Pace	Pat McDaniel	John Click
1975	Nov. 11-13	Topeka, KS	Luther M. Berry	George Goudie	Pat McDaniel	Calvin Miller
1976	Nov. 9-10	Wichita, KS	Doy L. Jones	Roger G. Easter	Pat McDaniel	Dennis Wood
1977	Nov. 8-10	Topeka, KS	Doy L. Jones	Roger G. Easter	R. Rex Lindsay	Gene Hawkins
1978	Nov. 13-15	Wichita, KS	Gene Hawkins	Roger G. Easter	R. Rex Lindsay	Doyle Smith
1979	Nov. 12-14	Great Bend, KS	Gene Hawkins	Roger G. Easter	R. Rex Lindsay	Ken Cumbie
1980	Nov. 11-12	Bellevue, NE	Doyle Smith	Mary Jo Robertson	R. Rex Lindsay	Alton Mathis
1981	Nov. 10-11	Prairie Village, KS	Doyle Smith	Mary Jo Robertson	R. Rex Lindsay	Ken Emerson
1982	Nov. 9-11	Garden City, KS	Dale Buchman	Mary Jo Robertson	R. Rex Lindsay	Jerry Barnes
1983	Nov. 15-17	Topeka, KS	Dale Buchman	Mary Jo Robertson	R. Rex Lindsay	Ray Emery
1984	Nov. 13-14	Kearney, NE	Mahlon Morley	Mary Jo Robertson	R. Rex Lindsay	Jimmy Cobb
1985	Nov. 12-13	Wichita, KS	Mahlon Morley	Mary Jo Robertson	R. Rex Lindsay	James Jones
1986	Nov. 11-12	Leawood, KS	John Click	Mary Jo Robertson	R. Rex Lindsay	Oscar L. Brown
1987	Nov. 10-11	Lincoln, NE	John Click	Mary Jo Robertson	R. Rex Lindsay	Daniel Shaeffer
1988	Nov. 14-16	Topeka, KS	Harold Finch	Mary Jo Robertson	R. Rex Lindsay	Gordon Dorian
1989	Nov. 13-15	Omaha, NE	Harold Finch	Mary Jo Robertson	R. Rex Lindsay	Mark Patton
1990	Nov. 12-14	Wichita, KS	Dave Sellars	Jimmy Cobb	R. Rex Lindsay	Andy St. Andre
1991	Oct. 21-23	Hutchinson, KS	Dave Sellars	Jimmy Cobb	R. Rex Lindsay	Calvin Miller
1992	Oct. 19-21	Overland Park, KS	N. N. Antonson	Bob Grayson	R. Rex Lindsay	Glenn Davis
1993	Oct. 25-27	Liberal, KS	N. N. Antonson	Mary Wolfington	R. Rex Lindsay	Randy Caddell
1994	Oct. 24-26	Lincoln, NE	Carl W. Garrett	Bryan Jones	R. Rex Lindsay	Jim Reynolds

Appendix II

Statistical Table of Convention Progress

Year	Sunday School	Total Members	Number of Churches	Gifts to All Causes	Baptisms	Gifts to Coop. Program	Church Property
1946	1,086	1,151	12	$30,868	133	$ 2,228.09	$78,678
1947	2,036	1,914	22	67,872	250	4,854.52	159,818
1948	2,797	2,602	31	78,168	404	6,745.77	210,814
1949	3,828	3,589	40	132,001	442	9,425.39	322,500
1950	5,496	5,057	54	195,268	788	15,172.46	566,862
1951	8,040	7,813	70	389,584	976	22,682.86	907,500
1952	8,973	9,449	78	490,938	1,013	35,771.08	893,850
1953	12,600	12,507	83	635,371	1,341	48,995.98	1,470,296
1954	15,548	14,858	103	849,778	1,728	62,777.08	2,208,474
1955	18,957	17,795	117	974,956	2,163	79,629.77	2,801,798
1956	21,609	20,561	121	1,133,816	2,084	94,263.12	3,499,644
1957	23,398	22,726	127	1,243,861	1,883	108,939.66	4,215,254
1958	25,025	24,970	135	1,451,190	2,054	130,315.96	4,746,850
1959	28,072	27,528	141	1,664,370	2,483	155,865.44	6,731,418
1960	30,282	30,483	152	1,925,955	2,463	172,933.07	8,551,893
1961	31,998	33,159	159	2,138,615	2,526	195,474.37	8,737,423
1962	33,645	35,903	165	2,365,533	2,410	213,972.68	11,129,792
1963	34,513	38,534	168	2,501,005	2,494	221,701.67	11,690,863
1964	37,461	41,007	172	2,759,635	2,398	220,668.91	12,599,859
1965	39,003	45,165	176	3,366,918	2,472	247,776.08	15,788,894
1966	39,441	46,995	183	3,438,156	2,342	252,195.47	16,465,946
1967	40,246	50,034	196	3,672,145	2,915	269,592.97	18,449,484
1968	40,502	51,902	197	4,139,163	2,731	285,963.50	19,695,306
1969	40,482	52,436	197	4,505,491	2,417	332,644.03	20,196,559
1970	38,902	54,522	197	4,670,143	2,391	307,286.84	21,042,374
1971	39,324	56,086	199	5,147,980	2,781	269,313.19	21,512,102
1972	39,106	58,028	200	5,455,544	3,190	283,658.42	23,589,968
1973	39,018	59,629	200	5,961,864	2,830	428,333.19	26,545,762
1974	39,079	61,797	203	6,991,132	2,959	502,616.49	29,999,240
1975	38,929	61,997	207	7,674,344	2,670	587,367.00	35,314,443
1976	42,088	64,009	211	8,774,057	2,692	640,054.76	38,581,119
1977	41,366	64,558	207	9,482,627	2,284	714,566.73	43,466,335
1978	40,078	65,283	211	10,718,378	2,359	744,903.19	50,170,358
1979	39,800	66,946	211	11,761,154	2,510	882,711.96	55,044,990
1980	42,198	69,883	223	14,071,539	3,054	1,043,031.53	61,171,676
1981	43,959	70,931	223	16,353,412	2,724	1,193,391.10	67,841,691
1982	45,193	73,186	227	18,263,433	3,065	1,270,983.32	76,178,421
1983	47,185	76,330	231	20,217,177	2,749	1,330,930.26	
1984	48,906	77,702	236	20,173,293	2,845	1,391,220.17	
1985	48,310	80,190	232	22,007,549	2,565	1,474,057.01	
1986	47,237	80,779	239	22,737,060	2,335	1,556,458.00	
1987	49,038	79,607	248	24,901,710	2,454	1,556,937.60	
1988	48,696	82,589	248	25,031,379	2,221	1,625,252.64	
1989	49,526	85,643	250	26,124,802	2,472	1,673,360.47	
1990	50,511	87,137	278	28,127,539	2,604	1,682,780.84	
1991	50,800	79,871	283	27,490,026	2,554	1,773,368.00	
1992	50,814	87,672	275	28,935,301	2,781	1,871,528.84	
1993	50,754	89,366	276	32,307,921	2,525	1,900,495.04	
1994	49,037	83,401	285	31,136,406	2,344	1,900,380.83	133,201,862

Appendix III

Timeline of Key Years and Events

Note: Some records are incomplete; the following is the best available evidence.

1814 Formation of General Missionary Convention of the Baptist Denomination in the U.S.A. for Foreign Missions.

1817 Triennial Convention appoints Isaac McCoy as the first Baptist missionary to present Kansas.

1823 McCoy opens manual training school at Carey Mission with thirty students.

1829 Triennial Convention appoints Johnston Lykins as a home missionary to work west of the Missouri.

1831 Lykins and John Pratt come to site where Shawnee Mission, KS, is now located to serve as missionaries to the Shawnee Indians.

1833 Ira Blanchard serves as missionary to the Delaware north of the present site of Edwardsville, KS.

1835 Missionary Moses Merrill comes to Bellevue, NE. Bellevue (meaning beautiful view) is the burial grounds for the Omaha, Pawnee, Otoe and other tribes. On April 1 he signs an agreement with John Dougherty to teach both sexes of the Otoe and Missouri tribes. He also begins to translate scripture into their languages.

1837 Jotham Meeker, missionary to the Ottawa, brings the first printing press to Kansas.

1837 Robert Simmerwell serves in a mission to the Pottawatomies located six miles south of Ottawa, in Linn County, near the Marais des Cygne River.

1842 Isaac McCoy organizes and is elected executive secretary of the American Indian Mission Association located in Louisville, KY. The official publication is *The Indian Advocate*.

1844 Elizabeth (Eliza) McCoy is appointed to work with the Pottawatomie near Topeka, and Sara Ann Osgood to work with Wea Indian Mission School located south of Kansas City. They are "set apart" with an "appropriate service" by the Lost River Church.

1845 Formation of the Southern Baptist Convention in Augusta, GA.

1846 Pottawatomie Indian treaties lead to establishment of the second Baptist mission known as the Pottawatomie Baptist Manual Labor Training School.

1847 Pottawatomies move from their homes at Council Bluffs on the Missouri and Osage Rivers to a new area purchased from the Kansas tribe. Johnston Lykins moves with them. Miami County, Kansas, was later called Lykins County.

1848 Baptists are selected to operate the Manual Training School for the Pottawatomies with sixteen students in temporary quarters.

1849 Johnston Lykins describes the new building which cost forty-eight hundred dollars and paid for by the U.S. Government. It is now located west of Topeka on the north side of Interstate 70. The Kansas Historical Museum is on its grounds.

1854 Negotiations open with the Board of Domestic Missions (present Home Mission Board) of the Southern Baptist Convention to take over work begun by the American Indian Mission Association.

1855 Domestic Mission Board assumes work of American Indian Mission Association. Pottawatomie School building is probably the oldest existing building in which the Home Mission Board conducted ministry.

1856 J. H. Luther departs for Kansas but does not enter because of the turmoil over slavery. Instead he operates a school for young ladies in Kansas City. He later pastors churches in Missouri and in 1866 becomes the editor of the *Missouri Baptist Journal*.

1856 John Jackson is sent to work with David Lykins, described as "Superintendent of all Baptist Missions in the Kansas Territories."

1857 W. Thomas appointed on October 1 to work in Delaware City, located on the north edge of the Delaware Reservation, near Leavenworth. He organizes the church in Delaware City with sixteen members. He helps write the constitution of "the first ever Baptist Association in Kansas."

1861 The Topeka Pottawatomie Mission School is closed due to the 1860 drought, the offer of citizenship to the Indians, and the Civil War.

1894 First Comity Agreement, Fortress Monroe, VA.

1900 Memorial Baptist Church of Pittsburg, KS, affiliates with Spring River Baptist Association in Missouri. This affiliation lasts until 1903.

1907 Northern Baptist Convention organized.

1909 New Mexico Conference on the Comity Agreement concerning mission work in New Mexico.

1911 Wirtonia (now Crestline) Baptist Church applies for membership with Missouri Convention. Church organized in 1892.

1930 Northeast Baptist Association of Oklahoma reports about the "new fields" with this statement: "Adding to this number a large population in Kansas served by our churches there."

1944 Five Kansas pastors (representing Chautauqua, Coffeyville Emmanuel, Ness City Trinity, Burden, and Ellinwood Calvary) gather for breakfast at the Oklahoma Baptist Convention and dream the Kansas Southern Baptist Fellowship.

1945 The same pastors who gathered in Oklahoma in 1944 meet again at the Oklahoma Convention and finalize the plans for an Evangelism Conference at Burden on November 21-22.

1945 First Baptist Church Burden is the site of the organization of the Kansas Southern Baptist Fellowship. Four churches join: Burden; Colleyville, Emmanuel; Ellinwood, Calvary; and Ness City, Trinity (November).

1945 A weekly news sheet is arranged.

1946 Relief and Annuity Board of SBC makes a retirement plan available to Kansas pastors (January).

1946 Baxter Springs hosts fellowship meeting for the Eastern Zone (January). Mrs. J. D. Williamson elected chair of the Women's Assembly. Before the March meeting the name is changed to Woman's Missionary Union.

1946 First Baptist Church of Cambridge hosts the Western Zone with a "Program of Evangelism" (February).

1946 On March 19 eleven churches meet in the First Baptist Church of Chetopa to organize the Kansas Convention of Southern Baptist Churches. Seven become charter members: Burden; Ness City, Trinity; Coffeyville, Immanuel; Chautauqua; Treece; Wichita, Airlane (later First Southern); and Chetopa. They elect N. J. Westmoreland part-time executive secretary-treasurer (he became full-time in June) and Ray Walker as president.

1946 Woman's Missionary Union is recognized as auxiliary to Kansas Convention of Southern Baptist Churches on March 20. Lois Clem is elected executive secretary-treasurer and Nellie Williamson, president.

1946 Orbie Clem elected editor of the news sheet which is renamed *The Southern Baptist Beams*. In July the first commercially printed issue appears.

1946 First State Camp at Cedar Bluff near Coffeyville—youth from eight Kansas churches and one Oklahoma church in attendance.

1946 The Five Year Plan is initiated to start one hundred churches in five years.

1946 Members of the "One Hundred Club" are asked to give one dollar per month to provide pastoral aid.

1946 The Convention assumes management of book store already in operation.

1946 First annual meeting of Convention in Burden, October 14-16. Convention authorizes Sunday School (Lonnie Wells, secretary) and Training Union (Floyd P. McDaniel) Departments. Both secretaries serve without pay.

1946 Name is changed to Kansas Convention of Southern Baptists. Executive Board authorizes the Pittsburg Student House at Pittsburg State College.

1948 First Baptist Student Union is organized at Pittsburg State College. Keith Hamm named president.

1948 First KCSB office and bookstore are located in the Westmoreland home.

1948 KCSB is recognized by the SBC in spite of a negative report by the study committee, breaking forever the comity agreement which confined the SBC to the South. The following year other states line up to join.

1948 D. E. Strahan, first missionary supported jointly by the Home Mission Board and KCSB, begins work.

1948 Brotherhood begins. President Robert Henry Hill serves without pay.

1949 Offices rented at 244 1/2 North Main Street, Wichita.

1949 First secretary of religious education, W. Ed Russell, is employed.

1949 Kansas Southern Baptist Foundation created.

1950 Northern Baptist Convention changes name to American Baptist Convention.

1951 Baptist Sunday School Board buys Baptist Book Store from Kansas Convention.

1952 KCSB purchases 130 acres on the Marais des Cygne River, near Quenemo, for a permanent camp.

1952 KCSB purchases Baptist Building at 231 Main, Wichita.

1954 *Kansas Southern Baptist Beams* changes name to *Baptist Digest*.

1955 First Southern Baptist Church (now Southview), Lincoln, constitutes to become the first Nebraska church. It affiliates with Kansas Southern Baptists through Wheatland Association (later Smoky Hill).

1955 Executive Board of Kansas Convention votes to sponsor work in Eastern Nebraska.

1957 Organization of Church Loan Association (CLA), Gordon Dorian, president, and Howard Whatley, executive vice-president.

1958 Membership of all Kansas-Nebraska churches reaches 25,148. By-law 18 of the SBC constitution is met and the KCSB is eligible to be represented on all SBC boards and agencies.

1958 Eastern Nebraska Association forms.

1959 On May 19 Rang Morgan, pastor, Sharon, Wichita, presents a gavel to SBC President, Brooks Hays, made from walnut lumber taken from the Pottawatomie Indian Baptist Mission building.

1959 First Kansas-Nebraska representatives elected to serve on SBC boards and agencies.

1963 Sunday School Board closes Baptist Book Store.

1963 Official opening of Baptist Building, 3000 West Kellogg, Wichita.

1966 Eight churches in Western Nebraska leave Colorado Convention and join Eastern Nebraska Association in forming the Nebraska Baptist Fellowship.

1968 In August the Kansas Securities and Exchange Commissioner deems the CLA to be insolvent. Since 1954, 254 loans totalling $4,900,000 have been issued to 115 churches.

1968 Bankruptcy is avoided during annual meeting at First Southern, Topeka, KS, as Convention deals with CLA crisis. Budget cuts result in release of two staff members (November).

1968 Howard H. Whatley resigns as executive vice-president of the Baptist Foundation and the Church Loan Association (December).

1969 Home Mission Board sends Pat McDaniel to Kansas-Nebraska to manage Convention financial affairs (January).

1969 Securities and Exchange Commission places Convention under a board of managers consisting of four laymen and one pastor (August).

1969 N. J. Westmoreland resigns as executive secretary-treasurer of the KCSB, having held this position since March 19, 1946 (September).

1969 "Strengthen Our Witness" instituted to raise five hundred thousand dollars to underwrite bonds.

1970 Churches pledge $672,108.62 through "Strengthen Our Witness."

1970 Pat McDaniel becomes executive director.

1971 Convention begins to rebuild staff by calling R. Rex "Peck" Lindsay as evangelism/missions director.

1973 KCSB becomes Kansas-Nebraska Convention of Southern Baptists (November).

1973 All bonds and coupons are called. No one loses a dime invested in the CLA. As churches repay loans a revolving loan fund is instituted by the foundation. Loan interest paid by churches goes to missions (December).

1977 Convention moves offices to 5410 West 7th Street, Topeka, and elects R. Rex "Peck" Lindsay as executive director (November).

1980 Convention votes to start two hundred new churches by the year 2000.

1980 Fifteen BSU members and four campus ministers spend three months in Malawi and Zambia.

1981 O. K. and Ila Belle Webster give eighty acres of "Camp Webster" to the Convention. In 1994 the conference center covers 231 acres.

1982 Convention names State Missions Offering in honor of Viola Webb.

1983 Kansas-Nebraska becomes first new work convention to enter into a foreign partnership agreement by joining with Malawi and Zambia.

1986 Musicians on Mission brings musicians from all over U.S. to Kansas-Nebraska.

1991 PraiSing II introduces new *Baptist Hymnal* to Kansas-Nebraska.

1992 Convention celebrates Viola Webb's eightieth birthday with celebration at Webster Conference Center which kicks off state missions offering. A record $155,000 is given.

1993 The KNCSB enters into partnership with Jordan.

1994 Agreement with Nevada makes Convention the first new work area to enter Home Mission Board partnership.

1995 Goal of 200 by 2000 (two hundred new church starts by the year 2000) accomplished.

1995 Convention celebrates fifty years of making a difference.

Appendix IV
Convention Executive Staff

Note: Some records are incomplete; the following is the best available evidence.

**EXECUTIVE SECRETARY-TREASURER/
EXECUTIVE DIRECTOR-TREASURER**
N. J. Westmoreland (1946-1969)
Pat McDaniel (1970-1976)
R. Rex "Peck" Lindsay (1977-Present)

ADMINISTRATIVE ASSISTANT
Bob Powell (1974-1976)
Anita Wilson (1977-Present)

ARCHITECTURE
Harold Inman (1979-1991)

**ASSISTANT EXECUTIVE
SECRETARY-TREASURER**
F. Paul Allison (1957-1964)

**ASSOCIATE EXECUTIVE
SECRETARY-TREASURER**
F. Paul Allison (1965-1967)
Sam D. Russell (1965)
F. Galen Irby (1967-1969)

ASSOCIATIONAL MISSIONS
R. Rex "Peck" Lindsay, Director (1979-Present)

BAPTIST CHAIR OF BIBLE, PITTSBURG
Z. Linston Brister, Professor (1954-1956)

BROTHERHOOD
J. O. Scheer, Secretary (1950-1954)
S. R. Belew, Secretary (1955-1956)
John Havlik, Secretary (1957-1960)
J. Frank Davis, Secretary (1962)
Garth Pybas, Secretary (1965-1968)
F. Galen Irby, Secretary (1969)
Pat McDaniel, Director (1970-1972)
Lynn P. Clayton, Director (1973-1975)
John Hopkins, Director (1976-1977, 1987-1989)
Dewey Hickey, Director (1978-1986)
Mark Clifton, Director (1990-Present)

**BUSINESS ADMINISTRATOR-
COMPTROLLER**
Harold C. Conley (1977-Present)

CAMPUS MINISTRY/STUDENT WORK
Ray Gilliland, Secretary (1956-1968)
Harold Inman, Secretary (1969-1970)

R. Rex "Peck" Lindsay, Director (1971-1986)
Roy Moody, Director (1987-Present)

CHRISTIAN SOCIAL MINISTRIES
John F. Hopkins, Area Consultant (1974-Present)

CHURCH SERVICES
Harold Inman, Division Director (1974-1978)
Harry Taylor, Associate Director (1974-1978)

CHURCH LOAN ASSOCIATION
Howard Whatley, Executive Vice-President (1957-1969)
Byron Tracy, Construction Supervisor (1965-1968)
Pat McDaniel, Director (1970-1973)

CHURCH ADMINISTRATION
Harry Taylor, Director (1979-Present)

EDITOR
Orbie R. Clem (1946-1952)
Tommie Hinson (1953)
Hoyt S. Gibson (1954-1956)
Joe Novak (1957-1958)
F. Paul Allison (1959-1965)
N. J. Westmoreland (1966-1970)
Pat McDaniel (1970-1972)
Lynn P. Clayton (1973-1978)
John F. Hopkins (1978-Present)
Eva Wilson, Associate Editor (1995-Present)

EVANGELISM
Jack Stanton, Secretary (1951-1955)
John Havlik, Secretary (1956-1960)
J. Frank Davis, Secretary (1962)
Garth Pybas, Secretary (1965-1968)
N. J. Westmoreland, Secretary (1969)
Pat McDaniel, Director (1970)
R. Rex "Peck" Lindsay, Director (1971-1972)
Lynn P. Clayton, Director (1973-1978)
Terry McIlvain, Intern (1979-1981); Area Consultant, Youth Evangelism (1982-1986, 1990-present)
Rennie J. Berry, Director (1981-1985)
Mike O'Donnell, Area Consultant, Youth Evangelism (1987-1988)
Roy Moody, Director (1986-Present)

EXTENSION
Dewey Hickey, Director (1978-1986)
Mark Clifton, Director (1990-Present)

FAMILY MINISTRY
Rennie J. Berry, Director (1981-1985)
Yvonne Keefer, Director (1986-Present)
Terry McIlvain, Director (1992-Present)

FMB VOLUNTEERS
Yvonne Keefer, Director (1992-Present)

FOUNDATION
Howard Whatley, Secretary (1951-1953);
    Executive Secretary-Treasurer (1954-1968)
Pat McDaniel, Executive Director-
    Treasurer (1970-1977)
R. Rex "Peck" Lindsay, Executive Director-
    Treasurer (1977-Present)
Harold C. Conley, Business Administrator/
    Comptroller (1977-Present)

HMB VOLUNTEER MISSIONS
John F. Hopkins, Director (1978-1989)
Terry McIlvain, Director (1990-Present)

INTERNATIONAL CONSULTANT
Viola Webb, Director (1979-1982)
Yvonne Keefer, Director (1983-1984)

MINISTER RELATIONS
Harry Taylor, Director (1992-Present)

MISSIONS
W. A. Burkey, Secretary (1951-1956)
Meeler Markham, Secretary (1960-1963)
Sam D. Russell, Secretary (1965)
F. Galen Irby, Secretary (1967-1969)
Pat McDaniel, Director (1970-1971)
R. Rex "Peck" Lindsay, Director (1971-1972);
    Division Director (1973-1976)
Lynn P. Clayton, Associate Division Director
    (1973-1976)

MUSIC
Ray Conner, Secretary (1963)
Harold Inman, Secretary (1964-1973)
Harry Taylor, Director (1974-Present)

PARTNERSHIP MISSIONS
Yvonne Keefer, Director (1983-Present)

PROMOTION
F. Paul Allison, Director (1957-1967)

PUBLIC RELATIONS
F. Paul Allison, Director (1962-1964)

RECREATION
Harry Taylor, Director (1977-Present)

RELIGIOUS EDUCATION
Ed Russell, Secretary (1949-1950)
Ray Gilliland, Secretary (1951-1955)
Harold Inman, Secretary (1969-1970);
    Department Director (1971-1972);
    Division Director (1973)

SPECIAL MISSION MINISTRIES
Terry McIlvain, Area Consultant (1982-1986)
Mike O'Donnell, Area Consultant (1987-1988)

STEWARDSHIP
W. A. Burkey, Secretary (1951-1952)
F. Paul Allison, Director (1957-1967)
F. Galen Irby (1967-1969)
Pat McDaniel, Director (1970-1976)
R. Rex "Peck" Lindsay, Director (1977-1980)
Harold C. Conley, Director (1981-1991)
Roy Moody (1992-Present)

SUNDAY SCHOOL
Lonnie Russell, Secretary (1946-?)
Ed Russell, Secretary (1950)
Hillary Brophy, Secretary (1956-1958)
Howard Halsell, Secretary (1960-1961)
Ray Conner, Secretary (1963)
Harold Inman, Secretary (1964-1968)

TEACHING/TRAINING
Harold Inman, Director (1979-1991)
Andy St. Andre, Director (1992-1995)

TRAINING UNION
F. P. McDaniel, Secretary (1946-?)
Ed Russell, Secretary (1950)
Ray Gilliland, Secretary (1956-1968)

WEBSTER CONFERENCE CENTER
Terry McIlvain, Director (1990-Present)

WOMAN'S MISSIONARY UNION
Lois Boundurant Clem, Executive
    Secretary-Treasurer (1946-1952)
Ida Polk, Executive Secretary-Treasurer
    (1953-1955)
Betty Freeman, Young People's Secretary
    (1955-1956)
Eva Berry, Executive Secretary (1956)
Viola Webb, Executive Director (1957-1982)
Beverly Hammack, Youth Director (1959-1960)
Yvonne Keefer, Executive Director (1983-Present)

YOUTH GOSPEL GROUP LEADER
Fred Hansen, Leader (1946-?)

Appendix V

Associational Directors of Missions

Note: Some records are incomplete; the following is the best available evidence.

STATE MISSIONARIES
D. E. (Gene) Strahan (1948-1949)
Ray T. Hart (1948-1949)
Keith Hamm (Student) (1949-1952)
L. L. Peninger (Student) (1950)
George Walker (1950-1955)

AREA MISSIONARIES
Cecil Finfrock, Eastern Area (1953-1955)
B. C. Stonecipher, Western Area (1953-)
E. G. Wright, Central Area (1953-1955)
Raymond Collier, Wichita (1955)
A. L. Busbee, Western Area (1954-1961)
Cecil Adams, Central Area (1955-1959)
Haskell Trask, Southeast Area (1955)
Loren Belt, Wichita Area (1956-1958)
I. Houston Lanier, Kansas City Area
   (1956-1960)
George Roberts, Northeastern (1957-1970)
Avery Wooderson, Southeast (1957-1961)

BLUE STEM
George Hair (1962-1964)
Gaylon Wiley (1966-1968)
Gerald Locke (1969-1982)
Les Arnold (1983-1986)
Frank Claiborne (1987)
Bill Kneisly (1988-Present)

CENTRAL
L. N. Stamper (1962-1963)
William G. O'Dell (1969-1973)
J. L. Williams (1973-1980)
Luther Berry (1980-1985)
Don Herman (1985-1991)
Roy Savage (1992-Present)

CHEYENNE
L. N. Stamper (1962-1963)

EASTERN NEBRASKA
Quentin Lockwood (1961-1968)
R. Rex "Peck" Lindsay (1968-1971)
C. Burtt Potter (1971-1974)
Harold Manahan (1974-Present)

HIGH PLAINS
A. L. Busbee (1959-1961)
Eugene Marley (1962-1968)
Jon Lurtz (1969-1972)
Jack Heath (1974-1975)

KANSAS CITY, KANSAS
Cecil Finfrock (1953-1955)
I. Houston Lanier (1956-1960)
Paul Elledge (1962-1974)
James Griffin (1975-1987)
Don Reed (1988-Present)

KAW VALLEY
Cecil Finfrock (1953-1955)
I. Houston Lanier (1956-1957)
George E. Roberts, Jr. (1957-1970)
Frank Claiborne (1970-1981)
Ken Townsend (1982-1989)
Tom Sykes (1990-1994)
Randy Callaway (1995-Present)

SEDGWICK
Raymond Collier (1955)
Loren J. Belt (1956-1958)
Sam D. Russell (1959-1965)
Paul G. Davis (1966-1988)
C. Don Beall (1990-1995)

SMOKY HILL
George E. Roberts (1956-1970)
Frank Claiborne (1970-1977)
Gerald Locke (1977-1982)
Les Arnold (1983-Present)

SOUTH CENTRAL
E. G. Wright (1954)
Cecil Adams (1955-1958)
William G. O'Dell (1960-1974)
Fred Garvin (1975-Present)

SOUTHERN PLAINS
A. L. Busbee (1954-1961)
Jon W. Lurtz (1961-1972)
Jack Heath (1974-1976)

TRI-COUNTY
Charles Himes (1950)
Roy Walker (1953-1956)
Dale Maddux (1959-1961)
T. D. Riddle (1962-1963)
James H. Shope (1965-1988)
Thomas Thorne (1990-Present)

TWIN VALLEY
Cecil Finfrock (1952)
Haskell Trask (1955-1957)
Avery Wooderson (1958-1961)
Gerald Locke (1961-1977)
James H. Shope (1977-1988)
Thomas Thorne (1990-Present)

WESTERN KANSAS
Jack Heath (1976-1985)
Andy St. Andre (1986-1990)
Charles Sharp (1992-Present)

WESTERN NEBRASKA
Quentin Lockwood (1960-1968)
R. Rex "Peck" Lindsay (1968-1971)
C. Burtt Potter (1971-1974)
Harold Manahan (1974)
Tom Wenig (1975-1994)

WHEATLAND ASSOCIATION
Harold Bergan (1962)
W. I. Barnett (1963)

Appendix VI

Campus Ministers/Student Directors

Note: The names of institutions have changed frequently. The names listed are current in 1995. Some records are incomplete; the following is the best available evidence.

STATE DIRECTORS
Ray Gilliland, Secretary (1956-1968)
Harold Inman, Secretary (1969-1970)
R. Rex "Peck" Lindsay, Director (1971-1986)
Yvonne Keefer, Executive Secretary (1977-1982)
Bob Anderson, Kansas Associate (1977-Present)
Brett Yohn, Nebraska Associate (1977-Present)
Roy Moody, Director (1987-Present)

BAKER UNIVERSITY, BALDWIN CITY, KS
Director:
David Webb (1981-1982)

CENTRAL COMMUNITY COLLEGE, HASTINGS, NE
Director:
Dale Phillips (1981)

CHADRON STATE COLLEGE, CHADRON, NE
Directors:
Doug Lee (1975)
Jerry Baumann (1981-1982)

COFFEYVILLE COMMUNITY COLLEGE, COFFEYVILLE, KS
Directors:
John Peck (1965)
Gerald Locke (1966)
C. F. Craighead (1967-1970)
C. Wayne Norton (1971)
C. L Lindsey (1972)

COLBY COMMUNITY COLLEGE, COLBY, KS
Director:
Daryl Riley (1990)

COWLEY COUNTY COMMUNITY COLLEGE, ARKANSAS CITY, KS
Director:
Carlene Pennel (1965-1967)

CREIGHTON UNIVERSITY, OMAHA, NE
Directors:
Ray Crawford (1978-1985)
Sally Watkins (1986-1987)
Jim McReynolds (1990)

DODGE CITY COMMUNITY COLLEGE, DODGE CITY, KS
Directors:
Mrs. Earl Newell (1967-1969)
David Hester (1988)

EMPORIA STATE UNIVERSITY, EMPORIA, KS
Directors:
James Powell (1960-1963)
Gaylene Bozarth Turner (1964-1966)
Dallas Roark (1967) (1969-1972)
Marilyn Brodie (1968)
Larry Duncan (1973)
Floyd Smith (1974-1981)
Jim Black (1984-Present)
Associates:
Linda Blain (1976-1981)
Bob and Leslie Lindsay (1993-Present)

FORT HAYS STATE UNIVERSITY, HAYS, KS
Directors:
James McMechan (1964-1965)
Floyd Littlepage (1966)
Bob Deen (1967-1968)
Steve Timken (1969)
Janice Overmiller (1970)
Mike Chlumsky (1972-1973)
Johnny Peters (1975-1976)
Lila Morrow (1977)
Gary Hayes (1981-1982)
Rusty Bush (1983-1987)

GARDEN CITY COMMUNITY COLLEGE, GARDEN CITY, KS
Directors:
Bill Long (1969-1971)
Pete Gipson (1972-1974)
Robert Underwood (1985)
Homer Rich (1986-1987, 1990)
Dan Cate (1986-1987)
David Hester (1988)

HASKELL INDIAN NATIONS UNIVERSITY
Directors:
Bill Crews (1960-1961)
Tom Muskrat (1962-1964)
James Goodner (1965-1967)
Sam Morris (1970-1973)
Gary and Jean Martin (1975)

Louise and Kenneth Holden (1976)
John Davis, Jr. (1977)
Glenn Lawson (1978-1979)
Frank Claiborne (1980)
Cloyd Harjo (1981-Present)
Associate:
Dorothy McLemore (1978)

HASTINGS COLLEGE, HASTINGS, NE
Directors:
Dennis Hampton (1978)
Dale Phillips (1979-1986)
Associate:
Cindy Marker (1978)

HUTCHINSON COMMUNITY COLLEGE, HUTCHINSON, KS
Director:
Todd Murray (1993-Present)

JOHNSON COUNTY COMMUNITY COLLEGE
Directors:
Lana Church (1973-1975)
Scott Smith (1982-1985)
Sheila Jones (1986)
Prabhakar Nemili (1987)

KANSAS CITY, KANSAS, COMMUNITY COLLEGE
Directors:
Lana Church (1973-1975)
Scott Smith (1982-1985)
Sheila Jones (1986)

KANSAS STATE UNIVERSITY, MANHATTAN, KS
Directors:
Lynn Stewart (1956-1961)
Faye Parrott Dunn (1962-1964)
Fred Hollomon (1965)
John Bolan (1966-1972)
Bob Anderson 1973-Present)
Associates:
Bob Anderson (1972)
Judy Smith Nelson (1973-1979)
Ramona Godkin (1980-1984)
Tarenda Wilbur (1984-1989)
Dick Jaques (1982-1987)
Deb Miller (1986-1987)
Jon Casimir (1988-1990)
Teresa Rose (1990-Present)
David Gevock (1991-Present)
Amy Reed (1992)
Lentz Upshaw (1993-Present)

KANSAS WESLEYAN UNIVERSITY, SALINA, KS
Director:
Rodney Penn (1993-Present)

MARY LANNING HOSPITAL SCHOOL OF NURSING, HASTINGS, NE
Director:
Dennis Hampton (1976)

OTTAWA UNIVERSITY, OTTAWA, KS
Director:
Fred Gibson (1969-1973)

PERU STATE UNIVERSITY, PERU, NE
Director:
Kevin Ware (1980-1981)

PITTSBURG STATE UNIVERSITY, PITTSBURG, KS
This was the first BSU. Three people gave early leadership: Keith Hamm, Stanley Gasswint, C. B. Coleman
Professor, Baptist Chair of Bible:
Z. Linston Brister (1954-1956)
Directors:
Dale Maddux (1957-1961)
Betty Parmele (1962)
Carl Swenson, Jr. (1963-1966)
Andy Hornbaker (1967)
Mr. and Mrs. Homer Watson (1968)
Don Lacy (1972-1975)
Dave Barteaux (1976-1981)
Gene Glenn (1982-1990)
Mike Trent (1991-Present)
Associates:
Debbie Peters (1979-1981)
Susan Carson (1994-Present)

PRATT COMMUNITY COLLEGE, PRATT, KS
Directors:
Jeff Mooney (1991-1992)
Bill and Kelly Gandy (1993-Present)

STERLING COLLEGE, STERLING, KS
Director:
Bob Smith (1980-1982)

UNIVERSITY OF KANSAS, LAWRENCE, KS
Directors:
Charles Beck (1954-1961)
Anderine Farmer (1962-1965)
Bill Marshall (1966-1969)

Yvonne Keefer (1969-1982)
Rick Clock (1983-Present)
Associates:
Kent Gee (1973)
Ben Broome (1974-1979)
Don Johnson (1976)
Luther C. Alexander (1978-1981)
Gary Ayers (1978)
Rick Clock (1980-1982)
Wendell Moore (1981)
Donna Lee (1981-1984)
Tim Sims (1985)
Leo Barbee (1986-Present)

**UNIVERSITY OF NEBRASKA—
LINCOLN, NE**
Directors:
Ted Hagen (1966-1967)
Jack Ritchie (1968)
Spots Crawford (1970)
Fred Garvin (1971)
Brett Yohn (1972-Present)
Associates:
Ted Boyls (1973)
Pam Nelson (1976-1978)
Missy Moss (1979-1982)
Scott Smith (1980-1981)
William Kennedy (1982)
Kevin Richardson (1983-1989)
Donna Carol Lee (1983-1984)
Kathy Bosworth (1985-1987)
Karl Nyquist (1986, 1990-1992)
Betsy Stanford (1988)
Kevin Shinn (1990-Present)
Melody Richeson (1993-Present)

**UNIVERSITY OF NEBRASKA AT
OMAHA, NE**
Directors:
Hallene Huddlestun (1964-1967)
Jim Martin (1968-1974)
Norman Clampitt (1975-1979)
Ray Crawford (1980-1985)
Sally Watkins (1986-1987)

**UNIVERSITY OF NEBRASKA AT
KEARNEY, NE**
Directors:
Scott Hadden (1980-1984)
Wayne Merklin (1985-1987)
Jeff Street (1988-Present)
Associate:
Missy Goodson (1992)

WASHBURN UNIVERSITY, TOPEKA, KS
Directors:
Yvonne Keefer (1966-1968)
Jon Sapp (1977-1980) (1981-1982)
Blaine Lemmons (1980-(1981)
Gregg Dennington (1984-1985)
Scott Hadden (1986)

WICHITA STATE UNIVERSITY, WICHITA, KS
Directors:
Mrs. Loren Belt (1956-1958)
James Powell (1958-1959)
Mrs. Stanley Nelson (1960-1961)
Forrest Burt (1962)
Edward Smith (1963)
Leo Poland (1964) (1971)
Darrell Wood (1965-1967)
Mrs. C. O. Little (1968)
Lynn Clayton (1970)
Jim Pickett (1972)
Art Mould (1975-1976)
Jim Herron (1978-1982)
John Denver Brooks (1983-1994)
Associates:
Melody Hufman (1976)
Martha McBride (1981-1982)
Cathy Shaughnessy (1985)
Ron Johnson (1986)
Gregory Symes (1989-1990)
Judy Bragdon (1990)
Brent Storrer (1992-Present)
Stacy Blackwell (1992-Present)

Appendix VII

Woman's Missionary Union Leadership

PRESIDENTS

1946-1952	Nellie Williamson
1952	Mrs. Mervin McGill
1952-1955	Mae Burdette
1955-1957	Gladys Braden
1957-1962	Elizabeth Lobaugh
1962-1967	Ethmer Kordis
1967-1968	Alma Tracy
1968-1971	Norma Briggs
1971-1976	Opal Bates
1976-1979	Maxine Barber
1979-1983	Renoma Foster
1983-1987	Jeanie Nolan
1987-1991	Bobbie Spradley
1991-1995	Millie Stengl
1995-Present	Mary Jo Troughton

EXECUTIVE DIRECTORS

1946-1952	Lois Boundurant Clem
1953-1956	Ida Polk
1/57-6/57	Eva Berry
1957-1982	Viola Webb
1983-Present	Yvonne Keefer

ASSOCIATES

Betty Freeman, Young People's Secretary (1955-1956)

Beverly Hammack, Youth Director (1959-1960)

323

Appendix VIII

Kansas-Nebraska Associations and How They Grew

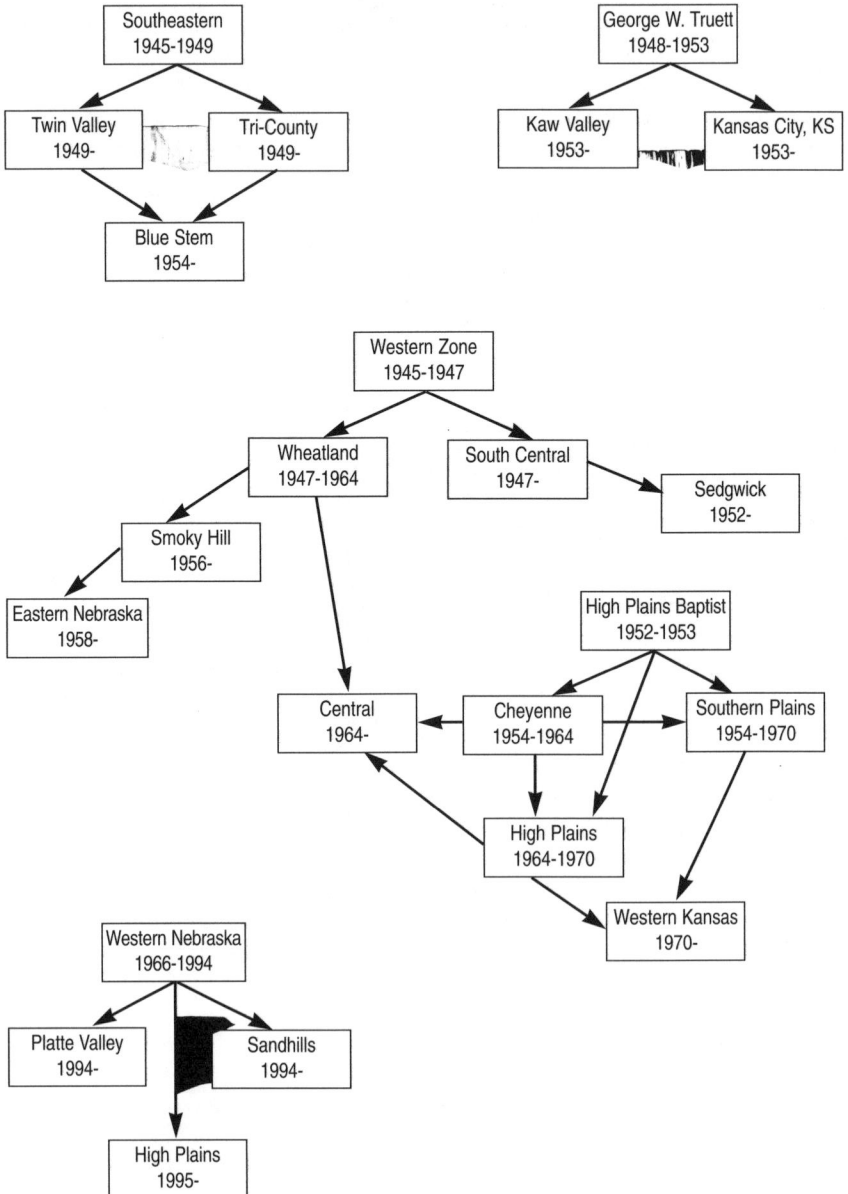

```
Southeastern                         George W. Truett
1945-1949                            1948-1953
   ↓        ↓                           ↓        ↓
Twin Valley   Tri-County          Kaw Valley    Kansas City, KS
1949-         1949-               1953-         1953-
      ↓    ↓
   Blue Stem
   1954-
```

```
                    Western Zone
                    1945-1947
              ↓                  ↓
        Wheatland            South Central
        1947-1964            1947-
      ↓          ↓                    ↓
  Smoky Hill                      Sedgwick
  1956-                           1952-
    ↓
Eastern Nebraska                    High Plains Baptist
1958-                               1952-1953
                                  ↓      ↓      ↓
           Central  ←  Cheyenne  →  Southern Plains
           1964-       1954-1964     1954-1970
                          ↓
                      High Plains
                      1964-1970
                              ↓
                          Western Kansas
                          1970-
```

```
Western Nebraska
1966-1994
  ↓          ↓
Platte Valley   Sandhills
1994-           1994-
      ↓
   High Plains
   1995-
```

324

Appendix IX

Kansas-Nebraska Southern Baptist Foundation Funds

Period Ended July 31, 1994

	Cash Balance	Fund Balance
Revolving Building Loan Fund	$64,020	$2,993,922

This fund has been in operation for several years, and a large portion of its corpus was created from funds remaining with the Church Loan Association after all bonds were redeemed. This fund was created and intended to be used for the development of new and existing Baptist churches cooperating with the KNCSB. It may be used in the purchase of land, construction of a building, or remodeling of an existing structure; and it is loaned with interest. All interest generated by this fund is placed in the Mission Support Fund.

Mission Support Fund	$7,109	$22,498

This fund was established in 1975 to receive all earnings (on loans and investments) generated by the Revolving Building Loan Fund to be used in meeting the needs of people and for promoting the general missionary purpose of the Kansas-Nebraska Southern Baptist Foundation. These funds are administered through the KNCSB.

Church Sites Loan Fund	$55,276	$55,424

This fund has been in existence for many years and was originally raised through the State Missions offering. It is loaned to churches for purchasing church sites only without interest for a period of time [generally three (3) years, but never more than five (5) years]. Since these loans earn little to no interest, the fund grows primarily as loans are paid off.

Kansas City Kansas Baptist Association Fund	$83,449	$83,672

This fund was created in 1974 as the "Carroll V. Day and Lew V. Day Mission Trust Fund" by the First Southern Baptist Church, Kansas City, Kansas. This endowment fund was created for the establishment of new mission work and strengthening churches of Southern Baptist faith in the Kansas City, Kansas, area. In 1993 an additional sum was added through a gift from the John E. Herndon Estate.

Eastern Nebraska Association Fund	$15,657	$54,988

This fund was started in 1979 resulting from the sales proceeds of the church property in Beatrice, Nebraska. The funds are to be invested and managed by the Kansas-Nebraska Southern Baptist Foundation for work in the Eastern Nebraska Southern Baptist Association.

Ed VanLandingham Music Scholarship Fund	$5,660	$5,675

This fund was started in 1979 by the Southview Baptist Church, Lincoln, Nebraska, with earnings from such fund only being used for annual music scholarships.

Allison Smith Memorial Fund	$5,334	$5,348

This fund was created in 1982 to provide a scholarship for a student committed to full-time Christian service from the Kansas-Nebraska Convention attending Midwestern Baptist Theological Seminary. The president and appropriate official of Midwestern Baptist Theological Seminary shall recommend a student subject to approval of the foundation board of directors. If no recommendation is received, a student from another Southern Baptist seminary can be considered.

State Missions Fund	$188,364	$226,206

This fund was created in 1981 to receive the 1981-82 and one-half of the 1982-83 State Missions Offering and will be loaned to acquire sites and build buildings exclusively for new churches and missions. The interest received from these loans will be to provide pastoral leadership for new churches and missions and support of Webster Conference Center.

Savings Holding Fund $17,119 $17,165
This fund was created in 1979 to receive, manage and invest for maximum secured earnings various sums held in building funds by our Kansas-Nebraska Southern Baptist churches and associations.

Operating Fund $1,027 $1,028
This fund appears to be one of the original funds of the foundation and was used for the operating expenses. All operating expenses of the Foundation are reimbursed by the Convention.

Baptist College/Seminary Scholarship Fund $10,360 $10,389
This fund was started in 1993 with endowment funds from the Student Loan Fund which was established many years ago to make loans to enable ministers to go to school. The fund shall assist students from Kansas-Nebraska churches committed to church-related vocational ministry with grants up to two hundred dollars. Such students must be enrolled in Baptist college/seminary supported by churches cooperating with the SBC. Requests for a grant must be submitted to the executive director of the KNCSB, accompanied by a letter of recommendation from his/her pastor and associational director of missions. Requests shall be evaluated on date of receipt, need, and availability of funds.

Evangelism Support Fund $5,693 $5,709
This fund was created in 1976 from royalties on the book entitled *No Second-Class Christians* by Lynn P. Clayton. It is to be used for equipping persons in evangelism and supporting evangelism projects as recommended by the KNCSB's director of evangelism subject to approval by the foundation board of directors.

Wohlgamuth Estate Fund $2,197 $2,203
This fund was started in 1975 with a gift from the estate of Mr. Edward Allen Wohlgamuth to be used for the "construction and maintenance of a home for the aged."

Property Fund $85,834
This fund was begun in 1975 as the "Abilene Property Fund" when the foundation received from the First Baptist Church, Madisonville, Texas, the deed to the property in Abilene, Kansas. The fund name was changed in 1984 to receive and hold in trust properties (real and personal) so given to the foundation.

Webster Conference Center Fund $250,000
This fund was established in 1982 to hold title to and manage real estate purchased under an "options agreement" by and between O. K. and Ila B. Webster and the KNCSB, and to receive gifts and bequests for Camp Webster.

J. Oscar Rhodes New Work Fund $45,077 $45,189
This fund was created in 1991 to provide pastoral aid, preferably for the first year of new work and no more than two years. The aid would be given to new work as recommended by the director-extension missions and/or the State Missions Committee.

Bertha Smith New Work Fund $246 $26,157
This fund was started in 1993 to provide pastoral aid, preferably for the first year of new work and no more than two years. The aid would be given as recommended by the church extension director of the KNCSB and/or the State Missions Committee.

Missions Assistance Fund $70,870 $71,065
This fund was established in 1983 when the foundation received title to assets in accordance with a December 31, 1982, contract for Transfer of Real Estate between the Eastside Baptist Church of Wichita, Inc., and the KNCSB, Inc., and approved by the Grace Community Baptist Church, Inc.

Webster Conference Center Endowment Fund $21,853 $21,912
This fund was created in 1984 with all income to be used to provide support and development for Webster Conference Center, Salina, Kansas.

Mr. & Mrs. T. J. McIlvain Living Memorial Trust Fund $6,516 $6,533
Established in 1986, this fund was designated with the interest earned to benefit youth ministry projects, youth evangelism projects, and new work projects in Kansas-Nebraska.

Foreign Missions Support Fund $21,857 $21,916
This fund was started in 1993 with a gift from the Georgia J. Hand Estate to support the ongoing work of Southern Baptist foreign missions.

WMU Endowment Fund $3,347 $3,356
This fund entitled "Supporting Missions Beyond My Lifetime" was started in 1989 by the WMU, KNCSB, to provide the opportunity to make a permanent investment in missions.

BSU Endowment Fund $19,227 $19,276
This endowment fund, initiated in 1992, receives gifts for investment, with the income distributed to Baptist Student Union projects in Kansas-Nebraska. Donors may designate primary campus beneficiary. Distributions to Baptist Student Union campus projects are initiated by Baptist Student Union directors' requests through or by the KNCSB's director of campus ministries.

Gift Annuity Fund $73,277 $299,155
Assets received in trust with an agreed income to donor and/or designees of donor for life or term, and then a designated Southern Baptist Christian cause will benefit from the gift.

Christian Trust Fund
Funds received in trust with income to grantor for life, and then to Southern Baptist Christian work as designated by grantor prior to his or her death.

Second Century Fund
This fund was started in 1990 by the WMU, SBC, to assist women in their support of missions.

Undesignated Fund $67,368 $67,549
Any gifts received by the Foundation in accordance with the general purpose of the Kansas-Nebraska Southern Baptist Foundation.

TOTALS $790,903 $4,402,169

Bibliography

Alexander, Thomas J. "Baptist Indian Missions." *The American Philatelist* 95, no. 2 (1981): 121-130.

Allen, Catherine. *Laborers Together with God.* Birmingham, Ala.: Woman's Missionary Union, 1987.

Annual, Southern Baptist Convention, 1959.

Armstrong, O. K., and Marjorie Armstrong. *The Baptists in America.* Garden City, N.Y.: Doubleday, 1979.

Barr, Thomas P. *The Pottawatomie Baptist Manual Labor Training School.* Reprinted from *Kansas Historical Quarterly* 43 (Winter 1977): 377-431.

Berkhoffer, Robert F., Sr. Introduction. *History of Baptist Indian Missions.* Isaac McCoy, 1840. Reprint, New York: Johnson Reprint Corporation, 1970.

Burkey, William Andrew. "A Study of the Department of Missions of Kansas Convention of Southern Baptists" (thesis, Central Baptist Theological Seminary, 1957).

Clayton, Lynn. "Runaway 'Yo Yo Days' Are Over on the Plains." *The Baptist Program* (May 1977): 8-9, 22.

Clem, Lois M. (Mrs. Orbie). "A History of the Beginning of Southern Baptist Work in Kansas" (scrapbook: 1940-1953): 1989 (copied).

Cox, Ethlene Boone. *Following in His Train.* Nashville, Tenn.: Broadman Press, 1938.

Coy, Lois. "A Cup of Cold Water." *Home Missions* (June 1960).

Encyclopedia Americana (1993).

Gibson, Hoyt. "Baptist Digest." *Encyclopedia of Southern Baptists* (1958): 114.

Gibson, Hoyt S. "Kansas Associations." *Encyclopedia of Southern Baptists. (1958): 718.*

Hamm, Keith. *The Battle for Recognition.* Topeka, Kan.: Kansas-Nebraska Historical Society, 1993.

Hayward, Elizabeth. *John McCoy: Life and Diaries.* New York: American Historical Co., 1948.

Hickey, Dewey, and James Shope. "Kansas-Nebraska Convention of Southern Baptists." *Encyclopedia of Southern Baptists* (1982): 2,300-2,301.

Hudson, Preston R. *Metro 10.* "A Historical Summary of Metropolitan Baptist Church of Wichita Celebrating Its 10th Anniversary in 1972" (Wichita, Kan: Metropolitan Baptist Church, 1972).

Huddlestun, J. B. *Decisive Decade* (A History of ENBA, 1955-1965). Published by ENBA upon authority of the Executive Board, 1966 (mimeographed).

Kansas Scrapbook.

Keefer, Yvonne. "Kansas-Nebraska Baptist Student Work." *Encyclopedia of Southern Baptists* (1982): 2,298-2,299.

Knight, Walker. "Beyond the Stormy Past, a Bright Future Is Emerging." *Home Missions* (September, 1974): 32.

Lindsay, R. Rex. "The Kansas-Nebraska Convention of Southern Baptists; Foundations and Strategies for Growth" (dissertation, Fuller Theological Seminary, 1982).

Lockwood, Alene. "WMU Circle Program . . . State Missions Emphasis, September 12-19, 1965," *State Missions '65 and Beyond* (Kansas Convention of Southern Baptists): 2.

McCormick, Calvin. *The Memoir of Miss Eliza McCoy.* Dallas, Tex.: Acebar, 1892.

McCoy, Isaac. *History of Baptist Indian Missions.* 1840. Reprint, New York: Johnson Reprint Corporation, 1970.

Miller, Calvin. Quoted by J. B. Huddlestun in *Decisive Decade* (A History of ENBA, 1955-1965).

Moore, Bessie Ellen. "Life and Work of Robert Simmerwell" (thesis, Washburn College, 1935).

Moratto, Mrs. H. O. "Kansas Convention of Southern Baptists." *Encyclopedia of Southern Baptists* (1971): 1,788-1,789.

Morgan, Kit. *Baptist History in the Making* (WNBA, Twenty-Fifth Anniversary). 1985 (mimeographed).

Sharp, W. A. *Baptist History of Kansas.* Holton, Kan.: Sharp, 1939.

Shope, James. "Kansas-Nebraska Associational Camps." *Encyclopedia of Southern Baptists* (1982): 2,298.

Shope, James. *Minutes,* Spring River Baptist Association. n.d.

Smith, Robert E., and James Shope. "Kansas-Nebraska Associations." *Encyclopedia of Southern Baptists* (1982): 2,298-2,299

Ware, Joseph S. *The Emigrants' Guide to California* (1849).

Westmoreland, N. J. *Kansas, 1955.* Wichita: KCSB, 1966 (filmstrip).

Westmoreland, N. J. "Kansas Associations." *Encyclopedia of Southern Baptists* (1971): 1,787.

Westmoreland, N. J. "Kansas' First Challenge to Southern Baptists." *Historical Quarterly Review* (July–Sept. 1955): 41-53, 56.

Westmoreland, N. J. "1947 Program for Day of Prayer for State Missions, Woman's Missionary Union, Kansas Convention of Southern Baptist Churches, 1947" (mimeographed).

Westmoreland, N. J., and Hoyt Gibson. "Kansas Convention of Southern Baptists." *Encyclopedia of Southern Baptists* (1958): 718-721.

White, W. R. "Comity Agreements." *Encyclopedia of Southern Baptists* (1958): 301-302.

Whitlow, June. "Lay Persons: Making a Difference in Today's World." *Baptist History and Heritage* (July 1994): 3-11.

Wyeth, Walter M. *Missionary Memorial: Isaac McCoy and Christina McCoy.* Philadelphia: W. N. Wyeth, 1995.

Information and quotations from the *Southern Baptist Beams* (*SSB*), the *Kansas Southern Baptist Beams* (*KSSB*), the *Baptist Digest* (*BD*), and State Convention *Annuals* were used extensively throughout the text. Citations are abbreviated as indicated.

Index

Index

333